Readings in Social Justice

Readings in Social Justice

Power, Inequality, and Action

First Edition

Edited by
Valerie Chepp
Cleveland Clinic

cognella®
SAN DIEGO

Bassim Hamadeh, CEO and Publisher
Seidy Cruz, Specialist Acquisitions Editor
Anne Jones, Project Editor
Susana Christie, Senior Developmental Editor
Jeanine Rees, Production Editor
Emely Villavicencio, Senior Graphic Designer
Trey Soto, Licensing Coordinator
Natalie Piccotti, Director of Marketing
Kassie Graves, Senior Vice President of Editorial
Jamie Giganti, Director of Academic Publishing

3970 Sorrento Valley Blvd., Ste. 500, San Diego, CA 92121

To all my students: past, present, and future.

Contents

Unit IV. Movements, Change, and Resistance 223
Valerie Chepp

Preface

Valerie Chepp

Readings in Social Justice: Power, Inequality, *and Action* offers a comprehensive resource for social justice teaching. This social justice anthology emerged as a result of my own experience teaching in and directing the Social Justice Program at Hamline University. When developing my Introduction to Issues in Social Justice class, I searched for an appropriate, wide-ranging, and critical course text. As a trained sociologist, I sought out texts that would not only help students learn about justice from philosophical/religious (ethics, morality, and values) or criminal/legal (retribution, punishment, and restorative justice) perspectives but that also located these examinations within social systems of power, inequality, and resistance. However, I found that most theoretical explorations of social justice were written from philosophical or religious perspectives, while applied explorations of social justice predominantly resided in the fields of education, law, or social services. I wanted a student-friendly, sociologically informed analysis of social justice that reflected the field's interdisciplinary roots. When I couldn't find one, I decided to develop one myself.

Below are some fundamental premises upon which this book is built as well as definitions of terms that will be used within it.

First, this book defines social justice as "efforts aimed at promoting a fair society that challenges inequality and oppression, and values diversity. Specific social justice concerns—such as racial, economic, gender, and environmental justice—fall within this definition" (Chepp 2018:271).[1] Another definition I like, which also informs the book, comes from Iris Marion Young: "the elimination of institutionalized oppression and domination" (p. 47 of this anthology). Don't worry if Young's definition is, at first glance, a little hard to understand. The readings in this anthology have been selected and organized in order to help. For now, notice that both definitions are action-oriented; each emphasizes efforts (or actions) that either promote justice or eliminate injustice. Thus, beyond merely description, an important feature of any definition of social justice involves the proscriptive necessity to do something about the problem. In this book, readers will learn about different types of social justice actions (or tactics) as well as historical and present-day examples of social justice activism.

Second, this book is grounded in literature on social change, liberation, ethics, and critical theory authored by prominent scholars, thinkers, practitioners, and activists in the field. I include a variety of interdisciplinary texts connected to social justice studies (e.g., philosophy, legal scholarship, religion, intersectionality scholarship, critical race, feminist, queer, postcolonial, disability scholarship, etc.). These (inter) disciplinary frameworks have been instrumental in developing the field of social justice studies and, in some cases, emerge out of social justice studies. Although the anthology is interdisciplinary in nature, sociological perspectives of justice serve as a unifying thread. Unlike other explorations of justice studies that privilege legal, criminal, religious, human rights, social welfare, conflict resolution, or peace elements of justice, this anthology emphasizes sociological standpoints, explicitly situating the social and systemic implications of justice at the center of analysis. The readings focus on the social contours of power, inequality, and actions for change and how these social phenomena have historically shaped and currently shape justice outcomes at every level of society: institutionally, interactionally, and individually.

Third, and related to the previous point, this interdisciplinary compilation of readings, collectively, provides readers with an introductory overview of the field of social justice studies. This includes key areas of study, foundational texts, core concepts, timely (and timeless) social justice issues, debates within the field, and future directions. Social justice studies is becoming increasingly institutionalized in higher education curriculums.[2] This development in the educational landscape is, in part,

---

1   Chepp, Valerie. 2018. "Social Justice." Pp. 271–273 in *Core Concepts in Sociology*, edited by J. M. Ryan. Hoboken, NJ: Wiley-Blackwell.

2   Smith, Mitch. 2012. "Social Justice Revival," *Inside Higher Ed*. January 31. Social justice studies has also experienced a backlash in institutions of higher education; see, e.g., Ellis, Lindsay. 2021. "No 'Social Justice' in the Classroom: Statehouses Renew Scrutiny of Speech at Public Colleges," *The Chronicle of Higher Education*. February 3.

a response to an increased awareness around the complexity of identity, the importance of diversity, rising levels of social inequality, the enduring legacy of systematic oppression, and the value of learning how to effectively navigate and address questions of justice and injustice. These issues, concerns, and skills are more important and relevant than ever before and contribute to the increased demand for social justice learning among present-day students. This anthology will help schools, programs, workplaces, civic groups, and universities meet this need of 21st-century learners.

Many audiences will find this book helpful. The book is designed to be accessible to anyone interested in deepening their understanding of social justice; this includes students, teachers, managers, parents, business owners, administrators, service providers, coaches, caseworkers, artists, activists, law enforcement officers, health care workers, government officials, policymakers, and everyday people who want to learn more about how systems of social power and domination profoundly shape our lives and what we can do to create a more fair, just, and dignified society.

Acknowledgements

THIS BOOK IS THE CULMINATION OF many people's help, kindness, and encouragement. Below, I express my gratitude to several of these individuals; however, there are countless others who have supported my ideas and work. I am deeply grateful to everyone who has nurtured my social justice perspectives and pedagogy.

First, I would like to thank the many students who I have taught over the years, particularly those in my social justice courses, including Introduction to Issues in Social Justice, Youth Activism, Storytelling and Social Justice, and Social Justice Capstone. I'm especially grateful to the students in my Social Justice Capstone in fall 2019—Kalu Abosi, Kathleen Butler, Taylor Curtis, Kiera Newson, Shaniah Smith, and Savannah Spirov—who provided valuable and insightful feedback on a preliminary version of the book. One student deserves special recognition. From early on in this project, Nico Van Ostrand was by my side, helping with the myriad tasks—big and small, fun and tedious—associated with curating an anthology. I benefited greatly from Nico's intellectual contributions, work ethic, and passion for social justice. I am privileged to now call Nico a friend and colleague, and I'm honored to have Nico's own words appear in the book's afterword.

This project also benefited from many friends and colleagues with whom I have discussed social justice pedagogy and curricula. Thanks, especially, to Lester Andrist, Kendra Barber, Colleen Bell, Valentine Cadieux, Paul Dean, Máel Embser-Herbert, Sarah Greenman, Josh Gumiela, Amy Irby-Shasanmi, Susi Keefe, Ryan LeCount, Sharon Preves, Maggie Struck, and Della Zurick, among others, including the dedicated educators at Hamline University who are committed to teaching in socially just ways. I have learned so much from all of you. I am thankful, also, for my own teachers and mentors who have modeled social justice teaching and learning.

To the team at Cognella who helped this book come to fruition, I appreciate your patience, flexibility, and support. Thanks especially to Jim Brace-Thompson, Susana Christie, Seidy Cruz, Anne Jones, Gem Rabanera, and Jeanine Rees, all of whom nurtured various aspects of publishing this book.

Over the years, this project has benefited from the supportive environment provided by Hamline University. I am grateful for my time directing Hamline's Social Justice Program, which offered ample opportunities to think deeply and in interdisciplinary ways about social justice curricula, coursework, assignments, assessment, advising, community-building, and programming. I am also grateful for the time and financial support I received from Hamline University in support of this anthology, which included a Humanities Grant.

Finally, thanks to my family, whose encouragement and love is a constant presence and inspiration. Thanks especially to my mom, Jean, whose generous gifts of time and talent allowed me to complete this work, and to my son, Zavier, who gives me endless opportunities to teach, parent, and reflect in socially just ways.

Introduction: What is Social Justice? (and Other Tough Questions)

Valerie Chepp

What is "social justice"? What does it mean to create a just society? Who decides what's "just" and how "unjust" situations should be fixed?

I N THE 21ST CENTURY, QUESTIONS ABOUT social justice are more pertinent than ever. Look around. Our era bears witness to racially charged tensions around police violence; increased visibility of alt-right/hate groups; unprecedented wealth inequality; deep-rooted anti-immigrant sentiment; religious intolerance; bans against transgender people in sports, bathrooms, and other social spaces; genocides; stubbornly high rates of sexual assault; inadequate access to quality shelter, education, and health care; human degradation of the environment; and rising global disparities between the "haves" and "have nots."

How do we make sense of these unequal arrangements? Why do they persist? A supposed hallmark of modernity and liberalism is the promise of progress. As a global society, shouldn't we have "evolved" beyond this? Is this what progress looks like?

Many would say no. Groups around the world and across the political spectrum speak out in opposition to these pressing social problems, all claiming to stand on the side of justice. Take, for example, debates around reproductive choice, drug policy, affirmative action, capital punishment, and unionization. Activists on opposing sides claim to advocate for the more "just" solution. Who's right? Are definitions of social justice contextual and culturally, geographically, and temporally relative? Or are there universal criteria by which to assess just and unjust claims?

This book will help readers think through these and other tough questions about justice. It will also, undoubtedly, raise new questions, perhaps leaving some unanswered. That's OK. In fact, one of the book's goals is to underscore the pervasiveness of these justice-related questions and the challenges associated with finding solutions. Whether we recognize it or not, justice-related concerns permeate our world and our individual and group experiences within it. There isn't a corner of social life left untouched. At every level of society, questions about social justice are not only relevant but are also instrumental building blocks, shaping our identities, interactions with others, and experiences with social institutions, such as schools, work sites, health care facilities, places of faith, military, politics, family life, and more.

As such, there's much at stake in resolving—or at least wrestling with—these tough questions. The challenge is learning to identify *how* justice and injustice operate, *who* benefits (and who doesn't), and *what*—if anything—should be done (also, how should it be done).

Social Justice as a Buzzword

In the early 21st century, the ubiquity, importance, and complexity of social justice issues and concerns have gained significant public visibility. It seems everywhere we look, the term "social justice" is being deployed. Turn on the television or skim your social media newsfeed and you see politicians, business people, celebrities, academics, service providers, health care workers, teachers, students, activists, news anchors, journalists, and everyday citizens use the term when talking about issues of fairness, equity, access, diversity, tolerance, violence, opportunity, empathy, choice, self-determination, resilience, resistance, and human dignity.

Beyond the media, the phrase "social justice" is commonplace in academic classrooms, workplace trainings, and other learning environments. In elementary and high schools, social justice frameworks inform school counseling approaches, classroom pedagogies, and subject matter content. Student organizations, such as gay-straight alliances and spoken word poetry clubs, have social justice goals built into their missions.

Social justice learning shows up in higher education, as well. Disciplinary curriculums as diverse as sociology, philosophy, religion, feminist/queer studies, critical race studies, psychology, computer science, public health, public policy, social work, education, rhetoric, legal studies, medicine, and business offer courses related to social justice. Institutionally, the term "social justice" appears in university mission statements, and campuses devote entire centers to social justice research and engagement. Increasingly, colleges and universities offer degrees and certificates in social justice learning. College students also participate in various social justice–oriented organizations, such as social justice theater troupes, sustainability clubs, racial justice groups, and interfaith organizations, among others.

Beyond academic environments, workplaces offer social justice learning opportunities, routinely providing workers with access to diversity and social justice trainings. Religious and faith-based organizations, as well as various advocacy, social service, and civic groups, also integrate social justice learning into their work profiles.

However, while the term "social justice" may be commonly used, its meaning is often taken for granted. At times, the term is contentious, with some claiming social justice is a noble aspiration, while others perceive the term as undesirable (as is the case with "social justice warrior"), empty, or cloaked with unnecessary political correctness.

How do *you* understand this frequently used but rarely defined term? Are discussions about justice and social justice synonymous, or is there something unique and significant about adding the word "social" before the word "justice"? How can we engage in robust democratic debate, and ultimately find solutions to pressing social problems, when the terms of the debate are ill defined? In short, how can we talk about social justice without clearly explicating its meaning?

Seeking Answers and Generating New Questions

When I ask students to define "social justice" on the first day of class, they offer many important and useful ideas. I write them all on the board. Eventually, we end up with a long list of relevant concepts, including equality versus equity; fairness; treating people the same, irrespective of identity or group membership; recognizing intersecting identities; amplifying marginalized voices and experiences; valuing diversity; and challenging racism, classism, sexism, heterosexism, ableism, and all the other power structures that systematically discriminate and disadvantage groups. These are all good starting points for a discussion about social justice and ultimately lead to a broader classroom conversation (and more questions) about such things as: What do we mean by equality? Paying everyone the same wage? What about those who work harder or go to school longer? Do they deserve more? Should social privilege be taken into account? If so, how? Does equality mean that everybody has equal access to the same "stuff" (e.g., jobs, money, education, marriage licenses)? Does anything besides stuff (i.e., material things) matter? For example, does access to prestige matter? What about decision-making power, or control over how one's culture is represented? What is fairness? Does justice always mean treating everybody the same, or does justice sometimes require that we treat people differently? What actions do people and groups deploy to advance their claims about justice? What are challenges to making social justice activism sustainable? Is social justice always a politically "liberal" fight, or is social justice compatible with politically conservative ideologies as well?

By now, your head might be spinning, trying to juggle potential—and perhaps competing—answers to all these questions about justice. Enjoy. This is just the tip of the iceberg. But read on, and you will become equipped with useful vocabulary, analytic tools, and theoretical ideas for helping you think through these and other tough questions. By the book's end, you will walk away with answers—or at least some food for thought—that will help you make sense of the world you live in, particularly as someone who experiences privilege, oppression, or (most likely) both.

Organization of the Anthology

In her well-known 2009 TED Talk, Nigerian writer Chimamanda Ngozi Adichie warns her audience of "the danger of the single story."[1] Adichie is referring to the harmful effects of reducing an entire group of people to a single, one-dimensional narrative. This results in stereotypes and deprives complex, heterogenous individuals of their humanity.

Adichie's words of caution apply to other types of stories as well, including the story I tell in this anthology. While this book is designed to help readers better understand the field of social justice studies and its emancipatory potential, my decisions about what to include and exclude are important to note. This anthology provides one, of many, possible introductory accounts of social justice studies. While it will necessarily have omissions and oversights in terms of content, issues, authors, perspectives, and disciplines, my hope is that it offers a solid introduction to the diverse, expansive, multidisciplinary field of social justice learning. I encourage readers to explore and discover other anthologies, books, novels, websites, audio stories, music, poetry, and films that critically engage topics related to social power, oppression, inequality, fairness, and dignity.

---

1   Adichie, Chimamanda Ngozi. 2009. "The Danger of the Single Story" [Video]. TED Conferences. July. Retrieved May 6, 2021 (https://www.ted.com/talks/chimamanda_ngozi_adichie_the_danger_of_a_single_story?). More recently, Adichie has received some criticism from social justice advocates; see, e.g., Camminga, B. 2020. "Disregard and Danger: Chimamanda Ngozi Adichie and the Voices of Trans (and Cis) African Feminists." *The Sociological Review* 68(4): 817–833.

The social justice story told in this anthology is intended to be concise, accessible, thought provoking, interdisciplinary, and comprehensive (though not exhaustive). Given my own academic training and area of expertise, the book's scope focuses primarily, though not exclusively, on the United States. As you approach each reading, note the date of publication listed after the title; these dates are included to convey a sense of time unfolding in which conversations about justice have taken place and a historical context that inevitably shapes authors' language and perspectives on social justice. How social justice issues are discussed has changed over time, and readers should keep this in mind. An example of this can be found in the current distinctions between inequality and inequity, designed to illustrate the difference between a social imbalance (i.e., inequality) and injustice or unfairness (i.e., inequity). Take, for instance, inequalities in health care, laid bare by the onset of the COVID-19 pandemic and the disproportionate impacts of the pandemic on marginalized communities. These health inequalities are the result of long-term inequities in access to health care as well as other social structural inequities, such as access to affordable housing and stable, well-paying jobs. While this distinction is often made in current social justice scholarship, it's less common in earlier texts.

This anthology is organized into four units. The first, "Foundations and Perspectives," lays out classical and foundational texts in the field of social justice studies as well as some key concepts, vocabulary, and theories. This foundation equips readers with a solid knowledge base from which to consider "real-world" social justice issues. Unit II, "Oppression, Privilege, and Intersectionality," draws upon more contemporary texts to examine social systems of power and how these systems intersect to result in social inequities for different social groups. The third unit, "Inequality, Institutions, and Systemic Power," consists of case studies, tangible examples, and empirically driven works that illustrate the material reality of injustice and inequality. The book's fourth and final unit, "Movements, Change, and Resistance," casts a forward-looking gaze and includes texts that imagine a path forward and argue for a particular future. The anthology concludes with an afterword by Nico Van Ostrand.

At the beginning of each unit, I offer a short introductory essay that situates and contextualizes the set of readings that follows. Throughout these unit introductions, I highlight some key terms (in **bold**) that readers might want to spend additional time thinking about and learning; some of these terms are defined in context, and others are defined in the sidebar. At the end of each unit introduction, I provide a set of post-reading questions to help deepen readers' comprehension of themes emerging from the texts and to encourage readers to place the different texts in conversation with one another.

As you read on, I leave you with two short quotes, both from prominent social justice activists of the U.S. civil rights movement. These quotes reflect key understandings from this anthology and from social justice studies more broadly. First, Dr. Martin Luther King Jr. famously wrote in his "Letter from the Birmingham City Jail" (see Reading 4.1), "Injustice anywhere is a threat to justice everywhere." The second quote comes from Ella Baker, who wisely stated, "We who believe in freedom cannot rest." As you read through these pages, carry these insights with you, and relate them to the ideas and experiences you learn about in this book. What do King and Baker mean? How are their comments connected, and how do they align with the possibility of a more just world?

Unit I

Foundations and Perspectives

Valerie Chepp

The readings in this unit draw upon classical and foundational texts to introduce key concepts, vocabulary, and theories in the field of social justice studies. The goal is to provide readers with a base of knowledge with which to understand and analyze various social justice issues.

This unit spans centuries of writing. The section is loosely, but not entirely, organized chronologically. What ties these readings together is that they profoundly shaped contemporary ideas about justice. Many of these ideas are firmly reflected and grounded in a tradition of **western liberal thought**. Emerging out of the Age of Enlightenment, this western liberal tradition, which also forms the bedrock of **social contract theory**, places an emphasis on human reason, choice, consent, the possibility for progress, and the opportunity to revolt against external rulers or governments who aren't of the people's consent. These core values, whether we uphold or critique them, shape modern-day discussions about justice; as such, this unit illuminates some of the origins that inform our most prominent ideas about what's right and wrong, fair and unfair.

> **social contract theory**: in moral and political philosophy, this theory purports that people mutually enter into tacit agreements in which they give up some of their individual rights and accept a central authority in exchange for governmental protection.

The opening reading, "Letter from Benjamin Banneker to the Secretary of State, with His Answer (1792)," is a correspondence between Banneker, a prominent African American astronomer and mathematician, and Thomas Jefferson who, at the time, was serving as the U.S. secretary of state. In his letter, Banneker seeks to rebut Jefferson's argument on the inferiority of Africans in his well-known *Notes on the State of Virginia*. Banneker's letter is heartfelt and articulated in a logical and moral fashion. In his brief response, Jefferson is polite yet dismissive and fails to address the political, religious, and ethical challenges raised by Banneker.

This correspondence presents some overarching questions threaded throughout the remainder of this anthology: What is our individual power in effecting change? How can we use our own positions of privilege to incite change? How does our social location shape our worldview? What is our belief in the possibility for progress and a more just future? How do we reconcile the discrepancy between the promise of justice manifested in words versus the reality manifested in actions? Especially striking in this correspondence is the juxtaposition between Banneker's eloquence and Jefferson's dismissal (here we can reflect upon the historical reverence bestowed upon Jefferson and how this history gets recorded, while others, like Banneker, are historically marginalized).

The next two readings represent different approaches to thinking about justice. In the brief selection from Homer's *Iliad*, the notion of "justice as vengeance" is introduced. This version of **retributive justice** delivers punishment based on one's group membership, as the Trojan warrior Adrestos was killed based on his affiliation with the Trojans rather than any wrongdoing he personally committed. The following reading, a series of biblical verses from the book of Leviticus, represents a different version of retributive justice, one in which punishment is delivered only to the wrongdoer and in a proportionate—or balanced—way (i.e., "eye for eye, tooth for tooth"). Justice as **proportionate punishment** can be found in other religious texts, such as the Koran.

retributive justice: a system of justice based on the punishment of lawbreakers or wrongdoers.

distributive justice: the fair distribution of wealth and goods among the members of a society based on merit.

The subsequent set of readings, focused on the writings of Plato and Aristotle, represent less of a concern with retributive justice and, instead, shift the discussion to concerns over social harmony, balance, and **distributive justice**, that is, fair and just exchange. In selections from Books I, IV, and V of the *Republic*, Plato argues that justice is the essential, most important virtue for humans, and through his "Ring of Gyges" parable, he seeks to prove that a harmonious republic (or society/city) is analogous to a harmonious soul (or individual). In both cases, whether the republic or individual, Plato underscores the importance of performing one's own job (what they're best suited for) and working together. This results in harmony/justice in the city as well as harmony/justice in the individual. In the reading selection from *Nichomachean Ethics*, Aristotle makes a clear case for distributive justice in his discussion of lawfulness, fairness, and equality. Emphasizing the importance of proportionality and balance, Aristotle not only advocates for a vision of justice that rectifies wrongs in a proportionate way (i.e., **rectificatory justice**) but also advocates for a similar sense of balance and fairness in his notion of distributive justice, arguing that goods and rewards should be distributed according to **merit** (what one "deserves"). On this point, it's worth noting that, for Aristotle, equality does not mean distributing goods and rewards equally to everyone. For Aristotle, this would be unjust since not everyone is equally deserving. The educational grading system is a good example of Aristotle's distributive justice, in which a "fair" system is one where students who are deemed more deserving earn higher grades, and students who are deemed less deserving earn lower grades. Plato's and Aristotle's ideas about justice are helpfully placed in conversation with one another in "Plato and Aristotle on Justice" by Gary Gabor, which compares and contrasts the two Greek philosophers' teachings about justice.

Writing more than 2,000 years later (closer to the time of Banneker and Jefferson), and building off the ideas of his predecessor Thomas Hobbes, John Locke's selection from *Second Treatise of Government* puts forth a case for justice informed by social contract theory. This selection also includes Locke's argument for private property as being central to justice. Writing nearly two centuries later, Karl Marx, in a sharp departure from Locke, is deeply critical of private property (a hallmark of capitalism) and the injustices it harbors. The corpus of work on and by Marx is vast; included in this volume is Lester Andrist's "The Curious Alienation of Cocoa Farmers from Their Chocolate," a short analysis (and accompanied video application) of Marx's thoughts on **alienation**, which is, as Andrist explains, "a condition that arises from the social relations that form within a system of capitalist production." In the following reading, "Justice as Fairness," Chris Brown provides an overview of the 20th-century philosopher John Rawls's notion of justice. In conversation with previous social contract theorists, Rawls argues that justice has to do with institutional arrangements and decision making. This reading covers two well-known concepts introduced by Rawls: **veil of ignorance** and **original position**.

veil of ignorance: a thought experiment designed to portray impartial choice in which people do not know their own abilities, preferences, or conception of the good.

original position: a state in which people decide how to establish a basic, impartial framework of institutions and rules, whereby people can pursue their own conception of the good.

Reading 1.1

Letter from Benjamin Banneker to the Secretary of State, with His Answer

(1792)

Benjamin Banneker, Thomas Jefferson

T HE BEST-KNOWN AFRICAN-AMERICAN SCIENTIST AND MECHANIC of the colonial period was undoubtedly Benjamin Banneker (1731–1806), who made clocks, taught himself astronomy, and published an acclaimed almanac. When Thomas Jefferson, then Secretary of State, published his famous *Notes on the State of Virginia* (written in 1781), it contained arguments for the inferiority of Africans and compared them unfavorably to "white" people. Knowing Jefferson to be a fellow scientist, Banneker sent him a copy of his almanac while it was still in manuscript form. His own technical virtuosity was a powerful rebuttal to Jefferson's racist judgments.

FIGURE 1.1   Portrait of Benjamin Banneker, reproduced on the title page of his almanac for 1795, printed for John Fisher. (Variant spellings of names were common in the eighteenth century.)

Carroll Pursell, "Letter from Benjamin Banneker to the Secretary of State, with His Answer (1792)," *A Hammer in Their Hands: A Documentary History of Technology and the African-American Experience*, pp. 15–16. Copyright © 2006 by MIT Press.

Copy of a Letter from Benjamin Banneker, & C.

Maryland, Baltimore County, August 19, 1791

Sir,

I am fully sensible of the greatness of that freedom, which I take with you on the present occasion; a liberty which seemed to me scarcely allowable, when I reflected on that distinguished and dignified station in which you stand, and the almost general prejudice and prepossession, which is so prevalent in the world against those of my complexion.

I suppose it is a truth too well attested to you, to need a proof here, that we are a race of beings, who have long labored under the abuse and censure of the world; that we have long been looked upon with an eye of contempt; and that we have long been considered rather as brutish than human, and scarcely capable of mental endowments.

Sir, I hope I may safely admit, in consequence of that report which hath reached me, that you are a man far less inflexible in sentiments of this nature, than many others; that you are measurably friendly, and well disposed towards us; and that you are willing and ready to lend your aid and assistance to our relief, from those many distresses, and numerous calamities, to which we are reduced.

Now Sir, if this is founded in truth, I apprehend you will embrace every opportunity, to eradicate that train of absurd and false ideas and opinions, which so generally prevails with respect to us; and that your sentiments are concurrent with mine, which are, that one universal Father hath given being to us all; and that he hath not only made us all of one flesh, but that he hath also, without partiality, afforded us all the same sensations and endowed us all with the same faculties; and that however variable we may be in society or religion, however diversified in situation or color, we are all of the same family, and stand in the same relation to him.

Sir, if these are sentiments of which you are fully persuaded, I hope that you cannot but acknowledge, that it is the indispensable duty of those, who maintain for themselves the rights of human nature, and who possess the obligations of Christianity, to extend their power and influence to the relief of every part of the human race, from whatever burden or oppression they may unjustly labor under; and this, I apprehend, a full conviction of the truth and obligation of these principles should lead all to.

Sir, I have long been convinced, that if your love for yourselves, and for those inestimable laws, which preserved to you the rights of human nature, was founded on sincerity, you could not but be solicitous, that every individual, of whatever rank or distinction, might with you equally enjoy the blessings thereof; neither could you rest satisfied short of the most active effusion of your exertions, in order to their promotion from any state of degradation, to which the unjustifiable cruelty and barbarism of men may have reduced them.

Benjamin Banneker and Thomas Jefferson, "Letter from Benjamin Banneker to Thomas Jefferson," 1791.

Sir, I freely and cheerfully acknowledge, that I am of the African race, and in that color which is natural to them of the deepest dye; and it is under a sense of the most profound gratitude to the Supreme Ruler of the Universe, that I now confess to you, that I am not under that state of tyrannical thraldom, and inhuman captivity, to which too many of my brethren are doomed, but that I have abundantly tasted of the fruition of those blessings, which proceed from that free and unequalled liberty with which you are favored; and which, I hope, you will willingly allow you have mercifully received, from the immediate hand of that Being, from whom proceedeth every good and perfect Gift.

Sir, suffer me to recall to your mind that time, in which the arms and tyranny of the British crown were exerted, with every powerful effort, in order to reduce you to a state of Servitude: look back, I entreat you, on the variety of dangers to which you were exposed; reflect on that time, in which every human aid appeared unavailable, and in which even hope and fortitude wore the aspect of inability to the conflict, and you cannot but be led to a serious and grateful sense of your miraculous and providential preservation; you cannot but acknowledge, that the present freedom and tranquility which you enjoy you have mercifully received, and that it is the peculiar blessing of Heaven.

This, Sir, was a time when you clearly saw into the injustice of a state of slavery, and in which you had just apprehensions of the horrors of its condition. It was now that your abhorrence thereof was so excited, that you publicly held forth this true and invaluable doctrine, which is worthy to be recorded and remembered in all succeeding ages: "We hold these truths to be self-evident, that all men are created equal; that they are endowed by their Creator with certain unalienable rights, and that among these are, life, liberty, and the pursuit of happiness."

Here was a time, in which your tender feelings for yourselves had engaged you thus to declare, you were then impressed with proper ideas of the great violation of liberty, and the free possession of those blessings, to which you were entitled by nature; but, Sir, how pitiable is it to reflect, that although you were so fully convinced of the benevolence of the Father of Mankind, and of his equal and impartial distribution of these rights and privileges, which he hath conferred upon them, that you should at the same time counteract his mercies, in detaining by fraud and violence so numerous a part of my brethren, under groaning captivity and cruel oppression, that you should at the same time be found guilty of that most criminal act, which you professedly detected in others, with respect to yourselves.

I suppose that your knowledge of the situation of my brethren, is too extensive to need a recital here; neither shall I presume to prescribe methods by which they may be relieved, otherwise than by recommending to you and all others, to wean yourselves from those narrow prejudices which you have imbibed with respect to them, and as Job proposed to his friends, "put your soul in their souls' stead;" thus shall your hearts be enlarged with kindness and benevolence towards them; and thus shall you need neither the direction of myself or others, in what manner to proceed herein.

And now, Sir, although my sympathy and affection for my brethren hath caused my enlargement thus far, I ardently hope, that your candor and generosity will plead with you in my behalf, when I make known to you, that it was not originally my design; but having taken up my pen in order to direct to you, as a present, a copy of an Almanac, which I have calculated for the succeeding year, I was unexpectedly and unavoidably led thereto.

This calculation is the production of my arduous study, in this my advanced state of life; for having long have unbounded desires to become acquainted with the secrets of nature, I have had to gratify my curiosity herein, through my own assiduous application to Astronomical Study, in which I need not recount to you the many difficulties and disadvantages, which I have had to encounter.

And although I had almost declined to make my calculation for the ensuing year, in consequence of that time which I had allotted therefor, being taken up at the Federal Territory, by the request of Mr. Andrew Ellicott, yet finding myself under several engagements to Printers of this state, to whom I had communicated my design, on my return to my place of residence, I industriously applied myself thereto, which I hope I have accomplished with correctness and accuracy; a copy of which I have taken the liberty to direct to you, and which I humbly request you will favorably receive; and although you may have the opportunity of perusing it after its publication, yet I choose to send it to you in manuscript previous thereto, that thereby you might not only have an earlier inspection, but that you might also view it in my own hand writing.

And now, Sir, I shall conclude, and subscribe myself, with the most profound respect,

Your most obedient humble servant,
Benjamin Banneker

To Mr. Benjamin Banneker.
Philadelphia, August 30, 1791

Sir,

I Thank you, sincerely, for your letter of the 19th instant, and for the Almanac it contained. No body wishes more than I do, to see such proofs as you exhibit, that nature has given to our black brethren talents equal to those of the other colors of men; and that the appearance of the want of them, is owing merely to the degraded condition of their existence, both in Africa and America. I can add with truth, that no body wishes more ardently to see a good system commenced, for raising the condition, both of their

Benjamin Banneker and Thomas Jefferson, "Letter from Thomas Jefferson to Benjamin Banneker," 1791.

body and mind, to what it ought to be, as far as the imbecility of their present existence, and other circumstances, which cannot be neglected, will admit.

I have taken the liberty of sending your Almanac to Monsieur de Condozett, Secretary of the Academy of Sciences at Paris, and Member of the Philanthropic Society, because I considered it as a document, to which your whole color had a right for their justification, against the doubts which have been entertained of them.

I am with great esteem, Sir,
Your most obedient
Humble Servant,
Thomas Jefferson

Reading 1.2

Selection from "Book 6" of the *Iliad* (ca. 800 B.C.)

Homer

Now MENELAOS OF THE GREAT WAR cry captured Adrestos alive; for his two horses bolting over the level land got entangled in a tamarisk growth, and shattered the curving chariot at the tip of the pole; so they broken free went on toward the city, where many beside stampeded in terror. So Adrestos was whirled beside the wheel from the chariot headlong into the dust on his face; and the son of Atreus, Menelaos, with the far-shadowed spear in his hand, stood over him. But Adrestos, catching him by the knees, supplicated: 'Take me alive, son of Atreus, and take appropriate ransom. In my rich father's house the treasures lie piled in abundance; bronze is there, and gold, and difficultly wrought iron, and my father would make you glad with abundant repayment were he to hear that I am alive by the ships of the Achaians.'

So he spoke, and moved the spirit inside Menelaos. And now he was on the point of handing him to a henchman to lead back to the fast Achaian ships; but Agamemnon came on the run to join him and spoke his word of argument: 'Dear brother, o Menelaos, are you concerned so tenderly with these people? Did you in your house get the best of treatment from the Trojans? No, let not one of them go free of sudden death and our hands; not the young man child that the mother carries still in her body, not even he, but let all of Ilion's people perish, utterly blotted out and unmourned for.'

The hero spoke like this, and bent the heart of his brother since he urged justice. Menelaos shoved with his hand Adrestos the warrior back from him, and powerful Agamemnon stabbed him in the side.

Homer, from The Iliad of Homer, trans. Richmond Lattimore. Copyright © 2003 by Wordsworth Editions Ltd.

Leviticus, Bible (NIV), 24:17–22

From the Bible

[17] "'Anyone who takes the life of a human being is to be put to death. [18] Anyone who takes the life of someone's animal must make restitution—life for life. [19] Anyone who injures their neighbor is to be injured in the same manner: [20] fracture for fracture, eye for eye, tooth for tooth. The one who has inflicted the injury must suffer the same injury. [21] Whoever kills an animal must make restitution, but whoever kills a human being is to be put to death. [22] You are to have the same law for the foreigner and the native-born. I am the Lord your God.'"

The Republic (excerpt)

(ca. 380 B.C.)

Plato

Book I

[...]

"Have we not agreed that justice is a virtue of the soul, and injustice a vice?", I (Socrates) said.

"Yes, we have," Thrasymachus replied.

"Then the just soul and the just person will live well, but the unjust badly?"

"Apparently," he said, "according to your argument."

"Again, the one that lives well is blessed and happy, the one that lives badly the opposite?"

"Agreed," he said.

"But it is not profitable to be miserable, but to be happy?"

"Undoubtedly."

"Then, my noble Thrasymachus, injustice is never more profitable than justice?"

"Well, Socrates," he said, "let that be your entertainment for the present feast."

"I have you to thank for it, Thrasymachus," I said, "since you became gentle with me, and stopped being disagreeable. But I have no satisfaction in my feast. That is my fault, not yours. I am like those greedy fellows who before they have properly enjoyed what is before them leave it to snatch at and taste every dish that comes their way. I have done the same. We left the original object of our inquiry, the definition of justice, before we have discovered it, and went off to consider whether it is a vice or ignorance, or wisdom and virtue. Then another argument appeared, to the effect that injustice is more profitable than justice. And I could not refrain leaving what we were at for this further point, so that now the result of our conversation is that I know nothing. For when I do not know what justice is, I am hardly likely to know whether it be a virtue or not, or whether the one that possesses it is unhappy or happy."

Adapted from Plato, The Republic of Plato, trans. A.D. Lindsay, pp. 38–39, 40–46, 133–139, 189, 204–205. J. M. Dent & Co., 1907.

Book II

"With these words I thought that I had finished. But this, it appeared, was after all only a prelude, for Glaucon with his usual fearlessness would not accept Thrasymachus' refutation, but said: Socrates, are you content with the appearance of conviction, or do you wish really to convince us that to be just is in every way better than to be unjust?"

"I should certainly prefer," I said, "to really convince you as far as lay in my power."

"Well, he said, you do not. [...] That is not the opinion of most people. They place it in the troublesome class of good things, which must be pursued for the sake of the reward and the high place in public opinion which they bring, but which in themselves are irksome and to be avoided."

"I know that people think so," I said. "It is on those grounds that Thrasymachus has always criticized justice and praised injustice. But I am apparently a slow pupil."

"Well," he said, "as Thrasymachus has spoken, let me speak also, and see then whether you are still of the same opinion. [...] I myself, Socrates, am not at all of this opinion. But I get confused; my ears are dinned with the arguments of Thrasymachus and countless others; but from none have I heard as yet the argument in defense of justice, and its superiority to injustice, as I want to hear it. For I want to hear the praises of justice for its own sake, and I have the greatest hopes that I shall do so from you. I shall speak vehemently therefore in favor of the unjust life, and in doing so I shall show you the way in which I want to hear you condemning injustice and praising justice." [...]

"By nature, men say, to do injustice is good, to suffer it evil, but there is more evil in suffering injustice that there is good in inflicting it. Therefore when men act unjustly towards one another, and thus experience both the doing and the suffering, those amongst them who are unable to compass the one and escape the other, come to this opinion: that it is more profitable they should mutually agree neither to inflict injustice nor to suffer it. Hence men began to establish laws and covenants with one another, and they called what the Law prescribed lawful and just. This, then, is the origin and nature of justice. It is a mean between the best—doing justice with impunity—and the worst—suffering injustice without possibility of requital. Thus justice, being a mean between those extremes, is looked upon with favor, not because it is good, but because the inability to inflict injustice makes it valuable. For no one who had the power to inflict injustice and was anything of a man would ever make a contract of mutual abstention from injustice with anyone else. He would be mad if he did. Such, Socrates, is the nature of justice, and such is its origin, according to the popular account."

"Now, that those who practice justice do so unwillingly and from inability to inflict injustice, will be seen most clearly if we make the following supposition. Suppose we take the just and the unjust man and give each power to do whatever he will, and then follow them and see where each is led by his desires. We shall catch the just man following undisguisedly the very same road as the unjust. He would be led on by his desire to outdo his fellows: every nature naturally pursues that as good, though law compels it to turn aside and reverence equality. The impunity I refer to would be best exemplified if they could have the power possessed by the ancestor of Gyges the Lydian in the story. For they say that he was a shepherd, a servant of the reigning king of Lydia. There was a great storm of rain and an earthquake where he was feeding his flock: the ground was rent, and a chasm appeared. In amazement he looked in, then descended into the chasm, and saw there many marvelous things which the story enumerates. Among them was a horse of bronze, hollow, with windows in its sides. He looked in and saw inside a dead body, which seemed of almost superhuman size. On the hand was a golden ring. He took this and nothing besides, then came away. When the shepherds held their usual gathering at which they arranged for the sending of their report on the flocks to the king, he came with the ring on his finger. As he was sitting with the others he happened to turn around the bezel of the ring until it came to the inside of his hand. On his doing so he became invisible to his companions, and they talked of him as of an absent man. In astonishment he touched his ring again and turned the bezel back to the outside of his hand. As he turned it he became visible again. Then he determined to test whether this power really lay in the ring, and he found that he became invisible when he turned the bezel inwards, visible when he turned it outwards. When he had made this discovery he at once contrived to be one of the messengers sent to the king. Arriving at the palace he seduced the queen, plotted with her against the king, killed him, and so obtained the crown."

"Now, if there were two such rings, and the just person took one and the unjust the other, no one, it is thought, would be of such adamantine nature as to abide to justice and have the strength to abstain from theft, and to keep their bands from the goods of others, when it would be in their power to steal anything they wished from the very marketplace with impunity, to enter people's houses and have intercourse with whom he would, to kill or to set free whomsoever they pleased; in short, to walk among people as a god. And, in so doing, the just person would act precisely as the unjust. Both would follow the same path. This, surely, may be cited as strong evidence that no person is just willingly, but only on compulsion. Justice is not a good to the individual, for everyone is unjust whenever they think injustice possible. Every person thinks that injustice is more profitable to the individual than justice, and thinks rightly, according to the supporters of this theory; for if any person who possessed this power we have described should yet refuse to do unjustly or to rob their fellows, all who knew of his conduct would think them the most miserable and foolish of people, but they would praise them to each other's faces, their fear of suffering injustice extorting that deceit from them. So much, then, for that. Now this question concerning the life of these two men we shall be able to decide aright only by contrasting the extremes of justice and injustice. How shall we make our contrast? In this way. Let us abstract nothing from the injustice of the unjust or from the justice of the just; each shall be perfect in their own way of life. Firstly, then, the unjust person shall be like a clever craftsman. The skillful captain or doctor can discern what is possible and what is impossible in their art. They attempt the one and leave the other alone; and if by any chance they make a mistake, they are able to retrieve it. Similarly the unjust person, if they are to be thoroughly unjust, shall show discernment in their unjust deeds and shall not be found out. If they are caught we must consider them a failure; for it is the extremity of injustice to seem just without being it. To the perfectly unjust person, then, we must give perfect injustice, and abstract nothing from it. We must allow them to do the fullest injustice and be reputed truly just. If ever they make a mistake, they must be able to retrieve it. If any of their unjust deeds are brought to light their eloquence will be convincing in their favor. They will be able to use force where force is needed, thanks to their courage, strength, and resources of friends and wealth. Such is the unjust person."

"Beside them, in accordance with the argument, let us place our just person, a simple and noble character, one who, as Aeschylus says, desires not to seem, but to be good. The semblance, indeed, we must take from them; for if they are reputed just, they will enjoy the honors and rewards that such a reputation earns, and thus it will not be apparent, it is objected, whether they are just for justice's sake or the honors' and rewards' sake. They must be stripped of everything except justice, and made the very counterpart of the other person. They shall do no injustice, and be reputed altogether unjust, that their justice may be tested as being proof against ill-repute and its consequences, and go on this way unchanged until death, all their life seeming unjust but being just. Thus these two will have come to the extremes of justice and of injustice, and we may judge which of them is the happier." [...]

"Well, given two such characters, it is not difficult now, I fancy, to go on, to discover what sort of life awaits each of them. Let me describe it. If my description is rather harsh, remember, Socrates, that those who praise injustice above justice are responsible, and not I. They will say that our just person will be scourged, racked, fettered, will have their eyes burnt out, and at last, after all manner of suffering, will be crucified and will learn that they ought to desire not to be but to seem just; for those words of Aeschylus applied much more truly to the unjust person. For it is the unjust person in reality, they will say, who, as his practice is akin to truth and his life not ruled by appearances, desires not to seem but to be unjust, 'and from the deep ploughed furrow of his heart reaps harvest rich of goodly purposes.' For, firstly, their semblance of justice brings them rule in their city. Then they may marry and give in marriage as they please; they may contract or enter into partnership with whom they will, and since they have no scruples against unjust dealings, they can besides make large profits. Therefore, when they enter into a contest, whether public or private, they come out victorious and get the better of their enemies. By so doing they become rich, help their friends and harm their enemies, and on the gods they bestow sacrifices and offerings fitting and magnificent. Far better than the just person can they serve the gods or whatsoever person they please. So that even the love of the gods is more appropriately theirs than the just person's. Thus they say, Socrates, that at the hands of gods and human beings life is made richer for the unjust than for the just."

[...]

After considering an idealized city for several books, Socrates returns to the question of the definition of justice and its benefits in response to Glaucon's challenge to describe its benefits compared to injustice:

Book IV

"How shall we find justice?," I (Socrates) asked.

"I certainly have no notion," Adeimantus said, "and in any case I have no desire to discover it first if we are to have no further inquiry into temperance. What I personally should prefer is that you should examine that first. [...]

"I will," I replied. "At first sight it is more like a harmony or a musical mode than the former virtues."

"In what way?"

"Temperance," I said, "is surely an ordering and a control of certain pleasures and desires, as is declared by the common but mysterious expression that a person is master of themselves, and there are other similar expressions which give a clue to its nature. Do you not agree?"

"Most certainly." [...]

"This expression, however," I said, "seems to me to mean that there is in the person themself, that is, in their soul, a better and a worse, and when the better has by nature control of the worse, then, as we say, the person is master of themselves; for the expression is one of approval. When, on the other hand, in consequence of bad training, or the influence of associates, the better is weaker than the worse, and is overcome by its superior numbers, this is condemned by the expression as something disgraceful., and the person who is in this condition is called overruled by themself, and intemperate."

"Consider then," I said, "our new city, and you will find one of those conditions realized in it. [...] But the simple and orderly desires which are guided by reason, and which accompany intelligence and right belief, you will find in a small number, in those who have the best natures." [...]

"For at the beginning when we were founding our city, the principle which we then stated should rule throughout was, I think, justice, or at least a form of it. We stated surely, and, if you remember, have often repeated our statement, that each individual should pursue that work in this city for which his nature was naturally most-fitted, each one man doing one work."

"Yes, we did."

"But we have often said ourselves, and heard others saying, that to mind one's own business and not be meddlesome is justice.[1] [...] Do you know how I infer this?"

"Do tell me," he said.

"We have examined," I said, "temperance and courage and wisdom, and I think that the remaining virtue in the city is that which enabled these to find a place in it, and after they have appeared, preserves them so long as it is present in the city. But we said that if we found the first three, the remaining one would be justice."

"Yes, inevitably," he said.

"Consider now whether this point of view brings us to the same conclusion. Will you make the rulers in the city judge lawsuits?"

"Surely."

"And in their decisions will not their aim be merely to prevent either party having what belongs to others or being deprived of what is their own?"

"Yes, that will be their aim."

"On the assumption that that is just?"

"Yes."

"So from this point of view the possession and practice of what belongs to us and is our own would be acknowledged to be justice?"

"True."

"Consider, now, whether you agree with me. Do you think it will do any notable harm to the city if a builder attempts a shoemaker's work, or a shoemaker a builder's, or if they rake one another's tools or pay, or even if the same man tries to do both, and there is a general interchange in such professions?"

"No," he said.

"But I fancy when be that is by nature a craftsman or a money-maker of some kind is so elated by his wealth, or his large connections, or his bodily strength, or some such qualities, that he essays to enter the warrior class, or when one of the warriors aspire to the counselling and guardian class when he is unworthy of it, and these take one another's tools and privileges, or when the same man tries to combine all these offices, then, I fancy, you think with me that such change and meddling among those classes is death to the city?"

---

1   An alternate translation of Plato's Greek here is "to do the things that belong to oneself." If a more accurate translation of Plato's language, this would raise further questions of what it means for an action or thing to belong to oneself, and not necessarily carry the potentially problematic notions of working towards social justice included in the phrase "minding one's own business."

"Most certainly."

"Our classes are three, and meddling and interchange among them is the greatest of injuries to the city, and might justly be described as the extreme of evil-doing."

"It is exactly as you say."

"Then will you not admit that the worst kind of evil-doing to one's own city is injustice?"

"Surely."

"This then is injustice; and conversely the opposite of this—when each class, money-makers, auxiliaries, and guardians, attends to what belongs to it, each doing its own work in the city—will be justice, and will make the city just." [...]

"Let us now complete the inquiry which we undertook in the belief that if we first managed to perceive justice in some bigger thing which possessed it, it would then be easier to see its nature in an individual. We thought that a city was a thing of this sort, and we therefore founded the best we could, knowing that justice would be found in the good city. Let us now apply to the individual the conception that has been revealed to us there, and if the result is consistent, so much the better. But if some other conception is revealed in the individual, then we shall go back to the city and test it there. And perhaps by looking at the two side by side, and rubbing them together, we may make justice blaze out, like fire from two sticks, and when it is revealed, we shall hold it firmly in our minds."

"Well," he said, "there is method in your proposal, and we must follow it."

"Then," I said, "when to two things, a greater and a smaller, we give the same name, will they, in so far as they are called the same, be unlike or like?"

"Like," he said.

"Then, so far as the mere form of justice is concerned, the just man will in no way differ from the just city, but will be the same?"

"He will," he said.

"But it has been seen that a city is just when the three kinds of natures in it do each their own work, and that it is also temperate, courageous, and wise through other similar dispositions and relations of those three kinds."

"True," he said.

"Then similarly, my friend, we shall expect that the individual has these same kinds in his soul, and the same dispositions of them, if they are rightly called by the same name as the city."

[...]

After several additional details of the nature of justice and necessary arrangements in the idealized city, speaking with Glaucon, Socrates turns to the topic of the relation between knowledge and rule:

Book V

"There is one change," I said, "which I think we could prove would bring about the revolution. It's certainly neither a small nor an easy change, but it is possible."

"What is it?" he said.

"Now," I said, "I am at the very topic which we likened to the greatest wave. Spoken, however, it shall be even though it is likely to deluge me with laughter and ridicule, like a wave breaking in merriment. Consider then what I am about to say."

"Say on," he said.

"Unless," I said, "philosophers bear kingly rule in cities, or those who are now called kings and princes become genuine and adequate philosophers, and political power and philosophy be brought together, and unless the numerous natures who at present pursue either politics or philosophy, the one to the exclusion of the other, be forcibly debarred from this behavior, there will be no respite from evil, my dear Glaucon, for cities, nor I fancy for humanity; nor will this constitution, which we have just described in our argument, come to that realization which is possible for it and see the light hesitate of day. It is this which has for so long made me hesitate to speak. I saw how paradoxical it would sound. For it is given to few to perceive that no other constitution could ever bring happiness either to states or individuals."

[...]

Nichomachean Ethics (excerpt)

(ca. 322 B.C.)

Aristotle, translated by D. P. Chase

Book Five

Part 1

With regards to justice and injustice we must (1) consider what kind of actions they are concerned with, (2) what sort of mean justice is, and (3) between what extremes the just act is intermediate. Our investigation shall follow the same course as the preceding discussions.

We see that all men mean by justice that kind of state of character which makes people disposed to do what is just and makes them act justly and wish for what is just; and similarly by injustice that state which makes them act unjustly and wish for what is unjust. Let us too, then, lay this down as a general basis. For the same is not true of the sciences and the faculties as of states of character. A faculty or a science which is one and the same is held to relate to contrary objects, but a state of character which is one of two contraries does not produce the contrary results; e.g. as a result of health we do not do what is the opposite of healthy, but only what is healthy; for we say a man walks healthily, when he walks as a healthy man would.

Now often one contrary state is recognized from its contrary, and often states are recognized from the subjects that exhibit them; for (A) if good condition is known, bad condition also becomes known, and (B) good condition is known from the things that are in good condition, and they from it. If good condition is firmness of flesh, it is necessary both that bad condition should be flabbiness of flesh and that the wholesome should be that which causes firmness in flesh. And it follows for the most part that if one contrary is ambiguous the other also will be ambiguous; e.g. if 'just' is so, that 'unjust' will be so too.

Now 'justice' and 'injustice' seem to be ambiguous, but because their different meanings approach near to one another the ambiguity escapes notice and is not obvious as it is, comparatively, when the meanings are far apart, e.g. (for here the difference in outward form is great) as the ambiguity in the use of kleis for the collar-bone of an animal and for that with which we lock a door. Let us take as a starting-point, then, the various meanings of 'an unjust man'. Both the lawless man and the grasping and unfair man

Aristotle, Nicomachean Ethics, trans. D. P. Chase, 1911.

are thought to be unjust, so that evidently both the law-abiding and the fair man will be just. The just, then, is the lawful and the fair, the unjust the unlawful and the unfair.

[...]

Part 2

[...]

The unjust has been divided into the unlawful and the unfair, and the just into the lawful and the fair. To the unlawful answers the aforementioned sense of injustice. But since unfair and the unlawful are not the same, but are different as a part is from its whole (for all that is unfair is unlawful, but not all that is unlawful is unfair), the unjust and injustice in the sense of the unfair are not the same as but different from the former kind, as part from whole; for injustice in this sense is a part of injustice in the wide sense, and similarly justice in the one sense of justice in the other. Therefore we must speak also about particular justice and particular and similarly about the just and the unjust. The justice, then, which answers to the whole of virtue, and the corresponding injustice, one being the exercise of virtue as a whole, and the other that of vice as a whole, towards one's neighbour, we may leave on one side. And how the meanings of 'just' and 'unjust' which answer to these are to be distinguished is evident; for practically the majority of the acts commanded by the law are those which are prescribed from the point of view of virtue taken as a whole; for the law bids us practise every virtue and forbids us to practise any vice. And the things that tend to produce virtue taken as a whole are those of the acts prescribed by the law which have been prescribed with a view to education for the common good. But with regard to the education of the individual as such, which makes him without qualification a good man, we must determine later whether this is the function of the political art or of another; for perhaps it is not the same to be a good man and a good citizen of any state taken at random.

[...]

Part 3

(A) We have shown that both the unjust man and the unjust act are unfair or unequal; now it is clear that there is also an intermediate between the two unequals involved in either case. And this is the equal; for in any kind of action in which there's a more and a less there is also what is equal. If, then, the unjust is unequal, just is equal, as all men suppose it to be, even apart from argument. And since the equal is intermediate, the just will be an intermediate. Now equality implies at least two things. The just, then, must be both intermediate and equal and relative (i.e. for certain persons). And since the equal intermediate it must be between certain things (which are respectively greater and less); equal, it involves two things; qua just, it is for certain people. The just, therefore, involves at least four terms; for the persons for whom it is in fact just are two, and the things in which it is manifested, the objects distributed, are two. And the same equality will exist between the persons and between the things concerned; for as the latter the things concerned—are related, so are the former; if they are not equal, they will not have what is equal, but this is the origin of quarrels and complaints—when either equals have and are awarded unequal shares, or unequals equal shares. Further, this is plain from the fact that awards should be 'according to merit'; for all men agree that what is just in distribution must be according to merit in some sense, though they do not all specify the same sort of merit, but democrats identify it with the status of freeman, supporters of oligarchy with wealth (or with noble birth), and supporters of aristocracy with excellence. [...]

Part 4

(B) The remaining one is the rectificatory, which arises in connexion with transactions both voluntary and involuntary. This form of the just has a different specific character from the former. For the justice which distributes common possessions is always in accordance with the kind of proportion mentioned above (for in the case also in which the distribution is made from the common funds of a partnership it will be according to the same ratio which the funds put into the business by the partners bear to one another); and the injustice opposed to this kind of justice is that which violates the proportion. But the justice in transactions between man and man is a sort of equality indeed, and the injustice a sort of inequality; not according to that kind of proportion, however, but according to arithmetical proportion. For it makes no difference whether a good man has defrauded a bad man or a bad man a good one, nor whether it is a good or a bad man that has committed adultery; the law looks only to the distinctive character of the injury, and treats the parties as equal, if one is in the wrong and the other is being wronged, and if one inflicted injury and the other has received it. Therefore, this kind of injustice being an inequality, the judge tries to equalize it; for in the case also in which one has received and the other has inflicted a wound, or one has slain and the other been slain, the suffering and the action have been unequally distributed; but the judge tries to equalize by means of the penalty, taking away from the gain of the assailant... [...]

These names, both loss and gain, have come from voluntary exchange; for to have more than one's own is called gaining, and to have less than one's original share is called losing, e.g. in buying and selling and in all other matters in which the law has left people free to make their own terms; but when they get neither more nor less but just what belongs to themselves, they say that they have their own and that they neither lose nor gain.

Therefore the just is intermediate between a sort of gain and a sort of loss, viz. those which are involuntary; it consists in having an equal amount before and after the transaction.

Plato and Aristotle on Justice
(2021)

Gary Gabor

ANCIENT GREEK PHILOSOPHERS LIKE PLATO AND Aristotle developed early, but not necessarily the first, systematic views on justice and society. By the time Plato began writing in the 4th century BCE, a deep moral tradition in Greek literature and society already existed, which likely drew not only on their original thinking, but potentially also Hittite, Near Eastern, and Egyptian precedents. People have likely reflected on the powers and structures of society for much longer than the existing written record can tell us. A continuity of ethical reflection in the Greek world, though, with poets, politicians, philosophers, and general populations all contributing and raising questions to themselves and others, along with the comparatively large amount of material that has been preserved from the Greek world, makes this a tradition still worth reflecting on today.

One of the main questions that recurs, both in ancient settings like these and today, is the relation between individual human happiness, and the happiness of society as a whole. As we shall see, Plato and Aristotle have much to say on this question. Their reflections, through later thinking and practices built on them, have also had a significant influence on contemporary society. Getting a better sense of their impact helps us to evaluate where we have come from, and where we should still go.

The Nature of Justice in Society—Plato's *Republic*

Plato's *Republic* is a long dialogue on the nature of society, the human person, justice, virtue, and the value of the good for both individual and collective action and life. It starts with several challenges to the value of justice—if it is possible to get away with secret unknown injustices, and not be punished for them, why not prefer that mode of life? It certainly seems, from experience and perhaps even inclination, that this would be preferable, or at least how most people would choose to live if given the possibility. Plato presents his teacher, Socrates, who was killed by an Athenian jury in 399 BCE for practicing philosophy, as providing an extended argument over ten books advocating for the internal benefit of justice and virtuous action, even if the consequences are not immediately advantageous. Through many twists and turns in the argument, Socrates collaboratively convinces his friends, some of which include

Plato's brothers Glaucon and Adeimantus, along with other famous foreigners who had moved to Athens.[1] Plato presents, in a concrete, real-life setting (even if such an exact dialogue between Socrates and his contemporaries didn't actually occur) the real consequences that thinking about justice and its nature has for the way we live our lives and construct society.

Socrates argues throughout the dialogue, in too many ways to describe here, the intrinsic value of justice for individuals and society. Justice, Socrates describes in Book 4, is like an inner harmony of the soul, where a person follows and pays attention to the best part of their soul, their reason, and allows that to help guide their more passionate or spirited parts (for instance, the competitive instinct to succeed Plato thinks exists in every human being) along with the appetites and desires that go along with every human life (for food, pleasure, comfort, good clothes and other things, sexual inter-course, the beauties of art and literature, and the "thousand other things" Socrates says humans want). This account of the human person shows, almost immediately Plato thinks, the need for reason, balance, and some kind of rule for a human life. Since it is possible to want literally thousands of different things—take a look at the diversity of what can be bought on Amazon today, similar to the plurality of things that could be bought in an ancient Athenian market in the fifth century BCE—it would literally be impossible to try to pursue all of these desires in the course of a human life. One would become far too tired or run out of resources, thus defeating the purpose of the sorts of pleasures that are supposed to come from our wants and needs to begin with. So Plato, along with Socrates, think there must be some balance, that we cannot be "ruled" by our desires, but must instead pursue them according to some rational measure. Thus, while the rational, and hence virtuous, life might at first appear more restrictive than an unbounded unjust pursuit of fulfilling one's inclinations, no matter the consequences, upon reflection we realize that such a life is intrinsically maddening, and that the ratio-nal, balanced life is far more intrinsically choice-worthy, and thus far more valuable and pleasant, than first appears.

The same goes for a society or state in Plato's mind. Some societies are practically mad and frenzied in their own pursuits of what they think will make for collective happi-ness, even if rational reflection shows the absurdity of that pursuit. Here Plato is clearly thinking about his home of rich and democratic Athens, but the parallels to many con-temporary capitalistic societies are clear. Thus Socrates later in the dialogue, especially in Books 8 and 9, but also occasionally at other points beforehand, will point to similar-ities, despite initial differences, between democracies and the tyrannical governments

---

[1]   This includes the weapon seller Cephalus and his adopted son Polemarchus, along with the famous sophist (and one of Socrates' strongest critics in the dialogue) Thrasymachus, who some think Aristotle mentions having set up a tyrannical government of his own later in life.

that they often take themselves to oppose and occasionally go to war with and over-throw. While these types of governments may be externally opposed, internally they also share deep similarities and agreements, since many democracies and tyrannies value the same things—material goods, superficial ideas of what constitutes a happy life, military and political power and security, etc. One of the most important in Plato's mind, and here Aristotle will follow, is whether the things that they choose to value are really the most valuable things for human life and human flourishing. Is it really mate-rial possessions, or social and political power, or fame and status, and things along those lines? Or are there some deeper goods that are much more important when it comes to human happiness? Whatever this deeper thing might be, Plato and Aristotle agree, would be the real thing that should count as human virtue and thus justice.

In addition to the task of identifying the most important virtue(s) for a flourishing and just human life, Plato also imagines the possibility of a radical change of oneself and society, even if he knows this will only rarely occur. So for instance in Book 1 of the dia-logue, Socrates engages with the foreigner Cephalus and his adopted son Polemarchus on whether justice really consists, as many people believed then (as today), in benefit-ting one's friends and getting back on one's enemies. Socrates asks, if this is justice, then how could something good ever cause harm to anyone—friend or enemy alike? It must only ever benefit, Socrates concludes, and Polemarchus ends up agreeing, but exactly what such a beneficial thing like this could be would take time to identify (this is where harmony in one's soul, led by reason, begins to look like an attractive answer, because it's hard to imagine how that could not be a good thing). So, while we might have to radically change the things we value, and many may not, it is still possible to begin to desire justice as a beneficial thing in itself, Plato thinks.

Similarly, later in Book 5, Socrates has an extended conversation on the many ways conventional Athenian society is structured to commit significant injustices on a sys-tematic level. For example, the educational opportunities, and other roles available to the citizens of cities, are significantly determined by the position of one's parents, as well as one's birth gender. Socrates argues that there are deep injustices on both counts—and that it is also simply not a smart idea for a society in general—when it squanders opportunities for all its members to flourish and succeed, based not on their position, but on their abilities and capacity. Socrates argues for several proposals that were rad-ical for the time—women should receive the same education as men; women should not be confined to the home and should be elevated to positions of rule; and children of rich or powerful people should not be able to retain their position if someone else is more deserving and capable, even if the latter comes from humble origins. All of these things, Socrates says, become clear when we begin to focus more on what the fine or the noble would demand, not for the individual, but for the whole, and that things should not simply be done out of tradition, but that a reconception of what it means to call something just has the potential to radically reconceptualize how we organize society.

These, among many other lessons, derive from Plato's reflections on morality and society in the *Republic*. He is quite aware that many conclusions raised in the dialogue will be challenging, both for individuals and societies, and that the concrete results arising from them may not always equal the radical proposals that philosophical discussions discover. But we're better for having such discussions, Plato thinks, because without them, we make no progress, neither as individuals, nor as societies. This is in part Plato's answer to his fellow Athenians about their decision to execute Socrates. Since they were afraid of philosophy, and afraid of thinking, in many ways they were afraid of trying to better themselves, as scary as such a task like that can be. Toward the end of the *Republic*, in Book 9, Socrates addresses a concern from some of his conversation partners, namely whether the ideal and beautiful city that they have been building up in dialogue over the course of several hours could ever come into being. Socrates says it is possible, if all of society was to embrace philosophy, that is to embrace thinking for itself, in some way. This is a hard task, but Plato's worldview is optimistic in that he thinks it is possible. But even if it is not possible for an entire society, or every society in history, to become this way, it is still always a possibility to embrace it for oneself—to answer the call of justice in oneself and one's soul, and how one lives one's life. Because of this, Plato thinks, the inspiration for justice to move individuals and societies to make their own lives, and the world, a better place, will remain.

Aristotle's Revision and Extension of Plato in the *Ethics* and *Politics*

Aristotle expands on Plato's thoughts on justice while also taking them in new directions. For instance, Aristotle distinguishes between justice as virtue in an individual, and the way it might operate in a state or other political community. Aristotle agrees with Plato that the two are closely connected, with many potential overlaps between the kind of actions that might make an individual and society "just." But there are also differences. For example, if an individual, or society, unjustly takes something of value from someone or some group, a 'restorative' justice is required in which the item must be repaid with compensation of equal value. But when it comes to 'proportional' justice, this appears to be something reserved more for individuals. For instance, if someone has the capacity, because of natural talent, inclination, or experience, to make a greater contribution to society than others, then Aristotle thinks it proper and fair for them to receive some recognition of that, greater than someone whose contribution is less. A similar example today might be, all other things being equal, if someone works harder and learns more than another in a class, it would be unfair for them to receive the same grade as someone who neither attended nor completed any of the work. These distinctions, made in their earliest form in Aristotle's *Nicomachean Ethics* and its continuation the *Politics*, significantly influenced contemporary legal theory and practice, through its intermediary influence on later medieval and early modern political philosophers like Thomas Aquinas, John Locke, and Montesquieu.

Another important conception of justice for Aristotle is what he describes as 'general justice'. General justice is just another name for morality or virtue as a whole. Such a characteristic can appropriately be applied to an individual, who has other important virtues like courage, moderation, honesty, good temper, and friendliness. When describing societies as a whole, however, Aristotle goes in a slightly different direction. He notes that, based upon what is valued in different societies, different characteristics get described as 'just' or 'good'. So for instance, in extremely capitalistic societies (or what Aristotle calls 'oligarchic' societies, where those with wealth predominantly have the most influence and rule), wealth is seen as the highest good, indeed, the greatest contribution one can make to society. By contrast, more egalitarian societies (what Aristotle calls 'democracies', where the larger majority of people have greater influence than any smaller subset) equality and freedom are seen as the most important goods. In the *Politics*, Aristotle notes that such different conceptions of the good often create friction—both within, and between, societies. Thus, the most valuable character traits in a capitalistic oligarchy would not necessarily be valued as highly (or perhaps even despised) in a more egalitarian democracy. Because of this, Aristotle raises the question in Book 3 of the *Politics* about whether there is any tension between being a good *citizen*, and being a good *person*. Such conflicts can even give rise to revolution and other similar internal social conflict (think about varying viewpoints about what constitutes just requirements and behavior between the American revolutionaries and their British overseers, or modern advocates of indigenous persons' claim on land rights in North America against historically perceived injustices performed by the United States, Canadian, and Mexican governments). Such differences of view about what constitutes valuable goods and justice can be found in many contemporary debates and disagreements about what is right and just today, on both the small and large scale, and across many different political and social spectrums.

Aristotle also thinks, when considering the goodness and justness of societies as a whole, that a very different but important question comes into play. The most important criterion, in Aristotle's mind, is not who rules—it could be possible to have a single ruler like in a monarchy, a small group, or the majority of the population—but rather for what purpose they rule. If rulers govern for the benefit of the whole, and not their own individual benefit, then we can call the government good and just. But if the group only rules for their own advantage (think for example of Thrasymachus' challenge to Socrates in the *Republic* again), then the government is clearly unjust in Aristotle's mind.

The differences between ruling for the good of the whole versus the good simply of the rulers is so significant for Aristotle that he prefers to use different names to describe such governments. Thus, a good government by a single (or perhaps two or three joint) king or queen Aristotle calls a 'monarchy'. The comparable bad government by a single person he labels a 'tyranny'. The bad form of government of the few Aristotle calls an oligarchy, meaning 'rule by a part'; large wealth often is the criterion for such selective rule most of the time. But a good rule by some small few, who have good character traits and virtue (aka 'arete' in the Greek), would be an 'aristocracy', or literally, rule by the good or the best. In such a society, these rulers would attempt to have some greater amount of wisdom, and not rule simply for their own benefit like in oligarchies. Finally, it is possible to have a 'tyranny of the majority', where some large portion of society has rule, but rules only for their own benefit and exploits some other minority or groups of minorities. This, Aristotle thinks, is actually how most democracies function—they say they value equality and freedom, but this is really often a mask for exploiting some other group. An actual rule by most (or all) of society, for the good of the whole of society, Aristotle says is so rare that it actually doesn't have a name. So he invents one, and simply calls it the 'polity' or 'constitution'. The ideal political framework, Aristotle thinks, is one that would blend the best aspects of each of the good forms of government—monarchy, aristocracy, and polity—so that both the whole of society, and those individuals with outstanding traits and skills, can contribute to the good of the whole. This significantly influences the modern French political philosopher Montesquieu in his *Spirit of the Laws* (1748), whose idea of shared governance and separation and contribution of different powers played a large role in the development of the United States Constitution in 1789, which also happens to be the longest running political constitution still extant in the world. Indeed, the United States can be seen as incorporating monarchical elements (in the Presidency), aristocratic elements (in the Supreme Court and Senate), and 'political' or democratic polity elements (in the House of Representatives, local state and city governments, and direct ballot initiatives), and which has been imitated in many other constitutions around the world. Without the writings of Plato then, and their later examination, revision, and critique by Aristotle, the world as we know it would be very different. Political and philosophical reflection on society has had a major impact on the way humans organize themselves and society, and will continue to do so as we try to figure out even better ways to live in society.

Second Treatise of Government (excerpt) (1690)

John Locke

Chapter II: Of the State of Nature.

Sect. 4. TO understand political power right, and derive it from its original, we must consider, what state all men are naturally in, and that is, a state of perfect freedom to order their actions, and dispose of their possessions and persons, as they think fit, within the bounds of the law of nature, without asking leave, or depending upon the will of any other man.

A state also of equality, wherein all the power and jurisdiction is reciprocal, no one having more than another; there being nothing more evident, than that creatures of the same species and rank, promiscuously born to all the same advantages of nature, and the use of the same faculties, should also be equal one amongst another without subordination or subjection, unless the lord and master of them all should, by any manifest declaration of his will, set one above another, and confer on him, by an evident and clear appointment, an undoubted right to dominion and sovereignty.

Sect. 5. This equality of men by nature, the judicious Hooker looks upon as so evident in itself, and beyond all question, that he makes it the foundation of that obligation to mutual love amongst men, on which he builds the duties they owe one another, and from whence he derives the great maxims of justice and charity. His words are,

> The like natural inducement hath brought men to know that it is no less their duty, to love others than themselves; for seeing those things which are equal, must needs all have one measure; if I cannot but wish to receive good, even as much at every man's hands, as any man can wish unto his own soul, how should I look to have any part of my desire herein satisfied, unless myself be careful to satisfy the like desire, which is undoubtedly in other men, being of one and the same nature? To have any thing offered them repugnant to this desire, must needs in all respects grieve them as much as me; so that if I do harm, I must look to suffer, there being no reason that others should shew greater measure of love to me, than they have by me shewed unto them: my desire therefore to be loved of my equals

John Locke, from Second Treatise of Government, 1690.

in nature as much as possible may be, imposeth upon me a natural duty of bearing to them-ward fully the like affection; from which relation of equality between ourselves and them that are as ourselves, what several rules and canons natural reason hath drawn, for direction of life, no man is ignorant, Eccl. Pol. Lib. 1.

Sect. 6. But though this be a state of liberty, yet it is not a state of licence: though man in that state have an uncontroulable liberty to dispose of his person or possessions, yet he has not liberty to destroy himself, or so much as any creature in his possession, but where some nobler use than its bare preservation calls for it. The state of nature has a law of nature to govern it, which obliges every one: and reason, which is that law, teaches all mankind, who will but consult it, that being all equal and independent, no one ought to harm another in his life, health, liberty, or possessions: for men being all the workmanship of one omnipotent, and infinitely wise maker; all the servants of one sovereign master, sent into the world by his order, and about his business; they are his property, whose workmanship they are, made to last during his, not one another's pleasure: and being furnished with like faculties, sharing all in one community of nature, there cannot be supposed any such subordination among us, that may authorize us to destroy one another, as if we were made for one another's uses, as the inferior ranks of creatures are for our's. Every one, as he is bound to preserve himself, and not to quit his station wilfully, so by the like reason, when his own preservation comes not in competition, ought he, as much as he can, to preserve the rest of mankind, and may not, unless it be to do justice on an offender, take away, or impair the life, or what tends to the preservation of the life, the liberty, health, limb, or goods of another.

Sect. 7. And that all men may be restrained from invading others rights, and from doing hurt to one another, and the law of nature be observed, which willeth the peace and preservation of all mankind, the execution of the law of nature is, in that state, put into every man's hands, whereby every one has a right to punish the transgressors of that law to such a degree, as may hinder its violation: for the law of nature would, as all other laws that concern men in this world be in vain, if there were no body that in the state of nature had a power to execute that law, and thereby preserve the innocent and restrain offenders. And if any one in the state of nature may punish another for any evil he has done, every one may do so: for in that state of perfect equality, where naturally there is no superiority or jurisdiction of one over another, what any may do in prosecution of that law, every one must needs have a right to do.

Sect. 8. And thus, in the state of nature, one man comes by a power over another; but yet no absolute or arbitrary power, to use a criminal, when he has got him in his hands, according to the passionate heats, or boundless extravagancy of his own will; but only to retribute to him, so far as calm reason and conscience dictate, what is proportionate to his transgression, which is so much as may serve for reparation and restraint: for these two are the only reasons, why one man may lawfully do harm to another, which is that we call punishment. In transgressing the law of nature, the offender declares himself to live by another rule than that of reason and common equity, which is that measure God has set to the actions of men, for their mutual security; and so he becomes dangerous to mankind, the tye, which is to secure them from injury and violence, being slighted and broken by him. Which being a trespass against the whole species, and the peace and safety of it, provided for by the law of nature, every man upon this score, by the right he hath to preserve mankind in general, may restrain, or where it is necessary, destroy things noxious to them, and so may bring such evil on any one, who hath transgressed that law, as may make him repent the doing of it, and thereby deter him, and by his example others, from doing the like mischief. And in the case, and upon this ground, EVERY MAN HATH A RIGHT TO PUNISH THE OFFENDER, AND BE EXECUTIONER OF THE LAW OF NATURE. [...]

Sect. 10. Besides the crime which consists in violating the law, and varying from the right rule of reason, whereby a man so far becomes degenerate, and declares himself to quit the principles of human nature, and to be a noxious creature, there is commonly injury done to some person or other, and some other man receives damage by his transgression: in which case he who hath received any damage, has, besides the right of punishment common to him with other men, a particular right to seek reparation from him that has done it: and any other person, who finds it just, may also join with him that is injured, and assist him in recovering from the offender so much as may make satisfaction for the harm he has suffered.

Sect. 11. From these two distinct rights, the one of punishing the crime for restraint, and preventing the like offence, which right of punishing is in every body; the other of taking reparation, which belongs only to the injured party, comes it to pass that the magistrate, who by being magistrate hath the common right of punishing put into his hands, can often, where the public good demands not the execution of the law, remit the punishment of criminal offences by his own authority, but yet cannot remit the satisfaction due to any private man for the damage he has received. That, he who has suffered the damage has a right to demand in his own name, and he alone can remit: the damnified person has this power of appropriating to himself the goods or service of the offender, by right of self-preservation, as every man has a power to punish the crime, to prevent its being committed again, by the right he has of preserving all mankind, and doing all reasonable things he can in order to that end: and thus it is, that every man, in the state of nature, has a power to kill a murderer, both to deter others from doing the like injury, which no reparation can compensate, by the example of the punishment that attends it from every body, and also to secure men from the attempts of a criminal, who having renounced reason, the common rule and measure God hath given to mankind, hath, by the unjust violence and slaughter he hath committed upon one, declared war against all mankind, and therefore may be destroyed as a lion or a tyger, one of those wild savage beasts, with whom men can have no society nor security: and upon this is grounded that great law of nature, Whoso sheddeth man's blood, by man shall his blood be shed. And Cain was so fully convinced, that every one had a right to destroy such a criminal, that after the murder of his brother, he cries out, Every one that findeth me, shall slay me; so plain was it writ in the hearts of all mankind.

Sect. 12. By the same reason may a man in the state of nature punish the lesser breaches of that law. It will perhaps be demanded, with death? I answer, each transgression may be punished to that degree, and with so much severity, as will suffice to make it an ill bargain to the offender, give him cause to repent, and terrify others from doing the like. Every offence, that can be committed in the state of nature, may in the state of nature be also punished equally, and as far forth as it may, in a commonwealth: for though it would be besides my present purpose, to enter here into the particulars of the law of nature, or its measures of punishment; yet, it is certain there is such a law, and that too, as intelligible and plain to a rational creature, and a studier of that law, as the positive laws of commonwealths; nay, possibly plainer; as much as reason is easier to be understood, than the fancies and intricate contrivances of men, following contrary and hidden interests put into words; for so truly are a great part of the municipal laws of countries, which are only so far right, as they are founded on the law of nature, by which they are to be regulated and interpreted.

Sect. 13. To this strange doctrine, viz. That in the state of nature every one has the executive power of the law of nature, I doubt not but it will be objected, that it is unreasonable for men to be judges in their own cases, that self-love will make men partial to themselves and their friends: and on the other side, that ill nature, passion and revenge will carry them too far in punishing others; and hence nothing but confusion and disorder will follow, and that therefore God hath certainly appointed government to restrain the partiality and violence of men. I easily grant, that civil government is the proper remedy for the inconveniencies of the state of nature, which must certainly be great, where men may be judges in their own case, since it is easy to be imagined, that he who was so unjust as to do his brother an injury, will scarce be so just as to condemn himself for it: but I shall desire those who make this objection, to remember, that absolute monarchs are but men; and if government is to be the remedy of those evils, which necessarily follow from men's being judges in their own cases, and the state of nature is therefore not to be endured, I desire to know what kind of government that is, and how much better it is than the state of nature, where one man, commanding a multitude, has the liberty to be judge in his own case, and may do to all his subjects whatever he pleases, without the least liberty to any one to question or controul those who execute his pleasure? and in whatsoever he doth, whether led by reason, mistake or passion, must be submitted to? much better it is in the state of nature, wherein men are not bound to submit to the unjust will of another: and if he that judges, judges amiss in his own, or any other case, he is answerable for it to the rest of mankind.

Sect. 14. It is often asked as a mighty objection, where are, or ever were there any men in such a state of nature? To which it may suffice as an answer at present, that since all princes and rulers of independent governments all through the world, are in a state of nature, it is plain the world never was, nor ever will be, without numbers of men in that state. I have named all governors of independent communities, whether they are, or are not, in league with others: for it is not every compact that puts an end to the state of nature between men, but only this one of agreeing together mutually to enter into one community, and make one body politic; other promises, and compacts, men may make one with another, and yet still be in the state of nature. The promises and bargains for truck, &c. between the two men in the desert island, mentioned by Garcilasso de la Vega, in his history of Peru; or between a Swiss and an Indian, in the woods of America, are binding to them, though they are perfectly in a state of nature, in reference to one another: for truth and keeping of faith belongs to men, as men, and not as members of society. [...]

Chapter III: Of the State of War.

Sect. 16. THE state of war is a state of enmity and destruction: and therefore declaring by word or action, not a passionate and hasty, but a sedate settled design upon another man's life, puts him in a state of war with him against whom he has declared such an intention, and so has exposed his life to the other's power to be taken away by him, or any one that joins with him in his defence, and espouses his quarrel; it being reasonable and just, I should have a right to destroy that which threatens me with destruction: for, by the fundamental law of nature, man being to be preserved as much as possible, when all cannot be preserved, the safety of the innocent is to be preferred: and one may destroy a man who makes war upon him, or has discovered an enmity to his being, for the same reason that he may kill a wolf or a lion; because such men are not under the ties of the common law of reason, have no other rule, but that of force and violence, and so may be treated as beasts of prey, those dangerous and noxious creatures, that will be sure to destroy him whenever he falls into their power. [...]

Sect. 19. And here we have the plain difference between the state of nature and the state of war, which however some men have confounded, are as far distant, as a state of peace, good will, mutual assistance and preservation, and a state of enmity, malice, violence and mutual destruction, are one from another. Men living together according to reason, without a common superior on earth, with authority to judge between them, is properly the state of nature. But force, or a declared design of force, upon the person of another, where there is no common superior on earth to appeal to for relief, is the state of war: and it is the want of such an appeal gives a man the right of war even against an aggressor, tho' he be in society and a fellow subject. Thus a thief, whom I cannot harm, but by appeal to the law, for having stolen all that I am worth, I may kill, when he sets on me to rob me but of my horse or coat; because the law, which was made for my preservation, where it cannot interpose to secure my life from present force, which, if lost, is capable of no reparation, permits me my own defence, and the right of war, a liberty to kill the aggressor, because the aggressor allows not time to appeal to our common judge, nor the decision of the law, for remedy in a case where the mischief may be irreparable. Want of a common judge with authority, puts all men in a state of nature: force without right, upon a man's person, makes a state of war, both where there is, and is not, a common judge.

Sect. 20. But when the actual force is over, the state of war ceases between those that are in society, and are equally on both sides subjected to the fair determination of the law; because then there lies open the remedy of appeal for the past injury, and to prevent future harm: but where no such appeal is, as in the state of nature, for want of positive laws, and judges with authority to appeal to, the state of war once begun, continues, with a right to the innocent party to destroy the other whenever he can, until the aggressor offers peace, and desires reconciliation on such terms as may repair any wrongs he has already done, and secure the innocent for the future; nay, where an appeal to the law, and constituted judges, lies open, but the remedy is denied by a manifest perverting of justice, and a barefaced wresting of the laws to protect or indemnify the violence or injuries of some men, or party of men, there it is hard to imagine any thing but a state of war: for wherever violence is used, and injury done, though by hands appointed to administer justice, it is still violence and injury, however coloured with the name, pretences, or forms of law, the end whereof being to protect and redress the innocent, by an unbiassed application of it, to all who are under it; wherever that is not bona fide done, war is made upon the sufferers, who having no appeal on earth to right them, they are left to the only remedy in such cases, an appeal to heaven.

Sect. 21. To avoid this state of war (wherein there is no appeal but to heaven, and wherein every the least difference is apt to end, where there is no authority to decide between the contenders) is one great reason of men's putting themselves into society, and quitting the state of nature: for where there is an authority, a power on earth, from which relief can be had by appeal, there the continuance of the state of war is excluded, and the controversy is decided by that power. Had there been any such court, any superior jurisdiction on earth, to determine the right between Jephtha and the Ammonites, they had never come to a state of war: but we see he was forced to appeal to heaven. The Lord the Judge (says he) be judge this day between the children of Israel and the children of Ammon, Judg. xi. 27. and then prosecuting, and relying on his appeal, he leads out his army to battle: and therefore in such controversies, where the question is put, who shall be judge? It cannot be meant, who shall decide the controversy; every one knows what Jephtha here tells us, that the Lord the Judge shall judge. Where there is no judge on earth, the appeal lies to God in heaven. That question then cannot mean, who shall judge, whether another hath put himself in a state of war with me, and whether I may, as Jephtha did, appeal to heaven in it? of that I myself can only be judge in my own conscience, as I will answer it, at the great day, to the supreme judge of all men. [...]

Chapter V: Of Property. [...]

Sect. 27. Though the earth, and all inferior creatures, be common to all men, yet every man has a property in his own person: this no body has any right to but himself. The labour of his body, and the work of his hands, we may say, are properly his. Whatsoever then he removes out of the state that nature hath provided, and left it in, he hath mixed his labour with, and joined to it something that is his own, and thereby makes it his property. It being by him removed from the common state nature hath placed it in, it hath by this labour something annexed to it, that excludes the common right of other men: for this labour being the unquestionable property of the labourer, no man but he can have a right to what that is once joined to, at least where there is enough, and as good, left in common for others.

Sect. 28. He that is nourished by the acorns he picked up under an oak, or the apples he gathered from the trees in the wood, has certainly appropriated them to himself. No body can deny but the nourishment is his. I ask then, when did they begin to be his? when he digested? or when he eat? or when he boiled? or when he brought them home? or when he picked them up? and it is plain, if the first gathering made them not his, nothing else could. That labour put a distinction between them and common: that added something to them more than nature, the common mother of all, had done; and so they became his private right. And will any one say, he had no right to those acorns or apples, he thus appropriated, because he had not the consent of all mankind to make them his? Was it a robbery thus to assume to himself what belonged to all in common? If such a consent as that was necessary, man had starved, notwithstanding the plenty God had given him. We see in commons, which remain so by compact, that it is the taking any part of what is common, and removing it out of the state nature leaves it in, which begins the property; without which the common is of no use. And the taking of this or that part, does not depend on the express consent of all the commoners. Thus the grass my horse has bit; the turfs my servant has cut; and the ore I have digged in any place, where I have a right to them in common with others, become my property, without the assignation or consent of any body. The labour that was mine, removing them out of that common state they were in, hath fixed my property in them. [...]

Sect. 31. It will perhaps be objected to this, that if gathering the acorns, or other fruits of the earth, &c. makes a right to them, then any one may ingross as much as he will. To which I answer, Not so. The same law of nature, that does by this means give us property, does also bound that property too. God has given us all things richly, 1 Tim. vi. 12. is the voice of reason confirmed by inspiration. But how far has he given it us? To enjoy. As much as any one can make use of to any advantage of life before it spoils, so much he may by his labour fix a property in: whatever is beyond this, is more than his share, and belongs to others. Nothing was made by God for man to spoil or destroy. And thus, considering the plenty of natural provisions there was a long time in the world, and the few spenders; and to how small a part of that provision the industry of one man could extend itself, and ingross it to the prejudice of others; especially keeping within the bounds, set by reason, of what might serve for his use; there could be then little room for quarrels or contentions about property so established.

The Curious Alienation of Cocoa Farmers from Their Chocolate

(2021)

Lester Andrist

IT IS QUITE COMMON TO HEAR people discuss Karl Marx's notion of alienation as a term that simply describes widespread feelings of unhappiness and psychological distress among workers. It's true that one result of alienation may be unhappiness, but the term was intended to describe much more than workers' feelings. It's important to remember that Marx wrote about alienation as a condition that arises from the social relations that form within a system of capitalist production.

Specifically, Marx was also interested in drawing attention to workers' relationships to their work, a form of alienation he called species-being. For example, prior to modern capitalism, a woodworker could express herself through her work by making unique decisions about how pieces of furniture were to be constructed. However, under capitalism workers are often not afforded the ability to express themselves through their work. Work has instead become a series of routinized movements, making every new piece of furniture identical to the last.

Marx also wrote about alienation, not just in terms of the relationship between workers and their work, but also in terms of the relationship between workers and the products they produce. Capitalism is a peculiar system in that it compels people to produce objects that do not belong to them and that they very often cannot even afford. Again, the woodworkers of long ago could conceivably keep the furniture they built, or if the mood struck them, they could give it away as a gift. But under modern capitalism, the furniture workers produce generally belongs to their employers. Although an Ikea employee might spend her day helping construct the components of low-cost furniture, her home may not actually contain a single product from Ikea.

Another rather vivid example of this last form of alienation can be observed in a video from VPRO Metropolis, a global collective of young reporters (to watch this video, visit https://tinyurl.com/563s2kft or scan the QR code below). The video features a small cocoa farmer named Alfonse, who is surprised to learn that something called chocolate is made from the beans he harvests. In fact, Alfonse confesses he has never even tasted chocolate.

Adapted from Lester Andrist, "Marxist Theory Explains Why These Cocoa Farmers Have Never Tasted Chocolate," The Sociological Cinema. Copyright © 2014 by *The Sociological Cinema*. Reprinted with permission.

While it is certainly striking that Alfonse is unfamiliar with chocolate, or as Marx would put it, that he is *alienated* from the product of his labor, it is arguably even more surprising that Alfonse seems to regard his alienation as if it were the natural state of affairs. The lesson here is that alienation can appear to those it infects as an unremarkable, mundane fact of existence, but it is important to note that this taken-for-granted-ness is one reason why the alienation persists. So convinced are people that their alienation is the natural state of affairs, they are often unable to even imagine a more meaning-ful connection to their work or the products they produce, much less articulate a call for change.

Justice as Fairness[1]

(2010)

Chris Brown

J OHN RAWLS IS PREDOMINANTLY CONCERNED TO determine the conditions under which the institutions of a society could be considered just; his aim is to write 'ideal theory', and to generate what he calls in the *Law of Peoples* a 'realistic utopia', which, for the moment, can be defined as an account of the world which is utopian in so far as it does not reflect existing social arrangements, but realistic in so far as it does not contravene anything we know about human nature.[2] His account, which he summarises as 'Justice as Fairness' employs the well-worn device of a fictional 'social contract'—the basic institutions of a society are just if the principles upon which they are based would be agreed to, under ideal conditions, by those they concern. Society is taken, for these purposes, to be a bounded 'co-operative scheme for mutual advantage', and we are invited as a thought-experiment to imagine the arrangements to which potential members of such a scheme would agree prior to its formation, in what is termed the 'original position'. These potential contractors make their choices under the 'veil of ignorance'; they know that there are certain 'primary goods' that all rational persons behind the veil can be assumed to want whatever else they want—and, in the revised version of *A Theory of Justice*, it is, importantly, made clear that these primary goods include what people need in their status as free and equal citizens as well as what they need for their general welfare and survival—but they do not know certain key facts about themselves, such as their race, talents, gender, or intelligence, or even their 'conceptions of the good or their special psychological propensities'.[3] We are to invited to consider what principles would be chosen under these conditions.

Rawls assumes contractors will be risk-averse, which rules out principles that dramatically disadvantage some to the gain of the rest; thus, for example, no one would choose a society based upon slavery unless they knew that they themselves would not be slaves, and this knowledge is denied them by the veil of ignorance. Accordingly, the

---

1   This section draws upon material first published in a brief review essay, Brown (2000a).

2   In what follows Rawlsian terms of art are placed in inverted commas on their first appearance in order to indicate that they actually *are* terms of art.

3   Rawls (1999a, p. 11).

first principle of justice that will be chosen by contractors is that 'each person is to have an equal right to the most extensive scheme of equal basic liberties compatible with a similar scheme of liberties for others'.[4] More controversially, Rawls suggests that the second principle concerning distribution of social and economic goods will have two parts; first, is what he calls 'fair equality of opportunity', that is a system in which positions are, as far as possible, available to all under conditions where the influence of social circumstances such as social class is eliminated. Second, he argues contractors will accept as just only those inequalities of outcome which can reasonably be expected to be to everyone's advantage, that is, those inequalities which work to the benefit of the least advantaged members of society; this is what he calls the 'difference principle' (because it concerns legitimate differences in responsibilities and authority). There is a lexical ordering here; providing the most extensive equal basic liberties takes priority over distributional principles—contractors will not trade freedom for increases in economic efficiency. This is why they will reject the principle of average utility which is one possible alternative to the 'difference principle' set out above. On the other hand, the other possible principle of justice is strict egalitarianism, but this will be rejected because it could leave *everyone* worse off than under the difference principle.

A key question is whether these principles are thought to be universal in application, or are only appropriate to societies composed of people committed to liberal principles. The original text of A *Theory of Justice* was confusing on this point. Rawls now argues that his theory was actually intended to provide principles for a liberal society; however, he argues, this theory was based on liberalism as a 'comprehensive doctrine' to which all were expected to adhere, and this was a mistake. In a 'well-ordered' society (a term Rawls adopts from Jean Bodin) there must be room for a plurality of 'reasonable comprehensive doctrines'. Justice must be understood as political, not metaphysical. This means it must be based on principles that are capable of being the object of an 'overlapping consensus' amongst such reasonable doctrines. To elaborate this point, while a just society as such is based on liberal principles, it is not necessary for its members themselves to be full-blown liberals; what is required of them is that when arguing for particular principles or policies they do not rely on comprehensive doctrines (including secular liberalism itself). Thus, for example, practising Roman Catholics may believe abortion to be contrary to God's law, but this is not an argument that they may validly employ in public debate, being required to defend their position via what Rawls calls 'public reason', that is, they must employ only those arguments to which believers in other reasonable comprehensive doctrines can reasonably be expected to respond.

This position is set out and defended in the essays that make up Rawls's second major work, *Political Liberalism*. It is fair to say that the majority of liberal theorists who were

---

4 Ibid. (p. 52).

inspired by *A Theory of Justice* have been much less enthusiastic about these later ideas, wishing, for the most part, to defend liberalism as a comprehensive doctrine.[5] On the other hand, it will be seen that the arguments of *Political Liberalism* are more consistent with Rawls's international thought than are those of *A Theory of Justice*, although it should be noted that the principles elaborated in *The Law of Peoples* were first set out in the earlier book, even though they sit more easily with the later development of Rawls's thought. It may not be too fanciful to suggest that the shift from A Theory of Justice to Political Liberalism was, at least in part, prompted by the realisation that there was a disjuncture in the earlier volume between Rawls's international and domestic thought.

Bibliography

Barry, B. (1995) 'Review Essay: John Rawls and the Search for Stability', *Ethics*, vol. 105, no. 4, July.

Brown, C. (2000a) 'John Rawls, "The Law of Peoples" and International Political Theory' in *Ethics and International Affairs*, vol. 14.

Ethics 'Symposium on John Rawls' (1994) *Ethics*, vol. 105, no. 1, October.

Rawls, J. (1971) *A Theory of Justice*, Oxford: Oxford University Press.

——— (1993) 'The Law of Peoples' in S. Shute and S. Hurley (eds) *On Human Rights: The Oxford Amnesty Lectures 1993*, New York: Basic Books.

——— (1995) *Political Liberalism*, Cambridge, MA: Harvard University Press.

——— (1999a) *A Theory of Justice*, rev. edn, Cambridge, MA: Belknap Press of Harvard University.

---

5   See, for example, the essays in *Ethics* (1994) and Barry (1995).

Post-Reading Questions for Unit I

Refer back to the reading selections in this unit to help you correctly respond to each of the questions below.

1. The *Iliad* and Bible were written a long time ago; however, we can still think about modern-day examples of retributive justice.

   - Can you provide a contemporary example of (a) justice as retaliation based on group membership and (b) justice as proportionate punishment?

2. Plato argued that we need wise rulers (i.e., "philosopher-kings") who have their priorities straight and will create good laws and decrees that everyone else can follow and from which they can get their own knowledge of goodness.

   - Do you agree with Plato that ignorance is what makes people bad/unjust, and thus, what we need is knowledge and wisdom to be good/just?

   - How does Plato's perspective play out when we look at our rulers today? Does his vision of leadership, knowledge, and justice hold true today? Why, or why not?

3. In the *Republic*, Plato identifies three classes that make up the ideal society: money-makers (also called craftsmen or producers), auxiliaries, and guardians. Do a quick internet search on how Plato defined each of these classes.

   - In Plato's mind, what do these three classes of society have to do with justice?

   - Do these three classes still hold true in our current society?

   - Or do we have more classes? Or less?

   - If alive today, would Plato need to update his argument regarding social classes, justice, and the ideal society? Why, or why not?

4. Watch Michael Sandel's 2010 TED Talk "The Lost Art of Democratic Debate" (available at tinyurl.com/y6s6p7rf), and respond to the following questions:

   - Who does Aristotle think should get the best flutes (and why)?

   - What did the Supreme Court decide in the case *PGA Tour Inc. v. Martin*?

   - How does this tie back to Aristotle's notion of justice?

   - Do you agree with Aristotle's notion of justice?

5. Explain why some people argue that Aristotle had an odd understanding of equality.

   - Do you agree that this is "odd," or does it make sense to you? Why, or why not?

6. Explain John Locke's logic for how he arrives at the conclusion that people have a natural right to own property.

   - According to Locke, what keeps this system of property ownership "in check" (i.e., assures that people won't get greedy)?

   - How do Locke's ideas about labor, property, and greed play out in our contemporary capitalistic context?

7. Locke claims that since people own their own labor, when they mix their labor with that which is unowned, it becomes their property. The philosopher Robert Nozick challenged this argument, using the example of mixing tomato juice one owns with the sea.

   - Nozick asks: When we mix something we own with something we don't own, why should we think we gain—instead of lose—property?

8. Compare and contrast John Locke's and Karl Marx's perspectives on private property.

   - What are Locke's beliefs about our right to own property?

   - For Locke, how does property ownership relate to justice?

   - What would Marx say about private property and its role in justice and injustice?

   - What do *you* think?

   - Do you think we have a right to own property?

   - How do you think the right to own property contributes to justice and/or injustice?

9. Read the 2020 *Washington Post* article "U.S. Says it Won't Join WHO-Linked Effort to Develop, Distribute Coronavirus Vaccine" (available at tinyurl.com/2k8t2acb).

   - According to John Rawls, what is the veil of ignorance?

   - For Rawls, how would making decisions behind a veil of ignorance have resulted in more just decision making about vaccine development and distribution?

   - Do you agree with Rawls's claims about the veil of ignorance and more just/fair decision making?

Unit II

Oppression, Privilege, and Intersectionality

Valerie Chepp

Building off the foundation of knowledge laid in the previous unit, Unit II readings use more contemporary texts to deepen readers' knowledge about social injustice, with special attention to oppression, privilege, and intersectionality. The core concepts introduced in this unit will further develop readers' ability to make sense of the social justice issues they encounter in their everyday lives.

In her reading "Displacing the Distributive Paradigm," Iris Marion Young offers an important intervention in discussions about justice, claiming justice isn't only about distribution, or "who has what." In this reading, Young is in conversation with prominent social justice thinkers, including Marx and Rawls, in order to show how justice includes nondistributive facets as well. She identifies three aspects of justice that do not primarily concern distribution: decision making, division of labor, and culture. This selection comes from the first chapter of her book *Justice and the Politics of Difference* (1990), and it is here where Young defines social justice as "the elimination of institutionalized **domination** and **oppression.**" She critiques earlier thinkers for failing to capture such a broad notion of justice and ultimately argues that, for justice to occur, we must institutionally recognize (but not oppress) different **social groups**. This can take the form of **group-conscious policies**, whereby different groups are treated differently in order to ensure social equity for oppressed groups (e.g., affirmative action policies).

domination: Young defines this as institutional constraints on self-determination.

oppression: Young defines this as institutional constraints on self-development. Young argues that oppression is a condition of social groups.

social groups: "a collective of people who have affinity with one another because of a set of practices or way of life; they differentiate themselves from or are differentiated by at least one other group according to these cultural forms" (Young, 1990, p. 186).

privilege: "when one group has something of value that is denied to others simply because of the groups they belong to, rather than because of anything they've done or failed to do" (Johnson, p. 57 of this anthology).

material consequences: tangible, "real" outcomes; "touchable" things of this world, such as people, relationships, money, raw materials, environment, and disease. Marx emphasized the importance of material conditions, rather than ideals, as a way of explaining history and social change.

double bind: situation in which choices are limited and all result in some sort of penalty; a catch-22 or no-win situation. Frye argues that the double bind is a characteristic feature of oppressed groups.

intersectionality: an analytic strategy that considers how systems of power (e.g., race, class, gender, sexuality, nationality, religion, ability, age, etc.) intersect in meaningful and complex ways, resulting in social inequity.

hegemony: ideas of the ruling class are seen as the norm, seen as universal ideologies perceived to benefit everyone while really only benefiting the ruling class; the process of getting people to unwittingly consent to their own oppression.

social structure: patterned social arrangements comprised of social institutions (e.g., family, religion, education, media, law, politics, economy) and patterned institutionalized relationships; these social institutions and relationships are interrelated and interdependent.

social location: the distinct social positions of individuals and groups within intersecting power relations; these positions produce patterns of privilege and disadvantage that shape individual and group experiences.

coalition building: the process by which groups who share similar values, interests, and goals form alliances in order to achieve a common purpose or activity; allows groups to pool their resources and become more powerful.

The next two readings, one by Allan Johnson and one by Marilyn Frye, offer additional opportunity to deepen our awareness of how social groups experience **privilege** and oppression. Consistent with Young's attention to social differences (and the importance of recognizing group difference for social justice), in "The Social Construction of Difference," Johnson provides important context for how to understand social differences: as **socially constructed**. That is, social differences such as race, gender, and disability are only rendered meaningful in a *social* context. We know this because meanings change across time and space (e.g., race and gender are organized differently across different cultures and time periods). Despite being social constructed, these social differences have very real **material consequences**. Johnson provides a list of tangible examples of what membership in a privileged (and, by extension, oppressed) group looks like.

Like Johnson, Frye argues we must be explicit about what oppression means, or else we risk misidentifying or obscuring it. In her well-known essay "Oppression," Frye makes clear that oppression is not the same as suffering, misery, or feeling limited, burdened, damaged, harmed, or frustrated. Her discussion of the **double bind** illuminates how social groups experience oppression, and her birdcage metaphor is useful for understanding how systemic, oppressive forces operate.

Frye's selection serves as the first of several readings that uses the case of feminism as a lens through which to examine core social justice concepts, including oppression, privilege, **intersectionality**, **hegemony**, social groups, **social structure**, politics of location (and **social location**), and **coalition building**. I encourage readers to ask themselves, what might be other case studies, aside from feminist history, thought, and activism, through which to apply these and other social justice concepts?

In the following excerpt, "Toward a New Vision: Race, Class, and Gender as Categories of Analysis and Connection," Patricia Hill Collins builds upon several of the concepts introduced in Frye's reading and encourages readers to consider how different systems of oppression (e.g., sexism, racism, classism) intersect to result in different experiences with domination and sub-ordination for different social groups. Collins advocates for new ways of thinking about the relationship among social categories such as race, class, and gender, which, she argues, helps us better understand how oppression operates across different dimensions (institutional, sym-bolic, and individual). Equipped with this better understanding, we are in a stronger position to build relationships and coalitions that will result in a more socially just society. A key insight emerging from this new, intersectional way of understanding oppression is that people simul-taneously experience oppression and privilege; no one is entirely oppressed, and no one is entirely privileged.

Originally presented in 1989, Collins's reading represents one of many intellectual efforts to articulate what eventually came to be known as "intersectionality." In a chapter from their graphic novel *A Brief History of Feminism*, the subsequent selection by Patu and Antje Schrupp (translated by Sophie Lewis) offers a quick introduction to intersectionality and, specifically, its relationship to the second wave feminist movement in the United States, which dispropor-tionately focused on White, middle-class women's liberation. This chapter offers a launching pad for critiquing what has more recently been dubbed "White feminism."

In "Tita Aida: Intimate Geographies of Suffering," Martin F. Manalansan IV builds upon this critique of exclusionary feminism and draws attention to the importance of colonial systems of domination in intersectional analyses. Specifically, speaking of his experience conducting ethno-graphic research on Filipino gay immigrants during the AIDS pandemic, Manalansan illustrates how race, ethnicity, nationality, sexuality, class, and health status come together (i.e., intersect) to construct what Manalansan calls "intimate geographies of suffering." This postcolonial anal-ysis illustrates how suffering is structured by time and space, both in the here and now as well as by what is remembered, and how this complex experience with suffering intersects with one's biography and history.

Building off Manalansan's attention to postcolonial theory and the political importance of place and space, in "Feminism and the Politics of Location," Kathy Davis underscores how a person's location—that is, where they are geographically situated—shapes their understand-ing of history, knowledge, and political alliances. Using feminist theory and practice as a case study, Davis encourages readers to resist "single story" readings of history and to consider how the politics of location calls on us to grapple with **epis-temology**, hegemony, and intersectionality in new and explicit ways.

> **epistemology**: a field of study in philosophy concerned with the question of how you know what you know.

Unit II concludes with the article "100 Defensive Tactics and Attributions Dodging the Dialogue on Cultural Diversity" by Cornel Pewewardy, which lists 100 linguistic practices that are frequently deployed in resistance to conversations about—and efforts to advance—social justice. This list is grounded in Pewewardy's decades of experience in social justice education and indigenous teaching. This list is helpful because it names and helps readers recognize the rhetorical hegemonic practices—whether carried out by others or by ourselves—that serve to undermine social justice work. This concluding text serves as a reminder to readers that social justice learning can be uncomfortable and met with resistance. As you read the works in this anthology, I encourage you to confront and reflect upon any discomfort you may experience. It is in this space, on our **learning edge**, when we are best positioned to expand our understanding.

learning edge: the state when we are on the edge of our comfort zone; this is often the best place to expand our understanding.

Reading 2.1

Displacing the Distributive Paradigm
(1990)

Iris Marion Young

> *It was in general a mistake to make a fuss about so-called distribution and put the principal stress on it. Any distribution whatever of the means of consumption is only a consequence of the distribution of the conditions of production themselves. The latter distribution, however, is a feature of the mode of production itself.*

—Karl Marx

THOUSANDS OF BUSES CONVERGE ON THE city, and tens of thousands of people of diverse colors, ages, occupations, and life styles swarm onto the mall around the Washington Monument until the march begins. At midday people move into the streets, chanting, singing, waving wild papier-mâché missiles or effigies of government officials. Many carry signs or banners on which a simple slogan is inscribed: "Peace, Jobs, and Justice."

This scene has occurred many times in Washington, D.C., in the last decade, and many more times in other U.S. cities. What does "justice" mean in this slogan? In this context, as in many other political contexts today, I suggest that social justice means the elimination of institutionalized domination and oppression. Any aspect of social organization and practice relevant to domination and oppression is in principle subject to evaluation by ideals of justice.

Contemporary philosophical theories of justice, however, do not conceive justice so broadly. Instead, philosophical theories of justice tend to restrict the meaning of social justice to the morally proper distribution of benefits and burdens among society's members. In this chapter I define and assess this distributive paradigm. While distributive issues are crucial to a satisfactory conception of justice, it is a mistake to reduce social justice to distribution.

I find two problems with the distributive paradigm. First, it tends to focus thinking about social justice on the allocation of material goods such as things, resources, income, and wealth, or on the distribution of social positions, especially jobs. This focus tends to ignore the social structure and institutional context that often help determine distributive patterns. Of particular importance to the analyses that follow are issues of decisionmaking power and procedures, division of labor, and culture.

One might agree that defining justice in terms of distribution tends to bias thinking about justice toward issues concerning wealth, income, and other material goods, and that other issues such as decisionmaking power or the structure of the division of labor are as important, and yet argue that distribution need not be restricted to material goods and resources. Theorists frequently consider issues of the distribution of such nonmaterial goods as power, opportunity, or self-respect. But this widening of the concept of distribution exhibits the second problem with the distributive paradigm. When metaphorically extended to nonmaterial social goods, the concept of distribution represents them as though they were static things, instead of a function of social relations and processes.

In criticizing distributively oriented theories I wish neither to reject distribution as unimportant nor to offer a new positive theory to replace the distributive theories. I wish rather to displace talk of justice that regards persons as primarily possessors and consumers of goods to a wider context that also includes action, decisions about action, and provision of the means to develop and exercise capacities. The concept of social justice includes all aspects of institutional rules and relations insofar as they are subject to potential collective decision. The concepts of domination and oppression, rather than the concept of distribution, should be the starting point for a conception of social justice. [...]

The Distributive Paradigm Presupposes and Obscures Institutional Context

Most theorizing about social justice focuses on the distribution of material resources, income, or positions of reward and prestige. Contemporary debates among theorists of justice, as Charles Taylor (1985) points out, are inspired largely by two practical issues. First, is the distribution of wealth and income in advanced capitalist countries just, and if not, does justice permit or even require the provision of welfare services and other redistributive measures? Second, is the pattern of the distribution of positions of high income and prestige just, and if not, are affirmative action policies just means to rectify that injustice? Nearly all of the writers I cited earlier who define justice in distributive terms identify questions of the equality or inequality of wealth and income as the primary questions of social justice (see also Arthur and Shaw, 1978). They usually subsume the second set of questions, about the justice of the distribution of social positions, under the question of economic distribution, since "more desirable" positions usually correspond to those that yield higher income or greater access to resources.

Applied discussions of justice too usually focus on the distribution of material goods and resources. Discussions of justice in medical care, for example, usually focus on the allocation of medical resources such as treatment, sophisticated equipment, expensive procedures, and so on (e.g., Daniels, 1985, esp. chaps. 3 and 4). Similarly, issues of justice enter discussion in environmental ethics largely through consideration of the impact that alternative policies might have on the distribution of natural and social resources among individuals and groups (see, e.g., Simon, 1984).

[...] the social context of welfare capitalist society helps account for this tendency to focus on the distribution of income and other-resources. Public political dispute in welfare corporate society is largely restricted to issues of taxation, and the allocation of public funds among competing social interests. Public discussions of social injustice tend to revolve around inequalities of wealth and income, and the extent to which the state can or should mitigate the suffering of the poor.

There are certainly pressing reasons for philosophers to attend to these issues of the distribution of wealth and resources. In a society and world with vast differences in the amount of material goods to which individuals have access, where millions starve while others can have anything they want, any conception of justice must address the distribution of material goods. The immediate provision of basic material goods for people now suffering severe deprivation must be a first priority for any program that seeks to make the world more just. Such a call obviously entails considerations of distribution and redistribution.

But in contemporary American society, many public appeals to justice do not concern primarily the distribution of material goods. Citizens in a rural Massachusetts town organize against a decision to site a huge hazardous waste treatment plant in their town. Their leaflets convince people that state law has treated the community unjustly by denying them the option of rejecting the plant (Young, 1983). Citizens in an Ohio city are outraged at the announcement that a major employer is closing down its plant. They question the legitimacy of the power of private corporate decisionmakers to throw half the city out of work without warning, and without any negotiation and consultation with the community. Discussion of possible compensation makes them snicker; the point is not simply that we are out of jobs and thus lack money, they claim, but that no private party should have the right to decide to decimate the local economy. Justice may require that former workers and other members of the community have the option of taking over and operating the plant themselves (Schweickart, 1984). These two cases concern not so much the justice of material distributions as the justice of decisionmaking power and procedures.

Black critics claim that the television industry is guilty of gross injustice in its depictions of Blacks. More often than not, Blacks are represented as criminals, hookers, maids, scheming dealers, or jiving connivers. Blacks rarely appear in roles of authority, glamour, or virtue. Arab Americans are outraged at the degree to which television and film present recognizable Arabs only as sinister terrorists or gaudy princes, and conversely that terrorists are almost always Arab. Such outrage at media stereotyping issues in claims about the injustice not of material distribution, but of cultural imagery and symbols.

In an age of burgeoning computer technology, organizations of clerical workers argue that no person should have to spend the entirety of her working day in front of a computer terminal typing in a set of mindless numbers at monitored high speeds. This claim about injustice concerns not the distribution of goods, for the claim would still be made if VDT operators earned $30,000 annually. Here the primary issues of justice concern the structure of the division of labor and a right to meaningful work.

There are many such claims about justice and injustice in our society which are not primarily about the distribution of income, resources, or positions. A focus on the distribution of material goods and resources inappropriately restricts the scope of justice, because it fails to bring social structures and institutional contexts under evaluation. Several writers make this claim about distributive theories specifically with regard to their inability to bring capitalist institutions and class relations under evaluation. In his classic paper, for example, Allen Wood (1972) argues that for Marx justice refers only to superstructural juridical relations of distribution, which are constrained by the underlying mode of production. Because they are confined to distribution, principles of justice cannot be used to evaluate the social relations of production themselves (cf. Wolff, 1977, pp. 199–208).

Other writers criticize distributive theories of justice, especially Rawls's, for presupposing at the same time that they obscure the context of class inequality that the theories are unable to evaluate (Macpherson, 1973; Nielsen, 1978). A distributive conception of justice is unable to bring class relations into view and evaluate them, Evan Simpson suggests, because its individualism prevents an understanding of structural phenomena, the "macroscopic transfer emerging from a complicated set of individual actions" (Simpson, 1980, p. 497) which cannot be understood in terms of any particular individual actions or acquisitions.

Many who make this Marxist criticism of the distributive focus of theories of justice conclude that justice is a concept of bourgeois ideology and thus not useful for a socialist normative analysis. Others disagree, and this dispute has occupied much of the Marxist literature on justice. I will argue later that a criticism of the distributive paradigm does not entail abandoning or transcending the concept of justice. For the moment I wish to focus on the point on which both sides in this dispute agree, namely, that predominant approaches to justice tend to presuppose and uncritically accept the relations of production that define an economic system.

The Marxist analysis of the distributive paradigm provides a fruitful starting point, but it is both too narrow and too general. On the one hand, capitalist class relations are not the only phenomena of social structure or institutional context that the distributive paradigm fails to evaluate. Some feminists point out, for example, that contemporary theories of justice presuppose family structure, without asking how social relations involving sexuality, intimacy, childrearing, and household labor ought best to be organized (see Okin, 1986; Pateman, 1988, pp. 41–43). Like their forebears, contemporary liberal theorists of justice tend to presume that the units among which basic distributions take place are families, and that it is as family members, often heads of families, that individuals enter the public realm where justice operates (Nicholson, 1986, chap. 4). Thus they neglect issues of justice within families—for example, the issue of whether the traditional sexual division of labor still presupposed by much law and employment policy is just.

While the Marxist criticism is too narrow, it is also too vague. The claim that the distributive paradigm fails to bring class relations under evaluation is too general to make clear what specific nondistributive issues are at stake. While property is something distributed, for example, in the form of goods, land, buildings, or shares of stock, the legal relations that define entitlement, possible forms of title, and so on are not goods to be distributed. The legal framework consists of rules defining practices and rights to make decisions about the disposition of goods. Class domination is certainly enacted by agents deciding where to invest their capital—a distributive decision; but the social rules, rights, procedures, and influences that structure capitalist decisionmaking are not distributed goods. In order to understand and evaluate the institutional framework within which distributive issues arise, the ideas of "class" and "mode of production" must be concretized in terms of specific social processes and relations. [...]

The general criticism I am making of the predominant focus on the distribution of wealth, income, and positions is that such a focus ignores and tends to obscure the institutional context within which those distributions take place, and which is often at least partly the cause of patterns of distribution of jobs or wealth. Institutional context should be understood in a broader sense than "mode of production." It includes any structures or practices, the rules and norms that guide them, and the language and symbols that mediate social interactions within them, in institutions of state, family, and civil society, as well as the workplace. These are relevant to judgments of justice and injustice insofar as they condition people's ability to participate in determining their actions and their ability to develop and exercise their capacities.

Many discussions of social justice not only ignore the institutional contexts within which distributions occur, but often presuppose specific institutional structures whose justice they fail to bring under evaluation. Some political theories, for example, tend to assume centralized legislative and executive institutions separated from the day-to-day lives of most people in the society, and state officials with the authority to make and enforce policy decisions. They take for granted such institutions of the modern state as bureaucracies and welfare agencies for implementing and enforcing tax schemes and administering services (see, e.g., Rawls, 1971, pp. 274–84). Issues of the just organization of government institutions, and just methods of political decisionmaking, rarely get raised.

To take a different kind of example, [...] when philosophers ask about the just principles for allocating jobs and offices among persons, they typically assume a stratification of such positions. They assume a hierarchical division of labor in which some jobs and offices carry significant autonomy, decisionmaking power, authority, income, and access to resources, while others lack most of these attributes. Rarely do theorists explicitly ask whether such a definition and organization of social positions is just.

Many other examples of ways in which theorizing about justice frequently presupposes specific structural and institutional background conditions could be cited. In every case a clear understanding of these background conditions can reveal how they affect distribution—what there is to distribute, how it gets distributed, who distributes, and what the distributive outcome is. With Michael Walzer, my intention here is "to shift our attention from distribution itself to conception and creation: the naming of the goods, the giving of meaning, and the collective making" (Walzer, 1983, p. 7). I shall focus most of my discussion on three primary categories of nondistributive issues that distributive theories tend to ignore: decisionmaking structure and procedures, division of labor, and culture.

Decisionmaking issues include not only questions of who by virtue of their positions have the effective freedom or authority to make what sorts of decisions, but also the rules and procedures according to which decisions are made. Discussion of economic justice, for example, often de-emphasizes the decisionmaking structures which are crucial determinants of economic relations. Economic domination in our society occurs not simply or primarily because some persons have more wealth and income than others, as important as this is. Economic domination derives at least as much from the corporate and legal structures and procedures that give some persons the power to make decisions about investment, production, marketing, employment, interest rates, and wages that affect millions of other people. Not all who make these decisions are wealthy or even privileged, but the decisionmaking structure operates to reproduce distributive inequality and the unjust constraints on people's lives that [...] name exploitation and marginalization. As Carol Gould (1988, pp. 133–34) points out, rarely do theories of justice take such structures as an explicit focus. [...]

Division of labor can be understood both distributively and nondistributively. As a distributive issue, division of labor refers to how pregiven occupations, jobs, or tasks are allocated among individuals or groups. As a nondistributive issue, on the other hand, division of labor concerns the definition of the occupations themselves. Division of labor as an institutional structure involves the range of tasks performed in a given position, the definition of the nature, meaning, and value of those tasks, and the relations of cooperation, conflict, and authority among positions. Feminist claims about the justice of a sexual division of labor, for example, have been posed both distributively and nondistributively. On the one hand, feminists have questioned the justice of a pattern of distribution of positions that finds a small proportion of women in the most prestigious jobs. On the other hand, they have also questioned the conscious or unconscious association of many occupations or jobs with masculine or feminine characteristics, such as instrumentality or affectivity, and this is not itself a distributive issue. [...]

Culture is the most general of the three categories of nondistributive issues I focus on. It includes the symbols, images, meanings, habitual comportments, stories, and so on through which people express their experience and communicate with one another. Culture is ubiquitous, but nevertheless deserves distinct consideration in discussions of social justice. The symbolic meanings that people attach to other kinds of people and to actions, gestures, or institutions often significantly affect the social standing of persons and their opportunities. [...]

References

Arthur, John and William Shaw, eds. 1978. *Justice and Economic Distribution*. Englewood Cliffs, N.J.: Prentice-Hall.

Daniels, Norman. 1985. *Just Health Care*. Cambridge: Cambridge University Press.

Gould, Carol. 1988. *Rethinking Democracy: Freedom and Political Cooperation in Politics, Economics, and Society*. Cambridge: Cambridge University Press.

Macpherson, C. B. 1973. *Democratic Theory: Essays in Retrieval*. Oxford: Oxford University Press.

Nicholson, Linda. 1986. *Gender and History*. New York: Columbia University Press.

Nielsen, Kai. 1978. "Class and Justice." In John Arthur and William Shaw, eds., *Justice and Economic Distribution*. Englewood Cliffs, N.J.: Prentice-Hall.

Okin, Susan. 1986. "Are Our Theories of Justice Gender-Neutral?" In Robert Fullinwider and Claudia Mills, eds., *The Moral Foundations of Civil Rights*. Totowa, N.J.: Rowman and Littlefield.

Pateman, Carole. 1988. *The Sexual Contract*. Stanford: Stanford University Press.

Rawls, John. 1971. *A Theory of Justice*. Cambridge: Harvard University Press.

Schweickart, David. 1984. "Plant Relocations: A Philosophical Reflection." *Review of Radical Political Economics* 16 (Winter): 32–51.

Simon, Robert. 1984. "Troubled Waters: Global Justice and Ocean Resources." In Tom Regan, ed., *Earthbound*. New York: Random House.

Simpson, Evan. 1980. "The Subject of Justice." *Ethics* 90 (July): 490–501.

Taylor, Charles. 1985. "The Nature and Scope of Distributive Justice." In *Philosophy and the Human Sciences*. Cambridge: Cambridge University Press.

Walzer, Michael. 1983. *Spheres of Justice*. New York: Basic.

Wolfe, Alan. 1977. *The Limits of Legitimacy: Political Contradictions of Contemporary Capitalism*. New York: Free Press.

Wood, Allen. 1972. "The Marxian Critique of Justice." *Philosophy and Public Affairs* 1 (Spring): 244–82.

Young, Iris. 1983. "Justice and Hazardous Waste." In Michael Bradie, ed., *The Applied Turn in Contemporary Philosophy*. Bowling Green, Ohio: Applied Philosophy Program, Bowling Green State University.

The Social Construction of Difference
(2000)

Allan G. Johnson

T HE LATE AFRICAN AMERICAN NOVELIST JAMES Baldwin once offered the provocative idea that there is no such thing as whiteness or, for that matter, blackness or, more generally, race. "No one is white before he/she came to America," he wrote. "It took generations and a vast amount of coercion, before this became a white country."
...

Baldwin isn't denying the reality that skin pigmentation varies from one person to another. What he is saying is that unless you live in a culture that recognizes such differences as significant, they are socially irrelevant and therefore, in a way, do not exist. A "black woman" in Africa, therefore, who has not experienced white racism, does not *think* of herself as black or experience herself as black, nor do the people around her. African, yes, a woman, yes. But not a *black* woman.

When she comes to the United States, however, where privilege is organized according to race, suddenly she becomes black because people assign her to a social category that bears that name, and they treat her differently as a result. ...

So Baldwin is telling us that race and all its categories have no significance outside systems of privilege and oppression in which they were created in the first place. This is what sociologists call the "social construction" of reality.

...

The same is true with the definition of what is considered "normal." While it may come as a surprise to many who think of themselves as nondisabled, disability and nondisability are socially constructed. This doesn't mean that the difference between having or not having full use of your legs is somehow "made up" without any objective reality. It does mean, however, that how people notice and label and think about such differences and how they treat other people as a result depend entirely on ideas contained in a system's culture.

Human beings, for example, come in a variety of heights, and many of those considered "normal" are unable to reach high places such as kitchen shelves without the assistance of physical aids—chairs and step-stools. In spite of their inability to do this simple task without special aids, they are not defined as disabled. Nor are the roughly 100 million people in the United States who cannot see properly without the aid of eyeglasses. ...

Disability and nondisability are ... constructed through the language used to describe people. When someone who cannot see is labeled a "blind person," for example, it creates the impression that not being able to see sums up the entire person. In other words, blind becomes what they *are*. The same thing happens when people are described as "brain damaged" or "crippled" or "retarded" or "deaf"—the person becomes the disability and nothing more. Reducing people to a single dimension of who they are separates and excludes them, marks them as "other," as different from "normal" (white, heterosexual, male, nondisabled) people and therefore as inferior. ...

There is a world of difference between using a wheelchair and being treated as a normal human being (who happens to use a wheelchair to get around) and using a wheelchair and being treated as invisible, inferior, unintelligent, asexual, frightening, passive, dependent, and nothing more than your disability. And that difference is not a matter of the disability itself but of how it is constructed in society and how we then make use of that construction in our minds to shape how we think about ourselves and other people and how we treat them as a result.

What makes socially constructed reality so powerful is that we rarely if ever experience it as that. We think the way our culture defines something like race or gender is simply the way things are in some objective sense. ... In the 19th century, for example, U.S. law identified those having *any* African ancestry as black, a standard known as the "one-drop rule," which defined "white" as a state of absolute purity in relation to "black." Native American status, in contrast, required at *least* one-eighth Native American ancestry in order to qualify. Why the different standards? ... Native Americans could claim financial benefits from the federal government, making it to whites' advantage to make it hard for anyone to be considered Native American. Designating someone as black, however, took *away* power and *denied* the right to make claims against whites, including white families of origin. In both cases, racial classification has had little to do with objective characteristics and everything to do with preserving white power and wealth.

This fact has also been true of the use of race to tag various ethnic groups. When the Chinese were imported as cheap laborers during the 19th century, the California Supreme Court declared them not white. Mexicans, however, many of whom owned large amounts of land in California and did business with whites, were considered white. Today, as Paul Kivel points out, Mexicans are no longer considered white and the Chinese are "conditionally white at times."

...

No matter what privileged group you belong to, if you want to understand the problem of privilege and difference, the first stumbling block is usually the idea of privilege itself. When people hear that they belong to a privileged group or benefit from something like "white privilege" or "male privilege," they don't get it, or they feel angry and defensive about what they do get. *Privilege* has become one of those loaded words we need to reclaim so that we can use it to name and illuminate the truth. ...

Privilege exists when one group has something of value that is denied to others simply because of the groups they belong to, rather than because of anything they've done or failed to do. If people take me more seriously when I give a speech than they would someone of color saying the same things in the same way, then I'm benefiting from white privilege. That a heterosexual black woman can feel free to talk about her life in ways that reveal the fact that she's married to a man is a form of heterosexual privilege because lesbians and gay men cannot casually reveal their sexual orientation without putting themselves at risk.

...

What Privilege Looks Like in Everyday Life

... Privilege shows up in the daily details of people's lives in almost every social setting. Consider the following examples of race privilege. ...

- Whites are less likely than blacks to be arrested; once arrested, they are less likely to be convicted and, once convicted, less likely to go to prison, regardless of the crime or circumstances. Whites, for example, constitute 85 percent of those who use illegal drugs, but less than half of those in prison on drug-use charges are white.

  ...

- Whites are more likely than comparable blacks to have loan applications approved and less likely to be given poor information or the runaround during the application process.

- Whites are charged lower prices for new and used cars than are people of color, and residential segregation gives whites access to higher-quality goods of all kinds at cheaper prices.

  ...

- Whites are more likely to control conversations and be allowed to get away with it and to have their ideas and contributions taken seriously, including those that were suggested previously by a person of color and ignored or dismissed.

- Whites can usually assume that national heroes, success models, and other figures held up for general admiration will be of their race.

  ...

- Whites can assume that when they go shopping, they'll be treated as serious customers not as potential shoplifters or people without the money to make a purchase. When they try to cash a check or use a credit card, they can assume they won't be hassled for additional identification and will be given the benefit of the doubt.

  ...

- Most whites are not segregated into communities that isolate them from the best job opportunities, schools, and community services.

- Whites have greater access to quality education and health care.

  …

- Whites can succeed without other people being surprised.

- Whites don't have to deal with an endless and exhausting stream of attention to their race. They can simply take their race for granted as unremarkable to the extent of experiencing themselves as not even having a race. Unlike some of my African American students, for example, I don't have people coming up to me and treating me as if I were some exotic "other," gushing about how "cool" or different I am, wanting to know where I'm "from," and reaching out to touch my hair.

- Whites don't find themselves slotted into occupations identified with their race, as blacks are often slotted into support positions or Asians into technical jobs.

  …

- Whites can reasonably expect that if they work hard and "play by the rules," they'll get what they deserve, and they feel justified in complaining if they don't. It is something other racial groups cannot realistically expect.

In the following list for male privilege, note how some items repeat from the list on race but other items do not.

- In most professions and upper-level occupations, men are held to a lower standard than women. It is easier for a "good but not great" male lawyer to make partner than it is for a comparable woman.

- Men are charged lower prices for new and used cars.

- If men do poorly at something or make a mistake or commit a crime, they can generally assume that people won't attribute the failure to their gender. The kids who shoot teachers and schoolmates are almost always boys, but rarely is the fact that all this violence is being done by males raised as an important issue.

  …

- Men can generally assume that when they go out in public, they won't be sexually harassed or assaulted just because they're male, and if they are victimized, they won't be asked to explain what they were doing there.

- Male representation in government and the ruling circles of corporations and other organizations is disproportionately high.

  …

- Men are more likely than women are to control conversations and be allowed to get away with it and to have their ideas and contributions taken seriously, even those that were suggested previously by a woman and dismissed or ignored.

- Most men can assume that their gender won't be used to determine whether they'll fit in at work or whether teammates will feel comfortable working with them.

- Men can succeed without other people being surprised.

- Men don't have to deal with an endless and exhausting stream of attention drawn to their gender (for example, to how sexually attractive they are).

- Men don't find themselves slotted into a narrow range of occupations identified with their gender as women are slotted into community relations, human resources, social work, elementary school teaching, librarianship, nursing, and clerical, and secretarial positions.

  ...

- The standards used to evaluate men as *men* are consistent with the standards used to evaluate them in other roles such as occupations. Standards used to evaluate women as women are often different from those used to evaluate them in other roles. For example, a man can be both a "real man" and a successful and aggressive lawyer, while an aggressive woman lawyer may succeed as a lawyer but be judged as not measuring up as a woman.

In the following list regarding sexual orientation, note again items in common with the other two lists and items peculiar to this form of privilege.

- Heterosexuals are free to reveal and live their intimate relationships openly—by referring to their partners by name, recounting experiences, going out in public together, displaying pictures on their desks at work—without being accused of "flaunting" their sexuality or risking discrimination.

- Heterosexuals can marry as a way to commit to long-term relationships that are socially recognized, supported, and legitimated. This fact confers basic rights such as spousal health benefits, the ability to adopt children, inheritance, joint filing of income tax returns, and the power to make decisions for a spouse who is incapacitated in a medical emergency.

  ...

- Heterosexuals can move about in public without fear of being harassed or physically attacked because of their sexual orientation.

- Heterosexuals don't run the risk of being reduced to a single aspect of their lives, as if being heterosexual summed up the kind of person they are. Instead, they can be viewed and treated as complex human beings who happen to be heterosexual.

- Heterosexuals can usually assume that national heroes, success models, and other figures held up for general admiration will be assumed to be heterosexual.

- Most heterosexuals can assume that their sexual orientation won't be used to determine whether they'll fit in at work or whether teammates will feel comfortable working with them.

- Heterosexuals don't have to worry that their sexual orientation will be used as a weapon against them, to undermine their achievements or power.

  ...

- Heterosexuals can live where they want without having to worry about neighbors who disapprove of their sexual orientation.

- Heterosexuals can live in the comfort of knowing that other people's assumptions about their sexual orientation are correct.

In the following list regarding disability status, note again items in common with the other lists and items peculiar to this form of privilege.

- Nondisabled people can choose whether to be conscious of their disability status or to ignore it and regard themselves simply as human beings.

- Nondisabled people can live secure in other people's assumption that they are sexual beings capable of an active sex life, including the potential to have children and be parents.

  ...

- Nondisabled people can assume that they will fit in at work and in other settings without having to worry about being evaluated and judged according to preconceived notions and stereotypes about people with disabilities.

  ...

- Nondisabled people don't have to deal with an endless and exhausting stream of attention to their disability status. They can simply take their disability status for granted as unremarkable to the extent of experiencing themselves as not even having one.

- Nondisabled people can ask for help without having to worry that people will assume they need help with everything.

- Nondisabled people can succeed without people being surprised because of low expectations of their ability to contribute to society.

- Nondisabled people can expect to pay lower prices for cars because they are assumed to be mentally unimpaired and less likely to allow themselves to be misled and exploited.

  ...

- Nondisabled people are more likely to control conversations and be allowed to get away with it and have their ideas and contributions taken seriously, including those that were suggested before by a person with disabilities and then dismissed or ignored.

- Nondisabled people can assume that national heroes, success models, and other figures held up for general admiration will share their disability status.

  ...

- Nondisabled people can generally assume that when they go out in public, they won't be looked at as odd or out of place or not belonging. They can also assume that most buildings and other structures will not be designed in ways that limit their access.

- Nondisabled people can assume that when they need to travel from one place to another, they will have access to buses, trains, airplanes, and other means of transportation.

- Nondisabled people can count on being taken seriously and not treated as children.

- Nondisabled people are less likely to be segregated into living situations—such as nursing homes and special schools and sports programs—that isolate them from job opportunities, schools, community services, and the everyday workings of life in a society.

  ...

Regardless of which group we're talking about, privilege generally allows people to assume a certain level of acceptance, inclusion, and respect in the world, to operate within a relatively wide comfort zone. Privilege increases the odds of having things your own way, of being able to set the agenda in a social situation and determine the rules and standards and how they're applied. Privilege grants the cultural authority to make judgments about others and to have those judgements stick. It allows people to define reality and to have prevailing definitions of reality fit their experience. Privilege means being able to decide who gets taken seriously, who receives attention, who is accountable to whom and for what. And it grants a presumption of superiority and social permission to act on that presumption without having to worry about being challenged.

To have privilege is to be allowed to move through your life without being marked in ways that identify you as an outsider, as exceptional or "other" to be excluded, or to be included but always with conditions. ...

Oppression: The Flip Side of Privilege

For every social category that is privileged, one or more other categories are oppressed in relation to it. ... Just as privilege tends to open doors of opportunity, oppression tends to slam them shut.

Like privilege, oppression results from the social relationship between privileged and oppressed categories, which makes it possible for individuals to vary in their personal experience of being oppressed ("I've never been oppressed as a woman"). This also means, however, that in order to have the experience of being oppressed, it is necessary to belong to an oppressed category. In other words, men cannot be oppressed *as men,* just as whites cannot be oppressed as whites or heterosexuals as heterosexuals, because a group can be oppressed only if there exists another group with the power to oppress them.

As we saw earlier, people in privileged categories can certainly feel bad in ways that can feel oppressive. Men, for example, can feel burdened by what they take to be their responsibility to provide for their families. Or they can feel limited and even damaged by the requirement that "real men" must avoid expressing feelings other than anger. But although access to privilege costs them something that may *feel* oppressive, to call it oppression distorts the nature of what is happening to them and why.

...

The complexity of systems of privilege makes it possible, of course, for men to experience oppression if they also happen to be of color or gay or disabled or in a lower social class, but not simply because they are male. In the same way, whites can experience oppression for many reasons, but not because they're white.

...

Finally, being in a privileged category that has an oppressive relationship with another isn't the same as being an oppressive *person* who behaves in oppressive ways. That males as a social category oppress females as a social category, for example, is a social fact. That doesn't, however, tell us how a particular man thinks or feels about particular women or behaves toward them. This can be a subtle distinction to hang on to, but hang on to it we must if we're going to maintain a clear idea of what oppression is and how it works in defense of privilege.

...

Reading 2.3

Oppression

(1983)

Marilyn Frye

I T IS A FUNDAMENTAL CLAIM OF feminism that women are oppressed. The word "oppression" is a strong word. It repels and attracts. It is dangerous and dangerously fashionable and endangered. It is much misused, and sometimes not innocently.

The statement that women are oppressed is frequently met with the claim that men are oppressed too. We hear that oppressing is oppressive to those who oppress as well as those they oppress. Some men cite as evidence of their oppression their much-advertised inability to cry. It is tough, we are told, to be masculine. When the stresses and frustrations of being a man are cited as evidence that oppressors are oppressed by their oppressing, the word "oppression" is being stretched to meaninglessness; it is treated as though its scope includes any and all human experience of limitation or suffering, no matter the cause, degree or consequence. Once such usage has been put over on us, then if ever we deny that any person or group is oppressed, we seem to imply that we think they never suffer and have no feelings. We are accused of insensitivity; even of bigotry. For women, such accusation is particularly intimidating, since sensitivity is one of the few virtues that has been assigned to us. If we are found insensitive, we may fear we have no redeeming traits at all and perhaps are not real women. Thus are we silenced before we begin: the name of our situation drained of meaning and our guilt mechanisms tripped.

But this is nonsense. Human beings can be miserable without being oppressed, and it is perfectly consistent to deny that a person or group is oppressed without denying that they have feelings or that they suffer.

We need to think clearly about this oppression, and there is much that mitigates against this. I do not want to undertake to prove that women are oppressed (or that men are not), but I want to make clear what is being said when we say it. We need this word, this concept, and we need it to be sharp and sure.

I

The root of the word "oppression" is the element "press." *The press of the crowd; pressed into military service; to press a pair of pants; printing press; press the button.* Presses are used to mold things or flatten them or reduce them in bulk, sometimes to reduce them by squeezing out the gases or liquids in them. Something pressed is something caught between or among forces and barriers which are so related to each other that jointly they restrain, restrict or prevent the thing's motion or mobility. Mold. Immobilize. Reduce.

The mundane experience of the oppressed provides another clue. One of the most characteristic and ubiquitous features of the world as experienced by oppressed people is the double bind—situations in which options are reduced to a very few and all of them expose one to penalty, censure or deprivation. For example, it is often a requirement upon oppressed people that we smile and be cheerful. If we comply, we signal our docility and our acquiescence in our situation. We need not, then, be taken note of. We acquiesce in being made invisible, in our occupying no space. We participate in our own erasure. On the other hand, anything but the sunniest countenance exposes us to being perceived as mean, bitter, angry or dangerous. This means, at the least, that we may be found "difficult" or unpleasant to work with, which is enough to cost one one's livelihood; at worst, being seen as mean, bitter, angry or dangerous has been known to result in rape, arrest, beating, and murder. One can only choose to risk one's preferred form and rate of annihilation.

Another example: It is common in the United States that women, especially younger women, are in a bind where neither sexual activity nor sexual inactivity is all right. If she is heterosexually active, a woman is open to censure and punishment for being loose, unprincipled or a whore. The "punishment" comes in the form of criticism, snide and embarrassing remarks, being treated as an easy lay by men, scorn from her more restrained female friends. She may have to lie to hide her behavior from her parents. She must juggle the risks of unwanted pregnancy and dangerous contraceptives. On the other hand, if she refrains from heterosexual activity, she is fairly constantly harassed by men who try to persuade her into it and pressure her into it and pressure her to "relax" and "let her hair down"; she is threatened with labels like "frigid," "uptight," "man-hater," "bitch," and "cocktease." The same parents who would be disapproving of her sexual activity may be worried by her inactivity because it suggests she is not or will not be popular, or is not sexually normal. She may be charged with lesbianism. If a woman is raped, then if she has been heterosexually active she is subject to the presumption that she liked it (since her activity is presumed to show that she likes sex), and if she has not been heterosexually active, she is subject to the presumption that she liked it (since she is supposedly "repressed and frustrated"). Both heterosexual activity and heterosexual nonactivity are likely to be taken as proof that you wanted to be raped, and hence, of course, weren't *really* raped at all. You can't win. You are caught in a bind, caught between systematically related pressures.

Women are caught like this, too, by networks of forces and barriers that expose one to penalty, loss or contempt whether one works outside the home or not, is on welfare or not, bears children or not, raises children or not, marries or not, stays married or not, is heterosexual, lesbian, both or neither. Economic necessity; confinement to racial and/ or sexual job ghettos; sexual harassment; sex discrimination; pressures of competing expectations and judgments about *women*, *wives* and *mothers* (in the society at large, in racial and ethnic subcultures and in one's own mind); dependence (full or partial) on husbands, parents or the state; commitment to political ideas; loyalties to racial or ethnic or other "minority" groups; the demands of the self-respect and responsibilities to others. Each of these factors exists in complex tension with every other, penalizing or prohibiting all of the apparently available options. And nipping at one's heels, always, is the endless pack of little things. If one dresses one way, one is subject to the assumption that one is advertising one's sexual availability; if one dresses another way, one appears to "not care about oneself" or to be "unfeminine." If one uses "strong language," one invites categorization as a "lady"—one too delicately constituted to cope with robust speech or the realities to which it presumably refers.

The experience of oppressed people is that the living of one's life is confined and shaped by forces and barriers which are not accidental or occasional and hence avoidable, but are systematically related to each other in such a way as to catch one between and among them and restrict or penalize motion in any direction. It is the experience of being caged in: all avenues, in every direction, are blocked or booby trapped.

Cages. Consider a birdcage. If you look very closely at just one wire in the cage, you cannot see the other wires. If your conception of what is before you is determined by this myopic focus, you could look at that one wire, up and down the length of it, and be unable to see why a bird would not just fly around the wire any time it wanted to go somewhere. Furthermore, even if, one day at a time, you myopically inspected each wire, you still could not see why a bird would have trouble going past the wires to get anywhere. There is no physical property of any one wire, *nothing* that the closest scrutiny could discover, that will reveal how a bird could be inhibited or harmed by it except in the most accidental way. It is only when you step back, stop looking at the wires one by one, microscopically, and take a macroscopic view of the whole cage, that you can see why the bird does not go anywhere; and then you will see it in a moment. It will require no great subtlety of mental powers. It is perfectly obvious that the bird is surrounded by a network of systematically related barriers, no one of which would be the least hindrance to its flight, but which, by their relations to each other, are as confining as the solid walls of a dungeon.

It is now possible to grasp one of the reasons why oppression can be hard to see and recognize: one can study the elements of an oppressive structure with great care and some good will without seeing the structure as a whole, and hence without seeing or being able to understand that one is looking at a cage and that there are people there who are caged, whose motion and mobility are restricted, whose lives are shaped and reduced.

The arresting of vision at a microscopic level yields such common confusion as that about the male door-opening ritual. This ritual, which is remarkably widespread across classes and races, puzzles many people, some of whom do and some of whom do not find it offensive. Look at the scene of the two people approaching a door. The male steps slightly ahead and opens the door. The male holds the door open while the female glides through. Then the male goes through. The door closes after them. "Now how," one innocently asks, "can those crazy women's libbers say that is oppressive? The guy *removed* a barrier to the lady's smooth and unruffled progress." But each repetition of this ritual has a place in a pattern, in fact in several patterns. One has to shift the level of one's perception in order to see the whole picture.

The door-opening pretends to be a helpful service, but the helpfulness is false. This can be seen by noting that it will be done whether or not it makes any practical sense. Infirm men and men burdened with packages will open doors for able-bodied women who are free of physical burdens. Men will impose themselves awkwardly and jostle everyone in order to get to the door first. The act is not determined by convenience or grace. Furthermore, these very numerous acts of unneeded or even noisome "help" occur in counter-point to a pattern of men not being helpful in many practical ways in which women might welcome help. What *women* experience is a world in which gallant princes charming commonly make a fuss about being helpful and providing small services when help and services are of little or no use, but in which there are rarely ingenious and adroit princes at hand when substantial assistance is really wanted either in mundane affairs or in situations of threat, assault or terror. There is no help with the (his) laundry; no help typing a report at 4:00 a.m.; no help in mediating disputes among relatives or children. There is nothing but advice that women should stay indoors after dark, be chaperoned by a man, or when it comes down to it, "lie back and enjoy it."

The gallant gestures have no practical meaning. Their meaning is symbolic. The door-opening and similar services provided are services which really are needed by people who are for one reason or another incapacitated—unwell, burdened with parcels, etc. So the message is that women are incapable. The detachment of the acts from the concrete realities of what women need and do not need is a vehicle for the message that women's actual needs and interests are unimportant or irrelevant. Finally, these gestures imitate the behavior of servants toward masters and thus mock women, who are in most respects the servants and caretakers of men. The message of the false helpfulness of male gallantry is female dependence, the invisibility or insignificance of women, and contempt for women.

One cannot see the meanings of these rituals if one's focus is riveted upon the individual event in all its particularity, including the particularity of the individual man's present conscious intentions and motives and the individual woman's conscious perception of the event in the moment. It seems sometimes that people take a deliberately myopic view and fill their eyes with things seen microscopically in order not to see macroscopically. At any rate, whether it is deliberate or not, people can and do fail to see the oppression of women because they fail to see macroscopically and hence fail to see the various elements of the situation as systematically related in larger schemes.

As the cageness of the birdcage is a macroscopic phenomenon, the oppressiveness of the situations in which women live our various and different lives is a macroscopic phenomenon. Neither can be *seen* from a microscopic perspective. But when you look macroscopically you can see it—a network of forces and barriers which are systematically related and which conspire to the immobilization, reduction and molding of women and the lives we live.

II

The image of the cage helps convey one aspect of the systematic nature of oppression. Another is the selection of occupants of the cages, and analysis of this aspect also helps account for the invisibility of the oppression of women.

It is as a woman (or as a Chicana/o or as a Black or Asian or lesbian) that one is entrapped.

"Why can't I go to the park; you let Jimmy go!"

"Because it's not safe for girls."

"I want to be a secretary, not a seamstress; I don't want to learn to make dresses."

"There's no work for negroes in that line; learn a skill where you can earn your living."[1]

When you question why you are being blocked, why this barrier is in your path, the answer has not to do with individual talent or merit, handicap or failure; it has to do with your membership in some category understood as a "natural" or "physical" category. The "inhabitant" of the "cage" is not an individual but a group, all those of a certain category. If an individual is oppressed, it is in virtue of being a member of a group or category of people that is systematically reduced, molded, immobilized. Thus, to recognize a person as oppressed, one has to see that individual *as* belonging to a group of a certain sort.

There are many things which can encourage or inhibit perception of someone's membership in the sort of group or category in question here. In particular, it seems reasonable to suppose that if one of the devices of restriction and definition of the group is that of physical confinement or segregation, the confinement and separation would encourage recognition of the group as a group. This in turn would encourage the macroscopic focus which enables one to recognize oppression and encourages the individuals' identification and solidarity with other individuals of the group or category. But physical confinement and segregation of the group as a group is not common to all oppressive structures, and when an oppressed group is geographically and demographically dispersed the perception of it as a group is inhibited. There may be little or no thing in the situations of the individuals encouraging the macroscopic focus which would reveal the unity of the structure bearing down on all members of that group.*

(*Coerced assimilation is in fact one of the *policies* available to an oppressing group in its effort to reduce and/or annihilate another group. This tactic is used by the U.S. government, for instance, on the American Indians.)

A great many people, female and male and of every race and class, simply do not believe that *woman* is a category of oppressed people, and I think that this is in part because they have been fooled by the dispersal and assimilation of women throughout and into the systems of class and race which organize men. Our simply being dispersed makes it difficult for women to have knowledge of each other and hence difficult to recognize the shape of our common cage. The dispersal and assimilation of women throughout economic classes and races also divides us against each other practically and economically and thus attaches *interest* to the inability to see: for some, jealousy of their benefits, and for some, resentment of the others' advantages.

To get past this, it helps to notice that in fact women of all races and classes *are* together in a ghetto of sorts. There is a women's place, a sector, which is inhabited by women of all classes and races, and it is not defined by geographical boundaries but by function. The function is the service of men and men's interests as men define them, which includes the bearing and rearing of children. The details of the service and the working conditions vary by race and class, for men of different races and classes have different interests, perceive their interests differently, and express their needs and demands in different rhetorics, dialects and languages. But there are also some constants.

Whether in lower, middle or upper-class home or work situations, women's service work always includes personal service (the work of maids, butlers, cooks, personal secretaries),* sexual service (including provision for his genital sexual needs and bearing his children, but also including "being nice," "being attractive for him," etc.), and ego service (encouragement, support, praise, attention). Women's service work also is characterized everywhere by the fatal combination of responsibility and powerlessness: we are held responsible and we hold ourselves responsible for good outcomes for men and children in almost every respect though we have in almost no case power adequate to that project. The details of the subjective experience of this servitude are local. They vary with economic class and race and ethnic tradition as well as the personalities of the men in question. So also are the details of the forces which coerce our tolerance of this servitude particular to the different situations in which different women live and work.

(*At higher class levels women may not *do* all these kinds of work, but are generally still responsible for hiring and supervising those who do it. These services are still, in these cases, women's responsibility.)

All this is not to say that women do not have, assert and manage sometimes to satisfy our own interests, nor to deny that in some cases and in some respects women's independent interests do overlap with men's. But at every race/class level and even across race/class lines men do not serve women as women serve men. "Women's sphere" maybe understood as the "service sector," taking the latter expression much more widely and deeply than is usual in discussions of the economy.

III

It seems to be the human condition that in one degree or another we all suffer frustration and limitation, all encounter unwelcome barriers, and all are damaged and hurt in various ways. Since we are a social species, almost all of our behavior and activities are structured by more than individual inclination and the conditions of the planet and its atmosphere. No human is free of social structures, nor (perhaps) would happiness consist in such freedom. Structure consists of boundaries, limits and barriers; in a structured whole, some motions and changes are possible, and others are not. If one is looking for an excuse to dilute the word 'oppression', one can use the fact of social structure as an excuse and say that everyone is oppressed. But if one would rather get clear about what oppression is and is not, one needs to sort out the sufferings, harms and limitations and figure out which are elements of oppression and which are not.

From what I have already said here, it is clear that if one wants to determine whether a particular suffering, harm or limitation is part of someone's being oppressed, one has to look at it *in context* in order to tell whether it is an element in an oppressive structure: one has to see if it is part of an enclosing structure of forces and barriers which tends to the immobilization and reduction of a group or category of people. One has to look at how the barrier or force fits with others and to whose benefit or detriment it works. As soon as one looks at examples, it becomes obvious that not everything which frustrates or limits a person is oppressive, and not every harm or damage is due to or contributes to oppression.

If a rich white playboy who lives off income from his investments in South African diamond mines should break a leg in a skiing accident at Aspen and wait in pain in a blizzard for hours before he is rescued, we may assume that in that period he suffers. But the suffering comes to an end; his leg is repaired by the best surgeon money can buy and he is soon recuperating in a lavish suite, sipping Chivas Regal. Nothing in this picture suggests a structure of barriers and forces. He is a member of several oppressor groups and does not suddenly become oppressed because he is injured and in pain. Even if the accident was caused by someone's malicious negligence, and hence someone can be blamed for it and morally faulted, that person still has not been an agent of oppression.

Consider also the restriction of having to drive one's vehicle on a certain side of the road. There is no doubt that this restriction is almost unbearably frustrating at times, when one's lane is not moving and the other lane is clear. There are surely times, even, when abiding by this regulation would have harmful consequences. But the restriction is obviously wholesome for most of us most of the time. The restraint is imposed for our benefit, and does benefit us; its operation tends to encourage our *continued* motion, not to immobilize us. The limits imposed by traffic regulations are limits most of us would cheerfully impose on ourselves given that we knew others would follow them too. They are part of a structure which shapes our behavior, not to our reduction and immobilization, but rather to the protection of our continued ability to move and act as we will.

Another example: The boundaries of a racial ghetto in an American city serve to some extent to keep white people from going in, as well as to keep ghetto dwellers from going out. A particular white citizen may be frustrated or feel deprived because s/he cannot stroll around there and enjoy the "exotic" aura of a "foreign" culture, or shop for bargains in the ghetto swap shops. In fact, the existence of the ghetto, of racial segregation, does deprive the white person of knowledge and harm her/his character by nurturing unwarranted feelings of superiority. But this does not make the white person in this situation a member of an oppressed race or a person oppressed because of her/his race. One must look at the barrier. It limits the activities and the access of those on both sides of it (though to different degrees). But it is a product of the intention, planning and action of whites for the benefit of whites, to secure and maintain privileges that are available to whites generally, as members of the dominant and privileged group. Though the existence of the barrier has some bad consequences for whites, the barrier does not exist in systematic relationship with other barriers and forces forming a structure oppressive to whites; quite the contrary. It is part of a structure which oppresses the ghetto dwellers and thereby (and by white intention) protects and furthers white interests as dominant white culture understands them. This barrier is not oppressive to whites, even though it is a barrier to whites.

Barriers have different meanings to those on opposite sides of them, even though they are barriers to both. The physical walls of a prison no more dissolve to let an outsider in than to let an insider out, but for the insider they are confining and limiting while to the outsider they may mean protection from what s/he takes to be threats posed by insiders—freedom from harm or anxiety. A set of social and economic barriers and forces separating two groups may be felt, even painfully, by members of both groups and yet may mean confinement to one and liberty and enlargement of opportunity to the other.

The service sector of the wives/mommas/assistants/girls is almost exclusively a woman-only sector; its boundaries not only enclose women but to a very great extent keep men out. Some men sometimes encounter this barrier and experience it as a restriction on their movements, their activities, their control or their choices of "lifestyle." Thinking they might like the simple nurturant life (which they may imagine to be quite free of stress, alienation and hard work), and feeling deprived since it seems closed to them, they thereupon announce the discovery that they are oppressed, too, by "sex roles."

But that barrier is erected and maintained by men, for the benefit of men. It consists of cultural and economic forces and pressures in a culture and economy controlled by men in which, at every economic level and in all racial and ethnic subcultures, economy, tradition—and even ideologies of liberation—work to keep at least local culture and economy in male control.*

(*Of course this is complicated by race and class. Machismo and "Black manhood" politics seem to help keep Latin or Black men in control of more cash than Latin or Black women control; but these politics seem to me also to ultimately help keep the larger economy in *white* male control.)

The boundary that sets apart women's sphere is maintained and promoted by men generally for the benefit of men generally, and men generally do benefit from its existence, even the man who bumps into it and complains of the inconvenience. That barrier is protecting his classification and status as a male, as superior, as having a right to sexual access to a female or females. It protects a kind of citizenship which is superior to that of females of his class and race, his access to a wider range of better paying and higher status work, and his right to prefer unemployment to the degradation of doing lower status or "women's" work.

If a person's life or activity is affected by some force or barrier that person encounters, one may not conclude that the person is oppressed simply because the person encounters that barrier or force; nor simply because the encounter is unpleasant, frustrating or painful to that person at that time; nor simply because the existence of the barrier or force, or the processes which maintain or apply it, serve to deprive that person of something of value. One must look at the barrier or force and answer certain questions about it. Who constructs and maintains it? Whose interests are served by its existence? Is it part of a structure which tends to confine, reduce and immobilize some group? Is the individual a member of the confined group? Various forces, barriers and limitations a person may encounter or live with may be part of an oppressive structure or not, and if they are, that person may be on either the oppressed or the oppressor side of it. One cannot tell which by how loudly or how little the person complains.

IV

Many of the restrictions and limitations we live with are more or less internalized and self-monitored, and are part of our adaptations to the requirements and expectations imposed by the needs and tastes and tyrannies of others. I have in mind such things as women's cramped postures and attenuated strides and men's restraint of emotional self-expression (except for anger). Who gets what out of the practice of those disciplines, and who imposes what penalties for improper relaxations of them? What are the rewards of this self-discipline?

Can men cry? Yes, in the company of women. If a man cannot cry, it is in the company of men that he cannot cry. It is men, not women, who require this restraint; and men not only require it, they reward it. The man who maintains a steely or tough or laid-back demeanor (all are forms which suggest invulnerability) marks himself as a member of the male community and is esteemed by other men. Consequently, the maintenance of that demeanor contributes to the man's self-esteem. It is felt as good, and he can feel good about himself. The way this restriction fits into the structures of men's lives is as one of the socially required behaviors which, if carried off, contribute to their acceptance and respect by significant others and to their own self-esteem. It is to their benefit to practice this discipline.

Consider, by comparison, the discipline of women's cramped physical postures and attenuated stride. This discipline can be relaxed in the company of women; it generally is at its most strenuous in the company of men.* Like men's emotional restraint, women's physical restraint is required by men. But unlike the case of men's emotional restraint, women's physical restraint is not rewarded. What do we get for it? Respect and esteem and acceptance? No. They mock us and parody our mincing steps. We look silly, incompetent, weak and generally contemptible. Our exercise of this discipline tends to low esteem and low self-esteem. It does not benefit us. It fits in a network of behaviors through which we constantly announce to others our membership in a lower caste and our unwillingness and/or inability to defend our bodily or moral integrity. It is degrading and part of a pattern of degradation.

Acceptable behavior for both groups, men and women, involves a required restraint that seems in itself silly and perhaps damaging. But the social effect is drastically different. The woman's restraint is part of a structure oppressive to women; the man's restraint is part of a structure oppressive to women.

(*Cf., *Let's Take Back OUR Space: "Female" and "Male" Body Language as a Result of Patriarchal Structures,* by Marianne Wex (Frauenliteratureverlag Hermine Fees, West Germany, 1979), especially p. 173. This remarkable book presents literally thousands of candid photographs of women and men, in public, seated, standing and lying down. It vividly demonstrates the very systematic differences in women's and men's postures and gestures.)

V

One is marked for application of oppressive pressures by one's membership in some group or category. Much of one's suffering and frustration befalls one partly or largely because one is a member of that category. In the case at hand, it is the category, *woman*. Being a woman is a major factor in my not having a better job than I do; being a woman selects me as a likely victim of sexual assault or harassment; it is my being a woman that reduces the power of my anger to a proof of my insanity. If a woman has little or no economic or political power, or achieves little of what she wants to achieve a major causal factor in this is that she is a woman. For any woman of any race or economic class, being a woman is significantly attached to whatever disadvantages and deprivations she suffers, be they great or small.

None of this is the case with respect to a person's being a man. Simply being a man is not what stands between him and a better job; whatever assaults and harassments he is subject to, being male is not what selects him for victimization; being male is not a factor which would make his anger impotent—quite the opposite. If a man has little or no material or political power, or achieves little of what he wants to achieve, his being male is no part of the explanation. Being male is something he has going for him, even if race or class or age or disability is going against him.

Women are oppressed, as *women*. Members of certain racial and/or economic groups and classes, both the males and the females, are oppressed as members of those races and/or classes. But men are not oppressed *as men*.

... and isn't it strange that any of us should have been confused and mystified about such a simple thing?

Notes

1.   This example is derived from *Daddy Was A Number Runner*, by Louise Meriwether (Prentice-Hall, Englewood Cliffs, New Jersey, 1970), p. 144.

Toward a New Vision: Race, Class, and Gender as Categories of Analysis and Connection

(1989)

Patricia Hill Collins

Reflexive Essay: *I originally presented this essay in 1989 as a keynote address at the Workshop on Integrating Race and Gender into the College Curriculum, sponsored by the Center for Research on Women at Memphis State University. "Toward a New Vision" outlines some of the core ideas that have framed much of my intellectual activism. Working from African American women's ideas and experiences, I focus on the ideas and experiences of historically oppressed groups and point out how taking on multiple points of view fosters empathy. I also introduce the basic ideas of intersectionality as a paradigm for conceptualizing social reality. Before this talk, I had been working with issues of race, class, and gender as separate concerns. Yet, like others during the 1980s, I saw the limitations of this monocategorical approach. I conclude with a call for political resistance, by developing coalitional politics that are attentive to power differences and grounded in empathy. Because it is a touchstone for my work, I have not updated this speech.*

> *The true focus of revolutionary change is never merely the oppressive situations which we seek to escape, but that piece of the oppressor which is planted deep within each of us.*
>
> —Audre Lorde, from *Sister Outsider* (123)

IN KEEPING WITH OTHER ESSAYS IN *On Intellectual Activism*, and because this essay has been widely reprinted, I have omitted the original endnotes and substituted a brief reading list from the original essay. This talk reflects the collective effort of the center and all of the people who attended its workshops in the late 1980s and early 1990s. I have also retained the original capitalization of "black" and "white" used in this volume.

Audre Lorde's statement raises a troublesome issue for scholars and activists working for social change. While many of us have little difficulty assessing our own victimization within some major system of oppression, whether it be by race, social class, religion, sexual orientation, ethnicity, age, or gender, we typically fail to see how our thoughts and actions uphold someone else's subordination. Thus, White feminists routinely point with confidence to their oppression as women but resist seeing how much their white skin privileges them. African Americans who possess eloquent analyses of racism often persist in viewing poor White women as symbols of white power. The radical left fares little better. "If only people of color and women could see their true class interests," they argue, "class solidarity would eliminate racism and sexism." In essence, each group identifies the type of oppression with which it feels most comfortable as being fundamental and classifies all other types as being of lesser importance.

Oppression is full of such contradictions. Errors in political judgment that we make concerning how we teach our courses, what we tell our children, and which organizations are worthy of our time, talents, and financial support flow smoothly from errors in theoretical analysis about the nature of oppression and activism. Once we realize that there are few pure victims or oppressors, and that each one of us derives varying amounts of penalty and privilege from the multiple systems of oppression that frame our lives, then we will be in a position to see the need for new ways of thought and action.

To get at that "piece of the oppressor which is planted deep within each of us," we need at least two things. First, we need new visions of what oppression is, new categories of analysis that are inclusive of race, class, and gender as distinctive yet interlocking structures of oppression. Adhering to a stance of comparing and ranking oppressions—the proverbial "I'm more oppressed than you"—locks us all into a dangerous dance of competing for attention, resources, and theoretical supremacy. Instead, I suggest that we examine our different experiences within the more fundamental relationship of domination and subordination. To focus on the particular arrangements that race or class or gender take in our time and place without seeing these structures as sometimes parallel and sometimes interlocking dimensions of the more fundamental relationship of domination and subordination may temporarily ease our consciences. But while such thinking may lead to short-term social reforms, it is simply inadequate for the task of bringing about long-term social transformation.

While race, class, and gender as categories of analysis are essential in helping us understand the structural bases of domination and subordination, new ways of thinking that are not accompanied by new ways of acting offer incomplete prospects for change. To get at that "piece of the oppressor which is planted deep within each of us," we also need to change our daily behavior. Currently, we are all enmeshed in a complex web of problematic relationships that grant our mirror images full human subjectivity while stereotyping and objectifying those most different from ourselves. We often assume that the people we work with, teach, send our children to school with, and sit next to in conferences such as this will act and feel in prescribed ways because they belong to given race, social class, or gender categories. These judgments by category must be replaced with fully human relationships that transcend the legitimate differences created by race, class, and gender as categories of analysis. We require new categories of connection, new visions of what our relationships with one another can be.

Our task is immense. We must first recognize race, class, and gender as interlocking categories of analysis that together cultivate profound differences in our personal biographies. But then we must transcend those very differences by reconceptualizing race, class, and gender to create new categories of connection.

My presentation today addresses this need for new patterns of thought and action. I focus on two basic questions. First, how can we reconceptualize race, class, and gender as categories of analysis? Second, how can we transcend the barriers created by our experiences with race, class, and gender oppression to build the types of coalitions essential for social change? To address these questions, I contend that we must acquire new theories of how race, class, and gender have shaped the experiences not just of women of color but also of all groups. Moreover, we must see the connections between these categories of analysis and the personal issues in our everyday lives, particularly our scholarship, our teaching, and our relationships with our colleagues and students. As Audre Lorde points out, change starts with self, and relationships that we have with those around us must always be the primary site for social change.

How Can We Reconceptualize Race, Class, and Gender as Categories of Analysis?

To me, we must shift our discourse away from additive analyses of oppression. Such approaches are typically based on two key premises. First, they depend on either/or, dichotomous thinking. Persons, things, and ideas are conceptualized in terms of their opposites. For example, black/white, man/woman, thought/ feeling, and fact/opinion are defined in oppositional terms. Thought and feeling are not seen as two different and interconnected ways of approaching truth that can coexist in scholarship and teaching. Instead, feeling is defined as antithetical to reason, as its opposite. Despite the fact that we all have "both/and" identities (I am both a college professor and a mother—I don't stop being a mother when I drop my child off at school, or forget everything I learned while scrubbing the toilet), we persist in trying to classify each other in either/or categories. I live each day as an African American woman, a race/gender-specific experience. And I am not alone. Everyone in this room has a race/gender/class-specific identity. Either/or, dichotomous thinking is especially troublesome when applied to theories of oppression because every individual must be classified as being either oppressed or not oppressed. The both/and position of simultaneously being oppressed and oppressor becomes conceptually impossible.

A second premise of additive analyses of oppression is that these dichotomous differences must be ranked. One side of the dichotomy is typically labeled "dominant" and the other "subordinate." Thus, whites rule blacks, men are deemed superior to women, and reason is seen as being preferable to emotion. Applying this premise to discussions of oppression leads to the assumption that oppression can be quantified, and that some groups are oppressed more than others. I am frequently asked, "which has been most oppressive to you, your status as a Black person or your status as a woman?" What I am really being asked to do is divide myself into little boxes and rank my various statuses. If I experience oppression as a both/and phenomenon, why should I analyze it any differently?

Additive analyses of oppression rest squarely on the twin pillars of either/or thinking and the necessity to quantify and rank all relationships to know where one stands. Such approaches typically see African American women as being more oppressed than everyone else because the majority of Black women experience the negative effects of race, class, and gender oppression simultaneously. In essence, if you add together separate oppressions, you are left with a grand oppression greater than the sum of its parts.

I am not denying that specific groups experience oppression more harshly than others—lynching is certainly objectively worse than being held up as a sex object. But we must be careful not to confuse this issue of the saliency of one type of oppression in people's lives with a theoretical stance positing the interlocking nature of oppression. Race, class, and gender may all structure a situation but may not be equally visible and/or important in people's self-definitions. In certain contexts, such as the antebellum American south and contemporary South Africa, racial oppression is more visibly salient, while in other contexts, such as Haiti, El Salvador, and Nicaragua, social class oppression may be more apparent. For middle-class White women, gender may assume experiential primacy unavailable to poor Hispanic women struggling with the ongoing issues of low-paid jobs and the frustrations of the welfare bureaucracy. This recognition that one category may have salience over another in a given time and place does not minimize the theoretical importance of assuming that race, class, and gender as categories of analysis structure all relationships.

To move toward new visions of what oppression is, I think that we need to ask new questions. How are relationships of domination and subordination structured and maintained in the American political economy? How do race, class, and gender function as parallel and interlocking systems that shape this basic relationship of domination and subordination? Questions such as these promise to move us away from futile theoretical struggles concerned with ranking oppressions and toward analyses that assume race, class, and gender are all present in any given setting, even if one appears more visible and salient than the others. Our task becomes redefined as one of reconceptualizing oppression by uncovering the connections among race, class, and gender as categories of analysis.

Institutional Dimension of Oppression

Sandra Harding's contention that gender oppression is structured along three main dimensions—the institutional, the symbolic, and the individual—offers a useful model for a more comprehensive analysis encompassing race, class, and gender oppression. Systemic relationships of domination and subordination structured through social institutions such as schools, businesses, hospitals, the workplace, and government agencies represent the institutional dimension of oppression. Racism, sexism, and elitism all have concrete institutional locations. Even though the workings of the institutional dimension of oppression are often obscured with ideologies claiming equality of opportunity, in actuality, race, class, and gender place Asian American women, native American men, White men, African American women, and other groups in distinct institutional niches, with varying degrees of penalty and privilege.

Even though I realize that many in the current administration would not share this assumption, let us assume that the institutions of American society discriminate, whether by design or by accident. While many of us are familiar with how race, gender, and class operate separately to structure inequality, I want to focus on how these three systems interlock in structuring the institutional dimension of oppression. To get at the interlocking nature of race, class, and gender, I want you to think about the antebellum plantation as a guiding metaphor for a variety of American social institutions. Even though slavery is typically analyzed as a racist institution, and occasionally as a class institution, I suggest that slavery was a race-, class-, and gender-specific institution. Removing any one piece from our analysis diminishes our understanding of the true nature of relations of domination and subordination under slavery.

Slavery was a profoundly patriarchal institution. It rested on the dual tenets of White male authority and White male property, a joining of the political and the economic within the institution of the family. Heterosexism was assumed, and all whites were expected to marry. Control over affluent White women's sexuality remained key to slavery's survival because property was to be passed on to the legitimate heirs of the slave owner. Ensuring affluent White women's virginity and chastity was deeply intertwined with maintenance of property relations.

Under slavery, we see varying levels of institutional protection given to affluent White women, working-class and poor White women, and enslaved African women. Poor White women enjoyed few of the protections held out to their upper-class sisters. Moreover, the devalued status of Black women was key in keeping all White women in their assigned places. Controlling Black women's fertility was also vital to the continuation of slavery, for children born to slave mothers themselves were slaves.

African American women shared the devalued status of chattel with their husbands, fathers, and sons. Racism stripped blacks, as a group, of legal rights, education, and control over their own persons. African American women could be whipped, branded, sold, or killed, not because they were poor, or because they were women, but because they were Black. Racism ensured that Blacks would continue to serve Whites and suffer economic exploitation at the hands of all Whites.

So we have a very interesting chain of command on the plantation—the affluent White master as the reigning patriarch; his White wife helpmate to serve him, help him manage his property, and bring up his heirs; his faithful servants, whose production and reproduction were tied to the requirements of the capitalist political economy; and largely property-less, working-class White men and women watching from afar. In essence, the foundations for the contemporary roles of elite White women, poor Black women, working-class White men, and a series of other groups can be seen in stark relief in this fundamental American social institution. While Blacks experienced the harshest treatment under slavery, and thus made slavery clearly visible as a racist institution, race, class, and gender interlocked in structuring slavery's systemic organization of domination and subordination.

Even today, the plantation remains a compelling metaphor for institutional oppression. Certainly, the actual conditions of oppression are not as severe now as they were then. To argue, as some do, that things have not changed all that much denigrates the achievements of those who struggled for social change before us. However, the basic relationships among Black men, Black women, elite White women, elite White men, working-class White men, and working-class White women as groups remain essentially intact.

A brief analysis of important American social institutions mostly controlled by elite White men should convince us of the interlocking nature of race, class, and gender in structuring the institutional dimension of oppression. For example, if you are from an American college or university, is your campus a modern plantation? Who controls your university's political economy? Are elite White men over-represented among the upper administrators and trustees controlling your university's finances and policies? Are elite White men being joined by growing numbers of elite White women helpmates? What kinds of people are in your classrooms grooming the next generation who will occupy these and other decision-making positions? Who are the members of the support staff who produce the mass mailings, order the supplies, fix the leaky pipes? Do African Americans, Hispanics, or other people of color form the majority of the invisible workers who feed you, wash your dishes, and clean up your offices and libraries after everyone else has gone home?

If your college is anything like mine, you know the answers to these questions. You may be affiliated with an institution that has Hispanic women as vice-presidents for finance, or substantial numbers of Black men among the faculty. If so, you are fortunate. Much more typical are colleges where a modified version of the plantation as a metaphor for the institutional dimension of oppression survives.

The Symbolic Dimension of Oppression

Widespread, societally sanctioned ideologies used to justify relations of domination and subordination comprise the symbolic dimension of oppression. Central to this process is the use of stereotypical or controlling images of diverse race, class, and gender groups. To assess the power of this dimension of oppression, I want you to make a list, either on paper or in your head, of "masculine" and "feminine" characteristics. If your list is anything like that compiled by most people, it reflects some variation of the following:

Masculine	*Feminine*
Aggressive	Passive
Leader	Follower
Rational	Emotional
Strong	Weak
Intellectual	Physical

Not only does this list reflect either/or dichotomous thinking and the need to rank both sides of the dichotomy but it also makes you ask yourself exactly which men and women you had in mind when compiling these characteristics. This list applies almost exclusively to middle-class White men and women. The allegedly "masculine" qualities that you probably listed are only acceptable when exhibited by elite White men, or when used by Black and Hispanic men against each other or against women of color. Aggressive Black and Hispanic men are seen as dangerous, not powerful, and are often penalized when they exhibit any of the allegedly "masculine" characteristics. Working-class and poor White men fare slightly better and are also denied the allegedly "masculine" symbols of leadership, intellectual competence, and human rationality. Women of color and working-class and poor White women also are not represented on this list because they have never had the luxury of being "ladies." What appear to be universal categories representing all men and women instead are unmasked as being applicable to only a small group.

It is important to see how the symbolic images applied to different race, class, and gender groups interact in maintaining systems of domination and subordination. If I were to ask you to repeat the same assignment, but this time, to make separate lists for Black men, Black women, Hispanic women, and Hispanic men, I suspect that your gender symbolism would be quite different. In comparing all of the lists, you might begin to see the interdependence of symbols applied to all groups. For example, the elevated images of White womanhood need devalued images of Black womanhood to maintain credibility.

While this exercise illustrates the interlocking nature of race, class, and gender in structuring the symbolic dimension of oppression, part of its importance lies in demonstrating how race, class, and gender pervade a wide range of what appears to be universal language. Attending to diversity in our scholarship, our teaching, and our daily lives provides a new angle of vision on interpretations of reality thought to be natural, normal, and "true." Moreover, viewing images of masculinity and femininity as universal gender symbolism, rather than as symbolic images that are race-, class-, and gender-specific, renders the experiences of people of color and of nonprivileged White women and men invisible. One way to dehumanize an individual or a group is to deny the reality of their experiences. So when we refuse to deal with race or class because they do not appear to be directly relevant to gender, we are actually becoming part of someone else's problem.

Assuming that the same interlocking set of symbolic images affects everyone differently allows us to move forward toward new analyses. Women of color and White women have different relationships to White male authority, and this difference explains the distinct gender symbolism applied to both groups. Black women encounter controlling images such as the mammy, the matriarch, the mule, and the whore, images that encourage others to reject us as fully human people. Ironically, the negative nature of these images simultaneously encourages us to reject them. In contrast, White women are offered seductive images, those that promise to reward them for supporting the status quo. And yet seductive images can be equally controlling. Consider, for example the views of Nancy White, a 73-year old Black woman, concerning images of rejection and seduction:

> My mother used to say that the Black woman is the White man's mule and the White woman is his dog. Now, she said that to say this: we do the heavy work and get beat whether we do it well or not. But the White woman is closer to the master and he pats them on the head and lets them sleep in the house, but he ain't gon' treat neither one like he was dealing with a person. (Gwaltney, 148)

Both sets of images stimulate particular political stances. By broadening the analysis beyond the confines of race, we can see the varying levels of rejection and seduction available to each of us due to our race, class, and gender identity. Each of us lives with an allotted portion of institutional privilege and penalty, and with varying levels of rejection and seduction inherent in the symbolic images applied to us. This is the context in which we make our choices. Taken together, the institutional and symbolic dimensions of oppression create a structural backdrop against which all of us live our lives.

The Individual Dimension of Oppression

Whether we benefit or not, we all live within institutions that reproduce race, class, and gender oppression. Even if we never have any contact with members of other race, class, or gender groups, we all encounter images of these groups and are exposed to the symbolic meanings attached to those images. On this dimension of oppression, our individual biographies vary tremendously. As a result of our institutional and symbolic statuses, all of our choices become political acts.

All of us must come to terms with the multiple ways in which race, class, and gender as categories of analysis frame our individual biographies. I have lived my entire life as an African American woman from a working-class family, and this basic fact has had a profound impact on my personal biography. Imagine how different your life might be if you had been born Black, or White, or poor, or of a different race/class/gender group than the one with which you are most familiar. The institutional treatment you would have received and the symbolic meanings attached to your very existence might differ dramatically from what you now consider to be natural, normal, and part of everyday life. You might be the same, but your personal biography might have been quite different.

I believe that we carry around the cumulative effect of our lives within multiple structures of oppression. If you want to see how much this has affected you, I ask you one simple question: who are your close friends? Who are the people with whom you can share your hopes, dreams, vulnerabilities, fears, and victories? Do they look like you? If they are all the same, circumstance may be the cause. For the first seven years of my life, I saw only low-income Black people. My friends from those years reflected the composition of my community. But now that I am an adult, can the defense of circumstance explain the patterns of people I trust as my friends and colleagues? When given other alternatives, if my friends and colleagues reflect the homogeneity of one race, class, and gender group, then these categories of analysis have indeed become barriers to connection.

I am not suggesting that people are doomed to follow the paths laid out for them by race, class, and gender as categories of analysis. While these three structures certainly frame my opportunity structure, as an individual, I always have the choice of accepting things as they are or trying to change them. As Nikki Giovanni points out, "we've got to live in the real world. If we don't like the world we're living in, change it. And if we can't change it, we change ourselves. We can do something" (quoted in Tate, 68). While a piece of the oppressor may be planted deep within each of us, we each have the choice of accepting that piece or challenging it as part of the "true focus of revolutionary change."

How Can We Transcend the Barriers Created by Our Experiences with Race, Class, and Gender Oppression to Build the Types of Coalitions Essential for Social Change?

Reconceptualizing oppression and seeing the barriers created by race, class, and gender as interlocking categories of analysis is a vital first step. But we must transcend these barriers by moving toward race, class, and gender as categories of connection, by building relationships and coalitions that will bring about social change. What are some of the issues involved in doing this?

Differences in Power and Privilege

First, we must recognize that our differing experiences with oppression create problems in the relationships among us. Each of us lives within a system that offers varying levels of power and privilege. These differences in power, whether structured along axes of race, class, gender, age, or sexual orientation, frame our relationships. African American writer June Jordan describes her discomfort on a Caribbean vacation with Olive, the Black woman who cleaned her room:

> Even though both "Olive" and "I" live inside a conflict neither one of us created, and even though both of us therefore hurt inside that conflict, I may be one of the monsters she needs to eliminate from her universe and, in a sense, she may be one of the monsters in mine. (Jordan, 47)

Differences in power constrain our ability to connect with one another, even when we think we are engaged in dialogue across differences. Let me give you an example. One year, the students in my course "sociology of the Black community" got into a heated discussion about the reasons for the increase in racial incidents on college campuses. Black students complained vehemently about the apathy and resistance they felt most White students expressed about examining their own racism. Mark, a White male student, found these comments particularly unsettling. After claiming that all the Black people he had ever known had expressed no such beliefs to him, he questioned how representative the viewpoints of his fellow students actually were. When pushed further, Mark revealed that he had participated in conversations over the years with the Black domestic worker employed by his family. Since she had never expressed such strong feelings about White racism, Mark was genuinely shocked by class discussions. Ask yourselves whether that domestic worker was in a position to speak freely. Would it have been wise for her to do so in a situation where the power between the two parties was so unequal?

In extreme cases, members of privileged groups can erase the very presence of the less privileged. When I first moved to Cincinnati, my family and I went on a picnic at a local park. Picnicking next to us was a family of White Appalachians. When I went to push my daughter on the swings, several of the children came over. They had missing, yellowed, and broken teeth, they wore old clothing—their poverty was evident. I was shocked. Growing up in a large eastern city, I had never seen such awful poverty among Whites. The segregated neighborhoods in which I grew up made White poverty all but invisible. More importantly, the privileges attached to my newly acquired social class position allowed me to ignore and minimize the poverty among Whites that I did encounter. My reactions to those children made me realize how confining phrases such as "well, at least they're not Black" had become for me. In learning to grant human subjectivity to the Black victims of poverty, I had simultaneously learned to demean White victims of poverty. By applying categories of race to the objective conditions confronting me, I was quantifying and ranking oppressions and missing the very real suffering that, in fact, is the real issue.

One common pattern of relationships across differences in power is one that I label "voyeurism." From the perspective of the privileged, the lives of people of color, of the poor, and of women are interesting for their entertainment value. The privileged become voyeurs, passive onlookers who do not relate to the less powerful but are interested in seeing how the "different" live. Over the years, I have heard numerous African American students complain about professors who never call on them except when a so-called Black issue is being discussed. The students' interest in discussing race or their qualifications for doing so appear unimportant to the professor's efforts to use Black students' experiences as stories to make the material come alive for the White student audience. Asking Black students to perform on cue and provide a Black experience for their White classmates can be seen as voyeurism at its worst.

Most members of subordinate groups do not willingly participate in such exchanges, but often do so because members of dominant groups control the institutional and symbolic apparatuses of oppression. Racial/ethnic groups, women, and the poor have never had the luxury of being voyeurs of the lives of the privileged. Our ability to survive in hostile settings has hinged on our capacity to learn intricate details about the behaviors and worldview of the powerful and adjust our behaviors accordingly. I need only point to the difference in perception of those men and women in abusive relationships. Where men can view their girlfriends and wives as sex objects, helpmates, and a collection of stereotypes—categories of voyeurism—women must be attuned to every nuance of their partners' behavior. Are women "naturally" better at relating to people with more power than themselves, or have circumstances mandated that men and women develop different skills?

Another pattern in relationships among people of unequal power concerns a different form of exploitation. In scholarly enterprises, relationships among students and teachers, among researchers and their subjects, and even among us as colleagues in teaching and scholarship can contain elements of academic colonialism. Years ago, a Black co-worker of mine in the Roxbury section of Boston described the academic colonialism he saw among the teachers and scholars in that African American community: "The people with notebooks from Harvard come around here and study us. They don't get to know us because they really don't want to and we don't want to let them. They see what they want to see, go back and write their books and get famous off of our problems." Under academic colonialism, more powerful groups see their subordinates as people whom they perceive as subordinate to them, not as sources of entertainment, as in voyeurism, but as a resource to be benignly exploited for their own purposes.

The longstanding effort to "colorize" feminist theory by inserting the experiences of women of color represents at best genuine efforts to reduce bias in Women's Studies. But at its worst, colorization also contains elements of both voyeurism and academic colonialism. As a result of new technologies and perceived profitability, we can now watch black-and-white movie classics in color. While the tinted images we are offered may be more palatable to the modern viewer, we are still watching the same old movie that was offered to us before. Movie colorization adds little of substance—its contributions remain cosmetic. Similarly, women of color allegedly can teach White feminists nothing about feminism, but must confine ourselves to "colorizing" preexisting feminist theory. Rather than seeing women of color as fully human individuals, we are treated as the additive sum of our categories.

In the academy, patterns of relationships among those of unequal power, such as voyeurism and academic colonialism, foster reformist postures toward social change. While reformists may aim to make the movie more fun to watch by colorizing their scholarship and teaching via paying increased lip service to diversity, reformists typically insist on retaining their power to determine what is seen and by whom. In contrast, transformation involves rethinking these differences in power and privilege through dialogues among individuals from diverse groups.

Coming from a tradition where most relationships across difference are squarely rooted in relations of domination and subordination, we have much less experience relating to people as different but equal. The classroom is potentially one powerful and safe space where dialogues among individuals of unequal power relationships can occur. The relationship between Mark, the student in my class, and the domestic worker is typical of a whole series of relationships that people have when they relate across differences in power and privilege. The relationship among Mark and his classmates represents the power of the classroom to minimize those differences so that people of different levels of power can use race, class, and gender as categories of analysis to generate meaningful dialogues. In this case, the classroom equalized racial difference so that Black students who normally felt silenced spoke out. White students like Mark, who are generally unaware of how they had been privileged by their whiteness, lost that privilege in the classroom and thus became open to genuine dialogue.

Reconceptualizing course syllabi represents a comparable process of determining which groups are privileged by our current research and pedagogical techniques and which groups are penalized. Reforming these existing techniques can be a critical first step in moving toward a transformed curriculum reflecting race, class, and gender as interlocking categories of analysis. However, while reform may be effective as a short-term strategy, it is unlikely to bring about fundamental transformation in the long term. To me, social transformations, whether of college curricula or of the communities in which we live and work, require moving outside our areas of specialization and groups of interest to build coalitions across differences.

Coalitions around Common Causes

A second issue in building relationships and coalitions essential for social change is to identify the real reasons for engaging in a coalition. Just what brings people together? The presence of a common enemy is one powerful catalyst that fosters group solidarity. African American, Hispanic, Asian American, and Women's Studies share the common intellectual heritage of challenging what passes for certified knowledge in the academy. But politically expedient relationships and coalitions like these are fragile because, as June Jordan points out, "it occurs to me that much organizational grief could be avoided if people understood that partnership in misery does not necessarily provide for partnership for change: When we get the monsters off our backs all of us may want to run in very different directions" (47).

Sharing a common cause assists individuals and groups in maintaining relationships that transcend their differences. Building effective coalitions involves struggling to hear one another and developing empathy for the other points of view. The coalitions that I have been involved in that lasted and that worked have been those where commitment to a specific issue mandated collaboration as the best strategy for addressing the issue at hand.

Several years ago, master's degree in hand, I chose to teach in an inner-city parochial school in danger of closing. The money was awful, the conditions were poor, but the need was great. In my job, I had to work with a range of individuals who, on the surface, had very little in common. We had White nuns, Black middle-class graduate students, and Blacks from the "community," some of whom had been incarcerated and/or were affiliated with a range of federal anti-poverty programs. Parents formed another part of this community, Harvard faculty another, and a few well-meaning White liberals from Colorado were sprinkled in for good measure.

As you might imagine, tension was high. Initially, our differences seemed insurmountable. But as time passed, we found a common bond. In spite of profound differences in our personal biographies, differences that, in other settings, would have hampered our ability to relate to one another, we found that we were all deeply committed to the education of Black children. By learning to value each other's commitment and by recognizing that we each had different skills that were essential to actualizing that commitment, we built an effective coalition around a common cause. Our school was successful, and the children we taught benefited from the diversity we offered them.

I think that the process of curriculum transformation will require a process comparable to that of political organizing around common causes. None of us alone has a comprehensive vision of how race, class, and gender operate as categories of analysis or how they might be used as categories of connection. Our personal biographies offer us partial views. Few of us can manage to study race, class, and gender simultaneously. Instead, we each know more about some dimensions of this larger story and less about others. While we each may be committed to an inclusive, transformed curriculum, the task of building one is necessarily a collective effort. Just as the members of the school had special skills to offer to the task of building the school, we all have areas of specialization and expertise, whether scholarly, theoretical, or pedagogical, or within areas of race, class, or gender. We do not all have to do the same thing in the same way. Instead, we must support each other's efforts, realizing that they are all part of the larger enterprise of bringing about social change.

Building Empathy

A third issue involved in building the types of relationships and coalitions essential for social change concerns the issue of individual accountability. Issues of race, class, and gender oppression form the structural backdrop against which we frame our relationships—these are the forces that encourage us to substitute voyeurism and academic colonialism for fully human relationships. But while we may not have created this situation, we are each responsible for making individual, personal choices concerning which elements race, class, and gender oppression we will accept and which we will work to change.

One essential component of this accountability involves developing empathy for the experiences of individuals and groups different from ourselves. Empathy begins with taking an interest in the facts of other people's lives, both as individuals and as groups. If you care about me, you should want to know not only the details of my personal biography but also a sense of how race, class, and gender as categories of analysis created the institutional and symbolic backdrop for my personal biography. How can you hope to assess my character without knowing the details of the circumstances I face?

Moreover, by taking a theoretical stance that we have all been affected by race, class, and gender as categories of analysis that have structured our treatment, we open up possibilities for using those same constructs as categories of connection in building empathy. For example, I have a good White woman friend with whom I share common interests and beliefs. Yet we know that our racial differences have provided us with different experiences. So we talk about them. We do not assume that, because I am Black, race has only affected me, and not her, or that because I am a Black woman, race neutralizes the effect of gender in my life, while accentuating it in hers. We take those same categories of analysis that have created cleavages in our lives, in this case, categories of race and gender, and use them as categories of connection in building empathy for each other's experiences.

Finding common causes and building empathy is difficult, no matter which side of privilege we inhabit. Building empathy from the dominant side of privilege is difficult, simply because individuals from privileged backgrounds are not encouraged to do so. For example, for those of you who are White to develop empathy for the experiences of people of color, you must grapple with how your white skin has privileged you. This is difficult to do because it not only entails the intellectual process of seeing how whiteness is elevated in institutions and symbols but also involves the often painful process of seeing how your whiteness has shaped your personal biography. Intellectual stances against the institutional and symbolic dimensions of racism are generally easier to maintain than sustained self-reflection about how racism has shaped all of our individual biographies. Were and are your fathers, uncles, and grandfathers really more capable than mine, or can their accomplishments be explained in part by the racism that members of my family experienced? Did your mothers stand by silently and watch all this happen? More importantly, how have they passed on the benefits of their whiteness to you?

These are difficult questions, and I have tremendous respect for my colleagues and students who are trying to answer them. Because there is no compelling reason to examine the source and meaning of one's own privilege, I know that those who do so have freely chosen this stance. They are making conscious efforts to root out the piece of the oppressor planted within them. To me, they are entitled to the support of people of color in their efforts. Men who declare themselves feminists, members of the middle class who ally themselves with anti-poverty struggles, and heterosexuals who support gays and lesbians are all trying to grow, and their efforts place them far ahead of the majority who never think of engaging in such important struggles.

Building empathy from the subordinate side of privilege is also difficult, but for different reasons. Members of subordinate groups are understandably reluctant to abandon a basic mistrust of members of powerful groups because this mistrust has traditionally been central to their survival. As a Black woman, it would be foolish for me to assume that White women, Black men, White men, or any other group with a history of exploiting African American women has my best interests at heart. These groups enjoy varying amounts of privilege over me, and therefore I must watch them carefully and be prepared for a relation of domination and subordination.

Like the privileged, members of subordinate groups must also work toward replacing judgments by category with new ways of thinking and acting—refusing to do so stifles prospects for effective coalition and social change. Let me use another example from my own experiences. When I was an undergraduate, I had little time or patience for the theorizing of the privileged. My initial years at a private, elite institution were difficult, not because the coursework was challenging (it was, but that wasn't what distracted me) or because I had to work while my classmates lived on family allowances (I was used to work). The adjustment was difficult because so many people who took their privilege for granted surrounded me. Most of them felt entitled to their wealth. That astounded me.

I remember one incident that occurred while I was watching a White woman who lived down the hall in my dormitory try to pick out which sweater to wear. The sweaters were piled up on her bed in all the colors of the rainbow, sweater after sweater. She asked my advice in a way that let me know that choosing a sweater was one of the most important decisions she had to make on a daily basis. Standing knee-deep in her sweaters, I realized how different our lives were. She did not have to worry about maintaining a solid academic average so that she could receive financial aid. Because she was in the majority, she was not treated as a representative of her race. She did not have to consider how her classroom comments or her basic existence on campus contributed to the treatment her group would receive. Her allowance protected her from having to work, so she was free to spend her time studying, partying, or in her case, worrying about which sweater to wear. The degree of inequality in our lives and her unquestioned sense of entitlement concerning that inequality offended me. For a while, I categorized all affluent White women as being superficial, arrogant, overly concerned with material possessions, and part of my problem. But had I continued to classify people in this way, I would have missed out on making some very good friends whose discomfort with their inherited or acquired social class privileges pushed them to examine their position.

Because I opened with the words of Audre Lorde, it seems appropriate to close with another of her ideas. As we go forth to the remaining activities of this workshop, and beyond this workshop, we might do well to consider Lorde's perspective:

> Each of us is called upon to take a stand. So in these days ahead, as we examine ourselves and each other, our works, our fears, our differences, our sisterhood and survivals, I urge you to tackle what is most difficult for us all, self-scrutiny of our complacencies, the idea that since each of us believes she is on the side of right, she need not examine her position. (Lorde 1985)

I urge you to examine your position.

Additional Resources

Bambara, Toni Cade, ed. 1970. *The Black Woman*. New York: signet.

Davis, Angela. 1981. *Women, Race and Class*. New York: Random House.

Dill, Bonnie Thornton. 1983. "Race, Class, and Gender: Prospects for an All-Inclusive Sisterhood," *Feminist Studies* 9(1):131–150

Gwaltney, John Langston. 1980. *Drylongso: A Self-Portrait of Black America*. New York: Vintage.

Jordan, June. 1985. *On Call: Political Essays*. Boston: South End Press.

Lorde, Audre. 1984. *Sister Outsider*. Trumansberg, N.Y.: Crossing Press.

———. 1985. Keynote Address, "Sisterhood and Survival," Conference on the Black Woman Writer and the Diaspora, Michigan State University.

Tate, Claudia, ed. 1983. *Black Women Writers at Work*. New York: Continuum.

Zinn, Maxine Baca, Lynn Weber Cannon, Elizabeth Higginbotham, and Bonnie Thornton Dill. 1986. "The Cost of Exclusionary Practices in Women's Studies." *SIGNS: Journal of Women and Culture in Society* 11(2):290–303.

Womanism and Intersectionality Against the Dominance of White, Bourgeois Women

(2017)

Patu/Antje Schrupp & Sophie Lewis

Patu/Antje Schrupp and Sophie Lewis, "Womanism and Intersectionality Against the Dominance of White, Bourgeois Women," *A Brief History of Feminism*, pp. 65–68, 255–256. Copyright © 2017 by MIT Press. Reprinted with permission.

*A 1932 law in the United States provided a mandate for forced sterilization. In practice, the policy became a vector for the racist population politics espoused by the government. Those affected were overwhelmingly indigenous, Chicana, Puerto Rican, and African-American women.

As early as the 1960s, more and more women raised their voices in criticism of the dominance of a white, bourgeois perspective on women's rights, for example the poet Audre Lorde (1934–1992) . . .

"If white American feminist theory need not deal with the differences between us, and the resulting difference in our oppressions, then how do you deal with the fact that the women who clean your houses and tend your children while you attend conferences on feminist theory are, for the most part, poor women and women of color?"

. . . or the philosopher Angela Davis (1944–), whose book *Women, Race, and Class* was published in 1981.

"As a black woman, my politics and political affiliation are bound up with and flow from participation in my people's struggle for liberation, and with the fight of oppressed people all over the world."

To underline these differences, black activist women coined the term "womanism." The linked nature of different relations of discrimination was also dealt with at the time under the term "triple oppression" (which meant the threefold oppression on the basis of sex, skin color, and class affiliation).

At the end of the 1980s, the legal theorist Kimberlé Crenshaw (1959–) coined the term "intersectionality," that is, crossroads. It speaks to the fact that different forms of discrimination can't just be added up: a person is discriminated against as a woman, a person of color, and a lesbian—a lesbian woman of color—all at once. The different axes of oppression are so interlinked that the specific character of each individual aspect transforms the others as well. For example, a black woman is treated differently as a woman than a white woman is.

The terminology proliferates ...

We cannot simply lift the American category of race and apply it to the European context.

Furthermore, it soon became clear that besides these three, numerous other kinds of systemic injustice demanded analysis, for example, discrimination on the basis of sexual orientation, bodily norms, age, and so on.

Tita Aida: Intimate Geographies of Suffering

(2003)

Martin F. Manalansan IV

I N 1991, I HAD WORKED AND lived for two years in what is touted to be the epicenter of the epicenter of the AIDS pandemic, the Chelsea district of Manhattan. I was working at the Gay Men's Health Crisis (an AIDS service organization), a few blocks from my basement studio apartment. A thought crossed my mind one day as I walked back from work to my apartment. By then, I had witnessed a friend and several acquaintances die of the disease. Because my neighborhood is basically considered to be the city's gay ghetto, images of AIDS proliferated on the walls of many buildings, restaurants, shops, bars, and business establishments in the neighborhood. On the walls of buildings, on storefronts, even on mailboxes, the red ribbon, the words "Safer Sex" and of course, "AIDS" were plastered all over. AIDS at least in my immediate surroundings was never more than a few feet away.

It suddenly occurred to me that the terror of living in the pandemic had dissipated into a routinized banality. More often than not, I walk away from any discussion about AIDS at parties and social gatherings. One of my office mates said huffily that if Michael Callen, an AIDS activist and performer, sang his signature song, "Love Don't Need a Reason" one more time, he would leave the room. The song was supposed to be the anthem of AIDS awareness, yet after more than a decade into the pandemic, the cultural practices and icons that have emerged from it have become boringly ordinary for many people.

I heard very black and cruel humor about the disease, some coming from AIDS sufferers themselves. I once heard a story of a guy who had AIDS and had a yeast infection. His doctor forbade him to eat cheese, which he loved. At a party, he couldn't resist the urge so he took a slice of havarti and said, "I have to feed my yeast." I know of one gay man who had three remaining T-cells and had given them pet names.

All these scenes made me think back to years ago when I was living in the Philippines under martial law and the Marcos dictatorship. At that time, despite the numerous repressive measures that left thousands of Filipinos dead or in dire poverty, there was a fatalism that found its voice in humor, gossip, and satire. I left in 1984, two years before the Marcos era came to an end. I know that living under a dictatorship and living under a pandemic have important differences. However, as in the Philippines of my memory, the horror of the disease has in some ways become a commonplace part of everyday life. Terror becomes muted. Yet one feels that underneath all these placid surfaces there are rumblings, explosions of anger, and silent acts of defiance.

...

AIDS, Identity, and Immigration: Some Vignettes

> When I was growing up [in the Philippines] there was this huge bridge that connected my town, which was on an island, with the mainland. When I came back [from America] after being away for more than a dozen years, I realized that it was not as big as I remembered it to be. Actually, it was very small. —jojo

These words of a gay Filipino informant who immigrated to America best symbolize most of the underlying issues I will explore in this section. I locate the interconnections between subjectivities or identities in conducting an ethnography of AIDS among Filipino gay immigrants with the larger framework of anthropological practice and transnational social, economic, and political processes. I argue that issues of self and other in this particular fieldwork situation illustrate the ambivalent, contingent, and shifting character of subjectivities in an increasingly migrant world. I discuss how immigration affects specific identities, such as being gay and being Filipino amid the AIDS pandemic, and how these, in turn, affect the position of a "native" anthropologist like myself in conducting research among his own people.

I have decided against focusing on reflexivity as an exclusively phenomenological or autobiographical experience, because I believe that the historical moment we live in today should shape the way we as anthropologists reexamine or revise our identities and experiences in the pandemic in particular and in the study of human societies in general. Amid a burgeoning global cultural and economic system where people, ideas, machines, and diseases cross terrains and borders, the need to connect seemingly individual/personal and local experiences of various life trajectories with a systemic and structural framework is more compelling than ever. Immigration, as Homi Bhabha (1992) has noted, brings to light the ambivalent, hybrid, and dissembling character of life away from the homeland. What this means is that difference, be it racial, ethnic, cultural, sexual, or economic, becomes central to the identification process of migrants and their engagement with the pandemic. However, this kind of difference is neither fixed nor clearly bounded by a specific territory. Moreover, the intrusions of spaces and memory brought about by immigration become part of the engagement.

I argue that these spaces and memories bring forth what can be called an intimate geography of suffering. By this I mean the various ways in which suffering under the pandemic is structured and constituted not just by the here and now, but by remembered spaces and time fragments of one's biography and history. Suffering in the case of Filipino gay men in the diaspora is experienced and understood through and refracted by the exigencies of home and the problems of displacement and settlement. Suffering is not a process imbued only with forlornness but rather is a purposive series of acts that build and create spaces for negotiating location and positionality. The spatial aspects of AIDS and Filipino gay men can be properly understood by other studies on AIDS. Cindy Patton (2002), for example, explores the creation of "official maps" that seek to contain and naturalize the pandemic in strictly geographic terms. Additionally, Paul Farmer's (1992) study of AIDS in Haiti critically examines what he calls the "geography of blame" that morally inscribes the spread and provenance of the disease in Haitian bodies and social landscapes. Building on these examples, I aim to create an alternative mapping of AIDS in Filipino gay men's lives that brings together public and official discourses with private and intimate ones.

What follows below is not a sorrowful portrait of these men. Rather, suffering is rendered, appropriated, and performed in ambivalent and complicated ways but always in relation to the operations of power (Kleinman, Das, and Lock 1997). Pleasure, humor, and gossip intersect with mourning and abjection as part of the attempt of Filipino gay men to wrestle with, understand, and survive the onslaught of the disease.

It is often assumed that Filipinos will readily and easily assimilate into American culture since they have had some kind of cultural head start from their colonial and postcolonial relationships with America. There is nothing further from the truth, as my years of fieldwork in New York City have shown. The shifts in the way Filipino gay men represent themselves, particularly in the idioms they use to construct a sense of being during this pandemic, illustrate, if not evoke, displacement or dislocation as well as the ambivalent qualities that are constitutive of the immigration experience.

I would like to present four stories, vignettes if you will, of gay Filipinos living in New York to explain this assertion. These four stories provide a way to view the multilocality and transcultural sources of identity formation of Filipino gay informants from the vantage points of class, race, homosexuality, and AIDS. In turn, the shifts in identities in the following stories explode the myth of a monolithic Other perpetuated not only by scholars but more importantly by health and AIDS experts.

The first two stories are about the lives of Eric and Leila. These two gay Filipinos extend what are seemingly traditional Filipino homosexual practices such as cross-dressing into an encounter with American gay lifestyles. In addition, they appropriate the racial exoticism accorded to Asians by dominant Western discourses either to obfuscate their "real" identities as Filipino or as men, or to rationalize their roles and ideas about the AIDS pandemic.

Eric, who was in his thirties, recounted his experiences as a migrant worker in Saudi Arabia, where he said that underneath the strict Islamic rules against homosexuality there were several venues for same-sex encounters. This was the milieu in which he came out. As long as things were kept under wraps from the conservative American multinational corporation for which he worked and the Saudi theocracy, which kept watch over all activities, he had what he called a "paradise" for his desires and practices, including having a Miss Gay Philippines-Saudi Arabia drag contest.

Interestingly, when he came to America, Eric was shocked at the rather open way gay men went about their business. He was disappointed, however, that these gay men were too open, too vulgar. There was no "mystery," he said, no excitement of doing things secretly. It was also about the time he came to America that AIDS started to unleash its devastating effects on the gay community. He started noticing other gay Filipinos coming down with the disease in 1986. Soon, his own friends started getting sick and dying. He was appalled to hear that Filipinos have the highest number of cases of AIDS among Asians and Pacific Islanders. He said, "As usual, Filipinos top the list again ... especially when it comes to 'bad lists' like the number of illegal immigrants or high school dropout rates." This was one of the reasons why he told people that he was Samoan or Guamanian or the ubiquitous "Hawaiian"; there was less stigma attached to these identities than being Filipino, and more importantly, these identities sounded more exotic.

Leila was the drag name of Mando, who was in his late thirties. For Leila cross-dressing was a way of getting men. Like Eric, he liked assuming more exotic identities and aliases such as Suzie Wong or Nancy Kwan. In the Philippines, he said, he was able to get men for sex, but he had to pay them. In America, he said, there was a market for his cross-dressing talent and exotic beauty, although he could not compete in the hypermasculine, gym-oriented world of mainstream gay life in New York. "With my slight build, who would even give me a second look if I were wearing a T-shirt?" he said. However, there were men, particularly those who were not gay-identified, who were attracted to beautiful Oriental cross-dressers. Here in America, Leila did not have to pay the man to have sex with him. Rather, it was the other way around. "Sometimes, I feel so cheap," he said. "The man will insist on paying for everything, including the pleasure of having sex with you. It's like everything goes on an opposite current here in America. I like it."

Because of the epidemic, Leila said that the contents of his purse now included a condom, which was meant for the use of the Caucasian partner. Being the "lady" in the encounters or relationships meant that he had to be like the "typical woman" and carry the burden of making sure that the sex was safe. Furthermore, he said, "The whites [Caucasians] are less concerned about safety ... they are not concerned about their family, so why would they be concerned with other people's lives, much less their own?"

The last two life vignettes are those of David and Raul. Both are HIV seropositive, and this situation creates, to use a term by Deleuze and Guattari (1987), a deterritorializing effect in the way they locate themselves in America and in the AIDS crisis. The intersections of class as consciousness and class as access to resources intersect with the process of immigration.

David, [...] was very proud of his aristocratic background in the Philippines. He found America to be funny because he was able to maintain relationships with people who were not of his class. David was in a hospital when I met him. After being undocumented for nearly ten years, he became a legal resident and was diagnosed with AIDS three years later. Already in the terminal stages of AIDS, he rationalized his AIDS diagnosis in terms of taking the bad with the good. He succeeded in his professional life after years of hardship living as an illegal alien. He said, "I have seen America. America has been kind to me, but I am ready to go home [to the Philippines]."

Raul, the fourth informant, was quite different from David. He did not want to go back to the Philippines. In fact, he was on his way to legalizing his stay in America when he discovered that he was positive in a mandatory HIV test for potential immigrants. He found out that he will never be granted the green card and attain the American citizenship he has dreamed of. Ironically, it was his condition too that allowed him to stay in America for humanitarian and medical reasons. One of his worries was that while he could stay in America, he could never acquire the full rights of being an American permanent resident or citizen. He could not go out of the country. He could not visit the Philippines. Not that he had any desire to go back. There were no treatment facilities or medical trials there during the late 1980s and early 1990s. The dilemma worsened when he heard that the Philippine government had discriminated against and even deported Filipinos who had AIDS who were now citizens of other countries. He heard a story about the body of a Filipino who had died of AIDS abroad. Philippine authorities refused entry of the remains to the Philippines unless the remains were cremated. "I don't want to be cremated," Raul said, "so that takes care of ever going back to the Philippines."

These short vignettes illustrate how AIDS and immigration emphasize the unboundedness of culture, people, and identities. In doing an ethnography of AIDS among immigrant gay populations, one comes across the appropriation and reconfiguration of identities, both mainstream and marginal. In the vignettes, the representations of self and others are seen from different angles or vantage points: class in the case of David, gay identities in the case of Eric and Leila, and legal/political identities in the case of Raul. Therefore, the demarcations between self and other are constantly being redrawn: Filipino and non-Filipino, "gay-identified men" and practitioners of same-sex encounters, white and nonwhite, legal residents/immigrants and illegal aliens, upper class and lower class.

The informants' experiences have brought me a keener sense of awareness of the paradoxical nature of identities, locales, and relationships present in the various individual and collective struggles in the pandemic. More importantly, this awareness has created a stronger conviction that despite all pronouncements of the exhilarating feelings of movement and travel, AIDS has ironically brought back the notions of "boundedness and fixity" and made more dramatic the experience of "in-betweenness" (Behar 1996) that exists in diasporic life. By in-betweenness, I mean the kind of spatial, emotional, and cultural displacements between homeland and new home.

Legal, political, economic, physical, and moral realities during this pandemic have rendered the celebratory image of the cosmopolitan immigrant into, at certain points and spaces, that of a war casualty or a political prisoner. However, under the shackles of disease and stigma there are moments of disruptions and interventions both in the realm of the everyday and in landmark events of illness, death, and mourning.

Works Cited

Behar, Ruth. 1996. *The Vulnerable Observer: Anthropology that Breaks Your Heart.* Boston: Beacon Press.

Bhabha, Homi. 1992. "The Other Question: The Stereotype and Colonial Discourse." In *The Sexual Subject: Screen Reader,* edited by Mandy Merck. London: Routledge.

Deleuze, Gilles, and Felix Guattari. 1987. *A Thousand Plateaus: Capitalism and Schizophrenia.* Minneapolis: University of Minnesota Press.

Farmer, Paul. 1992. AIDS and Accusation: Haiti and the Geography of Blame. Berkeley: University of California Press.

Kleinman, Arthur, Veena Das, and Margaret Lock. 1997. *Social Suffering.* Berkeley: University of California Press.

Patton, Cindy. 2002. *Globalizing* AIDS. Minneapolis: University of Minnesota Press.

Feminism and the Politics of Location (2007)

Kathy Davis

B ORN OF AN ENGAGEMENT BETWEEN FEMINIST theory and multiculturalism, cultural studies and postcolonial theory, the politics of location recognizes the importance of location as the ground from which one speaks and as shaping one's identity, knowledge of the world, and possibilities for political action. Initially coined by Adrienne Rich (1986),[1] the politics of location has variously been referred to as "locational feminism" (Friedman 1998), "feminist conjuncturalism" (Frankenberg and Mani 1993), "postmodern geographies" (Kaplan 1996), "diaspora space" (Brah 1996), and "theory from the borderlands" (Anzaldúa 1987). In the context of the present inquiry, it is impossible to do justice to the complexities involved in all these debates about location and what the linkages between the "global" and the "local" might mean for critical feminist inquiry (Grewal and Kaplan 1994; Kaplan 1996; Alexander and Mohanty 1997; Mohanty 2003). I will limit myself to how a concern for the politics of location has generated fundamentally different views about feminist history, feminist knowledge and knowledge practices, and the possibilities and limitations in political alliances among women both within and outside the United States.

The politics of location introduces spatiality or geography as essential for understanding women's *history* as well as histories of feminist struggle. While U.S. feminism had tended to valorize history, emphasizing the retrieval of the "lost" voices of women and making women's accomplishments visible, a politics of location recognizes that "the social production of history takes place in a certain geographical location" (Friedman 2001, 17). Symptomatic of the centrality given to history was the preoccupation of U.S. feminism with its "origins" and its ubiquitous temporal rhetoric of "awakening, revelation, and rebirth" (18) as epitomized in the notorious "click experience," which represented a

---

1   "I need to understand how a place on the map is also a place in history within which as a woman, a Jew, a lesbian, a feminist I am created and trying to create" (Rich 1986, 212). Rich was primarily interested in white U.S. feminists' becoming more reflexive about their location in the world. While acknowledging the importance of this intervention, Kaplan (1996) has criticized Rich for remaining "locked into the conventional opposition of the global-local nexus as well as the binary construction of Western and non-Western," thereby reducing the issue of accountability between women in the North and South rather than between women within the United States as a whole (166).

collective moment when women saw the light and became political subjects. The emphasis on the historical and temporal led many U.S. feminist historians to overlook the fact that feminism emerges in different forms in different places. Feminist ideas have a long and uneven history of being taken up and rearticulated in different locations across the globe throughout history, producing hybrid cultural formations that may bear only a passing resemblance to U.S. feminism in late modernity.[2] The assumption that feminism "began" (and "ended") in the United States separated women into the initiated and the uninitiated, a dualism that justified the view that U.S. feminists had achieved liberation while "traditional" or non-Western women were more severely oppressed and in need of salvation. The new emphasis on location involved a moving away from linear modernist histories of feminism to an exploration of how feminism "emerges, takes root, changes, travels, translates, and transplants in different spacio/temporal contexts" (15).

The politics of location has consequences for theorizing feminism as an *epistemological project*—that is, as a project that can generate knowledge and knowledge practices aimed at enhancing women's individual and collective empowerment. Initially, feminist epistemology employed a notion of location that referred to how an individual's (or group's) material position shaped her experiences, perceptions, and interactions with others. This particular conception of location provided the basis for feminist standpoint epistemology, which assumed that women use their material location not only as a resource for knowing what it means to be embodied as a woman in a particular social and cultural context but also as a place from which to construct a critical feminist subjectivity and perspective for social change.[3] Feminist standpoint epistemology has since generated considerable critical debate, most notably about the problems involved in privileging one aspect of women's experience—gender—while ignoring the ways in which race, class, and other categories of difference intersect in multiple and contradictory ways in women's everyday lives.[4] The issue of how to theorize intersecting identities, along with the

2   Frankenberg and Mani (1993) use a politics of location to criticize Eurocentric periodizations that reproduce the temporal logic of dominant histories, advocating instead a conception of historical processes as uneven and discontinuous. Criticizing the too hasty use of postcoloniality within contemporary feminist and postcolonial theory, they note that at "given moments and locations, the axis of colonialization/decolonialization might be the most salient one, at other times, not so" (304).

3   Nancy Hartsock (1983, 1998) deserves credit for this important intervention in feminist knowledge politics. It has since been taken up and elaborated by many others. See, for example, Keller 1985; Harding 1986, 1991, 1998; Smith 1987, 1990a; Haraway 1991b; Moya 1997, 2001; and Collins 2000. For a constructive discussion of the significance of standpoint thinking for feminist theory, see the discussion in the winter 1997 issue of the journal *Signs* (Heckman 1997a, 1997b; Hartsock 1997; Collins 1997; Harding 1997; Smith 1997).

4   See Henwood et al. 1998 for an illuminating discussion of the similarities and differences between feminist standpoint thinking and feminist discussions of differences in the ways women are situated in terms of race, class, sexuality, and nationality.

implications this has for feminist epistemology, has been one of the most productive and highly developed areas of contemporary feminist scholarship.[5] An important outcome has been a shift from viewing location in terms of identity to viewing it as a context in which complex and shifting relationships are constituted within a dynamic field of historical and geopolitical forces (Mani 1989). Under the influence of postcolonial theory, this contextual understanding of location has been used to understand international exchanges of knowledge in a global-local nexus. Feminists have become increasingly concerned not only with the—often selective—reception of feminist texts in the United States (King 1994) but also with how feminist knowledge circulates through translation and dissemination of feminist texts across the globe (Spivak 1988b, 1985; Kaplan 1996). Feminism—both as theory and practice—is now viewable as a kind of "traveling theory" (Said 1983) that circulates globally and is rearticulated and transformed in the course of its relocation from place to place.

The politics of location makes it essential to imagine and implement *feminist political alliances* across lines of difference rather than through a shared identity as women. U.S. feminism has often had an international vision of a unitary world of women, bringing together women from different parts of the globe by virtue of their assumed shared experience of oppression and their common struggles as women (Morgan 1984). The danger of this version of "global feminism," however, was the centrality it tended to give to white women within what was a decidedly Euro-American version of feminism. In addition to being ethnocentric, global feminism often celebrated "cultural differences," whereby global power relations were mystified and a stance of cultural relativism was adopted that precluded the necessary discussions about feminist accountability and a more serious engagement with practices and politics in other parts of the globe (Lugones and Spelman 1983; Kaplan 1996; Narayan 1997, 1998). The problems inherent in global feminism were countered by integrating the feminist desire for transnational feminist alliances with a feminist, anti-imperialist culture critique (Mohanty et al. 1991; Grewal and Kaplan 1994; Alexander and Mohanty 1997; Mohanty 2003). This version of the politics of location entailed recognition of the myriad ways in which women across the globe are already linked in diverse and unequal relations through historical, global processes of domination produced by global capitalism, colonialism, imperialism, or slavery. These transnational and historically contingent relations of power—or "scattered hegemonies" (Grewal and Kaplan 1994)—provide, paradoxically, a location from which feminists can recognize the inequalities that separate them yet can also join forces, forming alliances around common concerns. This notion of international feminist politics is not based on

---

5   Some of the best-known and most frequently cited examples include Davis 1981; Smith 1983; hooks 1981, 2000; Moraga and Anzaldúa 1983; Anzaldúa 1987, 1990; King 1988; Spelman 1988; Crenshaw 1989; Sandoval 1991; and Mohanty 2003.

women's biological identity or shared cultural identities. It takes as its starting point the tensions and divisions between women across divides of class, race, ethnicity, sexuality, and national borders (Mani 1989; Lugones 2003). It provides a vision of feminism that encompasses "imagined communities of women with divergent histories and social locations, woven together by the political threads of opposition to forms of domination that are not only pervasive but also systemic" (Mohanty 2003, 46–47).[6]

In conclusion, a politics of location identifies the grounds of historically specific differences and similarities among women in diverse and asymmetrical relations, creating alternative histories, knowledge practices, and possibilities for alliance. It opens up space for a new kind of critical feminist practice. Instead of being preoccupied with feminist history as a single story, multiple and diverse accounts of feminism in different places and at different points in time can be generated. It becomes possible to think about how feminism travels—that is, how feminist knowledge and knowledge practices move from place to place and are "translated" in different cultural locations. And, finally, we can consider how transnational feminist encounters emerge within a context of globally structured hierarchies of power and what this means for feminist encounters across lines of difference.

Bibliography

Alexander, M. Jacqui, and Chandra Talpade Mohanty. 1997. "Genealogies, Legacies, Movements." In *Feminist Genealogies, Colonial Legacies, Democratic Futures*, edited by M. Jacqui Alexander and Chandra Talpade Mohanty, xiii–xlii. New York: Routledge.

Anzaldúa, Gloria. 1987. *Borderlands/la Frontera: The New Mestiza*. San Francisco: Aunt Lute Books.

———, ed. 1990. *Making Face, Making Soul: Creative and Critical Perspectives by Feminists of Color*. San Francisco: Aunt Lute Books.

Brah, Avtar. 1996. *Cartographies of Diaspora: Contesting Identities*. London: Routledge.

Collins, Patricia Hill. 2000. *Black Feminist Thought: Knowledge, Consciousness, and the Politics of Empowerment*, 2nd ed. New York: Routledge.

———. 1997. "Comment on Hekman's 'Truth and Method: Feminist Standpoint Theory Revisited': Where's the Power?" *Signs* 22, no. 2: 375–81.

---

6 In describing this "vision of feminism," I have adopted Friedman's (2001) use of feminism in the singular, rather than feminisms, as encompassing "myriad and often conflicting cultural and political formations in a global context" (4). In her view, it was the specific U.S. context of identity politics that demanded the diversification of feminism. However, the risk of pluralization is a fetishization of [...]. As Audre Lorde (1984) wisely noted, "It's not our differences which separate women, but our reluctance to recognize these differences" (122).

Crenshaw, Kimberlé. 1989. "Demarginalizing the Intersection of Race and Sex: A Black Feminist Critique of Antidiscrimination Doctrine, Feminist Theory, and Antiracist Politics." *University of Chicago Legal Forum*: 139–67.

Davis, Angela Y. 1981. *Women, Race, and Class*. New York: Random House.

Frankenberg, Ruth, and Lata Mani. 1993. "Crosscurrents, Crosstalk: Race, 'Postcoloniality,' and the Politics of Location." *Cultural Studies* 7, no. 2 (May): 292–310.

Friedman, Susan Stanford. 2001. "Locational Feminism: Gender, Cultural Geographies, and Geopolitical Literacy." In *Feminist Locations: Global and Local, Theory and Practice*, edited by Marianne Dekoven, 13–36. New Brunswick, N.J.: Rutgers University Press.

———. 1998. *Mappings: Feminism and the Cultural Geographies of Encounter*. Princeton: Princeton University Press.

Grewal, Inderpal, and Caren Kaplan. 1994. "Introduction: Transnational Feminist Practices and Questions of Postmodernity." In *Scattered Hegemonies: Postmodernity and Transnational Feminist Practices*, edited by Inderpal Grewal and Caren Kaplan, 1–33. Minneapolis: University of Minnesota Press.

Haraway, Donna. 1991b. "Situated Knowledges: The Science Question in Feminism and the Privilege of Partial Perspective." In *Simians, Cyborgs, and Women*, 183–202. London: Free Association Books.

Harding, Sandra. 1998. *Is Science Multicultural? Postcolonialisms, Feminisms, and Epistemologies*. Bloomington: Indiana University Press.

———. 1997. "Comment on Hekman's 'Truth and Method: Feminist Standpoint Theory Revisited': Whose Standpoint Needs the Regimes of Truth and Reality?" *Signs* 22, no. 2: 382–91.

———. 1991. *Whose Science, Whose Knowledge? Thinking from Women's Lives*. Milton Keynes: Open University Press.

———. 1986. *The Science Question in Feminism*. Ithaca: Cornell University Press.

Hartsock, Nancy. 1998. *The Feminist Standpoint Revisited and Other Essays*. Boulder: Westview.

———. 1997. "Comment on Hekman's 'Truth and Method: Feminist Standpoint Theory Revisited': Truth or Justice?" *Signs* 22, no. 2: 367–74.

———. 1983. "The Feminist Standpoint: Developing the Ground for a Specifically Feminist Historical Materialism." In *Discovering Reality*, edited by Sandra Harding and Merrill B. Hintikka, 283–310. Dordrecht: Reidel.

Hekman, Susan. 1997a. "Response to Hartsock, Collins, Harding, and Smith." *Signs* 22, no. 2: 399–402.

———. 1997b. "Truth and Method: Feminist Standpoint Theory Revisited." *Signs* 22, no. 2: 341–65.

Henwood, Karen, Christine Griffin, and Ann Phoenix, eds. 1998. *Standpoints and Differences*. London: Sage.

hooks, bell. 2000. *Feminist Theory: From Margin to Center*. Cambridge: South End Press.

———. 1981. *Ain't I a Woman: Black Women and Feminism*. Boston: South End Press.

Kaplan, Caren. 1996. *Questions of Travel: Postmodern Discourses of Displacement*. Durham: Duke University Press.

Keller, Evelyn Fox. 1985. *Reflections on Gender and Science*. New Haven: Yale University Press.

King, Deborah. 1988. "Multiple Jeopardy, Multiple Consciousness: The Context of a Black Feminist Ideology." *Signs* 14, no. 1: 42–72.

King, Katie. 1994. *Theory in Its Feminist Travels: Conversations in U.S. Women's Movements*. Bloomington: Indiana University Press.

Lorde, Audre. 1984. *Sister Outsider*. Trumansburg, N.Y.: Crossing.

Lugones, María. 2003. *Pilgimages/Peregrinajes: Theorizing Coalition against Multiple Oppressions*. Lanham, Md.: Rowman and Littlefield.

Lugones, María, and Elizabeth V. Spelman. 1983. "Have We Got a Theory for You! Feminist Theory, Cultural Imperialism, and the Demand for 'The Woman's Voice.'" *Women's Studies International Forum* 6, no. 6: 573–81.

Mani, Lata. 1989. "Multiple Mediations: Feminist Scholarship in the Age of Multinational Reception." *Inscriptions* 5: 1–24.

Mohanty, Chandra Talpade. 2003. *Feminism without Borders: Decolonizing Theory, Practicing Solidarity*. Durham: Duke University Press.

Mohanty, Chandra Talpade, Ann Russo, and Lourdes Torres, eds. 1991. *Third World Women and the Politics of Feminism*. Bloomington: Indiana University Press.

Moraga, Cherríe, and Gloria Anzaldúa, eds. 1983. *The Bridge Called My Back: Writing by Radical Women of Color*. New York: Kitchen Table Press.

Morgan, Robin, ed. 1984. *Sisterhood Is Global: The International Women's Movement Anthology*. Garden City, N.Y.: Anchor.

Moya, Paula M. L. 2001. "Chicana Feminism and Postmodernist Theory." *Signs* 26, no. 2: 441–83.

———. "Postmodernism, 'Realism,' and the Politics of Identity: Cherríe Moraga and Chicana Feminism." In *Feminist Genealogies, Colonial Legacies, Democratic Futures*, edited by M. Jacqui Alexander and Chandra Talpade Mohanty, 125–50. New York: Routledge, 1997.

Narayan, Uma. 1998. "Essence of Culture and a Sense of History: A Feminist Critique of Cultural Essentialism." *Hypatia* 13, no. 2 (spring): 86–106.

———. 1997. *Dislocating Cultures: Identities, Traditions, and Third World Feminism*. New York: Routledge.

Rich, Adrienne. 1986. "Notes toward a Politics of Location." In *Blood, Bread, and Poetry: Selected Prose, 1979–1985*, 210–31. New York: Norton.

Said, Edward W. 1983. *The World, the Text, and the Critic*. Cambridge: Harvard University Press.

Sandoval, Chela. 1991. "U.S. Third World Feminism: The Theory and Method of Oppositional Consciousness in the Postmodern World." *Genders* 10 (spring): 1–24.

Smith, Barbara, ed. 1983. *Home Girls: A Black Feminist Anthology*. New York: Kitchen Table/Women of Color Press.

Smith, Dorothy E. 1997. "Comment on Hekman's 'Truth and Method: Feminist Standpoint Theory Revisited.'" *Signs* 22, no. 2: 392–98.

———. 1990a. *The Conceptual Practices of Power: A Feminist Sociology of Knowledge*. Boston: Northeastern University Press.

———. 1987. *The Everyday World as Problematic: A Feminist Sociology*. Toronto: University of Toronto Press.

Spelman, Elizabeth. 1988. *Inessential Woman: Problems of Exclusion in Feminist Thought*. Boston: Beacon.

Spivak, Gayatri Chakravorty. 1988b. *In Other Worlds: Essays in Cultural Politics*. New York: Routledge.

———. 1985. "Three Women's Texts and a Critique of Imperialism." *Critical Inquiry* 12, no. 1: 243–61.

100 Defensive Tactics and Attributions Dodging the Dialogue on Cultural Diversity

(2013)

Cornel Pewewardy

Introduction

Current battles against multicultural education are being waged on different fronts in the United States. In local schools and communities, culturally responsive teachers, serious parents, visionary administrators, and courageous students themselves, reject the alienating formulas and hegemonies of suppressive systems of schooling. Correspondingly, a resurgence of revolutionary scholars and researchers participate in this war, the battle for the minds of our own children. This article echoes the voices of many of those transformational leaders as well as presenting their standpoint about hegemonic voices in U.S. society.

As a professional educator who prepares future teachers for America's K-12 classrooms, I have come across a wide range of diverse conversations and discussions on topics of cultural diversity, multicultural education, and social justice in the U.S. The topics, terms, and definitions that are listed below are by no means complete, but are my attempt to create a foundation for *rhetoric sovereignty*[1] by exposing rhetorical hegemony that best expresses my holistic experiences as a male, Indigenous teacher educator.

There was an explosion of xenophobic-coded terms (e.g., politically correct, reverse discrimination, etc.) created when I became intensely involved in trying to eliminate American Indian mascots from school-sanctioned events. Thirty years of working on "Indian" mascot issues have helped me understand the social consciousness of many people about cultural diversity, multicultural education, and social justice in the U.S.

---

1   Rhetoric sovereignty is the inherent right and ability of Indigenous Peoples to determine their own communicative needs and desires in this pursuit, to decide for themselves the goals, modes of acquisition, styles of expression, and language of tribal dialect discourse.

The following list of defensive tactics and attributions is a direct result of my personal and professional experience with individuals in higher education who have the tendency to blame victims for their misfortune, so that one feels less likely to be victimized in a similar way.

To better organize my thinking of these defensive tactics and attributions, I sorted these actions into four categories: (1) Avoidance, (2) Disavowal, (3) Dismissal/Patronization, and (4) Re-centering. I started this list almost twenty years ago when I was a kindergarten teacher on the Navajo reservation in New Mexico. Moreover, it is a list that I have compiled throughout my professional career as an elementary teacher, principal, educational specialist, and teacher educator.

As I chronicled the terminology over the years, I began to compile and integrate this list into many of my professional workshops and conference presentations. Because of these presentations, many colleagues across the country volunteered additions to this list, which has helped to affirm these tactics and attributes.

One hundred terms is a list of sufficient length to demonstrate hegemonic educational (linguistic) practices in our society. However, this list is by no means complete. It is only a jump-start to naming the tactics that educators confront when engaging in social justice education. My prediction is that this list of hegemonic practices will continue to grow so long as there is resistance to social justice in this country.

Analytic tools that consist of looking at how systems of oppression interlock differ in emphasis from those that stress intersectionality. Interlocking systems need one another, and in tracing the complex ways in which they help to secure one another, we learn how underrepresented groups are placed in positions that exist symbiotically but hierarchically.

Avoidance

1. *The Sensitive Type*: Espouses sensitive racial and cultural issues, yet behaves discordantly. Contributed by Debbiesui Lee, doctoral student at Arizona State University.
2. *Confused*: Cannot quite "grasp" the culture issues being raised regardless of how clearly they are presented. Just does not get it. Contributed by Debbiesui Lee, doctoral student at Arizona State University.
3. *Color Blind*: When educated individuals say *"I don't see color"* in students, staff, faculty, or organization.
4. *The Cultural Schizophrenic*: When individuals are in a constant state of confusion about their cultural identity, characterized by vacillation about their ethnic or cultural identity for long periods of their life. Contributed by Sonia Nieto, University of Massachusetts.

5. *The Ethnic Cheerleader*: Good-minded individuals who bring in ethnic speakers, celebrate ethnic holidays, share ethnic foods, listen to ethnic music and so forth. This method of multicultural education never seriously infiltrates into the core discussions of cultural diversity and curricula in schools.

6. *The Nonengagement Type*: Classroom nonengagement embraces a process by students and teachers that can simultaneously be unconsciously conscious and/or consciously unconscious when entangled within the temporal and spatial dynamics of the pedagogical process. The term *"non* engagement" suggests a single/ dual/multiple process—the act of an individual withdrawing from a discourse that focuses on race and/or ethnicity. The word's simple identity that presupposes the ontogenetic desire to engage or not engage with the *Other* within a multicultural education terrain is apparent. A simple duality that is linear and deterministic in construction. Contributed by Rudolfo Chavez Chavez, New Mexico State University.

7. *The Trickster*: Persons who mask themselves from racial and cultural issues knowing full well of their intent to fool their opponent by pretending to be someone they are not.

8. *The Hard-of-Hearing*: Says, *"Speak up, I'm hard of hearing!"* Pretends he/she cannot hear, but can hear well enough to understand the complexity of racial and cultural issues.

9. *The Blind-Man's Bluff Theorist*: Pretends to have no visual perception and/or vision that is extremely limited, but can see well enough to get from one location to the other without any assistance.

10. *The Shouter*: Consciously elevates one's voice and volume trying to drown out racial and cultural discourse.

11. *The Double Agent*: Works underground for both hegemony and counter-hegemony in racial and cultural discourse.

12. *The Staller*: Outwardly speaks of diversity convincingly, but in the power structure stalls any meaningful change toward cultural diversity. Contributed by Denise Henning, Loras College.

13. *The Performance-Engager*: "Acts" multiculturally for the acquisition of a course grade ... after the course is over, the multicultural behavior disappears. Contributed by Jeanette Haynes Writer and Ruldolfo Chavez Chavez, New Mexico State University.

14. *The Ostrich*: Individuals who consciously choose not to engage in the discussions of race and diversity and would rather bury their heads in the sand or ground to avoid any serious discourse of this nature.

15. *The Faculty Will Just Be People*: Response by a college Dean about how faculty respond as people to issues of cultural diversity.

16. *The Hopeless*: Individuals who consciously believe that working toward a pluralistic society or social justice is absolutely hopeless or is never going to happen. They say *"so why try?"*

17. *The Arrogant Innocent*: Individuals who are well informed and versed in many issues of cultural diversity, yet they play *"opossum"* pretending that they don't know anything about the topical discussions.

18. *Don't Ask, Don't Tell*: President Clinton's policy regarding gays in the military, because if you don't ask, you won't be able to report them to military officials.

19. *Why Should I Learn about Multicultural Education, I'm Not Going to Teach Where There Are Any Minority Kids*: Common saying by monocultural teachers and/or teacher education students who don't plan to teach in communities where there are ethnic minority students.

20. *Playing Dumb*: Individuals who say, *"I don't know what you're talking about."* Contributed by Jill Stark, graduate student, Carnegie-Mellon University.

21. *Drama Queens*: Individuals who have their eyes averted, and actually have physical convulsions (I've seen it happen!). People who are so distraught by the accusation (even when there is no accusation made) of being a racist, that they are physically unable to discuss race issues. Contributed by Jill Stark, graduate student, Carnegie-Mellon University.

22. *The Toe-Tapper*: Individuals who are so afraid of offensive behavior that they avert their eyes and are overly nervous when they attempt to be respectful. They don't talk about or confront themselves about issues of race, but they will speak softly, look down, and not speak unless they are spoken to. Contributed by Jill Stark, graduate student, Carnegie-Mellon University.

23. *The Neutral Discussion Leader*: Individuals who are busy leading the discussion so they can't participate in the discussion of cultural diversity. Contributed by Jill Stark, graduate student at Carnegie-Mellon University.

24. *The Chameleon*: Attempts to fit in diverse cultural groups by attempting to be "just like" the members of the group. Contributed by Margery Ridgeway, University of Kansas.

25. *Comedians*: Individuals who take advantage of the stage by engaging in racial humor and making people laugh at the expense of underrepresented populations, rather than immersing themselves in a serious, articulate discussion on the topic. (The Rodney Dangerfield/Jay Leno style of cultural diversity).

26. *Why Can't We All Just Get Along?*: Individuals who dismiss race as a factor in race relations in the United States. The perpetual attitude is that race doesn't matter in this country. It's the Rodney King response to cultural diversity: "Why can't we all just get along?"

Disavowal (refusal to acknowledge)

27. *The Cognitive Dissonance Theorist*: When an individual finds himself/herself in a situation where he/she is expected to believe two mutually exclusive things, the subsequent tension and discomfort generates activity designed to reduce the dissonance or disharmony—individuals are faced with incompatible personal or professional beliefs.

28. *The Why Now?! Status Quo-iphile*: Person who constantly asks why people might contest a particular school-related policy/curriculum/pedagogy in the present day when this policy has been in place for a long period of time without any previously perceived criticism. "We've always done things this way, so why is there a problem now?" The underlying assumption is that current criticisms of a particular policy/ curriculum are unfounded, unwarranted, and/or unnecessary. Contributed by Jeff Corntassle, University of Victoria.

29. *The Mathematician*: Says, "Do the math, I wasn't born yet!" Dismisses racial and cultural issues by saying that historical cultural events happened before he/she was born, thereby letting themselves off the hook for oppressive histories before they were born. Contributed by Tony Clark, University of Kansas.

30. *The Crab Theorist*: Uses unkind words and negative rhetoric language trying to tear down someone's personal character—usually of the same ethnic group (e.g., apple, coconut, banana, oreo, zebra, cracker, etc.).

31. *The Dodger*: Tries to hide behind religion or other philosophical beliefs to maintain justification for various oppressions. Contributed by Jeannette Haynes Writer, New Mexico State University.

32. *"I Can't Believe You Played the Race Card"*: Colleagues who usually retaliate by saying this is a defense mechanism for being challenged for something they said or insinuated as culturally responsive. Contributed by Colleen Reed and Debra Ortiz, University of Kansas.

33. *The Traditionalist*: Individual who strongly believes in tradition, meaning that customs and attitudes have stayed constant so long that to change these elements would be conflict. Therefore, the traditionalist remains firmly grounded in the standpoint on certain multicultural issues.

34. *"But We Are Honoring You"*: Individuals whose standpoint is to keep their "Indian" mascot for sports teams because they honestly and consciously feel that using Indian mascots for sports teams is truly honoring Indigenous Peoples. From a consciously tribal perspective, this way to look at and honor "Indian" mascots for sports teams is culturally schizophrenic.

35. *Polite Avoidance*: Individuals who display polite mannerisms in public spaces, while consciously trying to block out and/or avoid serious conversations on issues of cultural diversity.

36. *Chip on the Shoulder*: Individuals who respond with this saying when they feel someone from an underrepresented group has a grudge against them and/or mainstream society and is therefore waiting for someone to say the wrong thing in hopes that they can instantly retaliate with heated vengeance. "*Unfortunately, I know many students who walk around with the 'chip' because they feel their own category (say, poor rural whites) are not properly included in benefit programs and scholarships and public awareness of their own hardships.*" Contributed by Annette Trefzer, University of Mississippi.

37. *Mix-It-Up*: Individuals who contradict themselves, hoping to muddle the topic. These people start talking about race, hoping that the questioner is so confused that he/she will change the topic. If the questioner persists, the questionee will say, "I just *told* you, don't you get it?" Contributed by Jill Stark, graduate student, Carnegie-Mellon University.

38. *The Qualifier*: Holds the idea that people are not racist, they just don't believe in "mixing races, or just aren't attracted to other races." Contributed by Jill Stark, graduate student, Carnegie-Mellon University.

39. *The Accusers*: Individuals who say, "You don't know what you're talking about." Contributed by Jill Stark, graduate student, Carnegie-Mellon University.

40. *Social Climbers*: People who won't speak about race with you unless you're some sort of authority on the issue. Contributed by Jill Stark, graduate student, Carnegie-Mellon University.

41. *Traders*: Individuals who play on the same-sounding word "traitor." The trader/traitor defends racist mascots and institutions in return for crumbs tossed her/his way. Contributed by Tony Clark, University of Kansas.

42. *Victims*: Individuals who go into a discussion on the defensive (everything gives the impression that they are under attack; their cowering stance, averted eyes, beaten expression, etc.) so it discourages anyone to disagree. Therefore, an honest discussion cannot be held because anyone who might make the "victim" look bad by disagreeing with him/her will make the "victim" appear to be under attack. This tactic tends to make anyone who disagrees look like accusatory shrews and promotes sympathy for the victim. Contributed by Jill Stark, graduate student, Carnegie-Mellon University.

43. *"You Don't Look Indian"*: Individuals who impose their cultural values and perceptions upon Indigenous Peoples by saying "you don't look Indian." This statement suggests that certain individuals have the authority to judge one's tribal identity based upon their self-proclaimed ethnic criteria of phenotype, lifestyle, spoken language, and overall general look. Most of the time, this ethnic look is referred to as the manufactured "Indian" image of something wild and inferior; their use implies a value judgement of white superiority created by

Hollywood scriptwriters with the intention of burning a psychological image into the American cultural imagination.

Dismissal/Patronizing

44. *The Intellectual Analyzer*: Capable of discussing issues of race and culture from an intellectual standpoint, but withdraws if there is any indication of affect or emotion. They feel no collective guilt about marginalized groups. Some will even evade and/or rationalize guilt. Contributed by Debbiesui Lee, doctoral student, Arizona State University.

45. *The Dysconscious Racist*: Accepts dominant white middle-class norms and privileges. It is not the absence of consciousness (that is, not unconsciousness) but an impaired consciousness or a distorted way of thinking about race and ethnicity as compared to, for example, critical consciousness. Contributed by Joyce King, Santa Clara University.

46. *The Multicultural Cops*: Individuals who take on the role of policing discussions of race and cultural diversity. Contributed by Carlos Cortez, University of California, Riverside.

47. *The Ethnic Fraud Police*: Individuals who take on the role of telling others that they don't belong in prescribed race boxes and/or tribal enrollment categories.

48. *The Racial Profiler*: When authority figures consciously identify a particular ethnic group as a target of suspicion. This usually occurs when mainstream police target and/or suspect ethnic groups as alleged lawbreakers.

49. *The Labeler*: Labels students of multicultural education "savvy" and lets those students carry the ball (conversation).

50. *The Cultural Critic*: Attacks comments made about racial/cultural issues without consideration of any other cultural perspective.

51. *The Patronizer*: Assumes superiority and advises strategies for someone not in his/her ethnic group to "get ahead" in life.

52. *The Cultural Appropriator*: Persons who engage in some cursory "research" on a particular group (other than their own) and then "enlighten" friends and colleagues with their own perspective on that group's history, cultural practices, identities, etc. The indigenous voices of ethnic group members are deemed less important than these persons' perspective regarding cultural diversity and multicultural education.

53. *The Older Boomer*: Retells or relives the Civil Rights Movement and violence without recognizing the state of racism and diversity today. For example, these are people who may have lived through turmoil regarding change of racial and cultural issues, but cannot move along the continuum of transformation from there. Frequent comments are "been there—done that" or "in my day. ..." They never

can get beyond the past to see the racial situation as it stands now. Contributed by Denise Henning, Loras College.

54. *The Sufferer*: A privileged individual who tries to invoke pity by proclaiming, "But I've been discriminated against, too!" in very superficial situations. Contributed by Jeanette Haynes Writer, New Mexico State University.

55. *The Colonizer*: Justifies oppression by saying: *"But where would you people be if this happened? It was good for you. So just get over it!"* Contributed by Jeanette Haynes Writer, New Mexico State University.

56. *The Director*: Works aggressively to gain control of the discourse and set a hostile climate within the group so no one will challenge him/her. Contributed by Jeanette Haynes Writer, New Mexico State University.

57. *The Wise One*: Dismisses the voices of others due to her/his acquired wisdom through age and/or experience in life. Contributed by Jeanette Haynes Writer, New Mexico State University.

58. *The Saviors*: Place themselves always in a "superior position" to their partners and are always trying to "help" those people. Frequently boast *"I'm not prejudiced, I treat all cultures in the same way."* Always reaching "down" to grasp the hand of someone whom they believe is below them—helps them "rise to the top" or "elevates" them because "the savior" believes they can.

59. *"Please, Give Me a Break!"*: Individuals who have already passed off or dismissed the opportunity to seriously engage in a conscious, intellectual discussion about cultural diversity. They will say, *"please, give me a break"* as if to suggest that your cultural diversity agenda is totally irrelevant to them.

60. *"We Want to Hire the Best Qualified"*: In hiring practices, this saying is used by individuals who dismiss the issues of affirmative action, distribution of wealth in this country, white privilege, cultural genocide, and legalized apartheid.

61. *The Tokenizers*: Individuals who can literally count on one hand that they know people or are friends of people of different cultures so that they don't have any "issues" with cultural diversity, and therefore, they don't need to expand their multicultural consciousness. Contributed by Gloria Ng, University of California, Davis.

62. *The Rhetoric Shot-putters*: Individuals (probably schooled in higher education) who throw around all the multicultural rhetoric, but have no concept of how the dirt thuds on impact—how the rhetoric masks the trauma of others' lived experiences. They get lost in the meanings of words and negate the feelings behind the words, especially when they haven't lived through the experience themselves. This is somewhat akin to the intellectual analyzer. Contributed by Gloria Ng, University of California, Davis.

63. *"Speak English, You're in America"*: Common saying by individuals who feel English should be the official language in the U.S., dismissing voluntary and involuntary immigrant languages in this country. They also dismiss all the Indigenous Peoples' languages because their mindset is programmed for monolingual English as the norm for language discourse in this country.

64. *The Race Umpires*: Individuals who say, *"They're just pulling the race card because they didn't get their way."* Contributed by Jill Stark, graduate student, Carnegie-Mellon University.

65. *The Exotificationer*: Individuals who subscribe to the idea that if you present cultures as exotic, you are paying homage to them, when in reality, you are characterizing and objectifying them. Contributed by Sonali Mishra, graduate student, Carnegie-Mellon University.

66. *The Historians (His Story)*: Those who will rewrite history and change the facts around so they won't look like racists, and will try to belittle any opposition. Contributed by Jill Stark, graduate student, Carnegie-Mellon University.

67. *The American Loyalist*: Regards non-English speakers as "the foreign problem." Espouses the English-Only Movement with "sink-or-swim" teaching practices. Completely disregards the fact that non-English speakers are often American-born U.S. citizens. Contributed by Margery Ridgeway, University of Kansas.

68. *The Segmenter*: Celebrates Black History Month, Hispanic Awareness Month, Native American Month, etc., but never mentions any culture other than white the rest of the time in the classroom. Contributed by Margery Ridgeway, University of Kansas.

69. *The Socially Polite Put-down*: When confronted with anything different from white upper-middle class culture and values, says "how interesting," while really insinuating the meaning, "how weird." Contributed by Margery Ridgeway, University of Kansas.

70. *The Multicultural Sidekick*: Individual in a position of authority and power in cultural diversity who assigns (and must have) an individual or two who accompanies him/her at all official multicultural functions.

71. *The Hidden Agenda*: This phenomenon occurs when a mainstream media interviewer has a preconceived (hidden) agenda when interviewing someone about cultural diversity. Many times they already have written a draft of their story, but have to go through the official interviewing process for the validity of their publication schedule.

72. *The Rock and the Hard Place*: When individuals in authority positions impose their ethnic stereotypes on their clients and/or subordinates. For example, a clinical psychologist (white male) who assigns homework to Indigenous clients by telling

them to inquire about their tribal role with spirit animals and sweat lodge ceremonies, completely dismissing the tribal-specific nature of this assignment.

73. *The Strategy of Innocent Gestures*: Individuals who say, "*I don't understand how my innocent gesture could be perceived as racist, homophobic, etc.*," and with this strategy, the rules have been established, the tables turned and one is now suddenly not accountable for what one releases from one's mouth or for how one chooses to act. Underlying the innocent gestures are really dangerous assumptions that everyone around will agree with the statement or the action. But it is impossible to see or comprehend that someone could possibly disagree because the majority culture like to "know it all." It is incomprehensible not to "know" something or "to be wrong." Therefore all they say is what they "know" and they assume that everyone else knows or should know in the same manner they know it. Contributed by Sandra Rios Balderama, The American Library Association.

74. *The Selective Endorsement of Ethnicity*: Individuals who may act like your best friend (who are usually racists whom you only see every ten years), always patting you on the back, telling all their friends how you are "not like the rest of them," and that you are a "good (Indian) minority." This individual reinforces tokenism and quickly reverts back to being a racist as soon as you leave the room. Contributed by Richard Williams, American Indian College Fund.

75. *"It's For Your Own Good"*: Individuals who see their actions as serving the critical mass, therefore, knowing what is good for selective groups and/or individuals. There is no rationale for their decisions other than patronizing.

Re-centering

76. *The Silencer*: Ignores comments concerning race and culture by changing the topic or by not responding at all. Contributed by Debbiesui Lee, doctoral student, Arizona State University.

77. *The Interpreter*: Re-interprets messages about racial/cultural issues in a way that reduces the power of the original message. Contributed by Debbiesui Lee, doctoral student, Arizona State University.

78. *The Questioner*: Asks a continuous barrage of questions regarding race/culture without consciously absorbing the original, centered content materials.

79. *The Minimizer*: Accepts comments about racial and cultural influences, but minimizes the impact of such influences. Contributed by Jeff Corntassle, University of Victoria.

80. *The Compromiser*: Person who is anxious to find a compromise on any given topic of cultural diversity and/or multicultural issue. He/she desperately seeks out people who can "meet in the middle" on an issue so that it will somehow be "resolved" in his/her own mind. Contributed by Jeff Corntassle, University of Victoria.

81. *The Politician*: Trivializes racial and cultural issues by making it political and/or using xenophobic-coded language like "politically correct," "politically incorrect," "reverse discrimination," "racial quotas," etc.

82. *The Distracter*: Deflects the diversity discussion by moving the conversation off center or to another topic.

83. *The Devil's Advocate*: Individual who immediately takes on the role of the opposing voice in racial/cultural issues without fully analyzing and/or processing the original content.

84. *The Projector*: Projects that the multicultural "problems" lie within the instructor/facilitator/speaker (individual) rather than owning the internal issues that he/she is throwing off. Contributed by Jeanette Haynes Writer, New Mexico State University.

85. *"Let's Talk Sports"*: Individuals who engage in discussions of cultural diversity only when it pertains to sports and/or athletics. Once the discussions shift outside of the sport/athletics discourse, these individuals become very uncomfortable and attempt to disengage from their original sports/athletics conversation. Contributed by Scott N. Brooks, doctoral student, University of Pennsylvania.

86. *Buck-Passers*: Individuals who choose to pass on the conversation by consciously referring the discourse of cultural diversity on to someone they feel is better qualified to continue the discussion. Another popular tactic is directing the issue to another ethnic group, like "well, Latinos are racist too," "Blacks don't like Asians," "Indians fight amongst themselves" and so forth. They fear that their standpoint on cultural diversity issues is too threatening to them, therefore too dangerous to openly discuss in public spaces. Contributed by Nocona Pewewardy, University of Kansas.

87. *"There Are More Important Issues to Discuss Than..."*: Outsiders who tell target groups that their issues are not important or do not have priority in cultural diversity discussions. These individuals are unaware of the target group's major issues and have never been seriously involved in their group's struggles. They would rather pass judgment (as outsiders) on target groups and their efforts toward liberation.

88. *The Great Negotiator*: Individual who would rather negotiate cultural issues and quickly come to a settlement rather than invest a lot of time and energy in a debate or discussion about cultural diversity. Contributed by Annette Trefzer, University of Mississippi.

89. *The Re-definer*: Individual who says, "I'm not racist because I don't hate *all* races." Contributed by Jill Stark, graduate student, Carnegie-Mellon University.

90. The Time-Liners: Individuals who say, "That happened ____ years ago," on the principle that because something happened in the past and was acceptable, that

it is OK, but not discussing that it happens today. Contributed by Jill Stark, graduate student, Carnegie-Mellon University.

91. *The Reverser*: Individuals who say, "What about me and my race? X culture was racist against my culture." Contributed by Jill Stark, graduate student, Carnegie-Mellon University.

92. *The Transmitters*: Individuals who say, *"I'm not from the majority race, therefore I can't be racist."* It's the idea that racism is restricted to the White elite, and therefore they don't have to address issues of racism. Contributed by Jill Stark, graduate student, Carnegie-Mellon University.

93. *The Whitewashers*: People who aren't comfortable with other cultures, but use whitewashed alternatives. With the *El Dia de los Muertos*, the Committee was not comfortable with true Mexican culture, so they "offered a compromise" of Cinco de Mayo, which is celebrated in America, but not in Mexico. It's more White culture than Mexican culture, and therefore they were comfortable with it. Contributed by Jill Stark, graduate student, Carnegie-Mellon University.

94. *The Family Pride Advocate*: *"My grandparents came to this country with nothing and spoke no English. With hard work they succeeded."* Regards lack of economic and social success in this country as purely the result of laziness or mental defect. Contributed by Margery Ridgeway, University of Kansas.

95. *The Interveners*: Individuals who "take the heat" or intervene on behalf of other people when someone in a cultural group challenges an assumption or cultural stereotype. They consciously try to deflect questions and/or inquiries that they know the original person being asked cannot answer or feels uncomfortable responding to. Contributed by Nocona Pewewardy, University of Kansas.

96. *The Ethnic Jokesters or Clowns*: Individuals who shift into "funny" characteristics and behaviorisms when discussing issues of cultural diversity. These people do not represent traditional clown societies of some tribes whose task it is to make their tribal groups laugh during celebrations and ceremonies. But the clown born of American popular culture, much like the European "jester" (or the fool), is the inferior one who was responsible for making his superior laugh. For example, many of these ethnic "Sambo" clowns were born out of the closed nature of North American slavery, in contrast to Latin American and African American slavery. These ethnic caricatures, with their racial fantasies, were portrayed as docile but irresponsible, loyal but lazy, humble but chronically given to lying and stealing; behaving with infantile silliness and inflated child talk and attachment. The racial fantasies of African American and First Nations Peoples' backwardness characterized as incapable of technological advancement and by superstitious and humanly regressive acts of savagery were all constructed in Hollywood films. They engage in slapstick ethnic humor and many times play out their own

internal ethnic stereotypes in public spaces: falling down the stairs, getting elec-
trocuted, bumbling ethnic characters with heavy-slurred accents, stoic-broken
English dialects, big-nosed figures, etc.

97. *The Multicultural Groupie*: Individuals who "star-gaze" at known figures in the
field of multicultural education. They chronicle their heroines' and heroes' publication record, conference speaking engagements, book-signing tour schedule,
and they keep constant track of their heroines' and heroes' accomplishments by
bench-marking their favorite websites on the Internet.

98. *The "I'm OK, You're OK" Diversity*: Individuals who make each other "feel good"
about their cultural stories and diverse histories, thereby diminishing "truth to
power" issues in critical multicultural education. They never get to the core or
main thrust of multicultural education: the interrogation of unequal educational
structures and race superior ideologies.

99. *Anwerers*: Individuals who are not serious about engaging in two-way discussions of cultural diversity, because they are always too busy analyzing and
anticipating what the speaker will say next. They are too preoccupied with the
formulation of a quick response to defend their own position (usually a position
of social or white privilege). Contributed by Christine TenBarge, doctoral student, University of Texas.

100. *Usurpers of Language*: Individuals who change the meaning of words according to their mood—e.g., inclusivity became exclusivity, focus becomes narrow
thinking and so forth. In Spanish we say "cuando conviene"—"when it is convenient"—meaning that you cannot count on someone who flip-flops. Contributed
by Sandra Rios Balderama, The American Library Association.

Conclusion

Today's educators live in a culturally dynamic society, unimagined by former generations. We are at the crossroads of our multicultural history. The legacy of social justice
continues because of those transformational leaders who embrace education and its
vital connection to social change.

As a critical multicultural educator, I have struggled to understand and challenge
the existing relations of Western patriarchal capitalist domination. In this article I have
tried to name these defensive tactics and attributions and understand where they came
from. Only then can I begin to challenge them structurally and interpersonally within
a classroom context. I reflect upon my own successes and struggles as I teach at a predominantly White university. That said, I wish to contribute to a liberatory education,
rather than act as a placeholder of colonization or imperialism. I know, however, that
resistance to liberatory education remains possible in the face of domination.

By not educating about some people's privilege, which is enacted economically, politically, and socially through dominant culture forms and through overt acts of supremacy, the hegemonic power of Eurocentrism is validated rather than challenged. In educational theory and practice we assimilate to these norms by imposing them on our students and then supporting people who adapt to these demands, rather than by introducing new paradigms of knowledge.

This article provides a jump-start to understanding defensive tactics and challenges at the theoretical level. With more critical multicultural educators, we can next develop a list of counter-hegemonic strategies to implement in our classrooms. With your help, we can strive for all of these elements to happen in our lifetime. The question really is—do we have the "will" to make it happen? As I see it today, we live in a multi-cultural society, and when it comes to providing the best quality education for our children, we must provide an education for social justice.

Refer back to the reading selections in this unit to help you correctly respond to each of the questions below.

1. Iris Marion Young seeks to "displace" the distributive paradigm of justice, arguing that it "ignores and tends to obscure the institutional context within which those distributions take place."

   • According to Young, what is the distributive paradigm?

   • What does she mean by "institutional context"?

   • How does the distributive paradigm ignore institutional contexts and presuppose institutional structures?

2. Young highlights three important aspects of justice that, she argues, a focus on distribution overlooks: (a) decision making, (b) culture, and (c) division of labor.

   • What examples does she give for each of these?

   • Do you agree with her argument?

3. Does Young think distributive justice doesn't matter? Do you agree with her? Explain your answer.

4. Why does Allan Johnson refer to oppression as "the flip side of privilege"? Give an example that illustrates Johnson's claim about oppression being the flip side of privilege.

5. Explain Marilyn Frye's birdcage metaphor for oppression. Give an example that supports Frye's metaphor.

6. Frye writes: "One of the most characteristic and ubiquitous features of the world as experienced by oppressed people is the double bind" (p. 64 of this anthology).

   • How does Frye define "the double bind"?

   • Give an example of a social group's experience with the double bind.

7. According to Marilyn Frye and Allan Johnson, can men experience oppression because they are men, or can White people experience oppression because they are White? Why, or why not?

8. Patu and Antje Schrupp illustrate how intersectional perspectives emerged from, and were relevant to, second wave feminist activism. Although her piece predates the use of the term "intersectionality," Patricia Hill Collins's reading articulates core tenets of intersectionality theory.

   - Using Collins's reading, name and describe some of the central features of intersectionality.

   - Besides second wave feminism, how have other past and present activist movements integrated or ignored intersectional perspectives?

9. Martin F. Manalansan IV writes about inequality and suffering during the AIDS pandemic.

   - Give an example from Manalansan's reading of how suffering was structured by one's biography and history.

   - More recently, the world has experienced another global pandemic: COVID-19. How has time and space contributed to intimate geographies of suffering during the COVID pandemic?

   - What systems of power have been especially significant in structuring suffering during the COVID pandemic?

10. Cornel Pewewardy provides numerous examples of rhetorical hegemony.

    - Reflecting on your own experiences, have you been subject to any of these examples of rhetorical hegemony?

    - Have you ever enacted them onto others?

    - Describe the situation(s) and how you felt at the time.

    - How, if at all, have your feelings changed?

Unit III

Inequality, Institutions, and Systemic Power

Valerie Chepp

The readings in Unit III draw upon **evidence** to demonstrate how inequality and injustice manifest in our everyday lives and institutions. The readings rely on diverse texts (e.g., personal narrative, scholarly articles, historical essays, popular press articles, photography, etc.), subject matters, and disciplines. Some readings use evidence grounded in **experiential knowledge** claims, that is, knowledge gleaned through one's lived experience. Other readings feature evidence based on **empiricism**, that is, observation and documentation of patterns and behavior through experimentation and other types of research. Readings in this unit are unified in that they all feature information about injustice and inequality that is substantiated in a verifiable (i.e., provable) reality. This focus on proof and verifiability is important given the tendency to encounter—and perpetrate—various defense tactics when learning about social injustice and inequality (see Reading 2.8). By focusing on verifiable evidence that is overwhelmingly confirmed and supported by a community of researchers and scientists, we can productively keep our attention on analyses and truths grounded in reality. So, for example, we don't spend time debating whether racism exists, since this social fact is backed by a staggering body of evidence. Rather, by focusing on verifiable data, we spend our time learning how racism manifests, and to what effect. This knowledge is fundamental to combatting racism and its legacy.

evidence: the available collection of information or facts that supports whether an idea or hypothesis is true or accurate.

The Unit III readings have been selected based on several criteria. First, the readings represent various ways injustice manifests in different everyday interactions, social processes, and institutional settings. This includes the justice system, policing, the economy, media, health care, immigration, technology, and climate change, among others. Second, the readings illustrate how injustice cuts across different (and intersecting) systems of power, such as race, ethnicity, nationality, class, and gender. Third, the readings illustrate how injustice is embedded in our cultural codes: language, symbols, stereotypes, cognitive schemas, discourses, and values. Fourth, the readings show how injustice manifests through time and space, highlighting how manifestations of inequality get produced, reproduced, and repackaged across—and within—generations, communities, societies, and national borders.

While the readings have been selected based on these criteria, they have also been selected with an eye toward demonstrating the **systemic nature of injustice**, that is, how institutions, interactions, and identity formation processes intersect and reinforce one another to result in an interlocking system of inequality. Here, readers can think back to Marilyn Frye's birdcage metaphor of oppression (see Reading 2.3), designed to illustrate how inequality in one social location is reproduced and reinforced in other settings, resulting in an oppressive structure. An understanding of the interlocking nature of inequality and injustice is important for designing and enacting **systemic solutions** that can challenge and chip away at injustice from many different angles (see Unit IV for more on social justice solutions).

systemic solutions: resolutions that address root causes of social problems that originate in the structure of the social system. Since these problems are structural (rather than individual or partial), solutions must fundamentally and holistically change how the entire system works, rather than alter just a portion of the system.

The readings in this unit are necessarily incomplete, with important aspects of social justice missing. This includes other institutional sites structured by inequality (such as the military, religion, education system, food systems, sports and leisure, tourism, housing, research methods, and science, to name a few), other systems of power that shape group experiences (e.g., sexuality, disability, body type, age, and language status, among others), as well as (many!) other significant times and places characterized by injustice. Some of these themes and topics are included in Unit I (e.g., see Reading 1.8 for work on oppressive labor relations within cocoa farming), Unit II (e.g., see Reading 2.6 on how sexuality, among other systems of power, shaped experiences with the AIDS pandemic), and Unit IV (e.g., see Readings 4.3, 4.4, 4.6, 4.7, 4.8, and 4.10 for discussions of liberatory education, disability rights, Zen and critical disability perspectives to confronting global neoliberal capitalism, youth activists, and combatting body terrorism).

Unit III begins with Evelyn Alsultany's personal narrative "Los Intersticios: Recasting Moving Selves." Writing of her experience as a graduate student in New York City, Alsultany taps into some of the themes introduced in Unit II, which are expanded upon in this unit. This includes Alsultany's examination of the political significance of location and "dislocation," intersectionality, and the power-laden nature of categorizing people into groups. In her reading "No Country for White Men," Arlie Hochschild builds upon the significance of group formation, power, and social justice. Drawing upon her ethnographic research on political conservativism, Hochschild sheds light on how perceptions of modern-day justice in the United States are fueled by anxieties around entitlement, shame, ambition, and the role of government in our lives. Hochschild skillfully shows how increasing political polarization, as well as race, class, gender, and other systems of power, shape many of the deep feelings that get attached to notions of justice, fairness, and political worldviews.

The next set of readings use criminalization as a lens through which to examine the interlocking nature of injustice and demonstrate how inequality and injustice manifest in our everyday lives and institutions. Radley Balko offers a historical overview of the emergence of our present-day police force and some of the dynamics that shape today's system (e.g., professionalism, militarization). Balko's selection includes different policing models—and the rationales behind them—throughout history; readers might consider how these different models could work (or not work) in the contemporary context. In "Multiple Manhoods," Victor Rios's ethnographic account of police interactions with gang-associated young men illustrates how constructions of masculinity, criminalization, and policing intersect and how race and class marginality shape these power-laden interactions. In the following reading "The New Jim Crow," Michelle Alexander offers an additional account of how groups' experiences with the criminal justice system are shaped by race, class, and gender discrimination, and she highlights how discriminatory policing and incarceration practices have resulted in the political disenfranchisement of poor communities of color.

The next two readings, in combination with what's been featured thus far, further demonstrate the interlocking, systemic nature of inequality. While previous readings show how race, class, and gender (among other factors) shape political worldviews and experiences with the systems of justice and law enforcement, the next set of readings examine how inequality manifests in two other institutional settings: the economy and health care.

In the reading "Are Emily and Greg More Employable Than Lakisha and Jamal?" Marianne Bertrand and Sendhil Mullainathan share findings from their field experiment to show how racial discrimination manifests in one component of the U.S. labor market: unequal callback rates based on employers' perceptions of applicants' race. When we consider other components of the labor market (e.g., promotion rates, wages, social networks, etc.), inequality is compounded. Paula Braveman's selection "Racial Disparities at Birth: The Puzzle Persists" points to how racism and social inequality can physically manifest in our bodies, leading to health inequity. She examines this through the case of birth outcomes. Braveman's article also serves as a nice example of the distinction and relationship between social inequality and inequity.

Min Zhou's reading "Becoming American: Identity Formation" picks up on themes introduced in Alsultany's "Los Intersticios" around categorization, cognitive schemas, labeling, and stereotypes. Focused on Asian American identity, Zhou's selection engages important questions around pan-Asianism and how the stereotypes of the "model minority" and "perpetual foreigner" have resulted in a "paradox of assimilation" for many Asian Americans.

In the reading "The Undead: Notes on Photography in the Philippines, 1898–1920s," Vicente Rafael also examines social justice implications of categorizing social groups. In his examination of colonial photography, Rafael shows how historical photographs functioned as a mechanism for categorizing groups into an ethnoracial hierarchy, which served to shore up imperial power. Rafael's piece can also be used to critically engage western liberal narratives around "progress" and how technological advancements (e.g., the camera, but we might consider contemporary technologies, such as the internet and social media) can reinforce, as well as subvert, systems of power and oppression.

Keeping our analysis on the intersecting systems of racism, capitalism, colonialism, and imperialism, the following reading considers the social injustices endemic to criminal justice and exclusionary migration policies. "Thinking (and Moving) Beyond Walls and Cages: Bridging Immigrant Justice and Anti-Prison Organizing in the United States" engages recurring themes we've encountered thus far: the significance of boundaries, locations, mobility, and categories. Illustrating the "convergence between cages and walls" (i.e., prisons and national borders), the authors seek to illuminate opportunities for coalition building between prison abolition and immigrant justice movements.

The intersection of criminalization and immigration policies makes for an interesting context in which to consider Christopher Todd Beer's reading on climate justice. Beer's piece empirically demonstrates the disproportionate impact of climate change on different groups; we might consider how this unequal impact results in increasing numbers of environmental migrants (sometimes referred to as "climate refugees")—that is, groups of people for whom environmental factors push them to leave their homes. While Beer's selection helpfully reiterates Unit III's focus on systemic manifestations of injustice across social settings, he also primes us for what's to come in Unit IV: an attention to the many people, groups, ideas, techniques, skillsets, and disciplines needed to effect change and enact justice.

Los Intersticios: Recasting Moving Selves

(2002)

Evelyn Alsultany

> *Ethnicity in such a world needs to be recast so that our moving selves can be acknowledged. ... Who am I? When am I? The questions that are asked in the street, of my identity, mold me. Appearing in the flesh, I am cast afresh, a female of color—skin color, hair texture, clothing, speech, all marking me in ways that I could scarcely have conceived of.*
>
> —Meena Alexander (66)

I'M IN A GRADUATE CLASS AT the New School in New York City. A white female sits next to me and we begin "friendly" conversation. She asks me where I'm from. I reply that I was born and raised in New York City and return the question. She tells me she is from Ohio and has lived in New York for several years. She continues her inquiry: "Oh ... well, how about your parents?" (I feel her trying to map me onto her narrow cartography; New York is not a sufficient answer. She analyzes me according to binary axes of sameness and difference. She detects only difference at first glance, and seeks to pigeonhole me. In her framework, my body is marked, excluded, not from this country. A seemingly "friendly" question turns into a claim to land and belonging.) "My father is Iraqi and my mother Cuban," I answer. "How interesting. Are you a U.S. citizen?"

I am waiting for the NYC subway. A man also waiting asks me if I too am Pakistani. I reply that I'm part Iraqi and part Cuban. He asks if I am Muslim, and I reply that I am Muslim. He asks me if I am married, and I tell him I'm not. In cultural camaraderie he leans over and says that he has cousins in Pakistan available for an arranged marriage if my family so desires. (My Cubanness, as well as my own relationship to my cultural identity, evaporates as he assumes that Arab plus Muslim equals arranged marriage. I can identify: he reminds me of my Iraqi relatives and I know he means well.) I tell him that I'm not interested in marriage but thank him for his kindness. (I accept his framework and respond accordingly, avoiding an awkward situation in which he realizes that I am not who he assumes I am, offering him recognition and validation for his [mis]identification.)

I am in a New York City deli waiting for my bagel to toast. The man behind the counter asks if I'm an Arab Muslim (he too is Arab and Muslim). I reply that yes, I am by part of my father. He asks my name, and I say, "Evelyn." In utter disdain, he tells me that I could not possibly be Muslim; if I were truly Muslim I would have a Muslim name. What was I doing with such a name? I reply (after taking a deep breath and telling myself that it's not worth getting upset over) that my Cuban mother named me and that I honor my mother. He points to the fact that I'm wearing lipstick and have not changed my name, which he finds to be completely inappropriate and despicable, and says that I am a reflection of the decay of the Arab Muslim in America.

I'm on an airplane flying from Miami to New York. I'm sitting next to an Ecuadorian man. He asks me where I'm from. I tell him. He asks me if I'm more Arab, Latina, or American, and I state that I'm all of the above. He says that's impossible. I must be more of one ethnicity than another. He determines that I am not really Arab, that I'm more Latina because of the camaraderie he feels in our speaking Spanish.

I am in Costa Rica. I walk the streets and my brown skin and dark hair blend in with the multiple shades of brown around me. I love this first-time experience of blending in! I walk into a coffee shop for some café con leche, and my fantasy of belonging is shattered when the woman preparing the coffee asks me where I'm from. I tell her that I was born and raised in New York City by a Cuban mother and an Arab father. She replies, "Que eres una gringa."

I am shocked by the contextuality of identity: that my body is marked as gringa in Costa Rica, as Latina in some U.S. contexts, Arab in others, in some times and spaces not adequately Arab, or Latina, or "American," and in other contexts simply as *other*.

My body becomes marked with meaning as I enter public space.[1] My identity fractures as I experience differing dislocations in multiple contexts. Sometimes people otherize me, sometimes they identify with me. Both situations can be equally problematic. Those who otherize me fail to see a shared humanity and those who identify with me fail to see difference; my Arab or Muslim identity negates my Cuban heritage. Identification signifies belonging or home, and I pretend to be that home for the mistaken person. It's my good deed for the day (I know how precious it can be to find a moment of familiarity with a stranger). The bridge becomes my back as I feign belonging, and I become that vehicle for others, which I desire for myself. Although it is illusory, I do identify with the humanity of the situation—the desire to belong in this world, to be understood. But the frameworks used to (mis)read my body, to disconnect me, wear on me. I try to develop a new identity. What should I try to pass for next time? Perhaps I'll just say I'm Cuban to those who appear to be Arab or South Asian. A friend suggests I say I'm an Italian from

---

1   Although such episodes are not exclusive to "public space," I will not be dealing with the complex dynamics of "private space" in this piece.

Brooklyn. I wonder if I could successfully pass for that. Ethnicity needs to be recast so that our moving selves can be acknowledged.

> *They would chop me up into little fragments and tag each piece with a label*
> *Who, me confused? Ambivalent? Not so. Only your labels split me.*

—Gloria Anzaldúa, "La Prieta" (205)

This Bridge Called My Back revolutionized how we saw ourselves as women of color. Our experiences—unacknowledged by the dominant culture and by feminist, ethnic, and/or queer movements—were finally named. *This Bridge* insisted on a theory of the flesh through which to bridge the contradictions in our lives: "We do this bridging by naming our selves and by telling our stories in our own words" (Moraga, 23). *Bridge* authors powerfully addressed the multiple displacements women of color often experience, or what Gloria Anzaldúa calls "los intersticios: 'Alienated from her mother culture,' 'alien' in the dominant culture, the woman of color does not feel safe within the inner life of her Self. Petrified, she can't respond, her face caught between los intersticios, the spaces between the different worlds she inhabits" (*Borderlands*, 20). Many multiethnic women identify strongly with this experience of being alienated in different ways from our various communities, trapped in a space of dislocation. Our complex selves can't be acknowledged as unified and whole.

When we're not acknowledged as complex unitary subjects, we become caught in los intersticios, haciendo caras to get by. Lisa Suhair Majaj, born to a Palestinian father and a white American mother, growing up in Lebanon and Jordan, has spent much of her life in los intersticios: "I learned to live as if in a transitional state, waiting always for the time that we would go to Palestine, to the United States, to a place where I would belong. But trips to Iowa and to Jerusalem taught me that once I got there, 'home' slipped away inexplicably materializing again just beyond reach. If a sense of rootedness was what gave life meaning, as my parents' individual efforts to ward off alienation implied, this meaning seemed able to assume full import only in the imagination" ("Boundaries," 71). Majaj's lived experiences are not mapped out; there are no ready frameworks to understand her identity as complex and simultaneously Arab and American. She never felt like she fully belonged anywhere and found herself searching for "home," a space of belonging. Yet she recurringly experienced belonging as deferment: "In my experience cultural marginality has been among the most painful of alienations. My childhood desire, often desperate, was not so much to be a particular nationality, to be American or Arab, but to be wholly one thing or another: to be *something* that I and the rest of the world could understand, categorize, label predict" (79, author's emphasis).

We carry this pain with us as we live in los intersticios. To "belong," we must fragment and exclude particular parts of our identity. Dislocation results from the narrow ways in which the body is read, the rigid frame-works imposed on the body in public space. At the end of the day, I'm tired of wearing masks, being misunderstood, projected upon, otherized, erased. "I am tired of being afraid to speak who I am: American and Palestinian, not merely half one thing and half of another, but both at once—and in that inexplicable melding that occurs when two cultures come together, not quite either, so that neither American nor Arab find themselves fully reflected in me, nor I in them" (Majaj, "Boundaries," 68). Identity must be reconceptualized so that we can speak our own identities as we live and interpret them in multiple contexts. But how can we create a space for the articulation of multiethnic identities as unitary and whole rather than fragmented and dislocated?

If we change the reading/framework/lens, we can transform dislocation into location. We must reconstruct "belonging" to embrace the experiences of all human beings. As Adrian Piper (a light-skinned African-American woman who grew up in los intersticios, alienated from the black community for her light skin complexion and alienated from the white community for her blackness) has stated, "the racial categories that purport to designate any of us are too rigid and oversimplified to fit anyone accurately. But then, accuracy was never their purpose" (110).

Racial categories' purpose has usually been geopolitical. In "Dislocated Identities: Reflections of an Arab Jew," Ella Shohat discusses how today's dominant frameworks do not account for her identity as an Arab Jew and illustrates the ways in which these categories have been recently constructed as antithetical. Such frameworks have a political function. For her grandmother's generation and for hundreds of prior generations, Jewishness was inextricably linked to Arabness; they were not binary categories but logically linked: an Arab could be Muslim, Jewish, Christian, or any other faith. It was when she arrived in Israel from Iraq (as a refugee) that her grandmother had to learn such imposed constructed distinctions. New cartographies were created within which her identity became dislocated: "For Middle Easterners, the operating distinction had always been 'Muslim,' 'Jew,' and 'Christian,' not Arab versus Jew. The assumption was that 'Arabness' referred to a common shared culture and language, albeit with religious differences." In the U.S. context this binarism between Arab and Jew operates, allowing for the narration of "a singular Jewish memory, i.e., a European one."

Shohat's experience points to the political nature of categorization. Meanings attached to identities shift not only over time and space but also according to political circumstance. That such meanings change indicates that we can alter them. We can create a new cartography. An inability to conceptualize multiethnic persons reflects a colonial ideology of categorization and separation based on a "pure blood" criteria—a system constructed for the white colonists to maintain power. Rigid racial categories keep us separate. Multiethnic identity comes as a surprise and a danger within this framework as people attempt to place us, to make sense within the schemas available for understanding people and the world. Our identities transgress the constructed categories and become threatening. As Piper explains, "These incidents and others like them had a peculiar cognitive feel to them, as though the individuals involved felt driven to make special efforts to situate me in their conceptual mapping of the world, not only by naming or indicating the niche in which they felt I belonged, but by seeking my verbal confirmation of it ... [an attempt to] locate me within the rigid confines of [their] stereotype of black people" (83).

I seek to decolonize these essentialized frameworks, so that I can move through public space without strategizing a performance, selecting a mask for each scenario. I want to expand los intersticios, creating a space for us all in our multiplicities to exist as unified subjects. It is a nonessentialist way of relating that creates a space to articulate multiple identifications and unlimited interpretations of those dimensions. This new space begins with a question: Ask me who I am. Don't project your essentialisms onto my body and then project hatred because I do not conform to your notions of who I'm supposed to be. There is no essentialized blueprint. Opening up the possibility of articulating the variety of ways we experience and negotiate our identities benefits everyone, not just the multi-ethnic. Recasting our moving selves begins with an openness and a willingness to listen, which leads to dialogue.

Note

I would like to thank Marisol Negrón, Alexandra Lang, María Helena Rueda, Ericka Beckman, Karina Hodoyan, Sara Rondinel, Jessi Aaron, and Cynthia María Paccacerqua for their feedback in our writing seminar at Stanford University with Mary Pratt. I would especially like to thank Mary Pratt for her invaluable feedback, and AnaLouise Keating and Gloria Anzaldúa for their thoughtful editing.

Works Cited

Alexander, Meena. *The Shock of Arrival: Reflections on Postcolonial Experience.* Boston: South End Press, 1996.

Anzaldúa, Gloria E. *Borderlands/La Frontera: The New Mestiza.* San Francisco: Aunt Lute, 1987.

———. "La Prieta." In Moraga and Anzaldúa, 198–209.

Majaj, Lisa Suhair. "Boundaries: Arab/American." In Kadi, 65–86.

Moraga, Cherríe, and Gloria Anzaldúa, eds. *This Bridge Called My Back: Writings by Radical Women of Color.* 1981. New York: Kitchen Table/Women of Color Press, 1983.

Piper, Adrian. "Passing for White, Passing for Black." In Shohat, 75–112.

Shohat, Ella. "Dislocated Identities: Reflections of an Arab Jew." *Movement Research: Performance Journal* 5 (1992): 8.

No Country for White Men

(2016)

Arlie Russell Hochschild

Sharon Galicia sells accident insurance to Louisiana laborers.

I N A FRAMED PHOTO OF HERSELF taken in 2007, Sharon Galicia stands, fresh-faced and beaming, beside first lady Laura Bush at a Washington, DC, luncheon, thrilled to be honored as an outstanding GOP volunteer. We are in her office in the Aflac insurance company in Lake Charles, Louisiana, and Sharon is heading out to pitch medical and life insurance to workers in a bleak corridor of industrial plants servicing the rigs in the Gulf of Mexico and petrochemical plants that make the plastic feedstock for everything from car seats to bubble gum.

After a 20-minute drive along flat terrain, we pull into a dirt parking lot beside a red truck with a decal of the Statue of Liberty, her raised arm holding an M-16. A man waves from the entrance to an enormous warehouse. Warm, attractive, well-spoken, Sharon has sold a lot of insurance policies around here and made friends along the way.

A policy with a weekly premium of $5.52 covers accidents that aren't covered by a worker's other insurance—if he has any. "How many of you can go a week without your paycheck?" is part of Sharon's pitch. "Usually no hands go up," she tells me. Her clients repair oil platforms, cut sheet metal, fix refrigerators, process chicken, lay asphalt, and dig ditches. She sells to entry-level floor sweepers who make $8 an hour and can't afford to get sick. She sells to flaggers in highway repair crews who earn $12 an hour, and to welders and operators who, with overtime, make up to $100,000 a year. For most, education stopped after high school. "Pipe fitters. Ditch diggers. Asphalt layers," Sharon says. "I can't find one that's not for Donald Trump."

I first met Sharon at a gathering of tea party enthusiasts in Lake Charles in 2011. I told them I was a sociologist writing a book about America's ever-widening political divide. In their 2008 book, *The Big Sort*, Bill Bishop and Robert Cushing showed that while Americans used to move mainly for individual reasons like higher-paid jobs, nicer weather, and better homes, today they also prioritize living near people who think like they do. Left and Right have become sub nations, as George Saunders recently wrote in *The New Yorker*, living like housemates "no longer on speaking terms" in a house set afire by Trump, gaping at one another "through the smoke."

I wanted to leave my subnation of Berkeley, California, and enter another as far right as Berkeley is to the left. White Louisiana looked like it. In the 2012 election, 39 percent of white voters nationwide cast a ballot for President Barack Obama. That figure was 28 percent in the South, but about 11 percent in Louisiana.

To try to understand the tea party supporters I came to know—I interviewed 60 people in all—over the next five years I did a lot of "visiting," as they call it. I asked people to show me where they'd grown up, been baptized, and attended school, and the cemetery where their parents had been buried. I perused high school yearbooks and photograph albums, played cards, and went fishing. I attended meetings of Republican Women of Southwest Louisiana and followed the campaign trails of two right-wing candidates running for Congress.

When I asked people what politics meant to them, they often answered by telling me what they believed ("I believe in freedom") or who they'd vote for ("I was for Ted Cruz, but now I'm voting Trump"). But running beneath such beliefs like an underwater spring was what I've come to think of as a *deep story*. The deep story was a feels-as-if-it's-true story, stripped of facts and judgments, that reflected the feelings underpinning opinions and votes. It was a story of unfairness and anxiety, stagnation and slippage—a story in which shame was the companion to need. Except Trump had opened a divide in how tea partiers felt this story should end.

"Hey Miss Sharon, how ya' doin'?" A fiftysomething man I'll call Albert led us through the warehouse, where sheet metal had been laid out on large tables. "Want to come over Saturday, help us make sausage?" he called over the *eeeeech* of an unseen electrical saw. "I'm seasoning it different this year." The year before, Sharon had taken her 11-year-old daughter along to help stuff the spicy smoked-pork-and-rice sausage, to which Albert added ground deer meat. "I'll bring Alyson," Sharon said, referring to her daughter. Some days they'd have 400 pounds of deer meat and offer her some. "They're really good to me. And I'm there for them too when they need something."

These men had little shelter from bad news. "If you die, who's going to bury you?" Sharon would ask on such calls. "Do you have $10,000 sitting around? Will your parents have to borrow money to bury you or your wife or girlfriend? For $1.44 a week, you get $20,000 of life insurance."

Louisiana is the country's third-poorest state; 1 in 5 residents live in poverty. It ranks third in the proportion of residents who go hungry each year, and dead last in overall health. A quarter of the state's students drop out from high school or don't graduate on time. Partly as a result, Louisiana leads the nation in its proportion of "disconnected youth"—20 percent of 16- to 24-year-olds in 2013 were neither in school nor at work. (Nationally, the figure is 14 percent.) Only 6 percent of Louisiana workers are members of labor unions, about half the rate nationwide.

Louisiana is also home to vast pollution, especially along Cancer Alley, the 85-mile strip along the lower Mississippi between Baton Rouge and New Orleans, with some 150 industrial plants where once there were sugar and cotton plantations. According to the American Cancer Society, Louisiana had the nation's second-highest incidence of cancer for men and the fifth-highest rate of male deaths from cancer. "When I make a presentation, if I say, 'How many of you know someone that has had cancer?' every hand is going to go up. Just the other day I was in Lafayette doing my enrollments for the insurance, and I was talking to this one guy. And he said, 'My brother-in-law just died. He was 29 or 30.' He's the third person working for his company that's been in their early 30s that's died of cancer in the last three years. I file tons and tons of cancer claims."

Sharon also faced economic uncertainty. A divorced mother of two, she supported herself and two children on an ample but erratic income, all from commission on her Aflac sales. "If you're starting out, you might get 99 'noes' for every one 'yes.' After 16 years on the job, I get 50 percent 'yeses.'" This put her at the top among Aflac salespeople; still, she added, "If it's a slow month, we eat peanut butter."

Until a few years ago, Sharon had also collected rent from 80 tenants in a trailer court. Her ex-husband earned $40,000 as a sales manager at Pacific Sunwear, she explained, and helped with child support; altogether it allowed her to pay her children's tuition at a parochial school and stay current on the mortgage of a tastefully furnished, spacious ranch house in suburban Moss Bluff. She lived in the anxious middle.

And from this vantage point, the lives of renters in her trailer park, called Crestwood Community, had both appalled and unnerved her. Some of her tenants, 80 percent of whom were white, had matter-of-factly admitted to lying to get Medicaid and food stamps. When she'd asked a boy her son's age about his plans for the future, he answered, "I'm just going to get a [disability] check, like my mama." Many renters had been, she told me, able-bodied, idle, and on disability. One young man had claimed to have seizures. "If you have seizures, that's almost a surefire way to get disability without proving an ailment," she said. A lot of Crestwood Community residents supposedly had seizures, she added. "Seizures? Really?"

As we drove through the vacated lot, we passed abandoned trailers with doors flung open, tall grass pockmarked with holes where mailboxes once stood. Unable to pay an astronomical water bill, Sharon had been forced to close the trailer park, giving residents a month's notice and provoking their resentment.

In truth, Sharon felt relief. Her renters, she said, had been a hard-living lot. A jealous boyfriend had murdered his girlfriend. Some men drank and beat their wives. One man had married his son's ex-wife. Beyond that, Sharon had felt unfairly envied by them. "I've been called a rich bitch. They think Miss Sharon lives the life of Riley." And while her home was a 25-minute drive away, the life of her renters had felt entirely too close for comfort. "You couldn't talk to anyone at Crestwood whose teeth weren't falling out, gums black, missing teeth," adding that she gave out toothbrushes and toothpaste one Christmas. "My kids make fun of me because I brush my teeth so much."

To her, the trailer park both did and did not feel worlds away. For one thing, a person's standard of living, their worldview and basic identity, seemed already set on a floor of Jell-O. Who could know for sure how you would fare in the era of an expanding bottom, spiking top, and receding middle class?

Sharon's maternal grandfather had established a successful line of local furniture stores and shown how far up a man with gumption could rise. Sharon herself had graduated magna cum laude from McNeese State University in Lake Charles and been elected president of Republican Women of Southwest Louisiana. But her youngest brother had dropped out of high school and, while very bright and able-bodied, had not found his way. Her father, a plant worker who'd left her mom when Sharon was a teen, had remarried and moved to a trailer in Sulphur with his new wife, a mother of four. Looking around her, Sharon saw family and friends who struggled with bad relationships and joblessness. Some collected food stamps. "I don't get it," she said, "and it drives me nuts."

For Sharon, being on the dole raised basic issues of duty, honor, and shame. It had been hard to collect rent that she knew derived from disability checks, paid, in the end, by hardworking taxpayers like her. "I pay $9,000 in taxes every year and we get nothing for it," she said. Like others I interviewed, she felt that the federal government—especially under President Obama—was bringing down the hardworking rich and struggling middle while lifting the idle poor. She'd seen it firsthand and it felt unfair.

As we drove from the trailer park to her home, Sharon reflected on human ambition: "You can just see it in some guys' eyes; they're aiming higher. They don't want a handout." This was the central point of one of Sharon's favorite books, *Barefoot to Billionaire*, by oil magnate Jon Huntsman Sr. (whose son ran in the 2012 Republican presidential primary). Ambition was good. Earning money was good. The more money you earned, the more you could give to others. Giving was good. So ambition was the key to goodness, which was the basis for pride.

If you *could* work, even for pennies, receiving government benefits was a source of shame. It was okay if you were one of the few who really needed it, but not otherwise. Indignation at the overuse of welfare spread, in the minds of tea party supporters I got to know, to the federal government itself, and to state and local agencies. A retired assistant fire chief in Lake Charles told me, "I got told we don't *need* an assistant fire chief. A lot of people around here don't like *any* public employees, apart from the police." His wife said, "We were making such low pay that we could have been on food stamps every month and other welfare stuff. And [an official] told our departments that if we went and got food stamps or welfare it would look bad for Lake Charles so that he would fire us." A public school teacher complained, "I've had people tell me, 'It's the teachers who need to pass the kids' tests.' They have no idea what I know." A social worker who worked with drug addicts said, "I've been told the church should take care of addicts, not the government." Both receivers and givers of public services were tainted—in the eyes of nearly all I came to know—by the very touch of government.

Sharon especially admired Albert, a middle-aged sheet metal worker who could have used help but was too proud to ask for it. "He's had open-heart surgery. He's had stomach surgery. He's had like eight surgeries. He's still working, though. He wants to work. He's got a daughter in jail—her third DUI, so he's raising her son—and this and that. But he doesn't want anything from the government. He's *such* a *neat* guy." There was no mention of the need for a good alcoholism rehab program for his daughter or afterschool programs for his grandson. Until a few days before his death Albert continued working, head high, shame-free.

Sharon's politics were partly rooted, it seemed, in the class slippage of her childhood. As the oldest of three, the "little mama" to two younger brothers, she said, "I got them up in the morning, made their beds for them, so my mama wouldn't come down hard on them." Sharon's mother, the daughter of that prosperous furniture store owner, had grown up with a black maid who'd made her bed for her. She'd married a highly intelligent but high-school-educated plant worker, a Vietnam vet who never spoke of the war and seemed in search of peace and quiet. Privileges came and went in deeply unsettling ways and made a person want to hold on to a reassuring past. "One time when I had to travel to Florida on work, I left the kids with my mom, and Bailey called me for help: 'Grandma's forcing me to make her bed!'" Sharon answered, "I'm really sorry, Bailey; make her bed."

With the proud memory of an affluent Southern white girlhood, her mother took a dim view of the federal government. She'd trained as a social worker, volunteered in a women's prison, and remembered its inmates in her daily prayer. A devoted Christian, Sharon's mother believed in a generous church. But government benefits were a very different story. Taking them meant you'd fallen and weren't proudly trying to rise back up.

A poultry worker in Lake Charles.

Dancing to a Cajun band at Fred's Lounge in Mamou, Louisiana.

As we pulled up to her home, Sharon reflected on various theories her mother had. "Have you heard of the Illuminati? The New World Order?" Sharon asked so as to prepare me. "I'm tea party," Sharon said, "but I don't go along with a lot that my mom does." Whether they clung to such dark notions or laughed them off, tea party enthusiasts lived in a roaring rumor-sphere that offered answers to deep, abiding anxieties. Why did President Obama take off his wristwatch during Ramadan? Why did Walmart run out of ammunition on the third Tuesday in March? Did you know drones can detect how much money you have? Many described these as suspicions other people held. Many seemed to float in a zone of half-belief.

The most widespread of these suspicions, of course—shared by 66 percent of Trump supporters—is that Obama is Muslim.

What the people I interviewed were drawn to was not necessarily the particulars of these theories. It was the deep story underlying them—an account of life *as it feels* to them. Some such account underlies all beliefs, right or left, I think. The deep story of the right goes like this:

You are patiently standing in the middle of a long line stretching toward the horizon, where the American Dream awaits. But as you wait, you see people cutting in line ahead of you. Many of these line-cutters are black—beneficiaries of affirmative action or welfare. Some are career-driven women pushing into jobs they never had before. Then you see immigrants, Mexicans, Somalis, the Syrian refugees yet to come. As you wait in this unmoving line, you're being asked to feel sorry for them all. You have a good heart. But who is deciding who you should feel compassion for? Then you see President Barack Hussein Obama waving the line-cutters forward. He's on their side. In fact, isn't he a line-cutter too? How did this fatherless black guy pay for Harvard? As you wait your turn, Obama is using the money in your pocket to help the line-cutters. He and his liberal backers have removed the shame from taking. The government has become an instrument for redistributing your money to the undeserving. It's not your government anymore; it's theirs.

I checked this distillation with those I interviewed to see if this version of the deep story rang true. Some altered it a bit ("the line-waiters form a new line") or emphasized a particular point (those in back are *paying* for the line-cutters). But all of them agreed it was their story. One man said, "I live your analogy." Another said, "You read my mind."

The deep story reflects pain; you've done everything right and you're still slipping back. It focuses blame on an ill-intentioned government. And it points to rescue: The tea party for some, and Donald Trump for others. But what had happened to make this deep story ring true?

Most of the people I interviewed were middle class—and nationally more than half of all tea party supporters earn at least $50,000, while almost a third earn more than $75,000 a year. Many, however, had been poor as children and felt their rise to have been an uncertain one. As one wife of a well-to-do contractor told me, gesturing around the buck heads hanging above the large stone fireplace in the spacious living room of her Lake Charles home, "We have our American Dream, but we could *lose it all* tomorrow."

Being middle class didn't mean you felt secure, because that class was thinning out as a tiny elite shot up to great wealth and more people fell into a life of broken teeth, unpaid rent, and shame.

Growing up, Sharon had felt the struggle it took for her family to "stand in line" in a tumultuous world. Three years after her father wordlessly left home when she was 17, Sharon married, soon embracing a covenant marriage—one that requires premarital counseling and sets stricter grounds for divorce. But then they did divorce, and Sharon, once the little mother to her own siblings, now found herself a single mother of two—a mom and dad both. She was doing her level best but wondered why the travails of others so often took precedence over families such as her own. Affirmative-action blacks, immigrants, refugees seemed to so routinely receive sympathy and government help. She, too, had sympathy for many, but, as she saw it, a liberal sympathy machine had been set on automatic, disregarding the giving capacity of families like hers.

Or as one tea partier wrote to me: "We're so broke. Where does this food & welfare money come from? How can free stuff (including college, which my 4.2 student needs) even be on the table when the US owes $19,343,541,768,824.00 as of July 1? Is it just me or does it seem like the only thing ANYONE cares about is themselves and their immediate circumstances?"

Pervasive among the people I talked to was a sense of detachment from a distant elite with whom they had ever less contact and less in common. And, as older white Christians, they were acutely aware of their demographic decline. "You can't say 'merry Christmas,' you have to say 'happy holidays,'" one person said. "People aren't clean living anymore. You're considered ignorant if you're for that." An accountant told me, "Other people say, 'You're too hard-nosed about [morals].' Better to be hard-nosed than to be like it is now, so permissive about everything." They also felt disrespected for holding their values: "You're a weak woman if you don't believe that women should, you know, just elbow your way through society. You're not in the 'in' crowd if you're not a liberal. You're an old-fashioned old fogey, small thinking, small town, gun loving, religious," said a minister's wife. "The media tries to make the tea party look like bigots, homophobic; it's not." They resented all labels "the liberals" had for them, especially "backward" or "ignorant Southerners" or, worse, "rednecks."

Liberal television pundits and bloggers took easy potshots at them, they felt, which hardened their defenses. Their Facebook pages then filled with news coverage of liberals beating up fans at Trump rallies and Fox News coverage of white policemen shot by black men.

For some, age had also become a source of humiliation. One white evangelical tea party supporter in his early 60s had lost a good job as a sales manager with a telecommunications company when it merged with another. He took the shock bravely. But when he tried to get rehired, it was terrible. "I called, emailed, called, emailed. I didn't hear a thing. That was totally an age discrimination thing." At last he found a job at $10 an hour, the same wage he had earned at a summer factory union job as a college student 40 years ago. Age brought no dignity. Nor had the privilege linked to being white and male trickled down to him. Like Sharon's clients in the petrochemical plants, he felt like a stranger in his own land.

BUT AMONG THOSE walking in this wilderness, Trump had opened up a divide. Those more in the middle class, such as Sharon, wanted to halt the "line-cutters" by slashing government giveaways. Those in the working class, such as her Aflac clients, were drawn to the idea of hanging on to government services but limiting access to them.

Sharon was a giving person, but she wanted to roll back government help. It was hard supporting her kids and being a good mom too. Managing the trailer park had called on her grit, determination, even hardness—which she regretted. She mused, "Having to cope, run the trailer court, even threaten to shoot a dog"—her tenant's pet had endangered children—"it's hardened me, made me act like a man. I hate that. It's not really *me*." There was a price for doing the right and necessary thing, invisible, she felt, to many liberals.

And with all the changes, the one thing America needed, she felt, was a steady set of values that rewarded the good and punished the bad. Sharon honored the act of giving when it came from the private sector. "A businessperson gives other people *jobs*," she explained. She was proud to have employed two people at the trailer park, and sad she'd had to let them go. "I promised, 'The whole month of October you're going to get paid because you're out looking for another job.' That's a whole month. I feel an obligation." If you rose up in business, you took others with you, and this would be a point of pride. There was nothing wrong with *having*; if you had, you gave. But if you took—if you took from the government—you should be ashamed.

It was the same principle evident across the conservative movement, the one Mitt Romney had hewed to when he disparaged 47 percent of Americans as people who "pay no income tax" and "believe that they are victims," or when Romney's running mate, Paul Ryan, spoke of "makers and takers." The rich deserve honor as makers and givers and should be rewarded with the proud fruits of their earnings, on which taxes should be drastically cut. Such cuts would require an end to many government benefits that were supporting the likes of Sharon's trailer park renters. For her, the deep story ended there, with welfare cuts.

But for the blue-collar workers in the plants she visited, the guys who *loved Donald Trump*, it did not. When Sharon and I last had dinner in March, shortly after Trump's 757 jet swooped into New Orleans for his boisterous rally ahead of his big win in the Louisiana primary, Sharon told me about conversations with her Aflac clients that had shocked her. "They were talking about getting benefits from the government as if it were a *good* thing—*even the white guys*."

Sharon was leery of Trump and tried to puzzle out his appeal for them. "For the first few weeks I was very intrigued. I was like, 'What is this guy talking about? He's a jerk, but I like some of what he says.' But when you really start listening, *no!*" What troubled her most was that Trump was not a real conservative, that he was for big government. "Is he going to be a dictator? My gut tells me yes, he's an egomaniac. I don't care if you're Ronald Reagan, I don't want a dictator. That's not America." So, I asked, what did her clients see in Trump? "They see him as very strong. A blue-collar billionaire. Honest and refreshing, not having to be politically correct. They want someone that's macho, that can chew tobacco and shoot the guns—that type of manly man."

But something else seemed at play. Many blue-collar white men now face the same grim economic fate long endured by blacks. With jobs lost to automation or offshored to China, they have less security, lower wages, reduced benefits, more erratic work, and fewer jobs with full-time hours than before. Having been recruited to cheer on the contraction of government benefits and services—a trend that is particularly pronounced in Louisiana—many are unable to make ends meet without them. In *Coming Apart: The State of White America*, conservative political scientist Charles Murray traces the fate of working-age whites between 1960 and 2010. He compares the top 20 percent of them—those who have at least a bachelor's degree and are employed as managers or professionals—with the bottom 30 percent, those who never graduated from college and are employed in blue-collar or low-level white-collar jobs. In 1960, the personal lives of the two groups were quite similar. Most were married and stayed married, went to church, worked full time (if they were men), joined community groups, and lived with their children.

A half-century later, the 2010 top looked much like their counterparts in 1960. But for the bottom 30 percent, family life had drastically changed. While more than 90 percent of children of blue-collar families lived with both parents in 1960, by 2010, 22 percent did not. Lower-class whites were also less likely to attend church, trust their neighbors, or say they were happy. White men worked shorter hours, and those who were unemployed tended to pass up the low-wage jobs available to them. Another study found that in 2005, men with low levels of education did two things substantially more than both their counterparts in 1985 and their better-educated contemporaries: They slept longer and watched more television.

How can we understand this growing gap between male lives at the top and bottom? For Murray, the answer is a loss of moral values. But is sleeping longer and watching television a loss of morals, or a loss of morale? A recent study shows a steep rise in deaths of middle-aged working-class whites—much of it due to drug and alcohol abuse and suicide. These are not signs of abandoned values, but of lost hope. Many are in mourning and see rescue in the phrase "Great Again."

Trump's pronouncements have been vague and shifting, but it is striking that he has not called for cuts to Medicaid, or food stamps, or school lunch programs, and that his daughter Ivanka nods to the plight of working moms. He plans to replace Obamacare, he says, with a hazy new program that will be "terrific" and that some pundits playfully dub "Trump-care." For the blue-collar white male Republicans Sharon spoke to, and some whom I met, this change was welcome.

Still, it was a difficult thing to reconcile. How wary should a little-bit-higher-up-the-ladder white person now feel about applying for the same benefits that the little-bit-lower-down-the-ladder people had? Shaming the "takers" below had been a precious mark of higher status. What if, as a vulnerable blue-collar white worker, one were now to become a "taker" oneself?

Trump, the King of Shame, has covertly come to the rescue. He has shamed virtually every line-cutting group in the Deep Story—women, people of color, the disabled, immigrants, refugees. But he's hardly uttered a single bad word about unemployment insurance, food stamps, or Medicaid, or what the tea party calls "big government hand-outs," for anyone—including blue-collar white men.

In this feint, Trump solves a white male problem of pride. Benefits? If you need them, okay. He masculinizes it. You can be "high energy" macho—and yet may need to apply for a government benefit. As one auto mechanic told me, "Why not? Trump's for that. If you use food stamps because you're working a low-wage job, you don't want someone looking down their nose at you." A lady at an after-church lunch said, "If you have a young dad who's working full time but can't make it, if you're an American-born worker, can't make it, and not having a slew of kids, okay. For any conservative, that is fine."

But in another stroke, Trump adds a key proviso: restrict government help to real Americans. White men are counted in, but undocumented Mexicans and Muslims and Syrian refugees are out. Thus, Trump offers the blue-collar white men relief from a taker's shame: If you make America great again, how can you not be proud? Trump has put on his blue-collar cap, pumped his fist in the air, and left mainstream Republicans helpless. Not only does he speak to the white working class' grievances; as they see it, he has finally stopped their story from being politically suppressed. We may never know if Trump has done this intentionally or instinctively, but in any case he's created a movement much like the anti-immigrant but pro-welfare-state right-wing populism on the rise in Europe. For these are all based on variations of the same Deep Story of personal protectionism.

DURING MY LAST dinner with Sharon, over gumbo at the Pujo Street Café in Lake Charles, our talk turned to motherhood. Sharon wanted to give Bailey and Alyson the childhood she never had. She wanted to expose them to the wider world, and to other ways of thinking. "When I was a kid, the only place I'd ever been, outside of Louisiana, was Dallas," she mused. "I want my kids to see the whole world." She'd taken them on an American-history tour through Boston, Philadelphia, New York, and Washington, DC, where nine years ago she'd lunched with Laura Bush. She'd taken them to Iceland, which "they loved," and she'd just scored three round-trip tickets for a surprise tour of Finland, Sweden, and Russia.

But Sharon's gift to her children of a wider world carried risks. Her thoughtful 17-year-old, Bailey, had been watching Bernie Sanders decry the growing gap between rich and poor, push for responsive government, and propose free college tuition for all. "Bailey likes Sanders!" Sharon whispered across the table, eyebrows raised. Sanders had different ideas about good government and about shame, pride, and goodness. Bailey was rethinking these values himself. "He can't stand Trump," Sharon mused, "but we've found common ground. We both agree we should stop criminalizing marijuana and stop being the world's policeman, though we completely disagree on men using women's bathrooms." The great political divide in America had come to Sharon's kitchen table. She and Bailey were earnestly, bravely, searchingly hashing it out, with young Alyson eagerly listening in. Meanwhile, this tea party mom of a Sanders-loving son was reluctantly gearing up to vote for Donald Trump.

A Quick History of Cops in America

(2013)

Radley Balko

> *Democratic law tends more and more to be grounded upon the maxim that*
> *every citizen is, by nature, a traitor, a libertine, and a scoundrel. In order to*
> *dissuade him from his evil-doing the police power is extended until it surpasses*
> *anything ever heard of in the oriental monarchies of antiquity.*

—H. L. Mencken, *Notes on Democracy*

C OLONIAL AMERICAN TOWNS WERE USUALLY FILLED with people who came from the same place, worshiped at the same altar, and shared the same sense of right and wrong. Historian and criminologist Sam Walker writes, "Crime and sin were synonymous; an offense against God was an offense against society, and vice versa."[1] Predatory crimes like murder, rape, and robbery were almost nonexistent. Far more common were punishments for crimes like blasphemy, adultery, or drunkenness. Not surprisingly, law and policing in prerevolutionary America were modeled fairly closely on the English example. Given the rugged conditions of frontier living and the lack of civic structures, trial and punishment were relatively rare.

Mores and shared values were generally sufficient, and when they weren't, shunning and other forms of informal justice usually worked to keep civic order. Not all colonial communities were the same, and laws varied from place to place depending on the prevailing religion and tradition, but there was little need for state agents to enforce the law. Communities tended to handle transgressors on their own. There were Crown-appointed sheriffs and constables, but again, they largely focused on administrative matters.

As the country grew, three distinctive policing traditions began to emerge, coinciding with three regions—the Northeast, the South, and the western frontier.

In the Northeast, as the cities grew larger and more diverse in the early eighteenth century, their residents encountered more crime. Throughout the seventeenth and eighteenth centuries, early American cities first installed *night watch patrols*, first voluntary and then paid. The night watches were fairly successful at rounding up drunks

---

1 Samuel Walker, *Popular Justice,* 2nd ed. (New York: Oxford University Press, 1998), p. 16.

and preventing petty infractions, but the low-paying positions would prove inadequate when cities began to experience riots, mobs, and more serious crimes.

The Southern colonies were more agrarian, less compact, and more homogeneous than the colonies of the Northeast. The primary threat to public safety in the South—at least in the minds of whites—was the possibility of slave revolts. As a result, the first real organized policing systems in America arguably began in the South with *slave patrols*. The patrols were armed and uniformed, and typically had broad powers to arrest, search, and detain slaves. The slave patrols' main responsibilities were to guard against rebellions and to look for escaped slaves. They had the power to enter slave quarters at will, whether or not they had permission from the slaves' owner. They could even enforce some laws against plantation owners, such as laws prohibiting the education of slaves. By the middle of the eighteenth century, every Southern colony had passed laws formalizing slave patrols. It became the primary policing system in the South. In many jurisdictions—most notably Charleston, South Carolina—slave patrols would eventually morph into the official police force.

On the western frontier, early policing was more piecemeal. Northern settlers tended to congregate together and set up systems in the Northern tradition, while pioneers from the South followed the Southern tradition. But the expanse of the frontier didn't always accommodate either system. Often there was just too much ground to cover, and the territory was too sparsely populated. That gap was often filled by *vigilantes* and private police for hire. The vigilante groups came together in response to some threat to public order, then dissolved once the threat had subsided. As the name implies, they tended to operate outside the formal legal system and were naturally more prone to pop up where the legal system either didn't exist or was too weak to maintain order. In some cases, vigilante groups were better than no justice at all. In other cases, they were quite a bit worse.

THE FIRST MODERN POLICE FORCE AS WE KNOW IT TODAY WAS created in 1829 in London by Sir Robert Peel. He and his father had been pushing the idea for decades, but British concerns over the nation's civil liberties tradition had repeatedly killed the idea. Concerned about the worsening conditions in the city, Parliament finally gave its approval in 1829, but only after Peel put in place assurances and checks to retain some local control over the force and ensure that police officers' responsibilities were limited to fighting crime and protecting individual rights—his task was to convince the city that a police force would not be an army enforcing the will of a centralized power.

The British police force began with three thousand officers. They wore uniforms to make themselves recognizable, but Peel made the uniforms blue to distinguish them from the red worn by the British military. Peel was sensitive to concerns about standing armies, but he also believed that a successful police force would need at least some of the structure and discipline of a military influence. Peel appointed a retired colonel as one of his two first supervising justices. Thus, the inaugural police force took on a military-like top-down administrative structure, and even borrowed some military titles. It's a tradition that continues in most police departments in the United States today.

Peel and his justices set out a strict code of conduct. Officers were to avoid confrontation when at all possible. They were to be civil and polite when interacting with citizens. Most of all, Peel hammered home the principle that his police force worked for the people of London, not against them. Nevertheless, it took a while for the public to warm to the idea.

Across the Atlantic in rapidly urbanizing America, larger cities began to adopt the British model, albeit with some Americanized adjustments. The first modern-style police department in the United States was established in New York in 1845. Boston and Philadelphia soon followed. New York began its experiment with eight hundred policemen. Fearing that the London force was already too much like an army, the New York cops began their patrols unarmed, and without uniforms. Early American police departments were also much more democratic than the system in London. Peel and his top aides handpicked the officers to work in London. In the United States, early police officers were nominated by ward leaders and political bosses, then appointed by the mayor. Cops were required to live in the wards they patrolled. All of this tended to make early police departments more like service agencies than law enforcement bodies. Since ward leaders were elected, they found they could pressure local commanders to prioritize police duties in ways that would help get them reelected. In some neighborhoods, police officers ran soup kitchens and homeless people were given shelter in police stations to sleep. This democratic style of policing also gave police (or more accurately, their commanders) discretion to enforce laws in ways that reflected the priorities of the communities they patrolled. Alcohol laws, for example, might be strictly enforced in one part of a city, but rarely if ever enforced in another.

In some ways, this wasn't all that dissimilar to the way laws had been enforced before police departments existed, when transgressions within a community were handled by its members. But there were some clear drawbacks. The job of police officer had quickly become a patronage position. The only qualification for becoming a cop was a political connection. Mass firings were common when power changed hands. The ethnicity of a ward's police force tended to be exclusively that of the majority of the ward's population. This could be problematic for, say, an Italian caught in a majority Irish neighborhood. Training was nonexistent, beatings were common, and, perhaps most importantly, the system had little effect on crime—neither preventing it nor helping to bring criminals to justice.

Ironically, the more centralized, less democratic London model proved to be more protective of individual rights than early American police departments. Centralization allowed Peel to set high, consistent hiring standards based on merit. Because he was so aware of the English public's fears about violations of their civil liberties, Peel knew that the survival of his police department was probably contingent on his ability to alleviate those fears.

And so by the end of the nineteenth century, London's "bobbies" (the nickname derived from Peel's name) had managed to win over the public within a couple of decades, while the reputation of the American police officer had hit bottom. With no training or standards, and with jobs based on patronage more than merit, the police in America were best known for corruption, brutality, and incompetence. Wealthy citizens looked instead to private organizations like the Pinkertons when they needed reliable security or knew of a crime they wanted solved.

By the early twentieth century, police reform had become a cause of the progressive movement, whose adherents saw corrupt cops as just another consequence of cities being run by political machines. There were two competing voices for reform. Progressive academics and elites wanted not only to rid police departments of patronage and corruption but to mandate a more paternalistic role for police. They wanted cops to enforce good habits and morals among the urban poor, especially immigrants.

The other voice for reform came from administrators within the law enforcement community. They too wanted to free police departments from the political machines, but they focused less on ideology and more on fighting crime. They wanted to give more freedom and autonomy to police chiefs, who were often held responsible for the actions of their officers but had very little power to actually change their behavior.

In the end, the administrators won the long-term debate by embracing the concept of *professionalism*. Through the adoption of best practices, they successfully transformed the job of police officer from a perk of patronage to a formal profession with its own standards, specialized knowledge, and higher personnel standards and entry requirements. To be a police officer was no longer just a job, it was a career. The first thirty or so years of the twentieth century saw the formation of professional societies like the Police Chiefs' Union; the sharing of knowledge and "police sciences" like fingerprinting; and the creation of specialized "squads" to tackle specific problems like alcohol, prostitution, and gambling.

The champion of the professionalism movement was August Vollmer, who served as chief of police in Berkeley, California, from 1905 to 1932. Vollmer pioneered the use of police radios, squad cars, bicycles, lie detector tests, and crime labs. As Walker writes, "The professionalism movement created the modern police organization: a centralized, authoritarian, bureaucracy focusing on crime control."[2]

---

2   Ibid., p. 170.

But the morals-oriented progressives also had some victories, at least in the short term. They succeeded in passing anti-obscenity laws, and in some cities (most notably New York) they were able to put shutting down brothels, adult-book stores, and other sex-related businesses high on the list of police priorities. Their biggest victory was of course the Eighteenth Amendment, which banned the production, sale, and importation of alcohol.

The amendment was enforced by the Volstead Act, passed in 1919. The prohibition of alcohol has some clear parallels with the modern drug war. Homicides spiked during Prohibition, as did public corruption. The federal government had created a lucrative new black market. In legal markets, businesses compete by providing a better product, a less expensive product, or better customer service. In black markets, they compete by warring over turf. Disputes are settled with guns, not in courtrooms. As the bootleggers obtained bigger guns to war with one another, law enforcement agencies felt that they needed bigger guns to go after the criminals. In larger cities, the ensuing arms race produced heavily armed police forces.

Like today's drug prohibition, the Volstead Act was a failure. It almost certainly reduced the amount of alcohol the country consumed, but it came nowhere near stamping out booze entirely. The true believers responded by calling for tougher crackdowns and less coddling of bootleggers and drinkers. In his book *The Spirits of America*, journalist Eric Burns writes that some politicians and civic leaders suggested sending drunks and booze distributors to Siberia or the South Pole. Burns notes that David Blair, the federal commissioner of internal revenue at the time, "recommended that all American bootleggers be lined up in front of a firing squad and shot to death."[3] Foreshadowing the cries the country would hear from drug warriors sixty years later, Henry Ford wanted the military to enforce the laws against illicit substances. Anti-alcohol activist Clarence True Wilson demanded that the Harding administration call up the Marines, "arm them to the teeth and send them to the speakeasies. Give the people inside a few minutes to depart, and if they choose not to, open fire anyhow."[4]

But as hard as the temperance activists tried, they couldn't demonize and dehumanize drinkers the way drug warriors have since succeeded in denigrating drug offenders. One likely reason was that the Volstead Act didn't criminalize the possession or consumption of alcohol, only its production and sale. So the feds could raid speakeasies, but they couldn't raid a home based on a tip that someone had a cupboard full of gin—unless they suspected there was a distillery inside. Since simply ingesting alcohol was not a criminal act, it was more difficult for Prohibition's supporters to cast drinkers as

3   Eric Burns, *Spirits of America: A Social History of Alcohol* (Philadelphia: Temple University Press, 2004) p. 229.

4   Burns, *Spirits of America*, p. 229.

villains. The country was also more federalist in the 1920s. Even after the Eighteenth Amendment passed, some states, cities, and counties simply refused to enforce it.

After the repeal of Prohibition in 1933, the professionalism model returned to police departments.

Although some of the aims of professionalism may have been noble, the story of early American policing is one of overcorrection. While the professionalism reformers were able to end the patronage system, in some cities they managed to insulate police departments from politics altogether, making it difficult for mayors and city councils to hold police officials accountable. At the level of individual cops, the use of squad cars and radios clearly brought a lot of benefits, but could also isolate police officers from the residents of the communities they patrolled. Cops out walking beats could chat with citizens, form relationships, and become a part of the community. Squad cars gave cops a faceless and intimidating presence. They tended not to get out of them except in the event of problems or confrontations. Police and citizens interacted only when police were ticketing or questioning someone, or when a citizen was reporting a crime. In poorer communities, that could bring about an increasingly antagonistic relationship between cops and the citizens on their beats.[5]

Perhaps no police chief better illustrated that double-edged sword of professionalism than William Parker in Los Angeles. Parker took over the LAPD in 1950 and imposed a rigid, hierarchical, militaristic bureaucracy. He took on corruption in the department—successfully—and stressed efficiency and crime fighting above all else. Parker had also worked in public relations for the military for a time, and he used that experience to sell his ideas about policing to the public. He helped create the show *Dragnet,* a virtual commercial for Parker-style police management—or at least an idealized form of it.[6]

But Parker also loathed community policing, the idea that cops should have a stake in the communities they served. He preferred to have a wall between cop and community. That sentiment probably stemmed from the goal of ridding the department of the sort of localized interests that existed in the patronage era. But completely walling off cops from their communities presented its own problems. Making cops indifferent to the areas they patrolled, instilling in them the notion that they were all that stood between order and anarchy—all of this could make police view the citizens in their districts as at

<hr />

5   The history of early policing in the United States is from Walker, *Popular Justice;* Roger Lane, "Urban Police and Crime in Nineteenth-Century America," and Eric H. Monkkonen, "History of Urban Police," both in *Modern Policing,* ed. Michael Tonry and Norval Morris (Chicago: University of Chicago Press, 1992); Robert H. Langworthy and Lawrence F. Travis III, *Policing in America* (Englewood Cliffs, NJ: Prentice-Hall, 2003); Burns, *Spirits of America*; and Samuel Walker and Charles M. Katz, *The Police in America,* 7th ed. (New York: McGraw-Hill, 2011).

6   See Walker, *Popular Justice,* pp. 173–175.

best the *other*, and at worst, the enemy. Consequently, while Parker's management rid the LAPD of political patronage and corruption, and instilled some needed structure and standards, he seemed oblivious to growing animosity toward police in the city's black and Latino populations.

Parker's efforts at instilling professionalism provide a good segue into the age of militarization for a couple of reasons. For one, as we'll see, when the racial tension in LA finally blew up in the form of the Watts riots, it went a long way toward scaring middle America about crime, to the point where they were willing to embrace an all-out "war" on crime and drugs to clean up the cities.

But Parker also had a much more direct impact on militarization. Shortly after taking office, the chief made a young LAPD cop barely a year into the job his personal chauffeur, and eventually his protégé. That set the young cop's career on a fast track. By the time of the Watts riots in 1965, Parker's young protégé would take command of the city police department's response. The experience would scar him. The protégé would eventually become LA's police chief himself. And in large part because of his experience in Watts, he did more to bring about today's militarized American police force than any other single person. His name was Daryl Gates.

Reading 3.4

Multiple Manhoods

(2017)

Victor M. Rios (with Rachel Sarabia)

W HEN I FIRST MET JASON, HE was twenty years old with a criminal record and considered himself an "active gang member."[1] Jason garnered respect from his "homies" because he had spent much of his teenage years "putting in work" on the streets, which meant fighting, dealing drugs, and stealing. Jason explained:

> Well, you have to earn respect. Nobody gives it to you. If you give respect to the right people, you get respect from the right people ... you hold your ground you know, just throw down [fight]. ... Like some fool tries make you look like a bitch, then you throw down [fight] and that's how they look at respect you know?

In my observations, I saw Jason "calling shots" in the neighborhood, giving orders to other young men, and avoiding victimization and incarceration by having other young men look out for him when conflict arose. But I also noticed that Jason was one of the few active gang members who escaped police searches and harassment.

One day, I was standing in front of Golden State Liquors with six boys, four of whom were drinking tall cans of Arizona Iced Tea. A Gang Suppression Team member—police officers responsible for monitoring gang members—pulled up to the curb, stepped out of his vehicle, and asked, "What are you drinking?" Most of the boys ignored him; two shrugged their shoulders. The officer signaled Julio to come closer, but Julio ignored him.

"If you don't come here," the officer warned, "I'm gonna make you look really bad in front of your homies."

Julio walked over, and the officer grabbed him by the shirt, pressuring him to sit on the curb. Then, he lifted Julio up by the shirt and emptied his pockets. Using his radio, the officer checked if Julio had a police record or any outstanding warrants. He proceeded to do the same for all the others—except for Jason.

Before driving off, the officer looked at Jason and said, "I'll see you at the bagel shop. ... Tell these boys they need to get a job like you."

Jason worked at a local bagel shop where police officers who patrolled the neighborhood often stopped, which is why he believed the police gave him more respect than some of the other young men. "Police know I am a hard worker," he said. "That's what they expect of me. I'm a family man and I don't commit crime anymore." Among more than eighty young men I encountered during my five-year study, Jason was one of only six homies who held a steady full-time job.

Jason often brought his four-year-old son, Junior, with him to hang out at the park or in front of the liquor store. Junior wore a blue bandana in his rear pocket, a sign representing the Mexican Mafia, and sometimes Jason urged him to play-fight with older neighborhood kids. He said he wanted Junior to learn to be a man, which entailed learning about street life, how to protect himself, and how to demand respect.

Although Jason believed that gang parents and older gang members sometimes played a negative role in the life of their younger kin, he did not realize that his own actions to socialize his son to be a tough man might also have a negative impact:

> It's like the families and older guys force them to join [the gang]. It's like a circle that can offer protection … well, not just force them, but also they don't have the money to buy this and that, so people join gangs for protection and go rob and shit. But my son, I don't want him doing all that nutty stuff.

Jason was an active father who wanted his son to have a bright future. Frequently, he could be seen pushing his son in a stroller through the neighborhood and tending to his needs. Yet, he did not as often consider how the actions and lessons of manhood performed around his boy might encourage Junior to join a gang in the future. To Jason, Junior was partaking in "child's play."

Jason always appeared incredibly loyal and respectful to his girlfriend, even on the street where other young women were called "bitches" and "hos" by their partners or other boys and could be physically or symbolically attacked. Jason had developed the ability to balance various manifestations of masculinity, which yielded diverse benefits: respect on the streets, acknowledgment from police, a healthy romantic relationship, and the reputation as a "manly son."

However, Jason's experience was unusual. Although all of the young men in this study adopted different forms of masculinity, Jason was one of the few who experienced associated positive outcomes. More commonly, young men displayed their masculinity in a way that resulted in their arrest for challenging or assaulting police officers and others. A comparison of Jason's experience with that of other young men yielded concrete examples of the various practices of masculinity in this South Riverland neighborhood.

These gang-associated young men used masculinity as a central vehicle by which to compensate for race and class subordination. In an effort to maintain dignity and respect, they used differing forms of masculinity (subordinate, street, working class, dominant, and hyper) at various times, a process we refer to as synthesized masculinities. The young men we studied synthesized masculinities to acquire social status and to contest various forms of subordination. Like other forms of gender and sexuality practice, the masculinities they practiced were fluid, situated, and shifting.

In addition to the morals and values of manhood the young men learned from being on the streets, they also found masculinity within criminalization—specifically, negative encounters with school, police, juvenile hall, and probation authorities. One consequence of criminalization and punitive social control for these boys was the development of a specific set of gendered practices that obstructed desistance from crime, positive social relationships, and social mobility. By analyzing the perceptions and actions of these young men, we uncovered how masculinity emerged from and reflected race, class, and gender subordination. Jason's discussion of "being a man" represented how many of the boys developed synthesized masculinities, a strategic and situational display of various masculinities. Various frames representing masculinity were meshed together to embody a masculinity that allowed the boys to feel empowered in multiple settings.

Like Jason, many of the other boys relied on masculinity to obtain respect and cope with race and class marginality; however, their approaches often led instead to victimization, stigmatization, and incarceration. With limited access to traditional pathways to accomplish conventional masculinity—that ideal in which a man works hard, makes good money, and supports his family—the boys sought alternative ways to achieve manhood. Synthesized masculinities allowed these young men to creatively accomplish masculinity throughout their lives in their effort to access resources they perceived to be lacking and to compensate for other forms of domination.

...

Law Enforcement, Masculinity Enforcement

A majority of the young men and women interviewed (forty-six of fifty-seven men, and fourteen of eighteen women) held negative worldviews about the police. All reported at least one negative interaction in which they felt victimized either through physical or verbal abuse. In my observations on the street and in ride-alongs with police, I observed a handful of positive interactions and many negative ones, although most interactions between youth and police were neutral. Often police simply questioned or cited the boys and let them go, but I witnessed times when police verbally degraded boys, used excessive force, and employed illegal searches. For many of the young men, the police represented one of many obstacles to their development and ability to find a place in the community. In their minds, the police, like others in society, grouped them as criminals and promoted that image to community members, potential employers, and school authorities. Through instilling fear of violence and incarceration, the police consistently tested, challenged, and degraded their masculinity.

Policing is a male-dominated and masculine field (Cooper 2009; Dodsworth 2007; Harris 2000), and machismo has been central in police culture (Herbert 2006). Many of the police-youth encounters I witnessed involved masculinity challenges. Through exerting their dominance, police officers were "doing" gender (e.g., Martin 1999) as they strategically emasculated the youths to symbolically demonstrate the officers were the "real" men.

Police responded to perceived attacks on their masculine self-identity and authority with violence or threats of violence, an observation consistent with other research (Harris 2000). When they believed neighborhood youths were disrespecting them, they used threats or physical power to restore their dignity. Police officers got "macho" with youths, staging masculinity contests with them—contests rife with meaning in these young men's lives. The youths interpreted such actions as taunts, efforts to provoke the boys' anger so they would talk back or lash out and do something that would justify an arrest (Gau and Brunson 2010; Harris 2000; Sollund 2006).

Dreamy, a seventeen-year-old Latino male once arrested for possessing a marijuana pipe, represented many of the other boys' perceptions:

> Cops are a bunch of bullies. ... They are always trying to act like they are bigger men than you. ... They think we are organized crime or something, and, like, damn, we are just a bunch of homies that are kicking it. ... I mean I think when you see a cop you should feel safe and you know kind of make you feel good, but hell no, when I see a cop I get fuckin' scared as hell! Even if I'm not doing anything wrong, I'm still fuckin' scared as hell!

Eighteen-year-old Angel, who had been arrested twice, once for a gang fight and once for violating probation, voiced similar interactions with police:

> They always say some fucked up shit to me. Once they told me, "Why don't you come work with us, *puta* [bitch]?" And sometimes they're like, "I promise I won't take you in if you do something for me [like giving them information on criminal activity]." *Pinche pendejos* [fucking idiots]. It's all a trick. They are always on top of us. ... They're like "look, I know you're on probation," and they just keep talking shit, talking shit. Cops don't respect us. They laugh at us. *En serio* [seriously], they're just like, oh, look at these fools, they're just a bunch of bitches.

Joker, a sixteen-year-old who hung out with the gang, but did well in school and avoided fighting, drinking, and staying out late, related an incident when an officer used physical force on him:

The cops do nothing but harass. I go to school. I try to stay out of trouble. Narc [undercover police] cars are always around. I see them driving back and forth on my way to school. Sometimes I think I'm just trippin'. It's like, fuck, why are they stopping here? You always gotta look over your shoulder, dog, you know what I mean? They roll up and they just stare at us. One time, they tried to stop me. I ran. I bounced because it was curfew. I tried to hide. They found me. I tried to tell them I got a fucked-up back, that I had been in a car accident. I told them not to slam me. That fool grabbed me from the neck, motherfucker, started cussing me out, fool. He fuckin' slams the shit out of me dog, fuckin' scraped my face, my chin and shit. And I'm just like, fuck, I got all dizzy. He was just talking shit. He was mad. He was like, "Yeah I fucked you up, motherfucker, keep running from me, you fuckin' little bitch. I'm gonna fuckin' bust you this time." They always mistreating us.

One afternoon, four boys in this study were arrested in front of a community center when three police officers arrived to disperse a crowd of twenty suspected gang members loitering outside. Five additional officers were called to provide backup. Jason started taking pictures of the officers. The officers approached Jason and started taking pictures of him with their cell phones. One officer got so close, according to Jason, that he was hit in the face a few times with the officer's phone. Jason pushed the officer's phone away. He was arrested for attempted robbery, resisting an officer, battery on a police officer, and participation in a criminal street gang. Three other boys were arrested for petty infractions.

Jason spent four months in jail for this incident. Tired of being photographed by police, he said he had decided to respond by taking a picture of the officers that day:

Why can't we take pictures of them, but they can take them of us? It's a bunch of bullshit. They just slap a bunch of shit on us. They always try to put us in the wrong and make it look they are the innocent ones, the good guys.

The camera incident demonstrates the masculinity battles waged between officers and the boys. Police demanded respect, and when it was not given, they reacted quickly and harshly. According to the boys, police "create bogus charges": attempted robbery, resisting an officer, battery of a police officer, or participation in a criminal street gang in an attempt to control and entrap them.

Police consistently challenged and mocked the boys for their way of talking, their dress, their friends and associates, and their failure to display conventional masculinity. More than enforcing the law, police were enforcing masculinity out of a desire to preserve their authority, prove their manhood, and maintain their dominant status on the streets

(Cooper 2009; Hahn 1971). The boys described officers as power-hungry individuals who had something to prove: that they were "manlier" than the gang. Criticizing police for overcompensating was an integral part of the boys' performances of masculinity. They believed they were the real men, and the police were weak individuals hiding behind badges and guns. But much of their manhood was constructed in direct response to power, in this case punitive police intervention in their lives.

Simultaneously, police attempted to reinforce a particular form of working-class masculinity that was less available to these particular young men than the officers seemed to understand. They pushed the idea that "a real man gets a job and provides for his family." Yet these boys' young age and poor education put them in the company of those with a 40 percent unemployment rate. If jobs existed, these boys were not among those getting hired.

Most of the officers serving the South Riverland community were white, and the boys viewed them as rich men with good jobs, even as they despised some of them. When officers gave advice to the boys, they used their profession as a reference point. "Right now you're just on probation for small stuff. You can still clean your record and become a cop one day," one officer told a group of four boys in front of the liquor store. Officers consistently made references to being "a real man" when they advised the boys. "Be a real man, get a job, leave the homies, go to school, and provide for your family," an officer told one boy as he stopped and searched him.

The boys understood the normative ideals for how to "become a man," even if they had yet to acquire the resources to do so. The following descriptions were representative:

> A man is someone that can support their family ... even with the struggle ... having a job ... putting support ... having food on the table, a roof over their head, and clothes on their backs ... that's a man. (Raul, 14)
>
> Knowing how to work makes you a man. Being responsible. A man is somebody that, you know, doesn't back down. To be a man, you gotta be down for whatever. You stick around, or stick to what you say you're gonna do. You don't learn this stuff overnight though; becoming a man is a process. (Tito, 17)
>
> I would want to be successful you know, and come back and help people that need it the most, like people that were ... or kids that went through the same shit that I went through or something you know, just trying to give back to the community. ... I mean hopefully college can help me figure that out, you know 'cause ... a lot of people don't even know what they want to do you know, and when they go to college that's where they figure shit out. So that's what I'ma try to do. (Jose, 16)

Most boys believed gang life was just a stage in their development, and that one day, they might be able to transition into a more productive path. First, they had to acquire the resources to become men capable of providing for their families by going to college or working. While this kind of masculinity—working hard, finishing school, and providing for families—could place the boys on a better trajectory, the boys encountered various obstacles on this path. Riverland lacked entry-level jobs and community programs to help this group of youths transition back into school, and the schools' zero-tolerance policies led many to be expelled for gang activity. Frequently, the boys viewed school as a place that targeted them as criminals and cared little for them. Thirty-two of the fifty-seven had dropped out of school or had been kicked out, and twelve told us they dropped out because they felt they did not belong or school officials did not care about them. On the streets, police gang units stopped, "tagged" (entered into a gang database), harassed, and arrested the boys, sometimes for something as simple as walking to the store to buy groceries.

When the boys attempted to get jobs or complete school, their avenues for opportunities often turned out to be dead ends. The realization that they were not able to be the kind of man mainstream society expected them to be inflicted stress, anger, and pain. As a result, they forged alternative forms of manhood—forms that often stressed being tough, gaining status and respect, and, like the police did onto them, demonstrating dominance over others.

References

Cooper, Frank. 2009. *Masculinities and the Law: A Multidimensional Approach*. New York: New York University Press.

Dodsworth, Francis. 2007. *Masculinity as Governance: Police, Public Service and the Embodiment of Authority, c. 1700–1850.*

Gau, Jacinta, and Rod Brunson. 2010. "Procedural Justice and Order Maintenance Policing: A Study of Inner City Young Men's Perceptions of Police Legitimacy." *Justice Quarterly* 27, no. 2: 255–79.

Hahn, Harlan. 1971. "Police in Urban Society." *American Behavioral Scientists* 16, no. 3.

Harris, A. P. 2000. "Gender, Violence, Race, and Criminal Justice." *Stanford Law Review*, 777–807.

Herbert, Steve. 2006. *Citizens, Cops, and Power: Recognizing the Limits of Community*. Chicago: University of Chicago Press.

Martin, Susan 1999. "Police Force or Police Service? Gender and Emotional Labor." *Annals of the American Academy of Political and Social Science* 561: 111–26.

Sollund, Ragnhild. 2006. "Racialization in Police Stop and Search Practice." *Critical Criminology* 14, no. 13: 265–92.

The New Jim Crow: How Mass Incarceration Turns People of Color Into Permanent Second-Class Citizens

(2011)

Michelle Alexander

THE FIRST TIME I ENCOUNTERED THE idea that our criminal-justice system functions much like a racial caste system, I dismissed the notion. It was more than 10 years ago in Oakland when I was rushing to catch the bus and spotted a bright orange sign stapled to a telephone pole. It screamed in large, bold print: "The Drug War is the New Jim Crow." I scanned the text of the flyer and then muttered something like, "Yeah, the criminal-justice system is racist in many ways, but making such an absurd comparison doesn't help. People will just think you're crazy." I then hopped on the bus and headed to my new job as director of the Racial Justice Project for the American Civil Liberties Union of Northern California.

What a difference a decade makes. After years of working on issues of racial profiling, police brutality, and drug-law enforcement in poor communities of color as well as working with former inmates struggling to "re-enter" a society that never seemed to have much use for them, I began to suspect that I was wrong about the criminal-justice system. It was not just another institution infected with racial bias but a different beast entirely. The activists who posted the sign on the telephone pole were not crazy, nor were the smattering of lawyers and advocates around the country who were beginning to connect the dots between our current system of mass incarceration and earlier forms of racial control. Quite belatedly, I came to see that mass incarceration in the United States has, in fact, emerged as a comprehensive and well-disguised system of racialized social control that functions in a manner strikingly similar to Jim Crow.

What has changed since the collapse of Jim Crow has less to do with the basic structure of our society than with the language we use to justify severe inequality. In the era of colorblindness, it is no longer socially permissible to use race, explicitly, as justification for discrimination, exclusion, or social contempt. Rather, we use our criminal-justice system to associate criminality with people of color and then engage in the prejudiced practices we supposedly left behind. Today, it is legal to discriminate against ex-offenders in ways it was once legal to discriminate against African Americans. Once you're labeled a felon, depending on the state you're in, the old forms of discrimination—employment discrimination, housing discrimination, denial of the right to vote, and exclusion from jury service—are suddenly legal. As a criminal, you have scarcely more rights and argu- ably less respect than a black man living in Alabama at the height of Jim Crow. We have not ended racial caste in America; we have merely redesigned it.

California Institution for Men, Chino, California

More than two million African Americans are currently under the control of the criminal-justice system—in prison or jail, on probation or parole. During the past few decades, millions more have cycled in and out of the system; indeed, nearly 70 percent of people released from prison are re-arrested within three years. Most people appre- ciate that millions of African Americans were locked into a second-class status during slavery and Jim Crow, and that these earlier systems of racial control created a legacy of political, social, and economic inequality that our nation is still struggling to over- come. Relatively few, however, seem to appreciate that millions of African Americans are subject to a new system of control— mass incarceration—which also has a devastating effect on families and communities. The harm is greatly intensified when prisoners are released. As criminologist Jeremy Travis has observed, "In this brave new world, pun- ishment for the original offense is no longer enough; one's debt to society is never paid."

The scale of incarceration-related discrimination is astonishing. Ex-offenders are routinely stripped of essential rights. Current felon-disenfranchisement laws bar 13 percent of African American men from casting a vote, thus making mass incarceration an effective tool of voter suppression—one reminiscent of the poll taxes and literacy tests of the Jim Crow era. Employers routinely discriminate against an applicant based on criminal history, as do landlords. In most states, it is also legal to make ex-drug offenders ineligible for food stamps. In some major urban areas, if you take into account prisoners—who are excluded from poverty and unemployment statistics, thus masking the severity of black disadvantage—more than half of working-age African American men have criminal records and are thus subject to legalized discrimination for the rest of their lives. In Chicago, for instance, nearly 80 percent of working-age African American men had criminal records in 2002. These men are permanently locked into an inferior, second-class status, or caste, by law and custom.

The official explanation for this is crime rates. Our prison population increased seven-fold in less than 30 years, going from about 300,000 to more than 2 million, supposedly due to rising crime in poor communities of color.

Crime rates, however, actually have little to do with incarceration rates. Crime rates have fluctuated during the past 30 years and today are at historical lows, but incarceration rates have consistently soared. Most sociologists and criminologists today will acknowledge that crime rates and incarceration rates have moved independently of each other; incarceration rates have skyrocketed regardless of whether crime has gone up or down in any particular community or in the nation as a whole.

What caused the unprecedented explosion in our prison population? It turns out that the activists who posted the sign on the telephone pole were right: The "war on drugs" is the single greatest contributor to mass incarceration in the United States. Drug convictions accounted for about two-thirds of the increase in the federal prison system and more than half of the increase in the state prison system between 1985 and 2000—the period of the U.S. penal system's most dramatic expansion.

Contrary to popular belief, the goal of this war is not to root out violent offenders or drug kingpins. In 2005, for example, four out of five drug arrests were for possession, while only one out five were for sales. A 2007 report from Sentencing Project found that most people in state prison for drug offenses had no history of violence or significant selling activity. Nearly 80 percent of the increase in drug arrests in the 1990s, when the drug war peaked, could be attributed to possession of marijuana, a substance less harmful than alcohol or tobacco and at least as prevalent in middle-class white communities and on college campuses as in poor communities of color.

The drug war, though, has been waged almost exclusively in poor communities of color, despite the fact that studies consistently indicate that people of all races use and sell illegal drugs at remarkably similar rates. This is not what one would guess by peeking inside our nation's prisons and jails, which are overflowing with black and brown drug offenders. In 2000, African Americans made up 80 percent to 90 percent of imprisoned drug offenders in some states.

The extraordinary racial disparities in our criminal-justice system would not exist today but for the complicity of the United States Supreme Court. In the failed war on drugs, our Fourth Amendment protections against unreasonable searches and seizures have been eviscerated. Stop-and-frisk operations in poor communities of color are now routine; the arbitrary and discriminatory police practices the framers aimed to prevent are now commonplace. Justice Thurgood Marshall, in a strident dissent in the 1989 case of *Skinner v. Railway Labor Executive Association*, felt compelled to remind the Court that there is "no drug exception" to the Fourth Amendment. His reminder was in vain. The Supreme Court had begun steadily unraveling Fourth Amendment protections against stops, interrogations, and seizures in bus stops, train stations, schools, workplaces, airports, and on sidewalks in a series of cases starting in the early 1980s. These aggressive sweep tactics in poor communities of color are now as accepted as separate water fountains were several decades ago.

If the system is as rife with conscious and unconscious bias, many people often ask, why aren't more lawsuits filed? Why not file class-action lawsuits challenging bias by the police or prosecutors? Doesn't the 14th Amendment guarantee equal protection of the law?

What many don't realize is that the Supreme Court has ruled that in the absence of conscious, intentional bias—tantamount to an admission or a racial slur—you can't present allegations of race discrimination in the criminal-justice system. These rulings have created a nearly insurmountable hurdle, as law-enforcement officials know better than to admit racial bias out loud, and much of the discrimination that pervades this system is rooted in unconscious racial stereotypes, or "hunches" about certain types of people that come down to race. Because these biases operate unconsciously, the only proof of bias is in the outcomes: how people of different races are treated. The Supreme Court, however, has ruled that no matter how severe the racial disparities, and no matter how overwhelming or compelling the statistical evidence may be, you must have proof of conscious, intentional bias to present a credible case of discrimination. In this way, the system of mass incarceration is now immunized from judicial scrutiny for racial bias, much as slavery and Jim Crow laws were once protected from constitutional challenge.

As a nation, we have managed to create a massive system of control that locks a significant percentage of our population—a group defined largely by race—into a permanent, second-class status. This is not the fault of one political party. It is not merely the fault of biased police, prosecutors, or judges. We have all been complicit in the emergence of mass incarceration in the United States. In the so-called era of colorblindness, we have become blind not so much to race as to the re-emergence of caste in America. We have turned away from those labeled "criminals," viewing them as "others" unworthy of our concern. Some of us have been complicit by remaining silent, even as we have a sneaking suspicion that something has gone horribly wrong. We must break that silence and awaken to the human-rights nightmare that is occurring on our watch.

We, as a nation, can do better than this.

Are Emily and Greg More Employable Than Lakisha and Jamal?: A Field Experiment on Labor Market Discrimination

(2004)

Marianne Bertrand & Sendhil Mullainathan

E VERY MEASURE OF ECONOMIC SUCCESS REVEALS significant racial inequality in the U.S. labor market. Compared to Whites, African-Americans are twice as likely to be unemployed and earn nearly 25 percent less when they are employed (Council of Economic Advisers, 1998). This inequality has sparked a debate as to whether employers treat members of different races differentially. When faced with observably similar African-American and White applicants, do they favor the White one? Some argue yes, citing either employer prejudice or employer perception that race signals lower productivity. Others argue that differential treatment by race is a relic of the past, eliminated by some combination of employer enlightenment, affirmative action programs and the profit-maximization motive. In fact, many in this latter camp even feel that stringent enforcement of affirmative action programs has produced an environment of reverse discrimination. They would argue that faced with identical candidates, employers might favor the African-American one. Data limitations make it difficult to empirically test these views. Since researchers possess far less data than employers do, White and African-American workers that appear similar to researchers may look very different to employers. So any racial difference in labor market outcomes could just as easily be attributed to differences that are observable to employers but unobservable to researchers.

To circumvent this difficulty, we conduct a field experiment that builds on the correspondence testing methodology that has been primarily used in the past to study minority outcomes in the United Kingdom. We send resumes in response to help-wanted ads in Chicago and Boston newspapers and measure callback for interview for each sent resume. We experimentally manipulate perception of race via the name of the fictitious job applicant. We randomly assign very White-sounding names (such as

Emily Walsh or Greg Baker) to half the resumes and very African-American-sounding names (such as Lakisha Washington or Jamal Jones) to the other half. Because we are also interested in how credentials affect the racial gap in callback, we experimentally vary the quality of the resumes used in response to a given ad. Higher-quality applicants have on average a little more labor market experience and fewer holes in their employment history; they are also more likely to have an e-mail address, have completed some certification degree, possess foreign language skills, or have been awarded some honors. In practice, we typically send four resumes in response to each ad: two higher-quality and two lower-quality ones. We randomly assign to one of the higher- and one of the lower-quality resumes an African-American-sounding name. In total, we respond to over 1,300 employment ads in the sales, administrative support, clerical, and customer services job categories and send nearly 5,000 resumes. The ads we respond to cover a large spectrum of job quality, from cashier work at retail establishments and clerical work in a mail room, to office and sales management positions.

We find large racial differences in callback rates. Applicants with White names need to send about 10 resumes to get one callback whereas applicants with African-American names need to send about 15 resumes. This 50-percent gap in callback is statistically significant. A White name yields as many more callbacks as an additional eight years of experience on a resume. Since applicants' names are randomly assigned, this gap can only be attributed to the name manipulation.

Race also affects the reward to having a better resume. Whites with higher-quality resumes receive nearly 30-percent more callbacks than Whites with lower-quality resumes. On the other hand, having a higher-quality resume has a smaller effect for African-Americans. In other words, the gap between Whites and African-Americans widens with resume quality. While one may have expected improved credentials to alleviate employers' fear that African-American applicants are deficient in some unobservable skills, this is not the case in our data.

The experiment also reveals several other aspects of the differential treatment by race. First, since we randomly assign applicants' postal addresses to the resumes, we can study the effect of neighborhood of residence on the likelihood of callback. We find that living in a wealthier (or more educated or Whiter) neighborhood increases callback rates. But, interestingly, African-Americans are not helped more than Whites by living in a "better" neighborhood. Second, the racial gap we measure in different industries does not appear correlated to Census-based measures of the racial gap in wages. The same is true for the racial gap we measure in different occupations. In fact, we find that the racial gaps in callback are statistically indistinguishable across all the occupation and industry categories covered in the experiment. Federal contractors, who are thought to be more severely constrained by affirmative action laws, do not treat the African-American resumes more preferentially; neither do larger employers or employers who explicitly state that they are "Equal Opportunity Employers." In Chicago, we find a slightly smaller racial gap when employers are located in more African-American neighborhoods.[1]...

Interpretation

Three main sets of questions arise when interpreting the results above. First, does a higher callback rate for White applicants imply that employers are discriminating against African-Americans? Second, does our design only isolate the effect of race or is the name manipulation conveying some other factors than race? Third, how do our results relate to different models of racial discrimination?

Interpreting Callback Rates

Our results indicate that for two identical individuals engaging in an identical job search, the one with an African-American name would receive fewer interviews. Does differential treatment within our experiment imply that employers are discriminating against African-Americans (whether it is rational, prejudice-based, or other form of discrimination)? In other words, could the lower callback rate we record for African-American resumes *within our experiment* be consistent with a racially neutral review of the *entire pool* of resumes the surveyed employers receive?

In a racially neutral review process, employers would rank order resumes based on their quality and call back all applicants that are above a certain threshold. Because names are randomized, the White and African-American resumes we send should rank similarly on average. So, irrespective of the skill and racial composition of the applicant pool, a race-blind selection rule would generate equal treatment of Whites and African-Americans. So our results must imply that employers use race as a factor when reviewing resumes, which matches the legal definition of discrimination.

But even rules where employers are not trying to interview as few African-American applicants as possible may generate observed differential treatment in our experiment. One such hiring rule would be employers trying to interview a target level of African-American candidates. For example, perhaps the average firm in our experiment aims to produce an interview pool that matches the population base rate. This rule could produce the observed differential treatment if the average firm receives a higher proportion of African-American resumes than the population base rate because African-Americans disproportionately apply to the jobs and industries in our sample.

Some of our other findings may be consistent with such a rule. For example, the fact that "Equal Opportunity Employers" or federal contractors do not appear to discriminate any less may reflect the fact that such employers receive more applications

---

1   For further details on this experiment, see Bertrand and Mullainathan (2004).

from African-Americans. On the other hand, other key findings run counter to this rule. As we discuss above, we find no systematic difference in the racial gap in callback across occupational or industry categories, despite the large variation in the fraction of African-Americans looking for work in those categories. African-Americans are under-represented in managerial occupations, for example. If employers matched base rates in the population, the few African-Americans who apply to these jobs should receive a higher callback rate than Whites. Yet, we find that the racial gap in managerial occupations is the same as in all the other job categories. This rule also runs counter to our findings on returns to skill. Suppose firms are struggling to find White applicants but are overwhelmed with African-American ones. Then they should be less sensitive to the quality of White applicants (as they are trying to fill in their hiring quota for Whites) and much more sensitive to the quality of Black applicants (when they have so many to pick from). Thus, it is unlikely that the differential treatment we observe is generated by hiring rules such as these.

Potential Confounds

While the names we have used in this experiment strongly signal racial origin, they may also signal some other personal trait. More specifically, one might be concerned that employers are inferring social background from the personal name. When employers read a name like "Tyrone" or "Latoya," they may assume that the person comes from a disadvantaged background. In the extreme form of this social background interpretation, employers do not care at all about race but are discriminating only against the social background conveyed by the names we have chosen.

While plausible, we feel that some of our earlier results are hard to reconcile with this interpretation. For example, we found that while employers value "better" addresses, African-Americans are not helped more than Whites by living in Whiter or more educated neighborhoods. If the African-American names we have chosen mainly signal negative social background, one might have expected the estimated name gap to be lower for better addresses. Also, if the names mainly signal social background, one might have expected the name gap to be higher for jobs that rely more on soft skills or require more interpersonal interactions. We found no such evidence.

There is one final potential confound to our results. Perhaps what appears as a bias against African-Americans is actually the result of *reverse discrimination*. If qualified African-Americans are thought to be in high demand, then employers with average quality jobs might feel that an equally talented African-American would never accept an offer from them and thereby never call her or him in for an interview. Such an argument might also explain why African-Americans do not receive as strong a return as Whites to better resumes, since higher qualification only strengthens this argument. But this interpretation would suggest that among the better jobs, we ought to see evidence of reverse discrimination, or at least a smaller racial gap. However, we do not find any such evidence. The racial gap does not vary across jobs with different skill requirements, nor does it vary across occupation categories. Even among the better jobs in our sample, we find that employers significantly favor applicants with White names.

Relation to Existing Theories

What do these results imply for existing models of discrimination? Economic theories of discrimination can be classified into two main categories: taste-based and statistical discrimination models. Both sets of models can obviously "explain" our average racial gap in callbacks. But can these models explain our other findings? More specifically, we discuss the relevance of these models with a focus on two of the facts that have been uncovered in this paper: (i) the lower returns to credentials for African-Americans; (ii) the relative uniformity of the race gap across occupations, job requirements and, to a lesser extent, employer characteristics and industries.

Taste-based models (Gary S. Becker, 1961) differ in whose prejudiced "tastes" they emphasize: customers, coworkers, or employers. Customer and co-worker discrimination models seem at odds with the lack of significant variation of the racial gap by occupation and industry categories, as the amount of customer contact and the fraction of White employees vary quite a lot across these categories. We do not find a larger racial gap among jobs that explicitly require "communication skills" and jobs for which we expect either customer or coworker contacts to be higher (retail sales for example).

Because we do not know what drives employer tastes, employer discrimination models could be consistent with the lack of occupation and industry variation. Employer discrimination also matches the finding that employers located in more African-American neighborhoods appear to discriminate somewhat less. However, employer discrimination models would struggle to explain why African-Americans get relatively lower returns to their credentials. Indeed, the cost of indulging the discrimination taste should increase as the minority applicants' credentials increase.

Statistical discrimination models are the prominent alternative to the taste-based models in the economics literature. In one class of statistical discrimination models, employers use (observable) race to proxy for *unobservable* skills (e.g., Edmund S. Phelps, 1972; Kenneth J. Arrow, 1973). This class of models struggle to explain the credentials effect as well. Indeed, the added credentials should lead to a larger update for African-Americans and hence greater returns to skills for that group.

A second class of statistical discrimination models "emphasize the precision of the information that employers have about individual productivity" (Altonji and Blank, 1999). Specifically, in these models, employers believe that the same observable signal is more precise for Whites than for African-Americans (Dennis J. Aigner and Glenn G. Cain, 1977; Shelly J. Lundberg and Richard Startz, 1983; Bradford Cornell and Ivo Welch, 1996). Under such models, African-Americans receive lower returns to observable skills because employers place less weight on these skills. However, how reasonable is this interpretation for our experiment? First, it is important to note that we are using the same set of resume characteristics for both racial groups. So the lower precision of information for African-Americans cannot be that, for example, an employer does not know what a high school degree from a very African-American neighborhood means (as in Aigner and Cain, 1977). Second, many of the credentials on the resumes are in fact externally and easily verifiable, such as a certification for a specific software.

An alternative version of these models would rely on bias in the observable signal rather than differential variance or noise of these signals by race. Perhaps the skills of African-Americans are discounted because affirmative action makes it easier for African-Americans to get these skills. While this is plausible for credentials such as an employee-of-the-month honor, it is unclear why this would apply to more verifiable and harder skills. It is equally unclear why work experience would be less rewarded since our study suggests that getting a job is more, not less, difficult for African-Americans.

The uniformity of the racial gap across occupations is also troubling for a statistical discrimination interpretation. Numerous factors that should affect the level of statistical discrimination, such as the importance of unobservable skills, the observability of qualifications, the precision of observable skills and the ease of performance measurement, may vary quite a lot across occupations.

This discussion suggests that perhaps other models may do a better job at explaining our findings. One simple alternative model is lexicographic search by employers. Employers receive so many resumes that they may use quick heuristics in reading these resumes. One such heuristic could be to simply read no further when they see an African-American name. Thus they may never see the skills of African-American candidates and this could explain why these skills are not rewarded. This might also to some extent explain the uniformity of the race gap since the screening process (i.e., looking through a large set of resumes) may be quite similar across the variety of jobs we study.

Conclusion

This paper suggests that African-Americans face differential treatment when searching for jobs and this may still be a factor in why they do poorly in the labor market. Job applicants with African-American names get far fewer callbacks for each resume they send out. Equally importantly, applicants with African-American names find it hard to overcome this hurdle in callbacks by improving their observable skills or credentials.

Taken at face value, our results on differential returns to skill have possibly import-ant policy implications. They suggest that training programs alone may not be enough to alleviate the racial gap in labor market outcomes. For training to work, some gener-al-equilibrium force outside the context of our experiment would have to be at play. In fact, if African-Americans recognize how employers reward their skills, they may ratio-nally be less willing than Whites to even participate in these programs.

References

Aigner, Dennis J. and Cain, Glenn G. "Statistical Theories of Discrimination in Labor Markets." *Industrial and Labor Relations Review,* January 1977, 30(1), pp. 175–87.

Altonji, Joseph G. and Blank, Rebecca M. "Race and Gender in the Labor Market," in Orley Ashenfelter and David Card, eds., *Handbook of labor economics,* Vol. 30. Amsterdam: North-Holland, 1999, pp. 3143–259.

Arrow, Kenneth, J. "The Theory of Discrimination," in Orley Ashenfelter and Albert Rees, eds., *Discrimination in labor markets.* Princeton, NJ: Princeton University Press, 1973, pp. 3–33.

Becker, Gary S. *The economics of discrimination,* 2nd Ed. Chicago: University of Chicago Press, 1961.

Bertrand, Marianne and Sendhil Mullainathan. "Are Emily and Greg More Employable Than Lakisha and Jamal? A Field Experiment on Labor Market Discrimination." *American Economic Review* 94 (September 2004): 991–1013.

Cornell, Bradford and Welch, Ivo. "Culture, Information, and Screening Discrimination." *Journal of Political Economy,* June 1996, 104(3), pp. 542–71.

Council of Economic Advisers. *Changing America: Indicators of social and economic well-being by race and Hispanic origin.* September 1998, http://w3.access.gpo.gov/eop/ca/pdfs/ca.pdf.

Lundberg, Shelly J. and Starz, Richard. "Private Discrimination and Social Intervention in Competitive Labor Market." *American Economic Review,* June 1983, 73(3), pp. 340–47.

Phelps, Edmund S. "The Statistical Theory of Racism and Sexism." *American Economic Review,* September 1972, 62(4), pp. 659–61.

Racial Disparities at Birth: The Puzzle Persists

(2008)

Paula Braveman

A BABY BORN TO AN AFRICAN-AMERICAN (BLACK) mother in the United States is twice as likely to die before reaching her first birthday as a baby born to a European-American (white) mother. A range of conditions contribute to infant mortality, but the most powerful predictors are being born too early (before 37 completed weeks of pregnancy) and/or too small (with a birth weight of less than 2,500 grams). Black infants are two to three times as likely as their white counterparts to be born prematurely and/or with low birth weight. Premature or low-birth weight infants who survive beyond infancy are far more likely than other infants to suffer major developmental problems, including cognitive, behavioral, and physical deficits during childhood, with lasting consequences in adulthood. They also have poorer prospects for employment and wages as adults. Prematurity and low birth weight (together referred to as adverse birth outcomes) also predict poor adult health, including diabetes, high blood pressure, and heart disease, all of which raise risks of disability and premature mortality. Caregiving to chronically ill and/or disabled survivors of adverse birth outcomes is a tremendous economic burden on families and society.

A growing body of research has been conducted in recent years into the causes of the racial disparities. The research has examined a wide range of possible factors, including differences in prenatal care, differences in women's health before they become pregnant, and infections. This research has produced useful insights but has not identified a clear cause for racial disparities. More recently, researchers have hypothesized a role for stress and adverse experiences throughout life, not just during pregnancy, as possible explanations. Much greater research investment is necessary if we are going to solve the puzzle of why racial disparities in birth outcomes persist.

At least in one major area there is now a strong scientific consensus: Differences in prenatal care are unlikely to explain racial disparities in prematurity and low birth weight. Black/white disparities in receipt of prenatal care have narrowed markedly over time, particularly with major expansions of Medicaid maternity care coverage beginning around 1990, without concomitant narrowing of birth-outcome disparities. In addition, a number of studies have failed to link prenatal care, as typically provided in the United States, to improved birth outcomes in general. The literature is inconclusive regarding effects on birth outcomes of prenatal care enhanced with various forms of psychosocial support; few studies have been conducted that meet rigorous criteria.

Given the scientific consensus that standard prenatal care does not hold much hope for reducing racial disparities in birth outcomes, there has been an increasing interest in focusing on the health of women before they become pregnant, including ensuring access to medical care for chronic conditions. It seems unrealistic to think that medical care given during a nine-month or shorter period could dramatically reverse the adverse effects of a lifetime of experience before conception. It also seems unlikely that medical care alone in the period before conception could reverse the effects of a lifetime of social disadvantage.

Well-established causes of being born too small or too early—without consideration of racial disparities—include prenatal exposure to tobacco, excessive alcohol, or illicit drugs; being underweight at the beginning of pregnancy and gaining insufficient weight during pregnancy; very short maternal stature; and chronic diseases. The known causes of low birth weight and/or preterm birth, however, do not explain the black/white disparities; studies taking these factors into consideration have not seen a narrowing of the racial gap in outcomes. For example, black women are less likely to smoke or to binge drink during pregnancy and less likely to be underweight before pregnancy than are white women.

Several factors have been hypothesized to explain birth-outcome differences by race. Among the more widely held hypotheses has been the notion that occult (hidden) infections may explain the racial gap. Rates of infection with bacterial vaginosis, a genital tract infection previously thought to be benign but recently associated with adverse birth outcomes, are higher among African-American women, as are periodontal infections. Although many clinicians have been optimistic that infections would turn out to be an important and relatively easily modifiable missing piece of the puzzle, treating infections has not consistently led to improved birth outcomes. This suggests that rather than infections being a cause of adverse birth outcomes, they may be a marker for some other factor or factors that are associated with both infections and adverse birth outcomes.

There has been a widespread assumption, without evidence, that genetic differences are the key to the black/white disparity in birth outcomes. In part, this assumption has rested on the observation that the black/white birth-outcome disparities have persisted even after taking into account mothers' educational attainment or family income around the time of pregnancy. However, no one has identified a gene or genes that are clearly linked to either prematurity or low birth weight, and the mechanisms involved appear different for the two outcomes and complex for both. It is likely that if genetic differences are involved in either, they would involve complex arrays or cascades of multiple genetic factors very unlikely to sort themselves out according to race. Although it is possible that genetic factors, particularly gene/environment interactions, could be involved, a primary role for genes is not supported by observed social patterns, which are discussed below.

Furthermore, current income and education reflect only a small part of the socioeconomic experiences of a woman, which could affect her birth outcomes through a range of biological and behavioral pathways. For example, among U.S. blacks and whites overall, the median net worth of whites ($86,573) is almost 4 times that of blacks ($22,914). In the bottom quintile of income, the median net worth of whites ($24,000) is 400 times that of blacks ($57). Wealth is probably more important than income for health because it can buffer the effects of temporarily low income, providing security as well as a higher standard of living. Furthermore, a black woman of a given educational or income level is far more likely than her similar-education-or-income white counterpart to have experienced lower socioeconomic circumstances when growing up. She also is far more likely to live (and to have lived in the past) in a neighborhood with adverse socioeconomic conditions, such as exposure to environmental toxins, crime, lack of sources of healthy foods and safe places to exercise, and/or poor-quality housing. There are many unmeasured socioeconomic differences between blacks and whites even in studies considering income and education; such studies should not but unfortunately often do conclude that observed racial differences must be genetic since they have "controlled for socioeconomic status."

Social patterns may give us valuable clues to the unsolved mystery of black/white disparities in birth outcomes. For example, although birth outcomes consistently improve with higher education or income, the relative disparities are largest among more affluent, better-educated women: nearly a threefold difference in our data from California and also observed to be large in national data. The racial disparity is also seen among poor and uneducated women, but it is much smaller, closer to 1.3 in 1 in recent study. Why would the racial disparity be greater among higher-socioeconomic status (SES) women? It is unlikely that higher-SES black women are genetically more different from their white counterparts than are lower-SES women. (This issue is discussed further below.)

Comparisons among black women according to birthplace may also provide important clues to likely and unlikely causes of the disparities in birth outcomes. Mirroring what has been called the "Hispanic paradox" of good birth outcomes for immigrant Hispanic women (despite poverty) and poor birth outcomes of their U.S.-born daughters (whose income and education levels are generally higher around the time of childbirth than those of their immigrant mothers), black immigrants also have better birth outcomes than U.S.-born black women. In contrast to the unfavorable (compared to whites) birth outcomes of black women born and raised in the United States, birth outcomes among black immigrants from Africa and the Caribbean are relatively favorable, especially after considering their income and education. As with the comparison of racial disparities in different socioeconomic groups noted above, it is very difficult to explain this disparity by maternal birthplace with genetic differences. If the basis for the differences in birth outcomes by maternal birthplace were genetic, one would expect the immigrants (presumably with a heavier "dose" of the adverse genes) to have worse outcomes, not better.

It makes scientific sense to focus on social advantage and disadvantage as plausible contributors to black/white disparities in birth outcomes.

Stress: A key piece of the puzzle?

In the past 15 to 20 years, knowledge has accumulated about the physiologic effects of stress, particularly chronic stress, in explaining racial differences in birth outcomes. Chronic stress could lead to adverse birth outcomes through neuroendocrine pathways. Neuroendocrine and sympathetic nervous system changes caused by stress could result in vascular and/or immune and inflammatory effects that could lead to premature delivery as well as inadequate fetal nutrition. Living in a crime-ridden neighborhood and facing constant pressures to cope with inadequate resources for housing, child care, transportation, and feeding and raising one's family are stressful, but such factors are rarely measured. Racial disparities in wealth and income are likely to translate into racial disparities in social networks that can provide financial and other material support during times of need. A growing body of literature on the health effects of subjective social status suggests that an awareness that one is in a group considered socially inferior could be a stressor with strong health effects.

Studies of stress as a possible contributor to adverse birth outcomes have not produced consistent findings. They have, however, tended to focus on stress experienced during pregnancy, rather than chronic stress across a woman's lifetime, despite the fact that current knowledge of the health effects of stress makes chronic (rather than acute) stress far more plausible as a causal factor in racial disparities in health. It could be a key mediator of many of the unmeasured socioeconomic factors that vary by race, including childhood socioeconomic adversity and neighborhood socioeconomic conditions.

It is biologically plausible that experiences associated with a legacy of racial discrimination are another potential source of unmeasured stress that may contribute to black/white disparities in birth outcomes, and some studies have demonstrated this connection. Incidents of overt racism against African-Americans in the United States are still pervasive, although probably becoming less frequent over time. More subtle experiences associated with racism, however, also could be stressful; for example, a constant awareness and state of arousal in anticipation of racist comments, whether subtle or overt, being made in one's workplace could be stressful. Vicarious experiences related to fears about one's children or other family members facing discrimination; or a background awareness of the long history of discrimination, including slavery, experienced by blacks in general; are other potential sources of chronic stress that also could exact a health toll, including on birth outcomes, even in the absence of overt incidents. The literature in this area is in the very early stages of development, and the results are not consistent; better measures of experiences of racism are needed to advance knowledge of the potential health effects of discrimination in various forms, not only dramatic overt incidents.

Could experiences of racism account for the counterintuitive finding of a greater racial disparity in birth outcomes among more affluent and educated women? One can only speculate, but unmeasured differences in socioeconomic factors during life appear to be a possibility, along with experiences related to racial discrimination. Unmeasured socioeconomic exposures (for example, in childhood and/or at the neighborhood level) could influence birth outcomes through pathways involving nutritional effects, exposure to toxins, and other adverse exposures related to low socioeconomic status, as well as stress. Paradoxically, a more educated black woman may, on a chronic basis, experience more discrimination and more constant awareness and fears of it, because she is far more likely than her less educated black counterpart to be working, playing, shopping, and traveling in a predominantly white world.

Implications for action

Given the staggering influence of birth outcomes on health during lifetimes, far more investment is needed in understanding the mechanisms that explain prematurity and low birth weight and racial disparities in them. Far more research is needed on social and psychological influences on birth outcomes, on how they are mediated biologically, and on how to intervene even before we completely understand all of the mechanisms at the molecular level. We have no firm answers now (except perhaps firm indications about some disproven explanations), but we have some very plausible hypotheses that require testing under a range of circumstances. Among the biologically plausible hypotheses are a major role for stress and adversity experienced throughout life, not only during pregnancy, which would mean that intervening during pregnancy may be too little and too late. Unmeasured experiences in early childhood and across a woman's life before conception could be important sources of stress that could explain racial disparities. These experiences could include unmeasured socioeconomic factors at the neighborhood and family levels as well as experiences related to racial discrimination and awareness of it, even in the absence of dramatic overt incidents. Gene/environment interactions cannot be ruled out as contributors to racial disparities in birth outcomes. If these interactions were involved, however, they would be very complex; biomedical solutions are not on the horizon at present and in any case would be a long way off, making it important to make vigorous efforts to identify and modify the triggers for the disparity in the social and physical environments. It makes scientific sense to focus on social advantage and disadvantage—including not only socioeconomic factors but also potentially subtle, chronically stressful experiences related to our legacy of racial discrimination—as plausible contributors to black/white disparities in birth outcomes. Even without definitive proof of their role in birth-outcome disparities, there are compelling ethical and human rights reasons to direct our attention to eliminating the profound and longstanding differences in social conditions that still break down along lines of skin color.

Becoming American: Identity Formation

(2009)

Min Zhou

Asian American versus Chinese American Identity

Post-1965 immigration has changed America's face. The U.S. population was 68 percent non-Hispanic white, 12 percent non-Hispanic black, 15 percent Hispanic, and 4 percent Asian at the dawn of the twenty-first century (compared with 80 percent white, 12 percent black, 6 percent Hispanic, and 1.5 percent Asian in 1980). It is projected that by the year 2050, the nation's face will be 51 percent white, 16 percent black, 24 percent Hispanic, and 8 percent Asian. In California, the concept of "white majority" no longer holds. The state's population as of 2006 was 43 percent non-Hispanic white, 6 percent non-Hispanic black, 36 percent Latino, and 12 percent Asian; and this single state concentrates about 30 percent of the nation's Hispanic population and 34 percent of the Asian-origin population (including a third of its Chinese Americans).[1] Not surprisingly, concerns about assimilation once again occupy a central place in public and academic discourse.

Just as the offspring of Irish, Italian, Jewish, and Polish immigrants are dropping their ethnic hyphens to melt into the indistinguishable category "white," we have seen new hyphens emerging in the American ethnic scene in the past few decades. These new hyphens are often based on racialized groupings beyond black and white (i.e., Latino, Chicano, and Asian), or on non-European national origins (Mexican, Chinese, Japanese, Korean, Filipino, Vietnamese, and Indian). Chinese Americans, like other Americans of Asian origin, are often lumped into a broad racial category of "Asian," as opposed to "white," "black," or "Hispanic," in official statistics. Unlike the racialized identity imposed upon Asian-origin Americans, however, "Asian American" is a self-empowering political identity. The term "Asian American" was coined by the late historian and

---

1   California—ACS Demographic and Housing Estimates from the 2006 American Community Survey, http://factfinder.census.gov/.

activist Yuji Ichioka during the ethnic consciousness movements of the late 1960s. To adopt this identity is to reject the western-imposed label of "Oriental."[2]

Before 1970, the Asian-origin population in the United States was largely made up of Chinese, Japanese, and Filipinos. Today, Americans of Chinese and Filipino ancestries are the largest subgroups (at 3.6 million and 3 million, respectively), followed by Indians, Koreans, Vietnamese, and Japanese (at more than one million). Some 20 other national-origin groups, such as Cambodians, Pakistanis, Lao, Thai, Indonesians, and Bangladeshis, were officially counted in government statistics only after 1980, and together amounted to more than 2 million residents at the dawn of the twenty-first century. Currently, about 60 percent of the Asian-origin population is foreign-born (the first generation); another 28 percent are U.S.-born of foreign-born parents (the second generation); and just 12 percent are born to U.S.-born parents (the third generation and beyond). The only exception to this pattern are Japanese Americans, who have a fourth generation and many U.S.-born elderly.

"Asian American" is now an umbrella category that includes both U.S. citizens and immigrants whose ancestors came from Asia east of Pakistan. However, differences in national origins, timing of immigration, affluence, and settlement patterns profoundly affect the formation of a stable panethnic identity. For example, recent arrivals are less likely than those born or raised in the United States to identify as Asian American. They are also so busy settling in that they have little time to think about being Asian or Asian American, or, for that matter, white. Their diverse origins evoke drastic differences in languages and dialects, religions, foodways, and customs. Many nationalities also brought to America their histories of conflict (such as the Japanese colonization of Korea and Taiwan, the Japanese invasion of China, and the Chinese armed conflict with Vietnam). Immigrants who are predominantly middle-class professionals (such as the Taiwanese and Indians) or predominantly small business owners (such as the Koreans) share few concerns and priorities with those who are predominantly uneducated, low-skilled refugees (such as Cambodians and Hmong). Finally, Asian-origin people living in San Francisco or Los Angeles among many other Asians and self-conscious Asian Americans develop sharper ethnic sensitivities than those living in, say, Latin-dominant Miami or white-dominant Minneapolis. A politician might get away with calling Asians "Orientals" in Miami but would get into big trouble in San Francisco. All of these differences can create obstacles to fostering a cohesive pan-Asian solidarity. As Yen Le Espiritu shows in her research, pan-Asianism is primarily a political ideology of U.S.-born, American-educated, and middle-class Asians rather than of Asian

---

2   Louie, "Searching for Roots in Contemporary China and Chinese America"; Wong and Chan, *Claiming America*; Yu, "The 'Oriental Problem' in America, 1920–1960."

immigrants, who are conscious of their national origins and overburdened with their daily struggles for survival.[3]

Although it is widely used in public discussions, most Asian-origin Americans are ambivalent about this label. Their reservations reflect the difficulty of being American and still keeping some ethnic identity: is one, for example, Asian American or Chinese American? In their private lives, few Americans of Chinese ancestry would spontaneously identify themselves as Asian or Asian American. They instead link their identities to specific places or ethnic origins, such as Chinese, Taiwanese, Cantonese, Fujianese, Hakka (Kejia), and so on. Although some Chinese Americans have family histories in the United States longer than those of many Americans of eastern or southern European origin, Chinese Americans as an ethnic group became numerous only after the passage of the Hart-Celler Act of 1965. According to the U.S. Citizenship and Immigration Services (USCIS), the United States admitted approximately 17 million immigrants between 1971 and 1995, matching the scale of the "old" immigration of the first quarter of the twentieth century (17.2 million between 1901 and 1925), and another 8.8 million between 1996 and 2005. About 1.7 million from China, Hong Kong, and Taiwan were admitted as permanent residents between 1970 and 2006.[4] High rates of contemporary immigration will continue to influence the identity formation of Chinese Americans, who are members of the nation's oldest immigrant group.

What Does It Mean to Be White?

In the United States, "white" is an arbitrary label having more to do with privilege than biology. Historically, some ethnic groups initially considered nonwhite, such as the Irish, Italians, and Jews, have attained membership in the "white" race by acquiring status and wealth. It is hardly surprising, then, that nonwhites would aspire to becoming "white" as a mark of and a tool for material success. However, becoming white can mean distancing oneself from "people of color" or selling out one's ethnicity. Panethnic identities—Asian American, African American, Hispanic American—are one way in which the politically vocal in these respective groups try to stem defections; yet these collective identities may restrain aspirations for individual mobility.

---

3   Espiritu, *Asian American Panethnicity*; Lien, "Homeland Origins and Political Identities among Chinese in Southern California"; Okamoto, "Toward a Theory of Panethnicity"; Zia, *Asian American Dream*.

4   The number was 716,916 between 1960 and 1989; 591,599 between 1990 and 1999; and 460,678 between 2000 and 2006. In comparison, the total number of Chinese immigrants legally admitted into the United States from 1850 to 1959 was 424,897, based on country of last residence. U.S. Department of Homeland Security, *Yearbook of Immigration Statistics: 2007*, table 2; see http://www.dhs.gov/ximgtn/statistics/publications/LPR07.shtm.

Are Chinese Americans becoming white? For many public officials, the answer to this question must be positive, because they classify Chinese (and other Asian) Americans with European-origin Americans for equal-opportunity programs; neither group is underrepresented, as blacks, Latinos, and American Indians are. But this answer is premature and based on false premises. Although Asian Americans as a group have attained the level of career and financial success equated with being white, and although many have moved near to or even married whites, they remain culturally distinct and suspect in a white society.

The paradox of Asian Americans being celebrated as a "model minority" while simultaneously viewed as "perpetual foreigners" is a case in point. The "model minority" image surfaced during World War II and became crystallized in the popular media in the mid-1960s, at the peak of the civil rights and ethnic consciousness movements but *before* the rising waves of immigration and the refugee influx from Asia.[5] Two articles from 1966—"Success Story, Japanese-American Style," by William Petersen in the *New York Times Magazine*, and "Success of One Minority Group in U.S.," by the *U.S. News & World Report* staff—marked a significant departure from the traditional depiction of Asian immigrants and their descendants in the media.[6] Both articles extolled Japanese and Chinese Americans for their persistence in overcoming extreme hardships and discrimination to achieve a level of success unmatched even by U.S.-born whites, through "their own almost totally unaided effort" and with "no help from anyone else," winning wealth and respect in American society through hard work, family solidarity, discipline, delayed gratification, nonconfrontation, and eschewing welfare.

The model-minority stereotype buttresses the myth that the United States is devoid of racism and accords equal opportunity to all, so that those who lag behind do so because of their own poor choices and inferior culture. Celebrating this model minority can help thwart other racial minorities' demands for social justice, pitting minority groups against each other. It can also pit Asian Americans against whites. On the surface, Asian Americans seem to be on their way to becoming white, just like the offspring of earlier European immigrants. But the model-minority image implicitly casts Asian Americans as different from whites. By placing Asian Americans above whites, it sets them apart from other Americans, white or nonwhite, in the public mind.

"What's wrong with being a model minority?" asked a black student in a class I taught on race. "I'd rather be in the model minority than in the downtrodden minority that nobody respects." Let me point to two less obvious effects. Whether people are in a model minority or a downtrodden minority, they are judged by a *different* standard. The

---

5   The model minority image began to take shape during World War II. See Wong, "From Pariah to Paragon." Also see Lee, *Orientals*.

6   See also Petersen, *Japanese Americans*.

model-minority stereotype holds Asian Americans to higher standards than average Americans. And it places particular expectations on members of the group so labeled, channeling them into specific avenues of success, such as science and engineering, and unintentionally reinforcing barriers for Asian Americans pursuing careers outside these designated fields. Falling into this trap, a Chinese immigrant father might be upset if his son told him that he had decided to change his major from engineering to English. Disregarding his son's passion and talent for creative writing, the father would rationalize his concern: "You have a 90 percent chance of getting a decent job with an engineering degree, but what chance would you have of earning income as a writer?" This rationale reflects more than the simple parental concern over career choices typical of middle-class families; it constitutes the self-fulfilling prophecy of a stereotype.

In the end, the celebration of Asian Americans as a model minority is based on the judgment that many Asian Americans perform at levels above the American average, which sets them apart not only from other minorities but also from whites. The truth of the matter is that the larger-than-average size of the middle and upper-middle class in some Asian-origin groups, such as the Chinese, Indians, and Koreans, paves the way for the immigrants and their offspring to regain their middle-class status in the new homeland. The financial resources that immigrants bring with them to this country also help build viable ethnic economies and institutions, such as private afterschool programs, that help the less fortunate members of the group to move ahead in society much faster than they would without these ethnic resources.

"It's Not So Much Being White as Being American"

> I never asked to be white. I am not literally white. That is, I do not have white skin or white ancestors. I have yellow skin and yellow ancestors, hundreds of generations of them. But like so many other Asian Americans of the second generation, I find myself now the bearer of a strange new status: white, by acclamation. Thus it is that I have been described as an "honorary white," by other whites, and as a "banana" by other Asians ... to the extent that I have moved away from the periphery and toward the center of American life, I have become white inside.—Eric Liu[7]

Many Chinese immigrants and their U.S.-born or -raised children seem to accept that "white" is mainstream, average, and normal, and they look to whites as their frame of reference for attaining a higher social position. Similarly, researchers often use

---

7   Liu, *The Accidental Asian*, p. 34.

non-Hispanic whites as the standard of comparison for other groups, even though there is great diversity among whites, too. Like most immigrants to the United States, Chinese immigrants tend to believe in the American dream and measure their achievements in material terms. Those with sufficient education, job skills, and money move into white middle-class suburban neighborhoods immediately upon arrival, while others work intensively to accumulate enough savings to move their families up and out of the old inner-city China-towns. Consequently, many children of contemporary Chinese immigrants spend their entire childhood in white communities, make friends with mostly white peers, and grow up speaking only English. In fact, Chinese Americans are one of the most acculturated non-European groups in the United States. By the second generation, most have lost fluency in their parents' native languages.[8] Chinese Americans also intermarry extensively with whites and with members of other minority groups.[9]

Yet U.S.-born or -raised Chinese Americans may be more ambivalent about becoming white than their immigrant parents. Many are cynical about the equation of "white" with "American." Although they recognize whites as a frame of reference, many children of Asian immigrants reject the idea of becoming white themselves: "It's not so much being white as being American," commented a Korean American student in my class on the new second generation. This aversion to becoming white is particularly common among well-educated and privileged second-generation college students who have taken ethnic studies courses, and among Asian American community activists. However, most of the second generation continues to strive for the privileged status associated with whiteness, just like their parents. For example, most U.S.-born or -raised Chinese American youths end up studying engineering, medicine, or law, believing that these areas of study guarantee well-paid jobs and middle-class lives, as well as enhancing social contact with whites.

Chinese Americans are also more conscious of the disadvantages associated with being nonwhite than their parents, who as immigrants tend to be optimistic about overcoming disadvantages. A second-generation Chinese American in her sixties succinctly described the situation in these words: "The truth is, no matter how American you think you are or try to be, you do not look *American*. If you have almond-shaped eyes, straight black hair, and a yellow complexion, you are a foreigner by default. People will ask where you come from but won't be satisfied until they hear you name a foreign country, and they will naturally compliment your perfect English. So you can certainly

---

8   Lopez, "Language Assimilation"; Portes, "English-Only Triumphs, but the Costs are High."
9   Kibria, "The Construction of 'Asian American'"; Lee and Bean, "America's Changing Color Lines"; Liang and Ito, "Intermarriage of Asian Americans in the New York City Region"; Sung, *Chinese American Intermarriage*; Wong, "A Look at Intermarriage among the Chinese in the United States in 1980."

be as good as or even better than whites, but you will never become accepted as white."[10] These remarks echo a common frustration among second-generation Asian Americans, who detest being treated as immigrants or foreigners. Their experience suggests that whitening has more to do with the beliefs of white America than with the actual situation of Asian Americans. Speaking perfect English, effortlessly adopting mainstream cultural values, and even marrying members of the dominant group may help reduce this "otherness" at the individual level, but it has little effect on the group as a whole. New stereotypes can emerge and un-whiten Asian Americans anytime and anywhere, no matter how "successful" and "assimilated" they have become. Congressman David Wu's story, quoted at the beginning of this chapter, is illustrative.

The stereotype of the "honorary white" or model minority goes hand in hand with that of the perpetual foreigner. At this point in time, Chinese Americans, like their Asian American peers, are in an ambivalent position as nonwhite and nonblack.[11] Globalization and U.S.-China relations, combined with continually high rates of immigration, affect how Chinese Americans are perceived in American society and how they evaluate themselves in relation to members of other racial and ethnic minorities, as well as their coethnics in China and the Chinese Diaspora.[12] Most of the historical stereotypes, such as the "yellow peril" and "Fu Manchu," have found their way into contemporary American life. Consider the murder of Vincent Chin, a Chinese American mistaken for Japanese and beaten to death by a disgruntled white auto worker in the 1980s; the trial of Wen Ho Lee, a nuclear scientist suspected of spying for the Chinese government in the mid-1990s; the 1996 presidential campaign finance scandal, which implicated Asian Americans in funneling foreign contributions to the Clinton campaign; and, in 2001, the Abercrombie & Fitch tee-shirts that depicted Chinese cartoon characters in stereotypically negative ways—with slanted eyes, thick glasses, and the Qing queue (a long pigtail at the back of the head).[13] The ambivalent, conditional nature of white acceptance of Chinese Americans prompts them to organize panethnically to fight back—which consequently heightens their racial distinctiveness. So becoming white or not may be beside the point, since Chinese Americans, like other Asian Americans, still constantly

---

10 Personal communication with a retired Chinatown activist in New York.

11 Wu, *Yellow*.

12 Chan, *Chinese American Transnationalism*; Koehn and Yin, *The Expanding Roles of Chinese Americans in U.S.-China Relations*; Lien, "Transnational Homeland Concerns and Participation in U.S. Politics"; Ma and Cartier, *The Chinese Diaspora*.

13 The Qing queue was a symbol of Han Chinese submission to the Qing dynasty ruled by the Manchus and was cut at the downfall of the Qing empire in 1912, but it became a feature of racist caricatures in the United States long after that date. See also Lee, *My Country Versus Me*; Lee and Zhou, "Conclusion"; Stober and Hoffman, *A Convenient Spy*; Wang, "Class, Race, Citizenship, and Extraterritoriality"; Wu, *Yellow*.

have to prove that they are truly loyal Americans, especially in situations where U.S.-China relations are in the spotlight.[14]

Ironically, it is the very fact that Asian Americans are assimilated but conditionally accepted that prompts them to organize on the basis of ethnicity. In the end, this Asian paradox overlaps the paradox of assimilation. In order to advance to the rank of average Americans, the first generation chooses the ethnic way and succeeds. In order to fight the negative stereotype of perpetual foreigners, the "assimilated" second generation falls back on ethnicity and ethnic self-consciousness for empowerment. Their ethnic strategy, which is qualitatively different from the one adopted by their parents, is effective: that is, becoming assimilated via the ethnic way and becoming American by becoming ethnic.[15]

Conclusion

The Chinese way, or the ethnic way, may not fit all Asian-origin groups, much less non-Asian groups, because of the different contexts and circumstances under which immigrants leave their various old countries and are received on American soil. In order to reach the goal in the race for social mobility, every group must find its own strategies and its own path. The truth is that ignorant and stupid bigots may still shout hysterically at Chinese Americans to "go back to China," but they cannot stop Chinese Americans, or any other "foreign-looking" groups, from making equal claims on this land they call home. As American society becomes increasingly multiethnic, and as ethnic communities and ethnic Americans become integral components of the society, the time will come, sooner or later, when the ethnic way is accepted as the American way. Whether "assimilation" is a meaningful concept remains arguable. After all, Chinatown and ethnic distinctiveness are quintessentially American.

Bibliography

Chan, Sucheng., ed. *Chinese American Transnationalism: The Flow of People, Resources, and Ideas between China and America during the Exclusion Era*. Philadelphia: Temple University Press, 2005.

---

14 Kibria, "The Construction of 'Asian American'"; Koehn and Yin, *The Expanding Roles of Chinese Americans in U.S.-China Relations*; Lien, "Transnational Homeland Concerns and Participation in U.S. Politics"; Lien, "Homeland Origins and Political Identities among Chinese in Southern California"; Wang, "The Structure of Dual Domination"; Wang, *The Dust That Never Settles*.

15 Kibria, *Becoming Asian American*; Louie, "Searching for Roots in Contemporary China and Chinese America"; Tuan, *Forever Foreigner or Honorary White?*; Tung, *Chinese Americans and Their Immigrant Parents*.

Espiritu, Yen Le. *Asian American Panethnicity: Bridging Institutions and Identities*. Philadelphia: Temple University Press, 1993.

Kibria, Nazli. *Becoming Asian American: Second-Generation Chinese and Korean American Identities*. Baltimore: Johns Hopkins University Press, 2002.

———. "The Construction of 'Asian American': Reflections on Intermarriage and Ethnic Identity among Second-Generation Chinese and Korean Americans." *Ethnic and Racial Studies* 20 (1997): 522–544.

Koehn, Peter H., and Xiaohuang Yin. *The Expanding Roles of Chinese Americans in U.S.-China Relations*. Armonk, NY: M. E. Sharpe, 2002.

Lee, Jennifer, and Frank D. Bean. "America's Changing Color Lines." *Annual Review of Sociology* 30 (2004): 221–242.

Lee, Jennifer, and Min Zhou. "Conclusion: Reflection, Thoughts, and Directions for Future Research." In Jennifer Lee and Min Zhou, eds., *Asian American Youth: Culture, Identity, and Ethnicity*. New York: Routledge, 2004. Pp. 313–324.

Lee, Robert G. *Orientals: Asian Americans in Popular Culture*. Philadelphia: Temple University Press, 1999.

Lee, Wen Ho (with Helen Zia). *My Country Versus Me*. New York: Hyperion, 2001.

Liang, Zai, and Naomi Ito. "Intermarriage of Asian Americans in the New York City Region: Contemporary Patterns and Future Prospects." *International Migration Review* 33 (1999): 876–900.

Lien, Pei-te. "Homeland Origins and Political Identities among Chinese in Southern California." *Ethnic and Racial Studies* 31 (2008): 1381–1403.

———. "Transnational Homeland Concerns and Participation in U.S. Politics: A Comparison among Immigrants from China, Taiwan, and Hong Kong." *Journal of Chinese Overseas* 2 (2006): 56–78.

Liu, Eric. *The Accidental Asian: Notes of a Native Speaker*. New York: Vintage Books, 1998.

Lopez, David. "Language Assimilation." In Roger Waldinger and Mehdi Bozorgmehr, eds., *Ethnic Los Angeles*. New York: Russell Sage Foundation, 1996. Pp. 139–163.

Louie, Andrea. "Searching for Roots in Contemporary China and Chinese America." In Sucheng Chan and Madeline Y. Hsu, eds., *Chinese Americans and the Politics of Race and Culture*. Philadelphia: Temple University Press, 2008. Pp. 195–217.

Ma, Laurence J. C., and Carolyn Cartier, eds. *The Chinese Diaspora: Space, Place, Mobility, and Identity*. Lanham, MD: Rowman & Littlefield, 2003.

Okamoto, Dina G. "Toward a Theory of Panethnicity: Explaining Asian American Collective Action." *American Sociological Review* 68 (2003): 811–842.

Petersen, Williams. *Japanese Americans: Oppression and Success*. New York: Random House, 1971.

Portes, Alejandro. "English-Only Triumphs, but the Costs Are High." *Contexts* 1 (2002): 10–15.

Stober, Dan, and Ian Hoffman. *A Convenient Spy: Wen Ho Lee and the Politics of Nuclear Espionage.* New York: Simon and Schuster, 2001.

Sung, Betty Lee. *Chinese American Intermarriage.* Staten Island, NY: Center for Migration Studies, 1989.

Tuan, Mia. *Forever Foreigners or Honorary White? The Asian Ethnic Experience Today.* New Brunswick, NJ: Rutgers University Press, 1999.

Tung, May Paomay. *Chinese Americans and Their Immigrant Parents.* New York: Haworth Press, 2000.

Wang, Ling-chi. "Class, Race, Citizenship, and Extraterritoriality: Asian Americans and the 1996 Campaign Finance Scandal." *Amerasia Journal* 24, no. 1 (1996): 1–21.

———. "The Structure of Dual Domination: Toward a Paradigm for the Study of the Chinese Diaspora in the United States." *Amerasia Journal* 21, nos. 1–2 (1995): 149–170.

Wang, Mei-ling T. *The Dust That Never Settles: The Taiwan Independence Campaign and U.S.-China Relations.* Lanham, MD: University Press of America, 1999.

Wong, K. Scott. "From Pariah to Paragon: Shifting Images of Chinese Americans during World War II." In Sucheng Chan and Madeline Y. Hsu, eds., *Chinese Americans and the Politics of Race and Culture.* Philadelphia: Temple University Press, 2008. Pp. 153–172.

Wong, K. Scott, and Sucheng Chan. *Claiming America: Constructing Chinese American Identities during the Exclusion Era.* Philadelphia: Temple University Press, 1998.

Wong, Morrison G. "A Look at Intermarriage among the Chinese in the United States in 1980." *Sociological Perspectives* 32, no. 1 (1989): 87–107.

Wu, Frank. *Yellow: Race in America Beyond Black and White.* New York: Basic Books, 2002.

Yu, Henry. "The 'Oriental Problem' in America, 1920–1960: Linking the Identities of Chinese Americans and Japanese Americans Intellectuals." In K. Scott Wong and Sucheng Chan, eds., *Claiming America: Constructing Chinese American Identities during the Exclusion Era.* Philadelphia: Temple University Press, 1998. Pp. 191–214.

Zia, Helen. *Asian American Dream: The Emergence of an American People.* New York: Farrar, Straus and Giroux, 2000.

The Undead: Notes on Photography in the Philippines, 1898–1920s

(2000)

Vicente L. Rafael

> Photography evades me. —Roland Barthes, *Camera Lucida*

One of the more visible legacies of the wars of 1898 was the explosion of photographic images, especially those of the lands and peoples that came under U.S. rule. Lighter and more mobile cameras allowed the photographing of sites and populations at greater distances, bringing these up close to a consuming public curious to see the recent "beneficiaries" of imperialist intervention. Photography transformed native peoples into images that could be wrenched from their origins and made to appear in novel contexts. Such images gave metropolitan viewers an acute sense of the technological and material expansiveness of the state and the mechanically reproducible proximity of its new subjects. Yet, photography as a means of expanding the aura, as it were, of the imperialist state, was also put to other uses productive of other effects in the colonies. In this chapter, I look into some of the ways in which photographic images as historical documents both confirmed and confounded the modernist vision of an imperial nation in one of its new possessions, the Philippines. For not only did photographic images reflect a tendentious notion of progress through disciplinary intervention; they also suggested the workings of a force that, as I shall try to show, eluded the demands of colonial and national ways of seeing.

Dead Images of the Living Many of the recent writings on colonial photography have tended to focus on the expropriative nature of the photographic enterprise. For this reason, they are often infused with a desire for revenge: the wish, as expressed in Malek Alloula's study of French photographs of Algeria, for example, to return the colonizer's gaze that had left its traces on the images of colonized natives.[1] In part, such projects have the effect of stirring anger, guilt, and embarrassment among contemporary readers. They remind us, whoever "we" are, of the violence that underlay the production and

---

1 Malek Alloula, *The Colonial Harem*, trans. Myrna Godzich and Wlad Godzich (Minneapolis: University of Minnesota Press, 1986), 5.

distribution of such images. They show the complicity of photographic representation with colonial policies as well as the ethnological and military means with which these were formulated and realized. Again and again, such approaches have demonstrated the tendentiousness of the eye that sees but remains unseen, resting on bodies that it both fixes and consumes for purposes alien to the lives of those it photographs.[2]

It is this capacity to convert the colonized into objects of foreign interests and subjects of colonial accounts that historically has lent to photography a predatory and cannibalistic quality. And it is all the more problematic, as critical studies have suggested, for its ability to provide an alibi of objectivity so that a photograph seems only to record what is in front of it while masking intentions, concealing selections, and rendering invisible the various frames that determine what is seen, how it is seen, and by whom. Photography has thus functioned as an apparatus of disavowal. Small wonder, then, that present-day discussions of colonial photography tend to incite an undercurrent of unease. They expose us to the relentless voyeurism that animated late imperial projects. In studying and, especially, looking at such photographs, we come into association with imperialist ways of looking and so feel unwittingly implicated in their workings. Like the gun, the camera has been part of the technology of subjugation, furnishing images to relay the workings of a prior and seemingly unassailable will. Colonial photographs seem like trophies of conquest. And to see them—even today—is to come in contact with this violence.

Looking through the photographic archive of U.S. colonial rule in the Philippines, it is not difficult—indeed, it would seem too easy—to confirm such arguments. One sees such photographs and feels compelled to respond.[3] Far from rendering Filipinos "invisible," colonialism instigated the proliferation of images of Filipino bodies. As part of a colonial regime of "compulsory visibility," photography was crucial in the depiction of a plural society as a target of imperialist reform.[4]

Particularly instructive in this regard are what might be called ethnological photographs: pictures that construct natives into distinct types. Appearing in a variety of

---

2   See, for example Donna Haraway, *Primate Visions: Gender, Race, and Nature in the World of Modern Science* (New York: Routledge, 1989), 1–18, 26–58; Mary Louise Pratt, *Imperial Eyes: Travel Writing and Transculturation* (New York: Routledge, 1992); and Alan J. Sekula, "The Body and the Archive," *October* 39 (winter 1986): 3–64.1 do not mean to suggest that all these works are alike and say the same thing, only that they have been among some of the more powerful and persuasive reformulations of photography's sociohistorical significance, furnishing indispensable touchstones for critiques of photography's colonial usages.

3   See, for example, the engaging book by Benito M. Vergara Jr., *Displaying Filipinos: Photography and Colonialism in Early-Twentieth-Century Philippines* (Quezon City: University of the Philippines Press, 1995).

4   I borrow the term *compulsory visibility* from Michel Foucault, *Discipline and Punish: The Birth of the Prison*, trans. Alan Sheridan (New York: Vintage Books, 1979).

texts, from popular magazines to academic studies, these sought to divide and classify the population into a hierarchy of ethno-racial differences.[5] [...] each group was situated in relation to its distance from or proximity to what was thought to be the norms of Anglo-Saxon civility. At one extreme were the non-Christian "tribes," such as the Negritos. They were routinely regarded as the most abject group because of their dark skin, short build, "nomadic" lifestyle, and lack of clothing (fig. 8). The more Malay-looking Igorots, the generic name for ethnic groups in the mountain regions of northern Luzon, elicited intense curiosity among white ethnologists, who often compared them to the Indians of North America. The Igorots—with their history of resistance against Spain, violent practices such as head-hunting, and muscular physique adorned with intricate tattoos—evoked fantasies about "noble savages" as natural allies of white colonizers on the tropical frontier (fig. 9).

FIGURE 8 **"Negritos in the island of Luzon"** (**William S. Bryan, ed.,** *Our Islands and Their People as Seen with Camera and Pencil* [**New York: N. D. Thompson and Publishing, 1899**])

FIGURE 9 **"An elaborate tattoo"** (**Albert E. Jenks,** *The Bontoc Igorot* [**Manila: Bureau of Public Printing, 1905**])

5 For a recent discussion of the use of photography in U.S. ethnological surveys conducted between 1900 and 1905, and the commercial uses, cultural effects, and political debates that such photographs instigated, see Paul A. Kramer, "The Pragmatic Empire: U.S. Anthropology and Colonial Politics in the Occupied Philippines, 1898–1916" (Ph.D. diss., Princeton University, 1998). See also Vergara, *Displaying Filipinos.*

Other groups on the southern island of Mindanao, both Muslim and non-Muslim, were regarded as slightly better-off in the ethno-racial hierarchy, given the allegedly improved nature of their material culture, but still requiring close colonial supervision (figs. 10 and 11). Finally, at the top of the hierarchy were the Christianized lowland groups, especially the Tagalogs. Thanks to centuries of Spanish rule, they had managed

FIGURE 10 **"Bagobos, island of Mindanao"** (*Annual Reports of the Philippine Commission, 1901–1908* [Washington, D.C.: U.S. Government Printing Office, 1902–1909])

FIGURE 11 **"Native chiefs of Mindanao, Philippines"** (Marrion Wilcox, ed. *Harper's History of the War in the Philippines* [New York: Harper and Brothers, 1900])

to come closer to the norms of civilization. But a history of racial mixing had supposedly weakened these groups, producing social divisions that installed an ambitious and corrupt mestizo upper class over a helpless lower class. These conditions made for a society that was as exotic as it was in need of discipline and reform (figs. 12, 13, and 14).

FIGURE 12 **"A pure Tagalog type of the lower class girl of Manila"** (William S. Bryan, ed., *Our Islands and Their People as Seen with Camera and Pencil* [New York: N. D. Thompson and Publishing, 1899])

FIGURE 13 **"Filipino Boy—Upper Class"** (William S. Bryan, ed., *Our Islands and Their People as Seen with Camera and Pencil* [New York: N. D. Thompson and Publishing, 1899])

Distinguishing between "uncivilized" and "civilized" "pure" and "mixed," "lower," "middle," and "upper" classes, such photographs reproduce a typology of native societies that had become commonplace in North American and European ethnology, one that viewed the world's people in social evolutionary terms. Fixing their subjects into timeless settings, these photographs effect the isolation and dissection of native bodies, converting them into specimens of colonial knowledge and reform. Rendered as dead objects, images of natives were cataloged as discrete items and made part of what I earlier termed a diorama of white love, better known as benevolent assimilation. That is to say, they were meant to represent less the particularities of native societies as the intentions and interests that posited their poses beyond and outside the photographs' frames. Looking at them from the standpoint of the present, we cannot but be aware of a presence exterior to the images that sets out to measure, calculate, and mummify, as it were, the bodies we see.

Ethnological photographs, then, had a kind of totemic significance. They served as supplements to a national identity in the United States that was suddenly expansive, and hence, coming under pressure throughout the late nineteenth century, but especially after 1898. Photographs of native bodies provided visual referents to the expansion of an imperial body politic in at least two ways. First, they signaled a frontier to be crossed and conquered, and second, they posed a limit to what could be assimilated into the nation. Put differently, these photographs of tribes, whether assumed to be savage or halfway civilized, functioned as fetishes of U.S. nationhood. Like the mass-produced images of Indian and African tribes on the North American continent itself, they were invested with the ability to incite phantasms of manifest destiny.[6]

For imperialist apologists, fulfilling this destiny meant not only the taking of lands and labor but also the giving back of civilization. U.S. colonization, as previously discussed, was conceptualized like other late European colonial projects as a modernizing and benevolent mission. As with any missionary undertaking, the key to success was securing the collaboration of converts and their disciplined

FIGURE 14 **"Type of high-class woman of Manila. The women of the Malay tribes are delicate of form and feature and more attractive than those of the Mongolian type, of whom many are found in the Philippines. The one whose portrait appears herewith has an admixture of Chinese blood."** (William S. Bryan, ed., *Our Islands and Their People as Seen with Camera and Pencil* [New York: N. D. Thompson and Publishing, 1899])

6 For example, ethnological photographs along with live specimens of Filipino types were displayed at the St. Louis Exposition of 1904. For a critical history of these exhibits, see Robert Rydell, *All the World's a Fair: Visions of Empire at American International Exhibitions, 1876–1916* (Chicago: University of Chicago Press, 1984), and *World of Fairs: The Century-of-Progress Exposition* (Chicago: University of Chicago Press, 1993). Also useful is Eric Breitbart, *A World on Display: Photographs from the St. Louis World Fair, 1904* (Albuquerque: University of New Mexico Press, 1997), which contains among other things tourist snapshots of the fair that show Igorot men watching other native types on display. For an astute account of the political and commercial failure of the St. Louis Exposition to promote the aims of the colonial government to publicize its accomplishments in the Philippines and the desire of exposition officials to make a profit, see Kramer, "The Pragmatic Empire," 200–252.

adherence to the state.[7] Again, photography registered the circulation of colonialism's gifts. Government reports, travel accounts, and historical narratives were generously illustrated with photographs of the natives' inevitable transformation under U.S. tutelage. For example, there were pictures of savages turned into soldiers (figs. 15, 16, and 17); prisoners turned into obedient citizens (fig. 18); lazy natives turned into productive laborers (fig. 19); and local elites turned into national politicians already destined for monumentalization by future generations (fig. 20).[8]

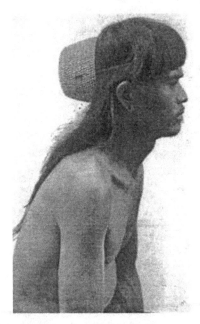  

FIGURE 15 **"Evolution of a Bontoc Igorot constabulary soldier—1901, when he was a head-hunting savage"** (Dean C. Worcester, *The Philippines Past and Present* [New York: Macmillan Publishing Co., 1914])

FIGURE 16 **"Evolution of a Bontoc Igorot constabulary soldier—1902, after he had been for a year in contact with Americans"** (Dean C. Worcester, *The Philippines Past and Present* [New York: Macmillan Publishing Co., 1914])

FIGURE 17 **"Evolution of a Bontoc Igorot constabulary soldier—1903, when he was a well disciplined and competent sergeant of a company of Philippine constabulary made up of his fellow tribesmen"** (Dean C. Worcester, *The Philippines Past and Present* [New York: Macmillan Publishing Co., 1914])

---

7   [...]

8   These photographs appear in such government publications as *Census of the Philippine Islands*, 4 vols. (Washington, D.C.: U.S. Government Printing Office, 1905); *Annual Reports of the Philippine Commission*, 1901–1908 (Washington, D.C.: US. Government Printing Office, 1902–1909); and in Dean C. Worcester, *The Philippines Past and Present*, 2 vols. (New York: Macmillan Publishing Co., 1914).

FIGURE 18 "The prison band 'sounding off' at retreat, Bilibid Prison" (U.S. Philippine Commission, *Annual Report of the Philippine Commission, 1901–1908* [Washington, D.C.: U.S. Government Printing Office, 1902–1909])

FIGURE 19 "Typical scene in a trade school. In institutions like this, young Filipinos are being taught the dignity of labor and are learning useful trades" (U.S. Philippine Commission, *Annual Report of the Philippine Commission, 1901–1908* [Washington, D.C.: U.S. Government Printing Office, 1902–1909])

FIGURE 20 **Filipino elites in the colonial legislature, 1918** (U.S. Bureau of the Census, *Census of the Philippine Islands, 1918,* 4 vols. [Manila: Bureau of Printing, 1920–1921])

FIGURE 21 **"Dead insurgent officer and soldier on the road to San Pedro Macati, after the charge of Gen. King's brigade"** (Marrion Wilcox, ed., *Harpers History of the War in the Philippines* [New York: Harper and Brothers, 1900])

FIGURE 22   "Burying the Filipino dead" (photo by J. D. Givens in General Oscar Fitzhalan Long's photographic album, "Our New Possessions in the Philippines," 1900, Bancroft Library, University of California, Berkeley)

As with ethnological photographs, these images convey the workings of an order outside their frames. We see individuals whose individuation seems to come from processes beyond what is visible. They appear as if composed by a power that is dispersed throughout the colony, inhabiting every aspect of everyday life and manifesting itself in and through the bodies of each subject. Their poses suggest their internalization of such a power. They come across as if they were recipients, and therefore also carriers, of promises that emanate from a hidden and distant elsewhere.

Living Images of the Dead So far, so obvious. What I've said about colonial photography in the Philippines could perhaps be said about photographic practices in many other colonial societies at the close of the nineteenth century and through the first half of the next one. That photography has been used to typify the relationship between colonizer and colonized, expanding the purview of the former while constraining that of the latter; that it has yielded images for the sake of compiling an encyclopedia of colonial visibilities; that it has served as a medium for the generation of imperialist desires and nostalgia: all these are true, and thus only partially so.

We might ask: what are the other sides of photography's truth? In treating colonial photographs as historical documents, to what extent do we find ourselves sliding into the temptation of seeing them as transparent emanations of the photographer's will? In insisting, as perhaps we must, that such images are conveyors of ideology chained to the determinations of sociopolitical contexts, do we risk reducing photographs to their frames, seeing them only to the degree that we look away, behind, or beyond that which appears in front of us? Seeing them by looking away from them, regarding them as mere appearances that carry messages whose meanings are already laid out in advance, do we not also submit to the force of a colonial reading practice that we might have wanted to expose and negate? And arriving at this moment of virtual complicity with colonial ways of seeing, as in fact nationalists tend to do, could the urge for a kind of violent separation not arise, fueled by the phantasms of humiliation and revenge, embarrassment and anger, critical smugness and moral superiority?

Perhaps there is no definitive way one can avoid turning to and returning the imperial gaze. It arguably continues to inform modern ways of seeing.[9] Nevertheless, it may be possible periodically to see otherwise. Images emerge at times from the archives that contain certain intractable elements, peculiar details, or distinct sensibilities that do not easily fit into the visual encyclopedia of colonial rule. Seeing them, one tends to linger, as I do, over those things that seem to peel away from one's expectations. Detaining one's eye, they give one pause about the nature of their illustrative function in narratives of various sorts. One looks, but isn't sure what one is looking at exactly. One feels the call to respond, but to what and to whom remain in doubt. As with all photographs, one senses a message. But not knowing what it might be, one is left with a communicative force suspended in the world.

There are, for instance, a number of arresting images from the Filipino-American War of 1899-1902. The most problematic—that is to say, persistently inconclusive—of these are the numerous photographs of Filipinos killed in battle. Images of death pervade photographs of the war. There are pictures of corpses left on the roadside (fig. 21), corpses lined up for mass burial (fig. 22), corpses on hillsides (fig. 23), and corpses dumped in mass graves (fig. 24). The circulation of these photographs was fairly widespread. They appeared in the private albums of colonial officers, newspaper accounts, and popular narratives of the war as well as historical studies of more recent years.[10] And

---

9 See Foucault, *Discipline and Punish*; and a number of works on colonialism inspired by this book, most notably Timothy Mitchell, *Colonizing Egypt* (Berkeley: University of California Press, 1991); and Allan Feldman, *Formations of Violence: The Narrative of the Body and Political Terror in Northern Ireland* (Chicago: University of Chicago Press, 1991).

10 See, for example, General Oscar Fitzhalan Long's photographic album, "Our New Possessions in the Philippines," with photographs by James David Givens, Bancroft Library, University of California, Berkeley; F. Tennyson Neely, *Fighting in the Philippines: Authentic and Original Photographs* (Chicago, 1899; Marrion Wilcox, ed., *Harper's History of the War in the Philippines* (New York: Harper and Brothers, 1900); William S. Bryan, ed., *Our Islands and Their People as Seen with Camera and Pencil* (New York: N. D. Thompson and Publishing, 1899; and Stuart Creighton Miller, *Benevolent Assimilation: The American Conquest of the Philippines, 1899–1903* (New Haven, Conn.: Yale University Press, 1982). As Jonathan Best has noted, some of these photographs were used as postcards, while others illustrated battles not even related to the Philippines, such as those of the Mexican Revolution. See his *A Philippine Album: American Era Photographs, 1900–1930* (Makati City, Philippines: Bookmark, Inc., 1998), 213.

FIGURE 23 "At the battle of Caloocan some shots were seen to come from a trench, and a single shell was sent toward it by the Utah Battery. When our troops advanced they found no less than ten men dead at this point" (Marrion Wilcox, ed., *Harpers History of the War in the Philippines* [New York: Harper and Brothers, 1900])

FIGURE 24 "The American Artillery did wonderful execution in the battles with the insurgents. In a trench at Santa Ana the Ta-gal [*sic*] dead lay in piles. The group shown in the picture consisted of thirty eight bodies" (Marrion Wilcox, ed., *Harpers History of the War in the Philippines* [New York; Harper and Brothers, 1900])

at one point, anti-imperialists in Boston were given to displaying these photographs as a way of decrying the brutality of the war.[11]

Photographs of war dead date back to the American Civil War with the work of Alexander Gardner, Timothy O'Sullivan, and Matthew Brady. Most of their images did not see publication until after the war, and did not become widely available until the end of the nineteenth century. By then, such photographs—usually labeled as the "harvest of war"—had come to signify, at least to a public two generations removed from the horrors of the Civil War, the "unimpeachable witness and irreducible essence" of the war's horrible truth.[12] Photographs of the dead in the Filipino-American War, however, to the best of my knowledge do not depict the American (or for that matter Spanish) dead lying on the battlefield. That photographic fate solely is reserved for Filipino bodies. One might think that in such a case, a different truth was at stake.

How is it possible to understand, much less look at these photographs? We might begin by speculating that such images of dead Filipinos were supposed to certify the mastery of the United States over death. Guerrilla warfare based on sporadic engagements, hit-and-run tactics, and techniques of camouflage rendered Filipino fighters relatively invisible, much to the frustration of U.S. soldiers. Photographing them dead meant making visible what could not previously be seen, fixing their once-mobile bodies into a set of unchanging images. Such images consolidate the memory of a prior confrontation. They were meant to prove less the skill of Filipino fighters as the courage of North Americans, who in setting aside their fear of death, showed themselves capable of risking their lives as well as taking the life of an other. But such risks in order to enter into history had to be acknowledged. Photographing the dead was a way to secure such recognition from those who survived the war. The captions that accompany each picture suggest as much in their description of each scene, accounting for Filipino deaths as if these were the natural outcome of U.S. superiority—moral, technological, and military. Unlike the American Civil War photographs, those of the Filipino-American War could then be read in triumphalist terms, whereby images of dead natives stood in stark contrast to those of living U.S. soldiers now united in a common cause on the other side of the world.[13]

---

11   This detail comes from Daniel B. Schirmer, *Republic or Empire? American Resistance to the Philippine-American War* (Cambridge, Mass.: Schenkman Publishing Co., 1972), 143.

12   I am grateful to Geoffrey Klingsporn for alerting me to this history in his unpublished essay, "'A Harvest of Death': War, Photography, and History" (1998), 3–6. Also suggestive is Alan Trachtenberg's stunning observations on war photography in *Reading American Photographs: Images as History, Matthew Brady to Walker Evans* (New York: Hill and Wang, 1989), 71–118.

13   Did the photographs of Filipino dead also lend themselves to ironic readings on the part of U.S. viewers? Certainly. James David Givens, for example, captions one such photograph as "War is Hell," which seems to resonate with the "harvest of war" motif associated with Civil War photographs. And anti-imperialists

But to photograph corpses also meant to keep them alive, after a fashion. It entailed preserving their death as a living legacy, beyond even one's own death. Thus the ghastly quality of these images. Where the ethnological photographs of natives could be understood as the dead images of living beings, images of corpses are what Roland Barthes would call "living images of [the] dead."[14] As the living dead, they refuse to be buried. Tendentious captions, colonial accounts, nationalist responses, and sociopolitical analysis can explain the conditions that may have led to such images but they cannot in the least bit transform them. For what appears in these photographs are neither individual bodies nor a body politic but a jumble of body parts that resist recognition and classification. They cannot be identified—that is to say, they cannot be read as signs or documents of a particular person or event. (In fact, calling them Filipino is itself freighted with a certain anxiety about their visibility and a wish to set them apart and put them in their proper place, or at least a place that might have some sociological depth.)

Pictures of corpses were taken shortly after military encounters by professional photographers working for U.S. newspapers or hired by the U.S. military as well as by U.S. soldiers who had cameras. They thus preserve the shock of contact. They are less the signs of war's traumatic effects so much as they are those effects themselves. They do not serve merely as representations of the past but relay a past event that cannot be assimilated into the present. The bodies that are scattered about are dead in a biological sense, or so we might assume, yet their status vis-à-vis the living remains in doubt. This is the source of their horror. Thanks to photography, they appear unchanged and therefore hopelessly out of place. Photographs capture their relentless dislocation and so make visible their scandalous presence. For after all, what sort of sociality could exist that did not have a place for the dead? What aesthetic practice would be possible that could not contain death but could only transmit what seemed like its unalterable and untranslatable thereness?

As enduring traces of the scandal at the heart of war, such images are eventful in their capacity to assail our present and convey the sense of something unreadable. In doing so, they act to limit not just the stretch of imperial vision and its narrative purchase over the interpretation of events; they also frustrate critical commentaries that might seek to re-frame and thereby bury them in the discursive graveyard of the archives. Thus do these photographs of corpses—what we might regard as the undead—resist the closure

---

used these pictures to illustrate what they felt was the unwarranted brutality of the war. Yet, as I discuss below, there is something about these photographs that escapes both triumphalist and ironic readings insofar as they bring to mind an event, death, whose eventfulness, as conveyed by photographs, defies interpretive closure.

14 Roland Barthes, *Camera Lucida: Reflections on Photography*, trans. Richard Howard (New York: Hill and Wang, 1981), 79.

of mourning. Unburied, they seem to have no place in the world and so cannot be put out of mind. Inhabiting the world of the living, images of the dead remain radically obscene to the viewer. Looking at them, our vision falters as we apprehend far more than we can ever comprehend. We cannot close a circle, square accounts, determine blame, much less seek revenge. Rather, we feel ourselves in the midst of spectral wanderings that recall, if that is the word for it, the trauma at the foundation of empire, the unaccountability of deaths in the course of war, and the inevitable failure to narrate the truth of a history that exceeds our capacity to see.

Thinking (and Moving) Beyond Walls and Cages: Bridging Immigrant Justice and Anti-Prison Organizing in the United States

(2009)

Jenna Loyd, Andrew Burridge, & Matthew Mitchelson

> *We continue to find that the prison is itself a border. This analysis has come from prisoners, who name the distinction between the "free world" and the space behind the walls of the prison. This is an important interpretation that undoes the illusions of the powerful nation-states on the one hand and the seeming disorganization and chaos of capital's travels on the other. There is a very specific political economy of the prison that brings the intersections of gender and race, colonialism and capitalism, into view (Davis and Dent, 2001: 1236–1237).*

U NDERSTANDING THE PRISON AS A BORDER enables us to tie the present intensification of border fortification and expansion within long and unique histories of slavery, colonialism, and imperialism. The important particularities of these histories, and the people whose lives have been shaped by them, are brought together through these borders as much as they are kept apart. At the 2008 Left Forum conference, for example, two of the current authors participated in a session on the connection between walls and cages and organizing strategies to move beyond them. One of the panel's speakers recounted a story about the difficulties of recognizing the commonalities of apparently different forms of migration policing in Queens, New York. Following September 11, South Asian and Muslim communities were rounded up here and nationwide in the name of national security and "fighting terrorism." Meanwhile, agents of the newly founded Immigration and Customs Enforcement were conducting raids in another Queens neighborhood, this time targeting West Indian people as criminals engaged in the drug trade. These groups were each subject to racial profiling, detention, and deportation, yet they were positioned differently in relation to the state and dominant racial formations. The groups were skeptical of one another, one declaring "We're not terrorists!" and the other "We're not criminals!"

These commonsense responses among neighbors living in one New York borough illustrate how practices of civil death, which have strikingly similar effects, nonetheless isolate groups discursively and politically from one another. Criminalization and exclusionary migration policy are forms of "civil death" that create categories of people who are not afforded the broadest range of rights and responsibilities afforded to the most privileged "citizens." Political organizing on these lines has the effect of legitimizing the racialization and state regulation of the other group, thereby bolstering at least one of what Andrea Smith (2006) calls the three pillars of white supremacy: slavery/capitalism, genocide/colonialism, and Orientalism/war. That is, such strategies reinforce the ways in which U.S. migration policy builds the domestic penal system and how nationalistic defenses of territorial integrity validate ongoing colonialism through a combination of military means *and* citizenship.

Walls and cages—the shorthand we use for U.S. migration policy and penal ("criminal justice") policy—facilitate contemporary processes of racialized dispossession and capitalist restructuring ("globalization"). Understanding how these differentiations work is thus consequential for people's lives and organizing possibilities. The dynamics that differentiate and isolate groups *simultaneously* converge and materialize in division's sturdy tools: the bullet, the chain, the cuff, coils of concertina wire, the wall and the cage.

On any given day, there are nearly 2.3 million people in U.S. jails and prisons, and more than twice as many people—5.1 million—are under direct state surveillance through the parole and probation systems (Glaze and Bonczar, 2009). The racial disparities of the punishment complex are well known. Some 58% of the people in prison are sentenced on nonviolent drug offenses and people of color comprise 75% of these prisoners (Ahrens, 2008; The Sentencing Project, n.d.; Wacquant, 2001). Women are being caged faster than any other group, and migrant detention is proliferating at a remarkable pace (West and Sabol, 2009). Over 30,000 migrants are detained on any given night, and over 1.6 million migrants have been deported since 1996 (this figure does not include those who have taken "voluntary departure").

The markedly increased caging of these particular groups is the predictable result, a decade later, of three infamous pieces of 1996 legislation signed into law under President Clinton: the Personal Responsibility and Work Act, which ended welfare as we knew it; the Antiterrorism and Effective Death Penalty Act (AEDPA), which imposed minimum sentencing requirements; and the Illegal Immigration Reform and Immigrant Responsibility Act (IIRIRA), which broadened the categories of criminal and deportable offenses, *and* made them enforceable retroactively. This is an important moment in the deepening ties between immigration and penal policy, which build on the longer rise of the carceral state in the second half of the 20th century.

From the Left Forum to the U.S. Social Forum, Critical Resistance 10, and more informal settings across the United States, people are engaging in inter-ethnic and inter-national conversations about the convergence between walls and cages. These conversations link different groups of folks who aim to break the ideological divisions that isolate struggles against prisons (and all forms of state violence) from struggles for immigrant and economic justice. We view our individual and collective work as part of this important dialogue and political project of bridging prison abolition and immigrant justice movements. As activist-geographers, we are co-editing a book entitled *Beyond Walls and Cages,* which brings together the writings of people directly affected by these systems with those of organizers, artists, advocates, and researchers.

Our goals in this piece are twofold: we wish to trace some of the scales of mobility and immobility through which walls and cages work; and we want to link some of the violent deformations marshaled (and entrenched) through these sites to some of the transformative, abolitionist alternatives we envision. Against the violently deformed meanings of justice, community, and safety that walls and cages produce, we promote abolitionist strategies for moving from prisons' "bedspaces" to the homes where people can freely rest and dream.

Audre Lorde (1984: 37) once wrote that "poetry is not only dream and vision; it is the skeleton and architecture of our lives. It lays the foundations for a future of change, a bridge across our fears of what has never been before." In throwing in our lot with generations of abolitionists, the mix of theory and practice is our poetry, creating bridges toward each other to walk through fear and toward another future. If, as Edward Said (1983: 226) suggests, the circulation of ideas is one "enabling condition of intellectual activity," then part of our work is marking the barriers and exclusions through which people and ideas and love struggle to traverse to create (momentary) places. Showing these connections comes out of being in the mix in our various movements and roles and is a condition for being in this mix (Gilmore in Murphy et al., 2005). Accounting for our locations as abolitionist scholar-activists means that documentation and theorizing blur at the edges so that the present and the possible may approach each other. To make desired changes in the world possible, the circulation of ideas is an essential part. And so this essay reflects a node in the circulation of social struggles, a report on the state of connections as they exist in dispersed conversations and murmurings of liberation that are seeking to be materialized more fully.

Scales of Mobility and Immobility

Detention and imprisonment are inherently multi-scalar projects. As a powerful site of state sovereignty, cages are places in which a variety of territorializations of economic and state power converge. The nation-state (border) and the city hold host to the powerful dialectics of fixity and flow, incapacitation and mobility, such as undocumented presence within a national territory, driving while Black or Brown, or being at "the wrong place at the wrong time" in the neighborhood. Very often, "the crime" being punished amounts to a transgression against the state's socio-spatial claims or the claims of private property. For now, walls and cages are deployed across these scales as the primary resolutions to these contradictions (Gilmore and Gilmore, 2008).

Thus, the cage links a host of places far beyond the prison's walls (e.g., the nation, the city, and the home). Places are linked such that the rural prison reproduces the "urban criminal" and policing the border reproduces the nationalistic categories and practices of citizenship and war-making. In this sense, imprisonment is a multi-scalar process that draws in multiple spaces, where they converge in the cage. Regardless of the scale at which territorial claims are invoked (or revoked), detention and imprisonment always relentlessly settle on a "local" site. The human body bares all penalties. Yet by twist of ideological alchemy, those most harmed by migration and penal policy become the origins of threat to the "good" citizen and nation, as are their own harms, rather than nationalist policy or racism. This displaces responsibility for known harms away from the state, obscuring state violence and reinforcing the legitimacy of the state to forcibly regulate "criminals" and "aliens."

Mobility is part of the human condition and international migration is part of the modern condition. Meanwhile, migration controls have become increasingly elaborate in tandem with the push toward freer international capital and commodity movement. Throughout the global South, neoliberal capitalist restructuring has resulted in the displacement of millions of people from rural livelihoods. This trend—in conjunction with industrial restructuring, privatization, deregulation, and worsening terms of trade—has resulted in international migration as a survival strategy for families, means of economic development for communities, and means of nation-states to pay off external debt.

Yet, even as freedom of movement becomes more imperative to economic survival, refugee and migration policies are becoming increasingly restrictive. We can see this at the nation-state and broader scales, with uniform boundary enforcement practices around what critics call Fortress Europe and Fortress NAFTA, and migrant interdiction occurring in sites far removed from national territories (Lahav, 1998; Mountz and Hyndman, 2007). These policies build on racialized colonial geographies and constitute a regime of selective mobility—global apartheid— inhibiting the free movement of the majority of the world's people (Nevins, 2008; Sharma, 2005). This is a reversal of the post-World War II to early 1980s moment of migration liberalization in the United States and Europe, whose economies were rapidly growing and which were under Cold War anti-colonial (and post-Holocaust) pressure to reform *de jure* racial policies.

With intensified economic competition and a steady shift of labor-intensive industries from the 1960s on, from the U.S. North to the U.S. South and then to the global

South, increasing sectors of the U.S.-born workforce face structural unemployment. And this economic restructuring was taking place as antiracist movements of the post-war era were breaking Jim Crow and demanding wholesale transformation of the racial economy. The disorder created by state and capitalist crises of the early 1970s on—and by the freedom, anti war, and women's movements—has (at least partially) been dealt with through mass incarceration (Gilmore, 1998/99; Parenti, 1999).

At the same time, migration to the United States has increased, with migrants often recruited into workplaces to break the organized power of the existing workforce. Far from economic globalization ushering in a liberalization of cross-border movement, U.S. migration policy since the mid-1980s has progressively relied on policing and penal strategies.[1] This is not paradoxical, because the racialized and nationalist enforcement of diminished rights creates a more exploitable and precarious workforce (Sharma, 2006). Repressive policing practices and nativist discourses create a climate of fear, which inhibits people's everyday movement and collective organizing for improved working and living conditions. This replicates the effect of hyper-policing in poor communities of color. The fallout of these structural adjustments affect men and women of color differently: women have shouldered the work of coping and working to keep families together, fed, housed, schooled, and loved. As these cuts continue to stretch women's capacities to respond, the criminalization of survival increasingly subjects women to direct policing and incarceration (Alexander, 2005: 181–254; Davis and Shaylor, 2001; Mohanty, 2003: 43–84).

Absolute control over boundaries, territory, and populations is a utopia (for some). The exclusionary premise of the nation and national territorial integrity is often legitimized through the idea of a shared national community and ideal of uniform treatment (justice). Yet the fiction of nationalist egalitarianism is revealed by racially differentiated citizenship (what Yen Le Espiritu [2003] calls "differential inclusion"). This is evident in racialized rates of involvement in the prison-industrial complex (PIC), and hence disenfranchisement from the vote and stripping of rights to entitlements, the permanent outsider status of some groups of people (regardless of how long they and their families have been here) based on racialized ideas of "unassimilable difference," and the popular belief (heard increasingly post-September 11) that non-citizens do not have the same constitutional rights as citizens (Loyd and Burridge, 2007).

Absolute control over movement and territory is an unachievable goal, and inevitable failures are used as justifications for new spatial strategies of deterrence and ever more repressive controls. Spatial solutions that involve increased militarization and

---

1   When Jorge Bustamante (2008), the Special Rapporteur on the human rights of migrants, delivered a report on U.S. migration and refugee policy to the United Nations Human Rights Council, he concluded: "In the past decade the use of detention as an immigration enforcement mechanism has become more the norm than the exception in United States immigration enforcement policy."

policing—zero-tolerance zones of all sorts, from interdictions on homelessness, drugs, assembly, and mere presence—shift unwanted activities *and people* elsewhere. These same activities continue, while a connected spatial infrastructure of walls and cages is built. As Gilmore and Gilmore (2008: 142) write, cages have become "catch-all solutions to social and political problems." These solutions categorize people by status, but fail to address the processes that create these conditions of living and powerful markers of difference. Meanwhile, the effects of these failures are blamed on the people who are most hurt by them. Criminalizing homelessness, drugs, and migration turns *people* into problems, but fails to build homes, reduce the harms of drug use, or facilitate the free movement of people. Instead, criminalization produces spaces of harm (for some) that are termed, most ironically and insidiously, "bedspace."

...

Sovereign Cages: Militarizing (Im)mobility at the Boundary

The multiple geographic scales through which prisons and borders (or incarceration and migration) constitute each other are nowhere more evident than at the U.S.-Mexico border. However, since the implementation of border militarization strategies, such as "Operation Hold the Line" and "Operation Gatekeeper" in the early 1990s, as well as of zero-tolerance programs by DHS's departments of Immigration and Customs Enforcement (ICE) and Customs and Border Protection (CBP), incarceration and deaths of undocumented border crossers have increased significantly.[2] As Heyman and Cunningham (2004: 294) write, such practices of spatial exclusion and management assign and enforce "differential rights and duties through enclosure." This necessarily "entails the allocation of unequal risk to various populations yet naturalizes such rights and risks as normal and proper consequences of territorial rules."

As a matter of strategic policy, CBP has funneled migrants into remote areas, such as the Altar Valley in southern Arizona, shutting off safer routes of travel. Yet the U.S. government places the blame upon migrants, or their guides, for their own deaths (Nevins, 2003). Indeed, Doris Meissner, former head of the INS, acknowledged that the U.S. government was well aware that fencing off urban areas, as in San Diego and El Paso, and relying on the geography of the desert would lead to a rise in deaths (Cornelius, 2001). Since 2000, the numbers of deaths have reached into the hundreds every year.

Since the formation of the DHS in 2003, when immigration enforcement was placed under the cabinet-level Department of Homeland Security, there has been a notable devolution of scale from the federal to the state and local levels within border policing

---

2   ICE was previously the Immigration and Naturalization Service (INS) and Customs and Border Protection was previously the United States Border Patrol.

and militarization policies along the U.S.-Mexico borderlands. Heyman (1998) refers to this as the "local state" of border enforcement. Although bills aimed at "comprehensive immigration reform," such as H.R. 4437 in 2006, failed to pass, the past few years have nonetheless seen a steady criminalization of unauthorized migration through a notably piecemeal approach to border militarization and interior enforcement practices.

Across the nine U.S. Border Patrol Sectors that comprise the southwest border, numerous border securitization projects and immigration policies have been implemented that are highly localized in their impact. Although the expansion of the USBP to 18,000 agents and the ongoing militarization of the borderlands through fencing and other methods have drawn attention, little noticed is how this process is further bolstered through the involvement of enforcement agents from agencies including the U.S. Fish and Wildlife Service, the U.S. Forest Service, Bureau of Land Management, local police and sheriff departments, and indigenous police forces such as on the Tohono O'odham reservation. This de facto marshalling of other federal agencies into migration policing bolsters the policing capacities of the CBP and further consolidates unauthorized presence as a criminal act for all government agencies to police.

Over the past decade, southern Arizona, and specifically the U.S. Border Patrol-designated "Tucson Sector," has become known as the busiest and most deadly region of the U.S.-Mexico borderlands for undocumented migration. First implemented in Del Rio, Texas, in 2005, followed by Yuma, Arizona, and then Laredo, Texas, in 2007, "Operation Streamline"—officially known as the Arizona Denial Prosecution Initiative (ADPI)—was put into effect in the Tucson sector on January 14, 2008. In a press release reporting on the fiscal year 2008 successes of Streamline in the sector, CBP stated that close to 10,000 undocumented migrants were prosecuted, "sending a clear message that there will be consequences for entering illegally into Arizona" (Customs and Border Protection, 2008). These expanding "zones of zero tolerance" (in CBP's terms) now comprise over 500 miles of the 2,000-mile U.S.-Mexico border, with plans to extend the program into other sectors of the border. These spatial strategies of criminalization create additional vulnerability for those crossing without the permission of the state *and* necessarily increase repression of borderland communities, citizens or not.

"Operation Streamline" is being enforced most vigorously in the 262-mile-wide Tucson Sector. Each weekday in the Evo A. DeConcini courthouse in downtown Tucson, undocumented migrants, mostly from Mexico and Central America, are criminally charged under Streamline for having entered illegally into the United States. Of the approximately 800 to 1,000 migrants detained by the Border Patrol in this sector each day, up to 70 persons are randomly selected and processed through the federal criminal court system. Migrants found crossing within the Tucson Sector are therefore subject to being placed within the Streamline process, and in turn are criminalized unlike others committing the same act elsewhere along the border who are "voluntarily deported" without a criminal record. Each of the 70 detainees face up to 180 days in an ICE-funded facility, a formal removal (deportation) process, and a five-year ban on legal reentry into the United States. Even those who are not interdicted and imprisoned are harmed by "deterrence" policies, which are designed to *create* hardships for those entering the United States without documents. As migrants and their *coyotes* attempt to avoid such criminalized spaces, they are inevitably pushed to take increasingly arduous and lengthy paths to cross through the borderlands and onward into the interior.

In March 2008, just two months after "Operation Streamline" began, the U.S. District Court proposed to move public hearings on the program to the detention center at Davis Monthan Air Force Base. Located on the outskirts of the city, it is home to the new CBP headquarters. As such, the only public aspect of the operation would have moved behind detention center walls. The migrant detention industry had already become increasingly privatized or hidden behind institutional walls, affording the public, media, and migrant rights groups little access. Through considerable pressure from grassroots groups active in Tucson and elsewhere, the District Court reversed the decision, instead maintaining public hearings at the federal courthouse.

The militarization of space and strengthened collaboration between law enforcement agencies have increased criminalization of undocumented migrants and those providing humanitarian aid in the U.S.-Mexico borderlands. This has been most significant in the Tucson Sector, where volunteers with humanitarian groups have been arrested and fined for providing aid, such as leaving gallon jugs of water for border crossers in the desert or transporting critically ill people to a hospital. By funneling migration into more remote desert corridors and interdicting life-saving humanitarian aid, the USBP and other law enforcement agents seek to disorganize the work of solidarity in the borderlands. Constrained mobility for migrants and aid workers makes the borderlands increasingly dangerous and deadly.

These piecemeal and arbitrary migration policies underscore how ideals of justice are deformed by absolutist nationalist desires. Localization of migration enforcement through the devolution of federal migration policy and enlistment of other agencies in interdiction measures has contributed significantly to the arbitrary nature of U.S. sovereign boundary enforcement. With law enforcement and land management agents acting as de facto border patrol agents, criminalization of migration has expanded. So, too, has the questioning of citizenship through increased surveillance and policing of who has the right to mobility in this region; for those deemed "out of place," this means further curtailment of their rights.

Situating "Interior" Enforcement: Migration and the City

Global cities are the paradigmatic sites where people who have been dispossessed and forced across national boundaries work to make possible the lives of the well-heeled, who may travel freely (Sassen, 2006). The inevitable failures of boundary policing to secure territorial integrity have brought cities to center stage in the debate over U.S. migration. Movements for sanctuary, identification cards, and voting rights expand the meaning of belonging beyond the bounds of national citizenship to incorporate residence and participating in the life of the city (Ridgely, 2008; Varsanyi, 2006, 2008). On the flip side are restrictionist, nationalist policies such as ordinances that prevent day labor sites or renting residential property to non-citizens, as well as the devolution of federal migration enforcement to local police agencies through formal 287(g) agreements and contracts with local jails for detention space.

Cities capture the contradictory convergence of freedom of movement and coercive mobility. Beyond being sites of flight, cities are also the target of the over two decade law-and-order rage that has built the prison-industrial complex. Thus, prisons are one site in an expansive institution of "coercive mobility" (Clear et al., 2001), a state-run system of circular migration linking poor, working-class, people of color neighborhoods with penal institutions typically located in sites far from where they live (Gilmore, 2007; Kurgan, 2007). Most of the 2.3 million caged people will return to their communities, making prisons part of a vast infrastructure and economy of people being warehoused and then transported back home.

These many rounds of forced migration do not create safety in highly policed neighborhoods, but further stretch—and shred—family and community relations of support, trust, and mutual aid (Clear et al., 2001). This is akin to what happens to social networks in neighborhoods that are displaced through large-scale redevelopment (Fullilove, 2004; Greenbaum, 2008). Thus, mass incarceration contributes to the structural violence of economic abandonment, racial segregation, and social infrastructural disinvestment, resulting in the accumulation of bodily harms in particular places (Greenberg and Schneider, 1994). It thereby amplifies already serious health crises in Black and Latina/o communities (Freudenberg, 2001; Golembeski and Fullilove, 2005; Lane et al., 2004; Willmott and Olphen, 2005).

By refusing to see migration in terms of the state definition—as crossing a national boundary—we can look at multiple scales of coercive migration, including that fostered by dispossession, economic dislocation, and mass imprisonment. The rights-stripping machinery of criminalization and migration policing builds on and consolidates racial hierarchies and ideologies, but "criminality" and "illegality" have the similar effect of naturalizing harms of dispossession and state coercion. Simultaneously, this machinery works to displace and disorganize, and thereby disempower, self-organized forms of care, mutual aid, and solidarity, whether known as the family, community, or labor unions. Thus, refusing this nationalist imaginary enables us to connect gentrification with rural land dispossession, and to see prisons—whether for people who have been charged with a criminal act or unauthorized presence in one sovereign space or other—as sites of dispossession. This, in turn, can open possibilities for creating places where death and exclusion are not effects of, or euphemized as, "safety" and "belonging."

Secure Communities or Right to the City?

There is nothing natural (or permanent) about bedspace, so questioning its limits and what kind of future it can build becomes urgent. As Larson, a man imprisoned in Sing Sing, reminds us: "Anyone planning a prison they're not going to build for ten or fifteen years is planning for a child, planning prison for somebody who's a child right now" (in Ahrens, 2008). What kinds of places might we build to replace these deforming spaces?

The immigrant justice and decarceration movements had a big win in August 2009 when the Department of Homeland Security announced that it would end its use of the T. Don Hutto family detention center. This win was overshadowed, though, by the promise of ICE head, John Morton, to transform the patchwork of migrant detention, which is "very much dependent on excess capacity in the criminal justice system," into a "truly civil detention system" (Bernstein, 2009b). This portends *additional* capacity for incapacitation of migrants and citizens, even as states struggle to pay for health care and schooling.

Lauded as a departure from George W. Bush's heavy-handed migration policies, President Barack Obama's administration nonetheless rejected a petition to create legally enforceable rules for immigrant detention (Bernstein, 2009a). He has pushed off promised "comprehensive" migration reform to 2010 and has failed to rein in the enforcement-only approach enshrined by his predecessor (Preston, 2009). Raids may officially be off the table, but these terrifying spectacles are only the most visible of interior enforcement practices. Criminal prosecutions for migration violations have increased, and Obama has expanded the notorious 287(g) program and intends to implement the Secure Communities program nationwide.

The 287(g) program trains and deputizes local police agents as federal migration cops. Civil and immigrant rights advocates criticize the program's lack of focus and the racial profiling engendered by the program. Secure Communities promises to rectify these problems, but actually creates conditions for more of the same. It will formalize existing extralegal practices whereby police officers notify ICE or the Border Patrol of suspected undocumented immigrants in their custody, and will formally turn the nation's 30,000-plus jails into migration posts. At any point during one's time in custody—whether at a traffic stop, being booked, formally charged, awaiting trial, or serving a sentence—authorities can pass a person's identification information to the FBI and DHS. These officials are not deputized as migration agents, but simply act as couriers; responsibility for discerning legal presence and potential for deportation remains at the federal level. This massive dragnet solves one of DHS's fundamental problems—pinpointing the over 11 million unauthorized migrants in their mission of "insuring departure of all removable aliens" from the country—while simultaneously avoiding the expense and undercutting opposition to federalizing local police (Barry, 2009).

How can we turn this exclusionary vision of a "secure community" into a truly egalitarian, safe, and free one? Just as transnational migration has forced a rethinking of national citizenship as the means of rights, responsibilities, and democratic governance (Glick Schiller, 2005; Varsanyi, 2006), Right to the City (RTTC) prompts a rethinking of the premise of citizenship itself as an institution structuring mobility, residence, and place-making. RTTC has been gaining theoretical and practical traction in recent years (Harvey, 2003; Holston and Appadurai, 1996; Isin, 2000; Purcell, 2003). One of the principles of the movement is that inhabitants should be able to create the city in which they want to live. This is an imperative that integrates commitments to economic justice with collective and individual self-determination. Inhabitance, not national citizenship, becomes the basis for asserting claims to the social wealth we all create, and for making commitments to building healthy, safe, and sustainable communities.

Abolitionism can find its grounding in the city. Poor and working-class groups, regardless of citizenship, share many vulnerabilities to residential and economic dislocation, and use the same crumbling health systems and schools. Conflicts over the city and its infrastructures are inevitable, but "criminality" and "illegality" are powerful, state-legitimized means of resolving conflicts through exclusion rather than more just, life-sustaining means. "Coercive mobility" shows linkages between what appear to be disconnected groups of people and can make the freedom to move and freedom to stay put joint demands that link reconstruction of urban *and* rural livelihoods. Local jails are important crossroads for migrants set into motion by neoliberal restructuring and criminalized responses to its dislocations. The Secure Communities migration policy builds on the tremendous growth in numbers of police officers that have been put on the streets *and* the excess capacity of this very system. Opportunities thus open for local anti-jail expansion campaigns to bring together immigrant justice, anti-prison, and prison reform groups.

As Rose Braz writes (in The CR10 Publications Collective, 2008), "abolition means a world where we do not use prisons, policing, and the larger system of the prison-industrial complex as an 'answer' to what are social, political, and economic problems." When it comes to migration, abolitionism supports the free movement of people and questions the use of national citizenship (or other arbitrary exclusionary boundaries) to determine who gets to move where and whose social needs are prioritized over another's (Cohen, 2006; Shantz, 2005; Sharma, 2003). Building economies and community institutions that foster creativity, care, self-determination, and mutual responsibility are among the abolitionist visions for a just society. That is, abolition is a vision for the future that can guide current action for making communities that create real safety and meet people's needs.

Abolitionist visions can contribute to making the Right to the City a reality. There is a necessary relation between freedom of movement and freedom to inhabit, both of which are fundamental to being able to (re)create strong communities and just, sustainable livelihoods. Geographic mobility and immobility are necessarily related to the power to claim and shape relations and movement between different places. This is evident at the urban and international scales, as illustrated by the twinned spatial injustices of segregation-gentrification and national border controls-rural dispossession. In conditions of spatial confinement, freedom to move under conditions of one's choosing is imperative. And in conditions of coercive mobility, being able to control space is also imperative. This makes freedom of movement and freedom to "stay home" or "stay put" (Bacon, 2008; Newman and Wyly, 2006) two sides of the same abolitionist efforts to create spaces for living with dignity and self-determination.

References

Ahrens, Lois 2008. *The Real Cost of Prisons Comix.* Oakland: PM Press.

Alexander, M. Jacqui 2005. *Pedagogies of Crossing: Meditations on Feminism, Sexual Politics, Memory, and the Sacred.* Durham, NC: Duke University Press.

Bacon, David 2008. "The Right to Stay Home." *Truthout* (July 14; at *www.truthout.org/articlelthe-right-stay-home*).

Barry, Tom 2009. "Immigrant Crackdown Joins Failed Crime and Drug Wars." *International Policy Report* (April 2; at *http://americas.irc-online.org/pdflreports/0904crackdown CIP.pdf*).

Bernstein, Nina 2009a. "U.S. Rejects Call for Immigration Detention Rules." *New York Times* (July 28; at *www.nytimes.com/2009/07/29lnyregionl29detain.html*).

———. 2009b. "U.S. to Reform Policy on Detention for Immigrants." *New York Times* (August 5; at *www.nytimes.com/2009/08/06luslpoliticslo6detain.htmT*).

Bustamante, Jorge 2008. *Report of the Special Rapporteur on the Human Rights of Migrants, Jorge Bustamante—Addendum—Mission to the United States of America.* New York: Human Rights Council, United Nations.

CCA 2008, 2007. *Annual Report.* Nashville, TN: Corrections Corporation of America.

Clear, Todd R., Dina R. Rose, Elin Waring, and Kristen Scully 2001. "Coercive Mobility and Crime: A Preliminary Examination of Concentrated Incarceration and Social Disorganization." *Justice Quarterly* 20, 1: 33–64.

Cohen, Steve 2006. *Deportation Is Freedom! The Orwellian World of Immigration Controls.* London: Jessica Kingsley Publishers.

Cornelius, Wayne A. 2001. "Death at the Border: Efficacy and Unintended Consequences of U.S. Immigration Control Policy." *Population and Development Review* 27, 4: 661–685.

Customs and Border Protection 2008. "Tucson Sector Makes Significant Gains in 2008." *Newsroom* (September 18; at *www.cbp.gov/xp/cgov/newsroom/news_releasesllo152008_7.xmT*).

Davis, Angela Y. and Gina Dent 2001. "Prison as a Border: A Conversation on Gender, Globalization, and Punishment." *Signs* 26, 4: 1235–1241.

Davis, Angela and Cassandra Shaylor 2001. "Race, Gender, and the Prison Industrial Complex: California and Beyond." *Meridians: Feminism, Race, Transnationalism* 2, 1: 1–25.

Department of Homeland Security Office of Inspector General 2009. *Immigration and Custom Enforcement Detention Bedspace Management.* Washington, DC: U.S. Department of Homeland Security.

Dyer, Joel 2000. *The Perpetual Prisoner Machine: How America Profits from Crime.* Boulder, CO: Westview Press.

Espiritu, Yen Le 2003. *Home Bound: Filipino American Lives Across Cultures, Communities, and Countries.* Berkeley: University of California Press.

Freudenberg, Nicholas 2001. "Jails, Prison, and the Health of Urban Populations: A Review of the Impact of the Correctional System on Community Health." *Journal of Urban Health* 78, 2: 214–235.

Fullilove, Mindy 2004. *Root Shock: How Tearing up City Neighborhoods Hurts America, and What We Can Do About It,* New York: Ballantine Books.

Geo Group 2008, 2007. *Annual Report.* Boca Raton, FL: The Geo Group, Inc.

Gilmore, Ruth Wilson 2007. *Golden Gulag: Prisons, Surplus, Crisis, and Opposition in Globalizing California.* Berkeley: University of California Press.

———. 1998–1999. "Globalisation and U.S. Prison Growth: From Military Keynesianism to Post-Keynesian Militarism." *Race and Class* 40, 2-3: 171–188.

Gilmore, Ruth Wilson and Craig Gilmore 2008. "Resisting the Obvious." M. Sorkin (ed.), *Indefensible Space: The Architecture of the National Insecurity State.* New York: Routledge: 141–162.

Glaze, Lauren E. and Thomas B. Bonczar 2009. *Probation and Parole in the United States, 2007 Statistical Tables.* Washington, DC: U.S. Department of Justice.

Glick Schiller, Nina 2005. "Transnational Urbanism as a Way of Life: A Research Topic, Not a Metaphor." *City and Society* 17, 1: 49–64.

Golembeski, Cynthia and Robert Fullilove 2005. "Criminal (In)Justice in the City and Its Associated Health Consequences." *American Journal of Public Health* 95, 10: 1701–1706.

Greenbaum, Susan 2008. "Poverty and the Willful Destruction of Social Capital: Displacement and Dispossession in African American Communities." *Rethinking Marxism* 20, 1: 42–54.

Greenberg, Michael and Dona Schneider 1994. "Violence in American Cities: Young Black Males Is the Answer, But What Was the Question?" *Social Science and Medicine* 39, 2: 179–187.

Gunn, Jerry 2009. "CCA Shows off Detention Center." *AccessNorthGA.com* (August 10; at *www.accessnorthga.com/detail.php?n=222377&c=10*).

Harvey, David 2003. "The Right to the City." *International Journal of Urban and Regional Research* 27, 4: 939–941.

Heyman, Josiah 1998. "Why Interdiction? Immigration Control at the United States-Mexico Border." *Regional Studies* 33, 7: 619–630.

Heyman, Josiah and Hilary Cunningham 2004. "Introduction: Mobilities and Enclosures at Borders." *Identities: Global Studies in Culture and Power* 11, 3: 289–302.

Holston, James and Arjun Appadurai 1996. "Cities and Citizenship." *Public Culture* 8, 2: 187–204.

Isin, Engin F. 2000. *Democracy, Citizenship, and the Global City.* London: Routledge.

King, Wayne 1984. "Contracts for Detention Raise Legal Questions." *The New York Times* (March 6): A10.

Kurgan, Laura 2007. "Postopolis." *SMAC Scribemedia Art Culture* (December 14; at *httpt://link.brightcove.com/services/layer/bcpid14306423001?bctid=1325126761*).

Lafer, Gordon 2003. "The Politics of Prison Labor." T. Herivel and P. Wright (eds.), *Prison Nation: The Warehousing of America's Poor.* New York, NY: Routledge: 120–128.

Lahav, Galiya 1998. "Immigration and the State: the Devolution and Privatisation of Immigration Control in the EU." *Journal of Ethnic and Migration Studies* 24, 4: 675–695.

Lane, Sandra D., Robert A. Rubinstein, Robert H. Keefe, Noah Webster, Donald A. Cibula, Alan Rosenthal, and Jesse Dowdell 2004. "Structural Violence and Racial Disparity in HIV Transmission." *Journal of Health Care for the Poor and Underserved* 15, 3: 319–335.

Lorde, Audre 1984. *Sister Outsider.* Trumansburg, NY: The Crossing Press.

Loyd, Jenna and Andrew Burridge 2007. "La Gran Marcha: Anti-Racism and Immigrant Rights in Southern California." *Acme* 6, 1: 1–35.

McKittrick, Katherine 2006. *Demonic Grounds: Black Women and the Cartographies of Struggle.* Minneapolis, MN: University of Minnesota Press.

Mitchelson, Matthew L. 2010. "'Alcatraz in the Sky': Engineering Earth in a Virginia (USA) Prison." S.D. Brunn (ed.), *Engineering Earth.* New York, NY: Springer.

Mohanty, Chandra Talpade 2003. *Feminism Without Borders: Decolonizing Theory, Practicing Solidarity.* Durham, NC: Duke University Press.

Morris, Norval and David J. Rothman (eds.) 1998. *The Oxford History of the Prison: The Practice of Punishment in Western Society.* Oxford, UK: Oxford University Press.

Mountz, Alison 2004. "Embodying the Nation-State: Canada's Response to Human Smuggling." *Political Geography* 23, 3: 323–345.

Mountz, Alison and Jennifer Hyndman 2007. "Refuge or Refusal: The Geography of Exclusion." D. Gregory and A. Pred (eds.), *Violent Geographies: Fear, Terror, and Political Violence.* New York: Routledge.

Murphy, Alexander B., H. J. de Blij, B.L. Turner 11, Ruth Wilson Gilmore, and Derek Gregory 2005. "The Role of Geography in Public Debate." *Progress in Human Geography* 29, 2: 165–193,

Nevins, Joseph 2008. *Dying to Live* (with photos by Mizue Aizeki). San Francisco: City Lights.

———. 2003 "Thinking out of Bounds: A Critical Analysis of Academic and Human Rights Writings on Migrant Deaths in the U.S.-Mexico Border Region." *Migraciones Internacionales* 2, 1: 171–190.

Newman, Kathe and Elvin Wyly 2006. "The Right to Stay Put, Revisited: Gentrification and Resistance to Displacement in New York City." *Urban Studies* 43, 1: 23–57.

Parenti, Christian 1999. *Lockdown America: Police and Prisons in the Age of Crisis.* London: Verso.

Preston, Julia 2009. "Firm Stance on Illegal Immigrants Remains Policy." *New York Times* (August 3; at *www.nytimes.com/2009/08/04/us/politics/04immig.html*).

Purcell, Mark 2003. "Citizenship and the Right to the Global City: Reimagining the World Capitalist Order." *International Journal of Urban and Regional Research* 27, 3: 564–590.

Ridgely, Jennifer 2008. "Cities of Refuge: Immigration Enforcement, Police, and the Insurgent Genealogies of Citizenship in U.S. Sanctuary Cities." *Urban Geography* 29, 1: 53–77.

Said, Edward W. 1983. "Traveling Theory." In *The World, the Text, and the Critic*. Cambridge, MA: Harvard Press: 226–247.

Sassen, Saskia 2006. "Cities and Communities in the Global Economy." N. Brenner and R. Keil (eds.), *The Global Cities Reader*. New York: Routledge. [First ed. 1996.]

Shantz, Jeff 2005. "No One Is Illegal: Organizing Beyond Left Nationalism in Fortress North America." *America, Socialism and Democracy* 19, 2: 179–185.

Sharma, Nandita 2006. *Home Economics: Nationalism and the Making of "Migrant Workers" in Canada*. Toronto: University of Toronto Press.

———. 2005. "Anti-trafficking Rhetoric and the Making of a Global Apartheid." *NWSA Journal* 17, 3:88–111.

———. 2003. "No Borders Movements and the Rejection of Left Nationalism." *Canadian Dimension* 37, 3: 37–39.

Smith, Andrea 2006. "Heteropatriarchy and the Three Pillars of White Supremacy: Rethinking Women of Color Organizing." INCITE! Women of Color Against Violence (ed.), *The Color of Violence: The Incite! Anthology*. New York: South End Press.

The CR10 Publications Collective 2008. *Abolition Now!: Ten Years of Strategy and Struggle Against the Prison Industrial Complex*. Oakland, CA: AK Press.

The Sentencing Project n.d., "Racial Disparity." The Sentencing Project homepage (December 14; at *www.sentencingproject.org/template/page.cfm?id=122*).

Turner, Joseph 2008. "Inmate Jobs on the Way Back." *The News Tribune* (August 25): A01.

Varsanyi, Monica W. 2008. "Immigration Policing Through the Back Door: City Ordinances, the 'Right to the City,' and the Exclusion of Undocumented Day Laborers." *Urban Geography* 29, 1:29–52.

———. 2006. "Interrogating 'Urban Citizenship' Vis-à-Vis Undocumented Migration." *Citizenship Studies* 10, 2: 229–249.

Wacquant, Loïc 2002. "The Curious Eclipse of Prison Ethnography in the Age of Mass Incarceration." *Ethnography* 3, 4: 371–397.

———. 2001. "Deadly Symbiosis: When Ghetto and Prison Meet and Mesh." *Punishment and Society* 3, 1: 95–134.

West, Heather C. and William J. Sabol 2009. *Prison Inmates at Midyear 2008—Statistical Tables*. Washington, DC: U.S. Department of Justice.

Willmott, Donna and Juliana van Olphen 2005. "Challenging the Health Impacts of Incarceration: The Role for Community Health Workers." *California Journal of Health Promotion* 3, 2: 38–48.

Wright, Paul 2003. "Making Slave Labor Fly." T. Herivel and P. Wright (eds.), *Prison Nation: The Warehousing of America's Poor*. New York, NY: Routledge: 112–119.

Climate Justice: Examining Climate Change through the Lens of Social Justice

(2021)

Christopher Todd Beer

L EARNING ABOUT CLIMATE CHANGE SHOULD NOT be limited to atmospheric science, chemistry, or other courses in the natural sciences for many reasons. Fundamentally, climate change is about the distribution of a primary modern resource—fossil fuel energy—and the positive and negative consequences of that distribution to various groups in local, national, and global society. The causes of climate change are rooted in social structures, values, and relationships within modern societies' primary economic mode of production—consumer capitalism. One way or another, addressing climate change will cause significant reorganization of national societies and collective global society in the coming decades. Additionally, the distribution of the causes and consequences of climate change are rooted in global and national inequality, political power, and the historical and modern structure of the global economy. It is for all of these reasons that sociology, anthropology, political science, and social justice are particularly well-suited to help us understand climate change.

At the very basic level, the empirical research of the collective scientific community indicates that the accumulation of what are commonly referred to as greenhouse gases (GHGs) (for their heat trapping ability) have reached levels unprecedented in human existence. These gases are emitted by human activity, primarily the burning of fossil fuels (coal, oil, and natural gas) in industrial processes, electricity production, and transportation, but also through deforestation and modern industrial agricultural practices. On average, the global emission of these gasses has increased annually since the beginning of the industrial revolution.

While climate change is a global problem, various groups of people have played different roles in causing it and will experience the negative impacts differently. Questions of justice emerge when we examine who has caused the problem and who will feel the negative impacts now and in the future, as well as who is responsible for addressing the challenges caused by global warming. The ideas of climate justice are rooted in the *unequal* distribution of the harms generated by climate change being felt by many *now* (not just in the coming decades), mostly by those who have contributed very little to the problem. While there are other justice perspectives regarding the political processes of global negotiations, this chapter will focus on the distribution of emissions and negative consequences—often referred to as distributional justice.

Broadly, justice involves holding those responsible for harm to others accountable in a fair manner. Because it is the emission of GHGs that has caused global warming and subsequent climate change, the source of those emissions must be examined. However, who is accountable can vary depending on how emissions are measured. Which emissions do we account for? Current emissions? Historical emissions? What unit of measure should be utilized? The individual? The nation state?

Commonly, net GHG emissions are reported on an annual basis for each nation. Nation-states remain the most powerful political structure and their individual sovereignty gives them the authority to generate policies and laws that reduce GHGs. Around 2004, China surpassed the U.S. as the nation emitting the most GHGs. However, China has *over four times* the population of the U.S. One of the basic arguments of climate justice is that emissions should be measured on a per capita basis. As of 2016, a person in China emits only half of what a person in the U.S. does on average.

However, GHGs don't just dissipate as they reach the atmosphere. Some of them (and their heat trapping qualities) linger for several decades and even millennia. Subsequently, the climate justice perspective argues that when holding those that caused the problem accountable, we should look at historical emissions. The emissions that are continuing to cause global warming are rooted in the industrial revolution, a process that emerged beginning in the late 1700s in some, but *not all* nations. Eventually, the mechanization of production replaced human, animal, or simple hydrologic power with fossil fuels. Burning these fuels in engines, machines, and power plants in the heavily industrialized West has subsequently been occurring for a solid couple of centuries—contributing to the changes in the climate we are experiencing today. This level of consumption of fossil fuels is not the case in nations of the world that were much delayed in their industrialization due to colonization and other forces—often referred today as the Global South. So, historically, certain nations are more responsible for climate change than others, especially when accounting for variations in population. Burning fossil fuels produced wealth and development for several nations—but also GHG emissions.

The climate justice perspective examines not only who is responsible, but also who is and will be harmed by climate change. Harm from climate change comes in many forms: rising sea levels due to melting glaciers and the expanding volume of warmer oceans will flood coastal cities and make many small island nations uninhabitable; greater frequency of droughts and floods due to changes in the hydrological cycle— warmer air holds more moisture—will damage infrastructure, crops, and livelihoods; warmer temperatures will spread the geographic range of many diseases; and warmer oceans produce more destructive hurricanes and typhoons. Heavily industrialized nations that developed using fossil fuels, have more resources and wealth to adapt to the harm of climate change. They will be able to and are: building walls and pumping systems to keep rising seas at bay; developing genetically engineered drought-resistant crops; and strengthening roads, bridges, and health systems to be more climate resilient. On the other hand, less developed nations that have contributed comparatively little to the problem of climate change lack the resources to adapt to many of the problems they face due to climate change. Subsistence farmers often lack irrigation systems to get them through a drought or rains arriving late in the planting season. Indigenous coastal communities in Alaska have already begun relocating inland, losing their traditional livelihoods. Small island nations' fresh water sources that provides their only drinking water are being inundated by the salt water of rising seas. The poor are less able to seek shelter in air conditioning when dangerous heat waves strike.

Demands of the varied climate justice movement organizations around the world include: millions of dollars of compensation from wealthy, developed, GHG-emitting nations to help less developed nations recover from and avoid damages from climate change; the open transfer of technology to developing nations to develop using alternative energy sources such as wind and solar; prioritizing poor communities that have been the hardest hit by climate change for new alternative energy jobs and infrastructure projects; and rejecting emissions trading markets and carbon offset projects that encourage land grabs, displacement of communities, and tree plantations in the Global South.

Climate change is a social issue and the unequal distribution of its causes and harmful consequences makes it a justice issue. To be fair and in order to make amends, those that caused climate change and live more comfortable lives should greatly assist those that are being harmed by it and already lived more tenuous livelihoods.

Refer back to the reading selections in this unit to help you correctly respond to each of the questions below.

1. The evidence-based readings in Unit III are a small sampling of how inequality and injustice manifest in our everyday lives and institutions.

   • What are other examples of institutional settings, systems of power, and historical events characterized by social injustice?

   • What types of evidence support these claims of injustice?

   • How are these examples of the systemic nature of injustice?

2. What does Arlie Hochschild mean by the "deep story"? What was the deep story according to the Louisiana residents she studied? How did this deep story inform people's political worldviews?

3. According to the reading by Radley Balko, when did policing start to become "professionalized"?

   • What changes to policing accompanied the professionalism movement?

   • What does Balko mean by the "double-edged sword of professionalism"?

   • Find examples of this double-edged sword in the readings by Victor Rios and Michelle Alexander.

4. What were Marianne Bertrand and Sendhil Mullainathan's research findings on job applicants? Which economic theory of discrimination model do the authors think best explain their findings: (a) taste-based, (b) statistical discrimination, or (c) lexicographic search by employers? Why do they believe this model might best explain their findings? This study was conducted in 2004; do you think the experiment would produce similar results today? Why, or why not?

5. Why does Paula Braveman argue that it makes scientific sense to focus on privilege and oppression as potential contributors to racial disparities in birth outcomes?

6. How does Min Zhou describe the "paradox of assimilation"? How is this similar to or different from Vicente Rafael's discussion of "benevolent assimilation"?

7. The themes of movement and borders are prominent throughout many Unit III readings. Select a reading from Unit III, analyze it through the framework of movement and borders, and then discuss the social justice implications of your analysis. For example, you might:

- Consider implications of the movement of images/people/discourses/messages across borders.

- Consider the space where people move and reside in between borders, which Evelyn Alsultany refers to as "los intersticios."

- Consider a lack of movement, or immobility, across borders, as Jenna Loyd, Andrew Burridge, and Matthew Mitchelson do in their analysis of detention and imprisonment.

- Consider the role of movement in opportunities for change, such as the synergies that exist between the immigrant justice and prison abolition movements.

8. Christopher Todd Beer's argument around climate justice is firmly grounded in a distributive framework.
   - What are some examples of Beer's distributive analysis?
   - Using Iris Marion Young's framework of identifying injustice that extends beyond distribution (see Reading 2.1), what might be some nondistributive aspects of climate injustice?

Unit IV

Movements, Change, and Resistance

Valerie Chepp

The readings in Unit IV present strategies for inciting and implementing social justice. These readings provide an important complement to the ideas presented in the previous units, which introduce, define, substantiate, and contextualize core knowledge in social justice studies. While understanding ideas and knowledge about injustice is crucial, the field of social justice is also necessarily action oriented, aimed at effecting change that results in a more fair, tolerant, and equitable society. In this more just world, all social groups are equipped with resources and capacities for self-determination and freedom from oppression.

The Unit IV selections encourage readers to imagine and envision paths forward toward this more just society, and they offer tools and tactics for how to make these visions a reality. Different types of social justice actions, as well as historical and present-day examples of social justice activism, are featured. Readers will walk away with an understanding of the myriad ways—both big and small—to become social justice change agents.

The unit opens with a reading by Martin Luther King Jr., "Letter from the Birmingham City Jail." Penned from jail in 1963 and addressed to his "fellow clergymen," King wrote the letter after being arrested for his involvement in a series of marches and sit-ins protesting racism and racial segregation in Birmingham, Alabama. The letter engages many important themes related to social justice change-making, and these themes are threaded throughout the remainder of Unit IV, including different activist strategies, the role of law in social justice and injustice (as well as strategic law breaking), legality versus morality, human dignity, and, as stressed in previous units, the importance of evaluating justice and injustice through the lens of social groups rather than individuals.

Consistent with insights from intersectionality, King also highlights the interconnectedness of social injustices and its relationship to social change-making, famously claiming that "injustice anywhere is a threat to justice everywhere."

Like King, Audre Lorde draws attention to the interconnectedness of injustices in her well-known selection "The Master's Tools Will Never Dismantle the Master's House." A classic example of early intersectionality scholarship, Lorde challenges readers to embrace and leverage (rather than retreat from) the power of social difference in movements for change. To do otherwise, she suggests, is to replicate racist, patriarchal structures. However, Lorde offers a slightly different perspective from King's approach to social justice change-making, and this difference in perspective runs throughout many debates about social change. Lorde's assertion about the limitations of using the master's tools to effect systemic social change differs from the approach embraced by many civil rights movement activists, who sought to strategically leverage and change laws in order to enact social justice. This distinction about change-making is sometimes described as working within the system (e.g., using laws to effect change) versus working outside the system to dismantle it and start anew. While rarely an either-or situation, this rough framework can be a useful starting place to situate and analyze social change strategies.

In her reading "Engaged Pedagogy," bell hooks examines the role of education and teaching practices in social justice change-making. Drawing upon the teachings of Paulo Freire and Thich Nhat Hanh, hooks presents a progressive, holistic approach to teaching and learning whereby education can serve as a site of freedom and liberation. While hooks discusses how this liberatory practice can be carried out in the classroom, readers might consider how engaged pedagogy could be implemented in other social contexts.

In "Free Spaces: Creating Oppositional Consciousness in the Disability Rights Movement," Sharon Groch taps into themes introduced by hooks—namely, the role of knowledge, consciousness, and freedom in social justice praxis. Using a comparative analysis and the disability rights movement as a case study, Groch illustrates how consciousness matters for liberation and primes social movement actors for activism. In the reading, Groch compares the different ways deaf and blind people created an oppositional consciousness and sense of **collective identity** within the disability rights movement. She pays particular attention to the role of **free spaces** in the development of oppositional consciousness. (Groch's full analysis examines three different groups within the disability community: the deaf, blind people, and people with mobility impairments.)

> **collective identity**: refers to a person's sense of belonging to a group or collective. In research on social movements, collective identity helps scholars explain how people come together and commit to a social movement over time.
>
> **free spaces**: physical space in which oppressed groups can "communicate and share perceptions of their experiences with relatively little interference from or control by the dominant group" (Groch, p. 249 of this anthology).

In "The Inuit Circumpolar Council: An Overview," Gary Wilson and Heather Smith also explore the complicated role of collective identity and advocacy among marginalized groups, focusing specifically on the diverse Inuit communities of the Arctic. Wilson and Smith examine different perspectives among Inuit groups on issues related to indigenous rights and environmental justice, particularly in regard to resource development, socioeconomic growth, and cultural sovereignty. The reading offers an opportunity to consider Inuit heterogeneity, opportunities and challenges of coalition building within and across social groups, and the role of policymaking and group self-determination in social justice work.

Capitalism is the overarching context in which these tensions around economic growth, self-determination, and cultural autonomy play out. In "Toward a Feminist Theory of Letting Go," Donna King examines contradictions presented by contemporary capitalist forces, focusing specifically on the economic and social pressures for women to be ultraproductive, high-achieving neoliberal subjects. In the face of these impossible performance standards, King draws upon Zen insight and feminist accounts of women with invisible chronic illness to suggest that "letting go" of these destructive external expectations is a liberating strategy. For King, letting go is a radical refusal to adopt, comply with, or buy into contemporary neoliberal capitalism's pressure to perform in ways that are never enough. This refusal to play by neoliberalism's rules presents opportunities for self-transformation, as well as social transformation.

The next two readings focus on youth activism, offering examples of how children and adolescents engage in social justice change-making. In "A Figment of Our (Civic) Imagination," Henry Jenkins, Sangita Shresthova, Liana Gamber-Thompson, and Neta Kligler-Vilenchik examine how young people use American popular culture and new media to politically engage with their peers. Jenkins and colleagues underscore the centrality of a **civic imagination** in social change efforts. This active and dynamic capacity to imagine alternatives to present-day social, political, or economic conditions is necessary for seeing beyond constraints to social problem solving and envisioning oneself as a political change agent. In "Kids Make History," Colleen Bell further illustrates the significance of a critical consciousness in social justice activism and opportunities for young people to cultivate this critical way of thinking. Bell draws attention to a social justice curriculum that centers kids' historical and contemporary roles in change-making. Illustrating how this curriculum serves as an important **counternarrative** to dominant **adultist** accounts of history, Bell argues for the necessity to understand young people and their activism in serious, dignified, and nonpatronizing ways.

> **civic imagination**: "the capacity to imagine alternatives to current social, political, or economic conditions" (Jenkins et al., p. 282 of this anthology).
>
> **counternarratives**: stories told from the perspective of those who have been historically marginalized; these alternative narratives counter or challenge dominant majoritarian, or "master," narratives.
>
> **adultism**: "a belief that adults are better than young people" (Bell, p. 292 of this anthology).

In "What Can We Do? Unraveling the Gender Knot," Allan Johnson revisits the systemic nature of oppression and privilege, and he highlights our own (even if unintentional) role in preserving the status quo. Johnson goes on to describes two powerful myths that get in the way of social justice change, and he ends with a list of tangible everyday actions that readers can do to chip away at systemic inequities. "A New Way Ordered by Love," by body-positive activist Sonya Renee Taylor, concludes Unit IV with a discussion of the role of radical self-love in social justice change-making. In the face of a capitalistic machine that profits from people's internalized body shame—what she refers to as the system of **body terrorism**—Taylor highlights the power and potential in loving oneself as an antidote to our structural, oppressive arrangements. Like Johnson, Taylor offers a list of tangible actions—what she calls "unapologetic agreements"—that help to cultivate new ways of communicating a more just world into existence.

body terrorism: the political, economic, and social systems that "uphold the marginalization of bodies based on race, gender, age, size, ability, sexual orientation, and a variety of other markers" (Taylor, p. 319 of this anthology).

Letter From the Birmingham City Jail
(1963)

Martin Luther King, Jr.

Birmingham City Jail
April 16, 1963

My dear Fellow Clergymen,

While confined here in the Birmingham City Jail, I came across your recent statement calling our present activities "unwise and untimely." Seldom, if ever, do I pause to answer criticism of my work and ideas. If I sought to answer all the criticisms that cross my desk, my secretaries would be engaged in little else in the course of the day and I would have no time for constructive work. But since I feel that you are men of genuine goodwill and your criticisms are sincerely set forth, I would like to answer your statement in what I hope will be patient and reasonable terms.

I think I should give the reason for my being in Birmingham, since you have been influenced by the argument of "outsiders coming in." I have the honor of serving as president of the Southern Christian Leadership Conference, an organization operating in every Southern state with headquarters in Atlanta, Georgia. We have some eighty-five affiliate organizations all across the South—one being the Alabama Christian Movement for Human Rights. Whenever necessary and possible we share staff, educational, and financial resources with our affiliates. Several months ago our local affiliate here in Birmingham invited us to be on call to engage in a nonviolent direct action program if such were deemed necessary. We readily consented and when the hour came we lived up to our promises. So I am here, along with several members of my staff, because we were invited here. I am here because I have basic organizational ties here. Beyond this, I am in Birmingham because injustice is here. Just as the eighth century prophets left their little villages and carried their "thus saith the Lord" far beyond the boundaries of their home town, and just as the Apostle Paul left his little village of Tarsus and carried the gospel of Jesus Christ to practically every hamlet and city of the Graeco-Roman world, I too am compelled to carry the gospel of freedom beyond my particular home town. Like Paul, I must constantly respond to the Macedonian call for aid.

Moreover, I am cognizant of the interrelatedness of all communities and states. I cannot sit idly by in Atlanta and not be concerned about what happens in Birmingham.

Martin Luther King, Jr., "Letter from a Birmingham Jail," 1963.

Injustice anywhere is a threat to justice everywhere. We are caught in an inescapable network of mutuality tied in a single garment of destiny. Whatever affects one directly affects all indirectly. Never again can we afford to live with the narrow, provincial "outside agitator" idea. Anyone who lives inside the United States can never be considered an outsider anywhere in this country.

You deplore the demonstrations that are presently taking place in Birmingham. But I am sorry that your statement did not express a similar concern for the conditions that brought the demonstrations into being. I am sure that each of you would want to go beyond the superficial social analyst who looks merely at effects, and does not grapple with underlying causes. I would not hesitate to say that it is unfortunate that so-called demonstrations are taking place in Birmingham at this time, but I would say in more emphatic terms that it is even more unfortunate that the white power structure of this city left the Negro community with no other alternative.

In any nonviolent campaign there are four basic steps: (1) Collection of the facts to determine whether injustices are alive; (2) Negotiation; (3) Self-purification; and (4) Direct action. We have gone through all of these steps in Birmingham. There can be no gainsaying of the fact that racial injustice engulfs this community. Birmingham is probably the most thoroughly segregated city in the United States. Its ugly record of police brutality is known in every section of this country. Its unjust treatment of Negroes in the courts is a notorious reality. There have been more unsolved bombings of Negro homes and churches in Birmingham than any city in this nation. These are the hard, brutal, and unbelievable facts. On the basis of these conditions Negro leaders sought to negotiate with the city fathers. But the political leaders consistently refused to engage in good faith negotiation.

Then came the opportunity last September to talk with some of the leaders of the economic community. In these negotiating sessions certain promises were made by the merchants—such as the promise to remove the humiliating racial signs from the stores. On the basis of these promises Rev. Shuttlesworth and the leaders of the Alabama Christian Movement for Human Rights agreed to call a moratorium on any type of demonstrations. As the weeks and months unfolded we realized that we were the victims of a broken promise. The signs remained. As in so many experiences of the past we were confronted with blasted hopes, and the dark shadow of a deep disappointment settled upon us. So we had no alternative except that of preparing for direct action, whereby we would present our very bodies as a means of laying our case before the conscience of the local and national community. We were not unmindful of the difficulties involved. So we decided to go through a process of self-purification. We started having workshops on nonviolence and repeatedly asked ourselves the questions, "Are you able to accept blows without retaliating?" "Are you able to endure the ordeals of jail?"

We decided to set our direct-action program around the Easter season, realizing that with the exception of Christmas, this was the largest shopping period of the year.

Knowing that a strong economic withdrawal program would be the by-product of direct action, we felt that this was the best time to bring pressure on the merchants for the needed changes. Then it occurred to us that the March election was ahead, and so we speedily decided to postpone action until after election day. When we discovered that Mr. Connor was in the run-off, we decided again to postpone action so that the demonstrations could not be used to cloud the issues. At this time we agreed to begin our nonviolent witness the day after the run-off.

This reveals that we did not move irresponsibly into direct action. We too wanted to see Mr. Connor defeated; so we went through postponement after postponement to aid in this community need. After this we felt that direct action could be delayed no longer.

You may well ask, Why direct action? Why sit-ins, marches, etc.? Isn't negotiation a better path?" You are exactly right in your call for negotiation. Indeed, this is the purpose of direct action. Nonviolent direct action seeks to create such a crisis and establish such creative tension that a community that has constantly refused to negotiate is forced to confront the issue. It seeks so to dramatize the issue that it can no longer be ignored. I just referred to the creation of tension as a part of the work of the nonviolent resister. This may sound rather shocking. But I must confess that I am not afraid of the word tension. I have earnestly worked and preached against violent tension, but there is a type of constructive nonviolent tension that is necessary for growth. Just as Socrates felt that it was necessary to create a tension in the mind so that individuals could rise from the bondage of myths and half-truths to the unfettered realm of creative analysis and objective appraisal, we must see the need of having nonviolent gadflies to create the kind of tension in society that will help men rise from the dark depths of prejudice and racism to the majestic heights of understanding and brotherhood. So the purpose of the direct action is to create a situation so crisis-packed that it will inevitably open the door to negotiation. We, therefore, concur with you in your call for negotiation. Too long has our beloved Southland been bogged down in the tragic attempt to live in monologue rather than dialogue.

One of the basic points in your statement is that our acts are untimely. Some have asked, "Why didn't you give the new administration time to act?" The only answer that I can give to this inquiry is that the new administration must be prodded about as much as the outgoing one before it acts. We will be sadly mistaken if we feel that the election of Mr. Boutwell will bring the millennium to Birmingham. While Mr. Boutwell is much more articulate and gentle than Mr. Connor, they are both segregationists dedicated to the task of maintaining the status quo. The hope I see in Mr. Boutwell is that he will be reasonable enough to see the futility of massive resistance to desegregation. But he will not see this without pressure from the devotees of civil rights. My friends, I must say to you that we have not made a single gain in civil rights without determined legal and nonviolent pressure. History is the long and tragic story of the fact that privileged groups seldom give up their privileges voluntarily. Individuals may see the moral light and voluntarily give up their unjust posture; but as Reinhold Niebuhr has reminded us, groups are more immoral than individuals.

We know through painful experience that freedom is never voluntarily given by the oppressor; it must be demanded by the oppressed. Frankly I have never yet engaged in a direct action movement that was "well timed," according to the timetable of those who have not suffered unduly from the disease of segregation. For years now I have heard the word "Wait!" It rings in the ear of every Negro with a piercing familiarity. This "wait" has almost always meant "never." It has been a tranquilizing thalidomide, relieving the emotional stress for a moment, only to give birth to an ill-formed infant of frustration. We must come to see with the distinguished jurist of yesterday that "justice too long delayed is justice denied." We have waited for more than three hundred and forty years for our constitutional and God-given rights. The nations of Asia and Africa are moving with jet-like speed toward the goal of political independence, and we still creep at horse and buggy pace toward the gaining of a cup of coffee at a lunch counter.

I guess it is easy for those who have never felt the stinging darts of segregation to say wait. But when you have seen vicious mobs lynch your mothers and fathers at will and drown your sisters and brothers at whim; when you have seen hate filled police-men curse, kick, brutalize, and even kill your black brothers and sisters with impunity; when you see the vast majority of your twenty million Negro brothers smothering in an air-tight cage of poverty in the midst of an affluent society; when you suddenly find your tongue twisted and your speech stammering as you seek to explain to your six-year-old daughter why she can't go to the public amusement park that has just been advertised on television, and see tears welling up in her little eyes when she is told that Funtown is closed to colored children, and see the depressing clouds of inferiority begin to form in her little mental sky, and see her begin to distort her little personal-ity by unconsciously developing a bitterness toward white people; when you have to concoct an answer for a five-year-old son asking in agonizing pathos: "Daddy, why do white people treat colored people so mean?"; when you take a cross-country drive and find it necessary to sleep night after night in the uncomfortable corners of your auto-mobile because no motel will accept you; when you are humiliated day in and day out by nagging signs reading "white" men and "colored"; when your first name becomes "nigger" and your middle name becomes "boy" (however old you are) and your last name becomes "John," and when your wife and mother are never given the respected title "Mrs."; when you are harried by day and haunted by night by the fact that you are a Negro, living constantly at tip-toe stance never quite knowing what to expect next, and plagued with inner fears and outer resentments; when you are forever fighting a degenerating sense of "nobodiness"—then you will understand why we find it diffi-cult to wait. There comes a time when the cup of endurance runs over, and men are no longer willing to be plunged into an abyss of injustice where they experience the bleakness of corroding despair. I hope, sirs, you can understand our legitimate and unavoidable impatience.

You express a great deal of anxiety over our willingness to break laws. This is certainly a legitimate concern. Since we so diligently urge people to obey the Supreme Court's decision of 1954 outlawing segregation in the public schools, it is rather strange and paradoxical to find us consciously breaking laws. One may well ask: "How can you advocate breaking some laws and obeying others?" The answer is found in the fact that there are two types of laws: There are just laws and there are unjust laws. I would be the first to advocate obeying just laws. One has not only a legal but moral responsibility to obey just laws. Conversely, one has a moral responsibility to disobey unjust laws. I would agree with Saint Augustine that "An unjust law is no law at all."

Now what is the difference between the two? How does one determine when a law is just or unjust? A just law is a man-made code that squares with the moral law or the law of God. An unjust law is a code that is out of harmony with the moral law. To put it in the terms of Saint Thomas Aquinas, an unjust law is a human law that is not rooted in eternal and natural law. Any law that uplifts human personality is just. Any law that degrades human personality is unjust. All segregation statutes are unjust because segregation distorts the soul and damages the personality. It gives the segregator a false sense of superiority and the segregated a false sense of inferiority. To use the words of Martin Buber, the great Jewish philosopher, segregation substitutes an "I-it" relationship for an "I-thou" relationship, and ends up relegating persons to the status of things. So segregation is not only politically, economically, and sociologically unsound, but it is morally wrong and sinful. Paul Tillich has said that sin is separation. Isn't segregation an existential expression of man's tragic separation, an expression of his awful estrangement, his terrible sinfulness? So I can urge men to obey the 1954 decision of the Supreme Court because it is morally right, and I can urge them to disobey segregation ordinances because they are morally wrong.

Let us turn to a more concrete example of just and unjust laws. An unjust law is a code that a majority inflicts on a minority that is not binding on itself. This is difference made legal. On the other hand a just law is a code that a majority compels a minority to follow that it is willing to follow itself. This is sameness made legal.

Let me give another explanation. An unjust law is a code inflicted upon a minority which that minority had no part in enacting or creating because they did not have the unhampered right to vote. Who can say that the legislature of Alabama which set up the segregation laws was democratically elected? Throughout the state of Alabama all types of conniving methods are used to prevent Negroes from becoming registered voters and there are some counties without a single Negro registered to vote despite the fact that the Negro constitutes a majority of the population. Can any law set up in such a state be considered democratically structured?

These are just a few examples of unjust and just laws. There are some instances when a law is just on its face but unjust in its application. For instance, I was arrested Friday on a charge of parading without a permit. Now there is nothing wrong with an ordinance which requires a permit for a parade, but when the ordinance is used to preserve segregation and to deny citizens the First Amendment privilege of peaceful assembly and peaceful protest, then it becomes unjust.

I hope you can see the distinction I am trying to point out. In no sense do I advocate evading or defying the law as the rabid segregationist would do. This would lead to anarchy. One who breaks an unjust law must do it openly, lovingly (not hatefully as the white mothers did in New Orleans when they were seen on television screaming "nigger, nigger, nigger") and with a willingness to accept the penalty. I submit that an individual who breaks a law that conscience tells him is unjust, and willingly accepts the penalty by staying in jail to arouse the conscience of the community over its injustice, is in reality expressing the very highest respect for law.

Of course there is nothing new about this kind of civil disobedience. It was seen sublimely in the refusal of Shadrach, Meshach, and Abednego to obey the laws of Nebuchadnezzar because a higher moral law was involved. It was practiced superbly by the early Christians who were willing to face hungry lions and the excruciating pain of chopping blocks, before submitting to certain unjust laws of the Roman Empire. To a degree academic freedom is a reality today because Socrates practiced civil disobedience.

We can never forget that everything Hitler did in Germany was "legal" and everything the Hungarian freedom fighters did in Hungary was "illegal." It was "illegal" to aid and comfort a Jew in Hitler's Germany. But I am sure that, if I had lived in Germany during that time, I would have aided and comforted my Jewish brothers even though it was illegal. If I lived in a communist country today where certain principles dear to the Christian faith are suppressed, I believe I would openly advocate disobeying these anti-religious laws.

I must make two honest confessions to you, my Christian and Jewish brothers. First, I must confess that over the last few years I have been gravely disappointed with the white moderate. I have almost reached the regrettable conclusion that the Negroes' great stumbling block in the stride toward freedom is not the White Citizen's "Counciler" or the Ku Klux Klanner, but the white moderate who is more devoted to "order" than to justice; who prefers a negative peace which is the absence of tension to a positive peace which is the presence of justice; who constantly says "I agree with you in the goal you seek, but I can't agree with your methods of direct action"; who paternalistically feels that he can set the timetable for another man's freedom; who lives by the myth of time and who constantly advises the Negro to wait until a "more convenient season." Shallow understanding from people of good will is more frustrating than absolute misunderstanding from people of ill will. Lukewarm acceptance is much more bewildering than outright rejection.

I had hoped that the white moderate would understand that law and order exist for the purpose of establishing justice, and that when they fail to do this they become dangerously structured dams that block the flow of social progress. I had hoped that the white moderate would understand that the present tension in the South is merely a necessary phase of the transition from an obnoxious negative peace, where the Negro passively accepted his unjust plight, to a substance-filled positive peace, where all men will respect the dignity and worth of human personality. Actually, we who engage in nonviolent direct action are not the creators of tension. We merely bring to the surface the hidden tension that is already alive. We bring it out in the open where it can be seen and dealt with. Like a boil that can never be cured as long as it is covered up but must be opened with all its pus-flowing ugliness to the natural medicines of air and light, injustice must likewise be exposed, with all of the tension its exposing creates, to the light of human conscience and the air of national opinion before it can be cured.

In your statement you asserted that our actions, even though peaceful, must be condemned because they precipitate violence. But can this assertion be logically made? Isn't this like condemning the robbed man because his possession of money precipitated the evil act of robbery? Isn't this like condemning Socrates because his unswerving commitment to truth and his philosophical delvings precipitated the misguided popular mind to make him drink the hemlock? Isn't this like condemning Jesus because His unique God consciousness and never-ceasing devotion to His will precipitated the evil act of crucifixion? We must come to see, as federal courts have consistently affirmed, that it is immoral to urge an individual to withdraw his efforts to gain his basic constitutional rights because the quest precipitates violence. Society must protect the robbed and punish the robber.

I had also hoped that the white moderate would reject the myth of time. I received a letter this morning from a white brother in Texas which said: "All Christians know that the colored people will receive equal rights eventually, but is it possible that you are in too great of a religious hurry? It has taken Christianity almost 2,000 years to accomplish what it has. The teachings of Christ take time to come to earth." All that is said here grows out of a tragic misconception of time. It is the strangely irrational notion that there is something in the very flow of time that will inevitably cure all ills. Actually time is neutral. It can be used either destructively or constructively. I am coming to feel that the people of ill will have used time much more effectively than the people of good will. We will have to repent in this generation not merely for the vitriolic words and actions of the bad people, but for the appalling silence of the good people. We must come to see that human progress never rolls in on wheels of inevitability. It comes through the tireless efforts and persistent work of men willing to be co-workers with God, and without this hard work time itself becomes an ally of the forces of social stagnation.

We must use time creatively, and forever realize that the time is always ripe to do right. Now is the time to make real the promise of democracy, and transform our pending national elegy into a creative psalm of brotherhood. Now is the time to lift our national policy from the quicksand of racial injustice to the solid rock of human dignity.

You spoke of our activity in Birmingham as extreme. At first I was rather disappointed that fellow clergymen would see my nonviolent efforts as those of the extremist. I started thinking about the fact that I stand in the middle of two opposing forces in the Negro community. One is a force of complacency made up of Negroes who, as a result of long years of oppression, have been so completely drained of self-respect and a sense of "somebodiness" that they have adjusted to segregation, and of a few Negroes in the middle class who, because of a degree of academic and economic security, and because at points they profit by segregation, have unconsciously become insensitive to the problems of the masses. The other force is one of bitterness and hatred and comes perilously close to advocating violence. It is expressed in the various black nationalist groups that are springing up over the nation, the largest and best known being Elijah Muhammad's Muslim movement. This movement is nourished by the contemporary frustration over the continued existence of racial discrimination. It is made up of people who have lost faith in America, who have absolutely repudiated Christianity, and who have concluded that the white man is an incurable "devil." I have tried to stand between these two forces saying that we need not follow the "do-nothingism" of the complacent or the hatred and despair of the black nationalist. There is the more excellent way of love and nonviolent protest. I'm grateful to God that, through the Negro church, the dimension of nonviolence entered our struggle. If this philosophy had not emerged I am convinced that by now many streets of the South would be flowing with floods of blood. And I am further convinced that if our white brothers dismiss us as "rabble rousers" and "outside agitators"—those of us who are working through the channels of nonviolent direct action—and refuse to support our nonviolent efforts, millions of Negroes, out of frustration and despair, will seek solace and security in black-nationalist ideologies, a development that will lead inevitably to a frightening racial nightmare.

Oppressed people cannot remain oppressed forever. The urge for freedom will eventually come. This is what has happened to the American Negro. Something within has reminded him of his birthright of freedom; something without has reminded him that he can gain it. Consciously and unconsciously, he has been swept in by what the Germans call the Zeitgeist, and with his black brothers of Africa, and his brown and yellow brothers of Asia, South America, and the Caribbean, he is moving with a sense of cosmic urgency toward the promised land of racial justice. Recognizing this vital urge that has engulfed the Negro community, one should readily understand public demonstrations. The Negro has many pent-up resentments and latent frustrations. He has to get them out. So let him march sometime; let him have his prayer pilgrimages to the city hall; understand why he must have sit-ins and freedom rides. If his repressed emotions do not come out in these nonviolent ways, they will come out in ominous expressions of violence. This is not a threat; it is a fact of history. So I have not said to my people, "Get rid of your discontent." But I have tried to say that this normal and healthy discontent can be channeled through the creative outlet of nonviolent direct action. Now this approach is being dismissed as extremist. I must admit that I was initially disappointed in being so categorized.

But as I continued to think about the matter I gradually gained a bit of satisfaction from being considered an extremist. Was not Jesus an extremist in love? "Love your enemies, bless them that curse you, pray for them that despitefully use you." Was not Amos an extremist for justice—"Let justice roll down like waters and righteousness like a mighty stream." Was not Paul an extremist for the gospel of Jesus Christ—"I bear in my body the marks of the Lord Jesus." Was not Martin Luther an extremist—"Here I stand; I can do none other so help me God." Was not John Bunyan an extremist—"I will stay in jail to the end of my days before I make a butchery of my conscience." Was not Abraham Lincoln an extremist—"This nation cannot survive half slave and half free." Was not Thomas Jefferson an extremist—"We hold these truths to be self-evident, that all men are created equal." So the question is not whether we will be extremist but what kind of extremist will we be. Will we be extremists for hate or will we be extremists for love? Will we be extremists for the preservation of injustice—or will we be extremists for the cause of justice? In that dramatic scene on Calvary's hill three men were crucified. We must never forget that all three were crucified for the same crime—the crime of extremism. Two were extremists for immorality, and thus fell below their environment. The other, Jesus Christ, was an extremist for love, truth, and goodness, and thereby rose above His environment. So, after all, maybe the South, the nation, and the world are in dire need of creative extremists.

I had hoped that the white moderate would see this. Maybe I was too optimistic. Maybe I expected too much. I guess I should have realized that few members of a race that has oppressed another race can understand or appreciate the deep groans and passionate yearnings of those that have been oppressed, and still fewer have the vision to see that injustice must be rooted out by strong, persistent, and determined action. I am thankful, however, that some of our white brothers have grasped the meaning of this social revolution and committed themselves to it. They are still all too small in quantity, but they are big in quality. Some like Ralph McGill, Lillian Smith, Harry Golden, and James Dabbs have written about our struggle in eloquent, prophetic, and understanding terms. Others have marched with us down nameless streets of the South. They have languished in filthy, roach-infested jails, suffering the abuse and brutality of angry policemen who see them as "dirty nigger lovers." They, unlike so many of their moderate brothers and sisters, have recognized the urgency of the moment and sensed the need for powerful "action" antidotes to combat the disease of segregation.

Let me rush on to mention my other disappointment. I have been so greatly disappointed with the white Church and its leadership. Of course there are some notable exceptions. I am not unmindful of the fact that each of you has taken some significant stands on this issue. I commend you, Rev. Stallings, for your Christian stand on this past Sunday, in welcoming Negroes to your worship service on a non-segregated basis. I commend the Catholic leaders of this state for integrating Spring Hill College several years ago.

But despite these notable exceptions I must honestly reiterate that I have been disappointed with the Church. I do not say that as one of those negative critics who can always find something wrong with the Church. I say it as a minister of the gospel, who loves the Church; who was nurtured in its bosom; who has been sustained by its spiritual blessings and who will remain true to it as long as the cord of life shall lengthen.

I had the strange feeling when I was suddenly catapulted into the leadership of the bus protest in Montgomery several years ago that we would have the support of the white Church. I felt that the white ministers, priests, and rabbis of the South would be some of our strongest allies. Instead, some have been outright opponents, refusing to understand the freedom movement and misrepresenting its leaders; all too many others have been more cautious than courageous and have remained silent behind the anesthetizing security of the stained glass windows.

In spite of my shattered dreams of the past, I came to Birmingham with the hope that the white religious leadership of this community would see the justice of our cause and with deep moral concern, serve as the channel through which our just grievances could get to the power structure. I had hoped that each of you would understand. But again I have been disappointed.

I have heard numerous religious leaders of the South call upon their worshippers to comply with a desegregation decision because it is the law, but I have longed to hear white ministers say follow this decree because integration is morally right and the Negro is your brother. In the midst of blatant injustices inflicted upon the Negro, I have watched white churches stand on the sideline and merely mouth pious irrelevancies and sanctimonious trivialities. In the midst of a mighty struggle to rid our nation of racial and economic injustice, I have heard so many ministers say, "Those are social issues with which the gospel has no real concern," and I have watched so many churches commit themselves to a completely other-worldly religion which made a strange distinction between body and soul, the sacred and the secular.

So here we are moving toward the exit of the twentieth century with a religious community largely adjusted to the status quo, standing as a tail-light behind other community agencies rather than a headlight leading men to higher levels of justice.

I have travelled the length and breadth of Alabama, Mississippi and all the other southern states. On sweltering summer days and crisp autumn mornings I have looked at her beautiful churches with their spires pointing heavenward. I have beheld the impressive outlay of her massive religious education buildings. Over and over again I have found myself asking: "Who worships here? Who is their God? Where were their voices when the lips of Governor Barnett dripped with words of interposition and nullification? Where were they when Governor Wallace gave the clarion call for defiance and hatred? Where were their voices of support when tired, bruised, and weary Negro men and women decided to rise from the dark dungeons of complacency to the bright hills of creative protest?"

Yes, these questions are still in my mind. In deep disappointment, I have wept over the laxity of the church. But be assured that my tears have been tears of love. There can be no deep disappointment where there is not deep love. Yes, I love the Church; I love her sacred walls. How could I do otherwise? I am in the rather unique position of being the son, the grandson, and the great-grandson of preachers. Yes, I see the Church as the body of Christ. But, oh! How we have blemished and scarred that body through social neglect and fear of being nonconformist.

There was a time when the Church was very powerful. It was during that period when the early Christians rejoiced when they were deemed worthy to suffer for what they believed. In those days the Church was not merely a thermometer that recorded the ideas and principles of popular opinion; it was a thermostat that transformed the mores of society. Wherever the early Christians entered a town the power structure got disturbed and immediately sought to convict them for being "disturbers of the peace" and "outside agitators." But they went on with the conviction that they were "a colony of heaven" and had to obey God rather than man. They were small in number but big in commitment. They were too God-intoxicated to be "astronomically intimidated." They brought an end to such ancient evils as infanticide and gladiatorial contest.

Things are different now. The contemporary Church is so often a weak, ineffectual voice with an uncertain sound. It is so often the arch-supporter of the status quo. Far from being disturbed by the presence of the Church, the power structure of the average community is consoled by the Church's silent and often vocal sanction of things as they are.

But the judgment of God is upon the Church as never before. If the Church of today does not recapture the sacrificial spirit of the early Church, it will lose its authentic ring, forfeit the loyalty of millions, and be dismissed as an irrelevant social club with no meaning for the twentieth century. I am meeting young people every day whose disappointment with the Church has risen to outright disgust.

Maybe again I have been too optimistic. Is organized religion too inextricably bound to the status quo to save our nation and the world? Maybe I must turn my faith to the inner spiritual Church, the church within the Church, as the true ecclesia and the hope of the world. But again I am thankful to God that some noble souls from the ranks of organized religion have broken loose from the paralyzing chains of conformity and joined us as active partners in the struggle for freedom. They have left their secure congregations and walked the streets of Albany, Georgia, with us. They have gone through the highways of the South on torturous rides for freedom. Yes, they have gone to jail with us. Some have been kicked out of their churches and lost the support of their bishops and fellow ministers. But they have gone with the faith that right defeated is stronger than evil triumphant. These men have been the leaven in the lump of the race. Their witness has been the spiritual salt that has preserved the true meaning of the Gospel in these troubled times. They have carved a tunnel of hope through the dark mountain of disappointment.

I hope the Church as a whole will meet the challenge of this decisive hour. But even if the Church does not come to the aid of justice, I have no despair about the future. I have no fear about the outcome of our struggle in Birmingham, even if our motives are presently misunderstood. We will reach the goal of freedom in Birmingham and all over the nation, because the goal of America is freedom. Abused and scorned though we may be, our destiny is tied up with the destiny of America. Before the pilgrims landed at Plymouth, we were here. Before the pen of Jefferson etched across the pages of history the majestic words of the Declaration of Independence, we were here. For more than two centuries our foreparents labored in this country without wages; they made cotton "king"; and they built the homes of their masters in the midst of brutal injustice and shameful humiliation—and yet out of a bottomless vitality they continued to thrive and develop. If the inexpressible cruelties of slavery could not stop us, the opposition we now face will surely fail. We will win our freedom because the sacred heritage of our nation and the eternal will of God are embodied in our echoing demands.

I must close now. But before closing I am impelled to mention one other point in your statement that troubled me profoundly. You warmly commend the Birmingham police force for keeping "order" and "preventing violence." I don't believe you would have so warmly commended the police force if you had seen its angry violent dogs literally biting six unarmed, nonviolent Negroes. I don't believe you would so quickly commend the policemen if you would observe their ugly and inhuman treatment of Negroes here in the city jail; if you would watch them push and curse old Negro women and young Negro girls; if you would see them slap and kick old Negro men and young Negro boys; if you will observe them, as they did on two occasions, refuse to give us food because we wanted to sing our grace together. I'm sorry that I can't join you in your praise for the police department.

It is true that they have been rather disciplined in their public handling of the demonstrators. In this sense they have been rather publicly "nonviolent." But for what purpose? To preserve the evil system of segregation. Over the last few years I have consistently preached that nonviolence demands the means we use must be as pure as the ends we seek. So I have tried to make it clear that it is wrong to use immoral means to attain moral ends. But now I must affirm that it is just as wrong or even more so to use moral means to preserve immoral ends. Maybe Mr. Connor and his policemen have been rather publicly nonviolent, as Chief Pritchett was in Albany, Georgia, but they have used the moral means of nonviolence to maintain the immoral end of flagrant injustice. T. S. Eliot has said that there is no greater treason than to do the right deed for the wrong reason.

I wish you had commended the Negro sit-inners and demonstrators of Birmingham for their sublime courage, their willingness to suffer, and their amazing discipline in the midst of the most inhuman provocation. One day the South will recognize its real heroes. They will be the James Merediths, courageously and with a majestic sense of purpose, facing jeering and hostile mobs and the agonizing loneliness that characterizes the life of the pioneer. They will be old, oppressed, battered Negro women, symbolized in a seventy-two year old woman of Montgomery, Alabama, who rose up with a sense of dignity and with her people decided not to ride the segregated buses, and responded to one who inquired about her tiredness with ungrammatical profundity: "My feets is tired, but my soul is rested." They will be the young high school and college students, young ministers of the gospel and a host of their elders courageously and nonviolently sitting-in at lunch counters and willingly going to jail for conscience sake. One day the South will know that when these disinherited children of God sat down at lunch counters they were in reality standing up for the best in the American dream and the most sacred values in our Judaeo-Christian heritage, and thus carrying our whole nation back to great wells of democracy which were dug deep by the founding fathers in the formulation of the Constitution and the Declaration of Independence.

Never before have I written a letter this long (or should I say a book?). I'm afraid it is much too long to take your precious time. I can assure you that it would have been much shorter if I had been writing from a comfortable desk, but what else is there to do when you are alone for days in the dull monotony of a narrow jail cell other than write long letters, think strange thoughts, and pray long prayers?

If I have said anything in this letter that is an overstatement of the truth and is indicative of an unreasonable impatience, I beg you to forgive me. If I have said anything in this letter that is an understatement of the truth and is indicative of my having a patience that makes me patient with anything less than brotherhood, I beg God to forgive me.

I hope this letter finds you strong in the faith. I also hope that circumstances will soon make it possible for me to meet each of you, not as an integrationist or a civil rights leader, but as a fellow clergyman and a Christian brother. Let us all hope that the dark clouds of racial prejudice will soon pass away and the deep fog of misunderstanding will be lifted from our fear-drenched communities and in some not too distant tomorrow the radiant stars of love and brotherhood will shine over our great nation with all their scintillating beauty.

Yours for the cause of
Peace and Brotherhood,
Martin Luther King, Jr.

Reading 4.2

The Master's Tools Will Never Dismantle the Master's House[1]

(1979)

Audre Lorde

I AGREED TO TAKE PART IN A New York University Institute for the Humanities conference a year ago, with the understanding that I would be commenting upon papers
dealing with the role of difference within the lives of american women: difference of
race, sexuality, class, and age. The absence of these considerations weakens any feminist discussion of the personal and the political.

It is a particular academic arrogance to assume any discussion of feminist theory
without examining our many differences, and without a significant input from poor
women, Black and Third World women, and lesbians. And yet, I stand here as a Black
lesbian feminist, having been invited to comment within the only panel at this conference where the input of Black feminists and lesbians is represented. What this says about
the vision of this conference is sad, in a country where racism, sexism, and homophobia
are inseparable. To read this program is to assume that lesbian and Black women have
nothing to say about existentialism, the erotic, women's culture and silence, developing feminist theory, or heterosexuality and power. And what does it mean in personal
and political terms when even the two Black women who did present here were literally found at the last hour? What does it mean when the tools of a racist patriarchy are
used to examine the fruits of that same patriarchy? It means that only the most narrow
perimeters of change are possible and allowable.

The absence of any consideration of lesbian consciousness or the consciousness of Third
World women leaves a serious gap within this conference and within the papers presented
here. For example, in a paper on material relationships between women, I was conscious
of an either/or model of nurturing which totally dismissed my knowledge as a Black lesbian. In this paper there was no examination of mutuality between women, no systems
of shared support, no interdependence as exists between lesbians and women-identified

---

1   Comments at "The Personal and the Political Panel," Second Sex Conference, New York, September
29, 1979.

women. Yet it is only in the patriarchal model of nurturance that women "who attempt to emancipate themselves pay perhaps too high a price for the results," as this paper states.

For women, the need and desire to nurture each other is not pathological but redemptive, and it is within that knowledge that our real power is rediscovered. It is this real connection which is so feared by a patriarchal world. Only within a patriarchal structure is maternity the only social power open to women.

Interdependency between women is the way to a freedom which allows the *I* to *be*, not in order to be used, but in order to be creative. This is a difference between the passive *be* and the active *being*.

Advocating the mere tolerance of difference between women is the grossest reformism. It is a total denial of the creative function of difference in our lives. Difference must be not merely tolerated, but seen as a fund of necessary polarities between which our creativity can spark like a dialectic. Only then does the necessity for interdependency become unthreatening. Only within that interdependency of different strengths, acknowledged and equal, can the power to seek new ways of being in the world generate, as well as the courage and sustenance to act where there are no charters.

Within the interdependence of mutual (nondominant) differences lies that security which enables us to descend into the chaos of knowledge and return with true visions of our future, along with the concomitant power to effect those changes which can bring that future into being. Difference is that raw and powerful connection from which our personal power is forged.

As women, we have been taught either to ignore our differences, or to view them as causes for separation and suspicion rather than as forces for change. Without community there is no liberation, only the most vulnerable and temporary armistice between an individual and her oppression. But community must not mean a shedding of our differences, nor the pathetic pretense that these differences do not exist.

Those of us who stand outside the circle of this society's definition of acceptable women; those of us who have been forged in the crucibles of difference—those of us who are poor, who are lesbians, who are Black, who are older—know that *survival is not an academic skill.* It is learning how to stand alone, unpopular and sometimes reviled, and how to make common cause with those others identified as outside the structures in order to define and seek a world in which we can all flourish. It is learning how to take our differences and make them strengths. For *the master's tools will never dismantle the master's house.* They may allow us temporarily to beat him at his own game, but they will never enable us to bring about genuine change. And this fact is only threatening to those women who still define the master's house as their only source of support.

Poor women and women of Color know there is a difference between the daily manifestations of marital slavery and prostitution because it is our daughters who line 42nd Street. If white american feminist theory need not deal with the differences between us, and the resulting difference in our oppressions, then how do you deal with the fact that the women who clean your houses and tend your children while you attend conferences on feminist theory are, for the most part, poor women and women of Color? What is the theory behind racist feminism?

In a world of possibility for us all, our personal visions help lay the groundwork for political action. The failure of academic feminists to recognize difference as a crucial strength is a failure to reach beyond the first patriarchal lesson. In our world, divide and conquer must become define and empower.

Why weren't other women of Color found to participate in this conference? Why were two phone calls to me considered a consultation? Am I the only possible source of names of Black feminists? And although the Black panelist's paper ends on an important and powerful connection of love between women, what about interracial cooperation between feminists who don't love each other?

In academic feminist circles, the answer to these questions is often, "We did not know who to ask." But that is the same evasion of responsibility, the same cop-out, that keeps Black women's art out of women's exhibitions, Black women's work out of most feminist publications except for the occasional "Special Third World Women's Issue," and Black women's texts off your reading lists. But as Adrienne Rich pointed out in a recent talk, white feminists have educated themselves about such an enormous amount over the past ten years, how come you haven't also educated yourselves about Black women and the differences between us—white and Black—when it is key to our survival as a movement?

Women of today are still being called upon to stretch across the gap of male ignorance and to educate men as to our existence and our needs. This is an old and primary tool of all oppressors to keep the oppressed occupied with the master's concerns. Now we hear that it is the task of women of Color to educate white women—in the face of tremendous resistance—as to our existence, our differences, our relative roles in our joint survival. This is a diversion of energies and a tragic repetition of racist patriarchal thought.

Simone de Beauvoir once said: "It is in the knowledge of the genuine conditions of our lives that we must draw our strength to live and our reasons for acting."

Racism and homophobia are real conditions of all our lives in this place and time. *I urge each one of us here to reach down into that deep place of knowledge inside herself and touch that terror and loathing of any difference that lives there. See whose face it wears.* Then the personal as the political can begin to illuminate all our choices.

Engaged Pedagogy
(1994)

bell hooks

T O EDUCATE AS THE PRACTICE OF freedom is a way of teaching that anyone can learn. That learning process comes easiest to those of us who teach who also believe that there is an aspect of our vocation that is sacred; who believe that our work is not merely to share information but to share in the intellectual and spiritual growth of our students. To teach in a manner that respects and cares for the souls of our students is essential if we are to provide the necessary conditions where learning can most deeply and intimately begin.

Throughout my years as student and professor, I have been most inspired by those teachers who have had the courage to transgress those boundaries that would confine each pupil to a rote, assembly-line approach to learning. Such teachers approach students with the will and desire to respond to our unique beings, even if the situation does not allow the full emergence of a relationship based on mutual recognition. Yet the possibility of such recognition is always present.

Paulo Freire and the Vietnamese Buddhist monk Thich Nhat Hanh are two of the "teachers" who have touched me deeply with their work. When I first began college, Freire's thought gave me the support I needed to challenge the "banking system" of education, that approach to learning that is rooted in the notion that all students need to do is consume information fed to them by a professor and be able to memorize and store it. Early on, it was Freire's insistence that education could be the practice of freedom that encouraged me to create strategies for what he called "conscientization" in the classroom. Translating that term to critical awareness and engagement, I entered the classrooms with the conviction that it was crucial for me and every other student to be an active participant, not a passive consumer. Education as the practice of freedom was continually undermined by professors who were actively hostile to the notion of student participation. Freire's work affirmed that education can only be liberatory when everyone claims knowledge as a field in which we all labor. That notion of mutual labor was affirmed by Thich Nhat Hanh's philosophy of engaged Buddhism, the focus on practice in conjunction with contemplation. His philosophy was similar to Freire's emphasis on "praxis"—action and reflection upon the world in order to change it.

In his work Thich Nhat Hanh always speaks of the teacher as a healer. Like Freire, his approach to knowledge called on students to be active participants, to link awareness with practice. Whereas Freire was primarily concerned with the mind, Thich Nhat Hanh offered a way of thinking about pedagogy which emphasized wholeness, a union of mind, body, and spirit. His focus on a holistic approach to learning and spiritual practice enabled me to overcome years of socialization that had taught me to believe a classroom was diminished if students and professors regarded one another as "whole" human beings, striving not just for knowledge in books, but knowledge about how to live in the world.

During my twenty years of teaching, I have witnessed a grave sense of dis-ease among professors (irrespective of their politics) when students want us to see them as whole human beings with complex lives and experiences rather than simply as seekers after compartmentalized bits of knowledge. When I was an undergraduate, Women's Studies was just finding a place in the academy. Those classrooms were the one space where teachers were willing to acknowledge a connection between ideas learned in university settings and those learned in life practices. And, despite those times when students abused that freedom in the classroom by only wanting to dwell on personal experience, feminist classrooms were, on the whole, one location where I witnessed professors striving to create participatory spaces for the sharing of knowledge. Nowadays, most women's studies professors are not as committed to exploring new pedagogical strategies. Despite this shift, many students still seek to enter feminist classrooms because they continue to believe that there, more than in any other place in the academy, they will have an opportunity to experience education as the practice of freedom.

Progressive, holistic education, "engaged pedagogy" is more demanding than conventional critical or feminist pedagogy. For, unlike these two teaching practices, it emphasizes wellbeing. That means that teachers must be actively committed to a process of self-actualization that promotes their own wellbeing if they are to teach in a manner that empowers students. Thich Nhat Hanh emphasized that "the practice of a healer, therapist, teacher or any helping professional should be directed toward his or herself first, because if the helper is unhappy, he or she cannot help many people." In the United States it is rare that anyone talks about teachers in university settings as healers. And it is even more rare to hear anyone suggest that teachers have any responsibility to be self-actualized individuals.

Learning about the work of intellectuals and academics primarily from nineteenth-century fiction and nonfiction during my pre-college years, I was certain that the task for those of us who chose this vocation was to be holistically questing for self-actualization. It was the actual experience of college that disrupted this image. It was there that I was made to feel as though I was terribly naive about "the profession." I learned that far from being self-actualized, the university was seen more as a haven for those who are smart in book knowledge but who might be otherwise unfit for social interaction. Luckily, during my undergraduate years I began to make a distinction between the practice of being an intellectual/teacher and one's role as a member of the academic profession.

It was difficult to maintain fidelity to the idea of the intellectual as someone who sought to be whole—well-grounded in a context where there was little emphasis on spiritual well-being, on care of the soul. Indeed, the objectification of the teacher within bourgeois educational structures seemed to denigrate notions of wholeness and uphold the idea of a mind/body split, one that promotes and supports compartmentalization.

This support reinforces the dualistic separation of public and private, encouraging teachers and students to see no connection between life practices, habits of being, and the roles of professors. The idea of the intellectual questing for a union of mind, body, and spirit had been replaced with notions that being smart meant that one was inherently emotionally unstable and that the best in oneself emerged in one's academic work. This meant that whether academics were drug addicts, alcoholics, batterers, or sexual abusers, the only important aspect of our identity was whether or not our minds functioned, whether we were able to do our jobs in the classroom. The self was presumably emptied out the moment the threshold was crossed, leaving in place only an objective mind—free of experiences and biases. There was fear that the conditions of that self would interfere with the teaching process. Part of the luxury and privilege of the role of teacher/professor today is the absence of any requirement that we be self-actualized. Not surprisingly, professors who are not concerned with inner wellbeing are the most threatened by the demand on the part of students for liberatory education, for pedagogical processes that will aid them in their own struggle for self-actualization.

Certainly it was naive for me to imagine during high school that I would find spiritual and intellectual guidance in university settings from writers, thinkers, scholars. To have found this would have been to stumble across a rare treasure. I learned, along with other students, to consider myself fortunate if I found an interesting professor who talked in a compelling way. Most of my professors were not the slightest bit interested in enlightenment. More than anything they seemed enthralled by the exercise of power and authority within their mini-kingdom, the classroom.

This is not to say that there were not compelling, benevolent dictators, but it is true to my memory that it was rare—absolutely, astonishingly rare—to encounter professors who were deeply committed to progressive pedagogical practices. I was dismayed by this; most of my professors were not individuals whose teaching styles I wanted to emulate.

My commitment to learning kept me attending classes. Yet, even so, because I did not conform—would not be an unquestioning, passive student—some professors treated me with contempt. I was slowly becoming estranged from education. Finding Freire in the midst of that estrangement was crucial to my survival as a student. His work offered both a way for me to understand the limitations of the type of education

I was receiving and to discover alternative strategies for learning and teaching. It was particularly disappointing to encounter white male professors who claimed to follow Freire's model even as their pedagogical practices were mired in structures of domination, mirroring the styles of conservative professors even as they approached subjects from a more progressive standpoint.

When I first encountered Paulo Freire, I was eager to see if his style of teaching would embody the pedagogical practices he described so eloquently in his work. During the short time I studied with him, I was deeply moved by his presence, by the way in which his manner of teaching exemplified his pedagogical theory. (Not all students interested in Freire have had a similar experience.) My experience with him restored my faith in liberatory education. I had never wanted to surrender the conviction that one could teach without reinforcing existing systems of domination. I needed to know that professors did not have to be dictators in the classroom.

While I wanted teaching to be my career, I believed that personal success was intimately linked with self-actualization. My passion for this quest led me to interrogate constantly the mind/body split that was so often taken to be a given. Most professors were often deeply antagonistic toward, even scornful of, any approach to learning emerging from a philosophical standpoint emphasizing the union of mind, body, and spirit, rather than the separation of these elements. Like many of the students I now teach, I was often told by powerful academics that I was misguided to seek such a perspective in the academy. Throughout my student years I felt deep inner anguish. Memory of that pain returns as I listen to students express the concern that they will not succeed in academic professions if they want to be well, if they eschew dysfunctional behavior or participation in coercive hierarchies. These students are often fearful, as I was, that there are no spaces in the academy where the will to be self-actualized can be affirmed.

This fear is present because many professors have intensely hostile responses to the vision of liberatory education that connects the will to know with the will to become. Within professorial circles, individuals often complain bitterly that students want classes to be "encounter groups." While it is utterly unreasonable for students to expect classrooms to be therapy sessions, it is appropriate for them to hope that the knowledge received in these settings will enrich and enhance them.

Currently, the students I encounter seem far more uncertain about the project of self-actualization than my peers and I were twenty years ago. They feel that there are no clear ethical guidelines shaping actions. Yet, while they despair, they are also adamant that education should be liberatory. They want and demand more from professors than my generation did. There are times when I walk into classrooms overflowing with students who feel terribly wounded in their psyches (many of them see therapists), yet I do not think that they want therapy from me. They do want an education that is healing to the uninformed, unknowing spirit. They do want knowledge that is meaningful. They rightfully expect that my colleagues and I will not offer them information without addressing the connection between what they are learning and their overall life experiences.

This demand on the students' part does not mean that they will always accept our guidance. This is one of the joys of education as the practice of freedom, for it allows students to assume responsibility for their choices. Writing about our teacher/student relationship in a piece for the *Village Voice,* "How to Run the Yard: Off-Line and into the Margins at Yale," one of my students, Gary Dauphin, shares the joys of working with me as well as the tensions that surfaced between us as he began to devote his time to pledging a fraternity rather than cultivating his writing:

> People think academics like Gloria [my given name] are all about difference: but what I learned from her was mostly about sameness, about what I had in common as a black man to people of color; to women and gays and lesbians and the poor and anyone else who wanted in. I did some of this learning by reading but most of it came from hanging out on the fringes of her life. I lived like that for a while, shuttling between high points in my classes and low points outside. Gloria was a safe haven ... Pledging a fraternity is about as far away as you can get from her classroom, from the yellow kitchen where she used to share her lunch with students in need of various forms of sustenance.

This is Gary writing about the joy. The tension arose as we discussed his reason for wanting to join a fraternity and my disdain for that decision. Gary comments, "They represented a vision of black manhood that she abhorred, one where violence and abuse were primary ciphers of bonding and identity." Describing his assertion of autonomy from my influence he writes, "But she must have also known the limits of even her influence on my life, the limits of books and teachers."

Ultimately, Gary felt that the decision he had made to join a fraternity was not constructive, that I "had taught him openness" where the fraternity had encouraged one-dimensional allegiance. Our interchange both during and after this experience was an example of engaged pedagogy.

Through critical thinking—a process he learned by reading theory and actively analyzing texts—Gary experienced education as the practice of freedom. His final comments about me: "Gloria had only mentioned the entire episode once after it was over, and this to tell me simply that there are many kinds of choices, many kinds of logic. I could make those events mean whatever I wanted as long as I was honest." I have quoted his writing at length because it is testimony affirming engaged pedagogy. It means that my voice is not the only account of what happens in the classroom.

Engaged pedagogy necessarily values student expression. In her essay, "Interrupting the Calls for Student Voice in Liberatory Education: A Feminist Poststructuralist Perspective," Mimi Orner employs a Foucauldian framework to suggest that

> Regulatory and punitive means and uses of the confession bring to mind curricular and pedagogical practices which call for students to publicly reveal, even confess, information about their lives and cultures in the presence of authority figures such as teachers.

When education is the practice of freedom, students are not the only ones who are asked to share, to confess. Engaged pedagogy does not seek simply to empower students. Any classroom that employs a holistic model of learning will also be a place where teachers grow, and are empowered by the process. That empowerment cannot happen if we refuse to be vulnerable while encouraging students to take risks. Professors who expect students to share confessional narratives but who are themselves unwilling to share are exercising power in a manner that could be coercive. In my classrooms, I do not expect students to take any risks that I would not take, to share in any way that I would not share. When professors bring narratives of their experiences into classroom discussions it eliminates the possibility that we can function as all-knowing, silent interrogators. It is often productive if professors take the first risk, linking confessional narratives to academic discussions so as to show how experience can illuminate and enhance our understanding of academic material. But most professors must practice being vulnerable in the classroom, being wholly present in mind, body, and spirit.

Progressive professors working to transform the curriculum so that it does not reflect biases or reinforce systems of domination are most often the individuals willing to take the risks that engaged pedagogy requires and to make their teaching practices a site of resistance. In her essay, "On Race and Voice: Challenges for Liberation Education in the 1990s," Chandra Mohanty writes that

> resistance lies in self-conscious engagement with dominant, normative discourses and representations and in the active creation of oppositional analytic and cultural spaces. Resistance that is random and isolated is clearly not as effective as that which is mobilized through systemic politicized practices of teaching and learning. Uncovering and reclaiming subjugated knowledge is one way to lay claims to alternative histories. But these knowledges need to be understood and defined pedagogically, as questions of strategy and practice as well as of scholarship, in order to transform educational institutions radically.

Professors who embrace the challenge of self-actualization will be better able to create pedagogical practices that engage students, providing them with ways of knowing that enhance their capacity to live fully and deeply.

Reading 4.4

Free Spaces: Creating Oppositional Consciousness in the Disability Rights Movement

(2001)

Sharon Groch

To DEVELOP OPPOSITIONAL CONSCIOUSNESS, OPPRESSED GROUPS usually need physical space in which to communicate and share perceptions of their experiences with relatively little interference from or control by the dominant group. These arenas, or "free spaces" (Allen 1970; Evans and Boyte 1986),[1] often provide the networks, funds, and repertoires of strategies and tactics that make social movements possible (see resource mobilization theory, e.g., McCarthy and Zald 1973, 1977; Oberschall 1973; Tilly 1978). In this chapter, however, I emphasize the effects of free spaces on the formation of oppositional culture and oppositional consciousness. Specifically, I examine how three different groups within the disability community—the deaf, blind people, and people with mobility impairments—took different routes in the creation of oppositional consciousness. Their differences, I argue, derive largely from their differing abilities to create autonomous free spaces.

Before members of oppressed groups can act collectively, they usually must develop an oppositional consciousness. That is, they must come to see themselves as members of a group, regard their life situations as unjust, find a common interest with other members of the group in opposing that injustice, consider the injustice due to structural inequalities, and believe the injustice can be diminished or ended through their collective actions. To come to this interpretation of their life situation, oppressed groups must create shared meaning. All three disability groups created shared meaning on each of the interdependent levels that Klandermans (1992) suggests: (1) through interactions within social networks; (2) through the conscious attempts of social actors to create shared meaning; and (3) through participating in collective actions or observing the collective actions of others. The first level, consensus formation, involves the

---

1   Other analysts have called these arenas "segregated spaces" (Morris and Braine, [...]), "sequestered social sites" (Scott 1990), "a world apart" (Taylor and Whittier 1992), "subaltern counterpublics" (Fraser 1992), or "enclaves" (Mansbridge 1994).

unplanned convergence of meaning. The second level, consensus mobilization, involves the deliberate attempts of activists to influence others' beliefs. The third level, action mobilization, involves the creation of shared meaning, planned or unplanned, through discussions that occur among participants and observers of collective action.

Consensus formation, the first level, occurred easily among both deaf and blind people who had been placed in residential schools at a young age. Interactions within these early schools created an early culture of opposition and eventually a sense of collective identity that included an understanding of identity of interests, an injustice frame that included opposition to those injustices, and a belief in the power of collective action. Once an oppositional consciousness with these components emerged, members of these groups perpetuated that consciousness deliberately (consensus mobilization) and developed that consciousness further through participation (action mobilization). By contrast, children with mobility impairments (i.e., who use wheelchairs, walkers, canes, and crutches) traditionally have not been segregated in residential schools. They have sometimes attended separate classes or even separate schools within local public school systems, and have sometimes attended classes with the non-mobility impaired. Consequently, although a strong sense of collective identity has eventually emerged among many members of this group, it has required conscious consensus mobilization and action mobilization through observing other groups. Unlike deaf people and blind people, people with mobility impairments have attempted to mobilize people with all types of disabilities, with the goal of creating an inclusive disability consciousness.

Images, slogans, literature, humor, rituals, and other cultural expressions facilitate the shared interpretations that animate oppositional culture. Some groups, such as African Americans, have developed strong oppositional cultures from which oppositional consciousness can arise (Morris 1984). Other oppressed groups, such as women, who also historically have formed injustice frames (Lerner 1993), have been less successful in creating all that is needed for a supportive oppositional culture.

The experiences of these three different segments of the disability rights movement supports Aldon Morris and Naomi Braine's contention that the degree of physical segregation that an oppressed group experiences influences the emergence of an oppositional consciousness [...]. Segregation does indeed make it easier for an oppressed group to create free spaces. However, the experience of the different disability groups suggests that both the *degree* and the *nature* of the segregation influence the formation of oppositional consciousness. Segregated groups that are controlled by nonmembers and allowed little unsupervised time have little opportunity to create free spaces. In such conditions, segregation facilitates a collective identity but inhibits the growth of either an oppositional culture or oppositional consciousness.

Two paths thus appear to developing an oppositional consciousness. First, a group can experience the kind of segregation that allows considerable group autonomy. Alternatively, a group that has experienced segregation without autonomy can build from its existing collective identity by applying the model of another group to its own conditions. In both paths "free spaces" play a critical role.

...

Deaf Consciousness

Recent measures of disability by the Census Bureau (McNeil 1993) find that among Americans fifteen years old and over, 10.9 million individuals have a hearing impairment; that is, they have difficulty hearing what is said in a normal conversation. Of this 10.9 million, 900,000 individuals are completely unable to hear what is said in such a conversation. Although these numbers do not tell us the degree of hearing difficulty most of these individuals experience, these numbers reveal that at least 900,000 Americans are profoundly deaf. Individuals within this subgroup of the hearing-impaired population, made up primarily of persons who were born deaf or became deaf at an early age, have forged an oppositional consciousness that they themselves call "deaf consciousness" (McWhinney 1991).

Individuals who possess a deaf consciousness express beliefs similar to those held by other oppressed groups who have developed an oppositional consciousness. These individuals (1) have a collective identity; (2) believe that, as a group, they are subject to unjust treatment and so reject the legitimacy of their subordinate position; (3) recognize a common interest in ending the unjust treatment, (4) blame that treatment on a system of domination created by hearing people; and (5) believe that collective action is their best form of redress. Persons who are blind or have mobility impairments have developed similar oppositional interpretations of their life situation. Unlike these groups, however, people with a deaf consciousness do not consider their impairment a disability.

Instead of identifying themselves as disabled, people who possess a deaf consciousness see themselves as members of a linguistic and cultural minority (Dolnick 1993; Lane 1992). They "share a language ... and a culture ... , have inherited their sign language, use it as a primary means of communication among themselves, and hold a set of beliefs about themselves and their connection to the larger society" (Padden and Humphries 1988, 2). To emphasize this point, deaf activists and scholars use the uppercase "Deaf" when referring to people who share the Deaf language and culture.

As with many linguistic minorities, the primary identifying characteristic of the Deaf community is its language. A visual language, American Sign Language (ASL) has a particular spatial grammar and unique syntax (Sacks 1990, 85–92). Deaf individuals consider ASL the natural, inherited language of their people and ridicule other means of communication such as lip reading or Signed English. Since ASL does not have a written form, Deaf individuals have created other expressions to preserve and pass on their language and culture. Signed poetry (Jepson 1993), plays such as those performed by the National Theatre of the Deaf, folktales (Padden and Humphries 1988, 32–33), and jokes (Gannon 1981 [...]) are shared through live performances and videotapes. These cultural forms often express the oppositional nature of deaf consciousness. In the poetry, plays, folktales, and jokes, people who hear are called "the others" and their mannerisms and habits ridiculed. Stories are told and retold of hearing educators insisting that Deaf children use oral communication techniques and discouraging students from marrying one another. Many cultural forms celebrate the Deaf community's ability to persevere, maintaining their language, culture, and social ties despite the oppression they have experienced.

Believing that the Deaf community constitutes a linguistic minority group, Deaf individuals value their deafness. When asked if they would rather hear, many Deaf people respond that they do not want to hear (Dolniek 1993). Deaf parents often refuse to let their Deaf children have cochlear implants, a procedure that provides some hearing (Barringer 1993; Dolniek 1993; Lane 1992). These parents argue that supporting cochlear implants is like supporting skin-lightening procedures for people of color. Both procedures attempt to change an integral characteristic of a person, a characteristic which should be a source of pride, not of shame.

Their experiences of oppression have caused many Deaf people to develop separatist views. Approximately nine out of ten Deaf individuals marry other Deaf people (Lane 1992, 17). Most Deaf parents send their Deaf children to residential schools for the deaf. Both intermarriage and separate schooling help ensure the continuation of a deaf consciousness. Deaf individuals also choose to socialize primarily with other Deaf people. As a result, Deaf individuals have established their own fraternal insurance society, travel agencies, social clubs, athletic associations, theater groups, and places of worship. These institutions function as free spaces in which Deaf people can interact with one another uninhibited by the presence of hearing people.

Political organizations form part of the network of organizations created and controlled by Deaf people. The oldest and largest of these organizations is the National Association of the Deaf (NAD). In 1880, Deaf individuals founded the NAD on the belief that Deaf people made up "a class by themselves" and "need[ed] to control their own destinies" (Van Cleve and Crouch 1989, 94). The members of the NAD held this belief so strongly that they denied hearing people membership for eighty-four years. NAD aims to secure the civil rights of Deaf people, to preserve and expand the language, culture, and heritage of the Deaf, and to develop future Deaf leaders. Members of NAD lobby state and national legislatures, provide legal defense funds in discrimination cases, organize workshops on ASL, sponsor summer youth camps, and award college scholarships to Deaf children. Implicit in these tactics is the goal of perpetuating deaf consciousness.

Gallaudet University plays an institutionally crucial role in the transmission of deaf consciousness. Founded in 1864 (Cannon 1981, 38), Gallaudet is the world's only liberal arts college for Deaf students. Many deaf individuals first encounter deaf consciousness at Gallaudet. Most deaf children born to Deaf parents form a deaf consciousness the way children of other ethnic and racial groups do, through their interactions with their parents and their communities. But only ten percent of all deaf children are born to Deaf parents (Lane 1992, 138). Moreover, most of the old segregated schools have been closed. By 1992, nearly three-quarters of the children who were deaf were attending integrated schools with hearing children (Lane 1992, 135). Integrated schools stress learning English in the form of speech, lip reading, written English, finger spelling, Signed English, or speech accompanied by ASL. In this system, deaf children of hearing parents typically graduate from high school knowing little about the culture of deaf consciousness. Some of these learn about deaf consciousness as adults when they seek out or stumble upon one of the organizations of the Deaf.

Many of the college oriented are introduced to deaf consciousness at Gallaudet, in what are not always easy lessons. A Deaf interviewee educated in integrated schools describes his initial experiences at Gallaudet as "a cultural shock. ... I actually had to interact with Deaf persons twenty-four hours a day!" Gallaudet gave this person his first lesson in ASL, his first Deaf adult role models in his teachers, his first group of Deaf friends, and his first awareness of deaf consciousness.

In 1988, Gallaudet University students forced the newly appointed hearing president to resign and replaced her with a Deaf president, the first in the university's history. The protest, called Deaf President Now (DPN), showed Deaf people beyond the university the power of collective action (see Christiansen and Barnartt 1995 for a comprehensive review of the protest). Although the mass media and many disability rights activists have claimed the DPN protest as "a touchstone event, a Selma or a Stonewall" for people with *disabilities* (Shapiro 1993, 74), for the Gallaudet students this was a specifically *Deaf* protest. The Gallaudet takeover was not the Selma of the disability rights movement; it was the Selma of the Deaf (Gannon 1989, 136; also see Barnartt 1994). While the DPN protest undoubtedly increased public awareness of the rights of disabled people, this broader aim was not the intent of the Gallaudet students.

The DPN protest sparked similar actions by the Deaf at residential schools across the nation. It has also drawn the attention of many journalists (Dolniek 1993; Solomon 1994) and social scientists (Barnartt 1994; Lane 1992; Sacks 1990) to deaf culture and consciousness. Many of these authors suggest that deaf consciousness is a relatively new phenomenon. However, a closer look at the history of Deaf people (Gannon 1981;

Van Cleve and Crouch 1989) reveals a long-standing tradition among the Deaf of collectively acting on their own behalf.

Consensus Formation in Deaf Consciousness

The beginnings of a deaf consciousness can be traced to the establishment of the first residential school for deaf children in 1817. Founded by three men, one of whom was a Deaf teacher in France who communicated using French Sign Language and writing, this school brought a substantial number of deaf children together for the first time. Having acquired or developed various forms of sign language before entering this school, these children, with the help of their Deaf teacher, began developing their own common language (which became ASL), along with their own beliefs, expressions, and practices. Upon graduating from school, many Deaf students passed on their culture by encouraging other states to open residential schools for the deaf and teaching in these institutions.

Although state funded, these early residential schools for the deaf were essentially indigenous institutions. Deaf administrators, staff, and teachers usually controlled the early schools. Within their schools, individuals communicated using ASL. Students lived segregated from the hearing world. They shared similar life experiences and had adult role models. The schools thus functioned as free spaces, within which deaf children developed the collective identity and "cultural attributes that marked deaf Americans as a distinct subculture within America" (Van Cleve and Crouch 1989, 30).

Upon graduating from these residential schools, Deaf friends maintained their ties by establishing alumni associations. Out of the alumni associations came many of the other organizations of the Deaf: their social clubs, political organizations, and independent newspapers. These organizations too functioned as free spaces, which helped create and transmit deaf consciousness as, after 1880, the schools for the deaf became increasingly controlled by hearing people. In this historical move, prominent educators led by Alexander Graham Bell convinced the world that Deaf children should no longer be taught ASL but should learn to communicate orally, by speaking and lip reading. With this change, what I will call "the culture of deaf consciousness" lost its influential position in the schools. Hearing teachers replaced Deaf teachers, eliminating important adult role models. Children were rewarded for their ability to speak and punished for using ASL. Yet by this time deaf consciousness had solid roots and continued to be passed on outside of the formal classroom settings, in the dormitories of the residential schools and in the many organizations founded by the Deaf.

Deaf people have believed in the power of collective action for over a century. In 1889, members of the NAD fought for equal employment in federal agencies by lobbying and writing letters. In 1913, a Nebraska Deaf group lobbied against teaching oralism in their schools. In the 1920s, Deaf groups across the nation fought successfully for the right to drive. The collective actions of Deaf people turned more disruptive in the early 1970s, as Deaf activists followed the lead of the Black civil rights movement and began to demonstrate publicly and to picket. Deaf students in residential schools organized demonstrations in Louisiana, New Jersey, and Pennsylvania over the lack of Deaf administrators and ASL instruction. Deaf actors picketed television stations to protest their use of hearing people to play Deaf individuals. The student protest at Gallaudet University in 1988 had many precursors.

Although the culture of deaf consciousness appears both stable and mature, individuals who are hearing impaired vary in many ways (Higgins 1980, 48–69). Any person who has a hearing impairment can become a member of the Deaf community by becoming proficient in ASL and accepting the values, norms, and behaviors of Deaf culture. However, variations in demographic characteristics such as race, socioeconomic level, and gender make some groups less likely to form a deaf consciousness than other groups.

People of color, for example, are less likely to become members of the Deaf community than are Whites. Although today most Deaf organizations actively recruit people of color, the Deaf community, created primarily by White deaf men, has traditionally either excluded or marginalized women and people of color.[2] As a White Deaf interviewee regretfully states, "Blacks and Latinos are not totally in the White man's Deaf world." The Deaf community's marginalization of people of color stems partly from past racist practices that segregated African American children in their own residential schools for the deaf. As a result of this early segregation, Deaf African Americans developed a distinct form of ASL. Although Black ASL and White ASL have many similarities, the differences between them are enough to produce occasional misunderstandings and to inhibit interactions between the groups (Higgins 1980, 52). Having created their own distinct oppositional culture and organizations to support this culture, African Americans have been reluctant to join the larger, mostly White, Deaf community.

Variations in time of onset and degree of deafness also influence the likelihood of a person joining the Deaf community. Individuals who become deaf as adults, either completely or partially, are far less likely to become members of the Deaf community than those who are born with profound deafness. People who have once heard usually find it hard to learn both ASL and a new culture that values deafness. Having grown up nondisabled, these individuals are likely to view their deafness as a disability and prefer to remain in the hearing world with their hearing families, friends, and associates. Because of these views and preferences, individuals who have lost their hearing

---

2   While women have been members of NAD since its beginning in 1880, African Americans were not allowed to become members until 1949 (Buchanan 1993, 197). Another of the earliest Deaf organizations, the National Fraternal Society of the Deaf (founded in 1901) excluded women until 1951 and African Americans until 1967 (National Fraternal Society of the Deaf n.d.).

as adults have founded their own organizations to express their unique identities and to address their specific issues.[3]

Hearing-impaired individuals outside of the Deaf community have nevertheless developed some degree of oppositional consciousness. The Deaf community and other organizations of the deaf have worked together on that basis to secure legislative protection for communication accessibility. However, the specific culture of deaf consciousness inhibits many members of these groups from developing a broad oppositional consciousness based on disability. This is particularly true for the Deaf who maintain that their group is not disabled but a linguistic minority.

Blind Consciousness

Census Bureau data (McNeil 1993) indicate that there are 9.7 million Americans fifteen years of age or older who have difficulty seeing words and letters in ordinary newsprint even when wearing corrective lenses. Of the 9.7 million people with visual impairments, 1.6 million individuals are completely unable to see words and letters in ordinary newsprint. Thus, nearly twice as many Americans are blind as are profoundly deaf.

Like the Deaf, a subgroup within the blind population has constructed a form of oppositional consciousness that I call "blind consciousness." Individuals who possess blind consciousness experience a collective identity with other blind people and believe that, as a group, they historically have been dominated and oppressed by the sighted. For these individuals being blind is much like being a member of any other minority group, not in a cultural sense as the Deaf assert, but in the sense that blind people are "subject to much the same differential treatment and suspicious regard as other minorities" (Matson 1990, 372). Blind activists argue that, in parallel with African Americans, blind people historically have been enslaved in asylums, exploited in workshops, and marginalized in education and employment opportunities.

With these beliefs comes the view, as a blind female interviewee asserts, that "blindness is a civil rights issue." Just as for the Deaf the problem is not being deaf, "the principle problem of blindness is not the blindness itself but the mistaken notions and ideas about blindness which are held by the general public" (Jernigan 1976, 20). Individuals with blind consciousness believe that the best way to change these ideas is to act collectively.

While many of the elements of blind consciousness are similar to those of deaf consciousness, blind consciousness differs from deaf consciousness in several important ways. Unlike persons with a deaf consciousness, those with a blind consciousness are more

---

3   The two largest groups are the Association of Late-Deafened Adults (ALDA) and Self Help for Hard of Hearing People (SHHH). The president of a local ALDA chapter recently called for members to identify themselves as "a group separate from the Deaf culture" (Tiering 1996, 1).

likely to believe that their impairment is a disability. Moreover, many blind individuals emphasize that blindness is a *sensory* disability, not a *physical* disability like paraplegia. In making this distinction, they imply that being blind differs from other physical disabilities.

People who have a blind consciousness do not value their blindness the way Deaf individuals value their deafness. Most say that, given the choice, they would prefer to see. However, these individuals do not view blindness as a tragedy, as many sighted people do. Instead, blind activists contend that blindness is a "serious inconvenience," a "constant annoyance," and a "nuisance."

Unlike the Deaf, individuals with a blind consciousness do not adopt a separatist stance. Rather, they insist on the complete integration of all blind people into the larger society. The value that blind activists place on integration appears in their rhetoric and daily actions. We have no statistical data on the degree to which blind individuals intermarry. Organizations of the blind report that data on intermarriages are not kept because their constituents have little interest in such data. Unlike the Deaf, who value intermarriages, blind interviewees explain that in their community intermarriage is neither encouraged nor discouraged; it is "simply not an issue."

Integration is also the goal for blind activists in educating their children. Like deafness, blindness can be hereditary. However, unlike the Deaf, blind parents whose children are blind seldom demand that their children attend residential schools for the blind. People who possess a blind consciousness neither value nor devalue educating their children with other blind children. These parents value schools that employ teachers who have high expectations for their children and can teach them important alternative skills, such as cane travel and braille.

People who are blind have created a network of institutions to meet their needs. Professional organizations, recreational clubs, alumni associations of blind residential schools, and theater groups offer the newly blinded as well as those who lost their sight at an early age the opportunity to meet other blind people, often for the first time. Like the organizations of the Deaf, the organizations of the blind foster the development of a collective identity among blind people. However, while a strong oppositional culture prevails in most Deaf organizations, this is not true of many blind organizations. The degree to which each group transmits a blind consciousness varies.

Individuals with a blind consciousness can be found primarily in two organizations: The National Federation of the Blind (NFB) and the American Council of the Blind (ACB). Founded as one organization by alumni associates of blind residential schools in 1940, these organizations split in 1961. Although these organizations have similar goals, much animosity remains between them. Seldom is a blind person a member of both the NFB and the ACB.

The purpose of the ACB is "to promote the independence, dignity, and well-being of blind and visually impaired people" by enhancing their civil rights, job opportunities, access to public services and facilities, and Social Security benefits. To achieve its purpose, the ACB monitors governmental policies, promotes public awareness, provides legal advice and assistance, and offers college scholarships. The ACB also advocates the public use of adaptive devices such as textured surfaces on curb cuts and alarm-sounding cross lights. Since the early 1970s, the ACB has worked in coalition with other disability organizations to secure the rights of all disabled people.

The NFB also promotes the independence, dignity, and well-being of blind people. However, the NFB adds a militant tone by demanding "the complete integration of the blind into society on a basis of equality." For NFB members, the "independence, dignity, and well-being" of the ACB are not enough. They demand as well security, opportunity, and equality. Many NFB tactics mirror the tactics used by the ACB. The NFB monitors governmental activities, lobbies for the passage of legislation, educates the public, and offers scholarships to blind students. However, unlike the ACB, the NFB does not support using adaptive devices for the blind. NFB members see these adaptations as perpetuating their second-class position. They declare, "We don't need the world re-engineered for us. We use it as it is. What we need is good training and good attitudes about ourselves" (National Federation of the Blind 1992).

The NFB also views working within disability coalitions differently from the ACB. An NFB member explains:

> There are very distinct and often rather devastating disadvantages to aligning ourselves with the large disability groups, and being involved, caught up in, the "pan-disability movement." We oppose it. We think it is definitely a bad idea. ... We feel that we are such a tiny minority, if we involve ourselves in a coalition, that the issues of the coalition will supersede and subvert our issues ... that our issues would not ordinarily get the kind of emphasis, the kind of commitment from a coalition that we feel is needed to get things done to benefit blind people.

In 1974, NFB members passed a resolution that prohibits them from joining in permanent coalitions with other disabled groups.

Although the NFB will not form coalitions, it remains one of the most aggressive disability organizations in America. When traditional methods of effecting social change fail, the NFB turns to more disruptive tactics. NFB members have held annual marches on Washington for increased representation in accreditation procedures and have picketed television stations for their negative portrayals of blind people. They also have organized strikes among sheltered-care workshop employees for better wages and for the right to form unions.

Like other groups that have developed a culture of oppositional consciousness, NFB members demand the right of self-definition. NFB members call themselves Federationists to distinguish themselves from ACB members, other blind people, and sighted people. They describe themselves as being "blind," not "visually impaired." To Federationists, refusing to use the word "blind" implies that being blind is shameful, and for them "it is respectable to be blind." Defining blindness broadly as the inability to drive a car, read ordinary print, or recognize faces at a distance, they believe that people who call themselves visually impaired are attempting to distance themselves from the blind community and denying their collective identity. Although NFB members do not use the uppercase "Blind" to refer to themselves, NFB members use the words "Federationist" and "blind" to express and build their oppositional consciousness.

NFB members also have created cultural symbols to express and transmit their oppositional consciousness. The NFB logo, with the initials "NFB" triangulated by the words "Security," "Opportunity," and "Equality," is printed on various everyday items such as coffee mugs and T-shirts. Members proudly wear NFB rings and lapel pins and use NFB white canes. Federationists have made the white cane itself an important cultural symbol. Unlike many individuals who see the white cane as stigmatizing, Federationists believe the white cane symbolizes freedom and independence. Members express their oppositional consciousness by walking briskly with their long NFB canes.

Braille is another symbol of blind consciousness. NFB members shun the use of talking books and computers, insisting that braille is the most effective means of writing and reading for blind people. At meetings, Federationists can be seen using braille slates and styluses and braille typewriters to take notes. For NFB members, using braille reaffirms that being blind is respectable; its use becomes an important symbol in building a culture of blind consciousness.

In addition to these other cultural symbols, NEB members have written songs to "promote the attitudes of the Federation." Using familiar melodies so that the songs can be learned and remembered easily, these "songs of freedom" tell of society's exploitation and marginalization of blind people (National Federation of the Blind 1991). Sung primarily during national conventions, the songs remind NFB members of past and ongoing struggles and victories, perpetuating a sense of blind consciousness.

Unlike deaf consciousness, the well-developed blind consciousness that Federationists have created is seldom seen outside this group. Members of the ACB also have a blind consciousness. Yet because of their animosity toward the NFB, they do not share the NFB's cultural expressions. Apart from the ACB and the NFB, most other organizations of the blind have a collective identity, but not an injustice frame.

Much of the difference in the degree to which deaf consciousness and blind consciousness have been developed and accepted by their respective populations derives from the fact that the Deaf share a language. ASL inherently sets the Deaf apart from those who speak. Blind people do not share such a language. Yet, like the Deaf, blind people historically have been segregated in residential schools. Today some segregation continues in work and recreational settings. Blind people also share a unique method of reading and writing, setting them further apart from those who see. These methods had particular salience before tape recorders, talking books, and computers were developed.

Consensus Formation in Blind Consciousness

The history of blind education in America (Koestler 1976; Lowenfeld 1975) indicates why blind people have never developed the same degree of oppositional consciousness as the Deaf. In 1832, fifteen years after deaf children had begun to be educated in residential schools, blind children began receiving their education in similar schools. Some of the blind schools opened as separate departments within schools for the deaf. Other blind schools were freestanding and, like most schools for the deaf, state administered and publicly funded. The major difference between these two school systems was that Deaf individuals helped create the residential schools for the deaf while sighted individuals founded the schools for the blind. Although many schools had some blind teachers, the schools for the blind were primarily controlled and run by sighted people. Moreover, influenced by the eugenics movement of the 1800s, sighted administrators and educators allowed little contact between the blind boys and girls. Although administrators of schools for the deaf had similar fears about perpetuating deafness, the educators of blind children went to a far greater extent to keep the sexes segregated. Separate classrooms for boys and girls were common. Casual conversations between the sexes outside of class often meant expulsion. Many schools prohibited class reunions. Some schools went so far as to open and close their schools at different times of day for the girls and for the boys so that the children would have no chance to meet on the trains.

Once blind children began to attend integrated day schools in the 1900s, the practice of placing boys and girls in separate classrooms ceased. However, even in these situations instructors and parents repeatedly stressed the dangers of two blind people dating and marrying. A blind respondent who went to a public grade school in the mid-1950s remembers that his teachers "made it seem nasty to socialize with other blind kids. It made you want to get away [from blind people] as far as you could!" Another recalls being in college in the 1960s and "purposely avoiding other blind students."

These educational practices reinforced the stigma that society places on individuals who are blind, inhibiting the growth of a positive, collective identity and an oppositional culture. Internalizing the views of their educators, early blind leaders, many of whom were educators themselves, actively discouraged the creation of organizations of the blind. In 1901, blind leader Robert Irwin declared that "every educator of the blind knows the deleterious effect of collecting the blind together in isolated groups" (Koestler 1976, 33).

In 1937, another blind leader, Henry Latimer wrote, "At best, blindness is a negative bond of common action. ... There is, nevertheless, no advantage accruing from membership in an all-blind organization which might not be acquired in greater measure through membership in a society of sighted persons" (Maurer 1993). These two men played key roles in the development of the American Foundation for the Blind, a nonmembership organization historically headed by sighted individuals. They did little to encourage and much to discourage the growth of an oppositional culture among the blind.

More recently, negative experiences in residential schools for the blind inspired some blind men to establish integrated schooling for blind children. The results were dramatic. Whereas in 1910, 96 percent of all blind children attended residential schools for the blind, by 1960 only 53 percent of the blind children attended residential schools. By 1970, this number had fallen to 32 percent (Koestler 1976) and by 1993 to only 9 percent (American Printing House for the Blind 1992–93, 26). This history contrasted with that of the deaf, who were mostly segregated in residential schools up until 1975.

Integrated in schools with the sighted and discouraged from socializing with one another, blind children had few opportunities to establish free spaces where an oppositional culture and consciousness could develop. The students of residential schools eventually created some crucial autonomous spaces by establishing alumni associations, indeed, the NFB grew from interactions within and between these alumni associations. Yet blind students did not establish their first alumni association until 1871, thirty-nine years after the first schools for the blind opened. Members of the alumni associations did not create a national organization of the blind until 1940, sixty-nine years later. By contrast, although it took them nearly as long (thirty-seven years) to establish their first alumni association, Deaf individuals created their first national organization within twenty-six years.

Because of the concern for integration among most of today's blind people, most residential schools for the blind have closed, with those remaining serving primarily children with multiple disabilities. The history of segregation without autonomy produced a greater acceptance of stigma, which in turn generated a resistance to self-segregation. Combined, these structural and cultural conditions have inhibited the "growth of a mature, widespread blind consciousness.

As in the deaf population, time of onset affects one's likelihood of forming a blind consciousness. Those most likely to form such a consciousness were born totally blind or became totally blind at an early age. However, today the majority of people who are blind have lost their sight later in their lives, after their sixty-fifth year. The needs and responses of these individuals differ from those who became blind early in life. Having lived most of their lives as sighted people, many in this group do not want to learn braille or how to use a white cane. Like the newly deaf, who prefer the hearing world, they prefer the sighted world. Those who have only a partial visual loss, regardless of time of onset, also often prefer to associate with sighted people. With little sense of collective identity, individuals who become blind late in life and/or are partially blind have found it hard to embrace the oppositional culture of blind consciousness.

Again, as among deaf people, race affects one's likelihood of developing a blind consciousness. The two organizations of the blind that perpetuate a blind consciousness have been founded and are still controlled primarily by White individuals. Many African Americans and Hispanic Americans who are blind find that these organizations fail to address their specific problems of living in a society with multiple systems of domination. Although some people of color are members of the NFB and the ACB, their numbers are few.

As the ACB has begun working in coalition with other disability groups, some blind individuals have transformed their blind consciousness into a broader disability consciousness. Nevertheless, although they see the advantage to such coalitions, most blind persons proceed cautiously for fear that the issues of the blind will be superseded by the issues of people whose disabilities are more visible and occur in greater numbers. As mentioned earlier, the most aggressive and culturally developed organization of the blind, the NFB, refuses to form permanent coalitions with other disability groups. Combined, these factors greatly hamper the growth of a broad disability consciousness among blind people.

Note

I would like to thank Jane Mansbridge and Aldon Morris for their insightful comments and suggestions on earlier drafts of this chapter. I am especially indebted to the individuals with disabilities who allowed me to interview them and to join in their protest activities.

References

Allen, Pamela. 1970. *Free Space: A Perspective on the Small Group in Women's Liberation.* New York: Times Change Press. Abridged in *Radical Feminism,* ed. Anne Koedt, Ellen Levine, and Anita Rapone. New York: Quadrangle, 1973.

American Printing House for the Blind. 1992–93. *Annual Report.* Louisville: American Printing House for the Blind.

Barnartt, Sharon N. 1994. "Action and Consensus Mobilization in the Beat President Now Protest and Its Aftermath." In *Research in Social Movements, Conflict and Change,* vol. 17. Ed. L. Kriesberg, M. Dobkowski, and I. Wallimann. Greenwich, Conn.: JAI.

Barringer, Felicity. 1993. "Pride in a Soundless World: Deaf Oppose a Hearing Aid." *New York Times,* 16 May, 1, 14.

Buchanan, Robert. 1993. "The Silent Worker Newspaper and the Building of a Deaf Community: 1890–1929." *In Deaf History Unveiled.* Ed. J. Van Cleve. Washington: Gallaudet University Press.

Christiansen, John B., and Sharon N. Barnartt. 1995. *Deaf President Now!* Washington: Gallaudet University Press.

Dolniek, Edward. 1993. "Deafness as Culture." *Atlantic Monthly.* September, 37–53.

Evans, Sara M., and Harry C Boyte. 1986. *Free Spaces: The Source of Democratic Change in America.* New York: Harper and Row.

Fraser, Nancy. 1992. "Rethinking the Public Sphere: A Contribution to the Critique of Actually Existing Democracy." In *Habermas and the Public Sphere.* Ed. C. Calhoun. Cambridge: MIT Press.

Gannon, Jack. 1981. *Deaf Heritage: A Narrative History of Deaf America.* Silver Spring, Md.: National Association of the Deaf.

Gannon, Jack. 1989. *The Week the World Heard Gallaudet.* Washington: Gallaudet University Press.

Hering, Kathie. 1996. *ALDA Chicago Style,* January-February, 1–2.

Higgins, Paul C. 1980. *Outsiders in a Hearing World: A Sociology of Deafness.* Beverly Hills: Sage.

Jepson, Jill. 1993. "Trends in Poetry by Deaf and Hard-of-Hearing Writers." In *The Disability Perspective: Variations on a Theme.* Ed. D. Preiffer, S. Hey, and G. Kiger. Salem, Oregon: Society of Disability Studies/Willamette University.

Jernigan, Kenneth. 1976. "Blindness: Of Visions and Vultures." *Vital Speeches of the Day* 43:19–24.

Klandermans, Bert. 1992. "The Social Construction of Protest and Multiorganizational Fields." In *Frontiers in Social Movement Theory.* Ed. Aldon Morris and Carol Mueller. New Haven: Yale University Press.

Koestler, Frances A. 1976. *The Unseen Minority: A Social History of Blindness in America.* New York: David McKay Company.

Lane, Harlan. 1992. *The Mask of Benevolence: Disabling the Deaf Community.* New York: Alfred A. Knopf.

Lerner, Gerda, ed. 1993. *The Creation of Feminist Consciousness: From the Middle Ages to 1870.* New York: Oxford University Press.

Lowenfeld, Berthold. 1975. *The Changing Status of the Blind: From Separation to Integration.* Springfield, Ill.: Charles C. Thomas.

Mansbridge, Jane. 1994. "Using Power/Fighting Power." *Constellations* 1:53–73.

Matson, Floyd. 1990. *Walking Alone and Marching: A History of the Organized Blind Movement in the United States, 1940–1990.* Baltimore: National Federation of the Blind.

Maurer, Mare. 1993. "The Continuity of Leadership: Twin Requirements." Reprint of the National Federation of the Blind President's Banquet Address at the annual convention, Dallas, Texas. Baltimore: National Federation of the Blind.

McCarthy, John D., and Mayer N. Zald. 1973. *The Trends of Social Movements in America: Professionalization and Resource Mobilization*. Morristown, N.J.: General Learning Press.

———. 1977. "Resource Mobilization and Social Movements: A Partial Theory." *American Journal of Sociology* 82:1212–11.

McNeil, John M. 1993. *Americans with Disabilities: 1991–92*. Washington: U.S. Government Printing Office.

McWhinney, Jeff. 1991. "Deaf Consciousness." *Signpost: Newsletter of the International Sign Linguistics Association*. Spring, 13–15.

Morris, Aldon. 1984. *The Origins of the Civil Rights Movement: Black Communities Organizing for Change*. New York: MacMillan/FreePress.

National Federation of the Blind. 1991. *NFB Song Book*. Baltimore: National Federation of the Blind.

———. 1992. *Architectural Barriers for the Blind: The Myth and the Reality*. Baltimore: National Federation of the Blind.

National Fraternal Society of the Deaf. N.d. *Our History*. Leaflet. Mount Prospect, III.: National Fraternal Society of the Deaf.

Oberschall, Anthony. 1973. *Social Conflict and Social Movements*. Englewood Cliffs, N.J.: Prentice-Hall.

Padden, Carol, and Tom Humphries. 1988. *Deaf in America: Voices from a Culture*. Cambridge: Harvard University Press.

Sacks, Oliver. 1990. *Seeing Voices: A Journey into the World of the Deaf*. New York: HarperPerennial.

Scott, James C. 1990. *Domination and the Arts of Resistance*. New Haven: Yale University Press.

Shapiro, Joseph P. 1993. *No Pity: People with Disabilities Forging a New Civil Rights Movement*. New York: Times Books.

Solomon, Andrew. 1994. "Defiantly Deaf." *New York Times Magazine*, 28 August, 40–45, 62, 65–68.

Taylor, Verta, and Nancy E. Whittier. 1992. "Collective Identity in Social Movement Communities: Lesbian Feminist Mobilization." In *Frontiers in Social Movement Theory*. Ed. Aldon Morris and Carol Mueller. New Haven: Yak University Press.

Van Cleve, John V., and Barry A. Crouch. 1989. *A Place of Their Own: Creating the Deaf Community in America*. Washington: Gallaudet University Press.

Reading 4.5

The Inuit Circumpolar Council: An Overview

(2011)

Gary N. Wilson & Heather A. Smith

T HE INUIT CIRCUMPOLAR COUNCIL (OR INUIT Circumpolar Conference, as it was originally called), a transnational organization that represents the approximately 155,000 Inuit in Russia, Alaska, Canada, and Greenland, was established in 1977 in Barrow, Alaska. Its creation followed a decade of political agitation and activity among the circumpolar Inuit and other aboriginal peoples throughout the Arctic in response to resource development in Alaska and the western Canadian Arctic.[1] At about the same time, the Greenlandic Inuit were pressing for greater autonomy from Denmark (and would be successful in achieving this goal with the establishment of home rule in 1979). As Eben Hopson, the first president of the ICC, argued in 1975, "[a] strong international Inuit community organization would provide us added strength in negotiating for more home rule. We feel that there is room for Eskimo sovereignty within the democratic traditions of our national government."[2]

The roots of the ICC may be found in issues of political autonomy and economic development but it would be misguided to interpret these roots solely through western conceptions of modernization. Such conceptions tend to compartmentalize knowledge and put different parts of our lived experiences into boxes with such labels as political, economic, social, or environmental. Western conceptions also apply universal understandings of knowledge. Indigenous knowledge, however, is holistic and simultaneously situated: culture, politics, economics, and the land are all woven together. For example, if we consider the ICC charter, we do see that this document includes elements that call for "self-determination and Inuit participation in policies and activities that affect our homeland."[3] The charter begins with the recognition that the "Inuit are an indigenous people, with a unique culture, ancestry and homeland" and that the purpose of the ICC

---

1   Jessica Shadian, "Remaking Arctic governance: The construction of an Arctic Inuit policy," *Polar Record* 42, no. 222 (2006): 249–59.

2   Ibid., 255.

3   Inuit Circumpolar Council charter, 2011, http://inuitcircumpolar.com.

is to promote Inuit rights and interests, strengthen Inuit unity, "ensure the endurance and growth of Inuit culture and societies for both present and future generations," and "promote wise management and use of non-renewable resources in the circumpolar region and incorporating such resources in the present and future development of Inuit economies, taking into account other Inuit interests."[4]

Rather than reading the charter as a list of itemized priorities, we are better served to consider it as a collection of interconnected values. Taking this perspective allows us to see the source of complicated identity claims where the Inuit are both a unified people and citizens of states. In addition, dispensing with our mainstream western interpretations allows us to see self-determination not simply in political terms, but rather as a call for "cultural sovereignty" understood as "the right to maintain an historical relationship with the Arctic land."[5]

While the issues of political autonomy and resource development were clearly entwined at the birth of the ICC, it is only more recently that these issues have once again reemerged to influence the development of the organization. For much of the 1980s and 1990s, the attention of the ICC was clearly focused on the broader questions of indigenous rights and environmental issues in the Arctic region. In 1983, it was granted NGO status in the United Nations economic and social council and actively assisted in the drafting of the universal declaration of the rights of indigenous peoples. In the 1990s, the ICC played a significant and visible role in the United Nations' deliberations on persistent organic pollutants and was also actively involved in the development of the Arctic environmental protection strategy both prior to and after the establishment of the Arctic Council in 1996. In the mid-1990s, the ICC spearheaded assistance to indigenous peoples, including the small Inuit community in northern Russia following the collapse of the Soviet Union. Finally, under the leadership of Sheila Watt-Cloutier (2002-06), it was very active on the issue of climate change. Framing climate change as a human rights question, Watt-Cloutier helped to put a human face on the otherwise abstract and intangible impacts of this contentious issue, as a result of which she was nominated for the Nobel peace prize in 2007.[6]

More recently, the issues of political autonomy and resource development have once again taken center stage on the ICC agenda. There has been renewed interest in resource development in the Arctic, facilitated by anticipated environmental changes in the Arctic environment, interstate competition over sea bed claims, and the world's

---

4   Ibid.

5   Shadian, "Remaking arctic governance," 251.

6   See Fenge, "POPs and Inuit"; Huebert, "New directions in circumpolar cooperation"; Wilson, "Inuit diplomacy in the circumpolar north"; Watt-Cloutier, "The Inuit journey towards a POPs-free world"; and Smith and Wilson, "Inuit transnational activism."

dependency on a depleting stock of fossil fuels. This, coupled with the evolution of Inuit political autonomy at the regional and subnational levels, has started to influence internal debates within the ICC. The organization has exhibited a great deal of collective unity over the years, but this has often occurred in response to external threats, including the resource development issues that galvanized support for the establishment of the ICC in the 1970s. Today, by contrast, ICC members hold a number of competing perspectives on resource development. These perspectives reflect the respective constituencies of particular leaders of Inuit peoples, different stages of self-determination, and competing political identities. Regardless of political location, however, these perspectives have shaped the discourse around the future direction of the ICC and its position on resource development. It is to these perspectives that we now turn.

Competing Inuit Perspectives on Resource Development

While the apparent divisions over resource development within the ICC have made media headlines, a more nuanced analysis of the issue reveals a range of different yet often overlapping perspectives. The Inuit discourse around resource development at the beginning of the 21st century cannot be categorized into a simple typology of pro- versus anti-development. Rather, we identify three perspectives. Although each constitutes a different response to the changed political circumstances of the Inuit, all of the various opinions and perspectives that have been advanced still contain a strong current of environmental stewardship and responsibility.

The difference between the three perspectives is often a matter of which values are foregrounded in the arguments relating to resource development. First, there are leaders and elites who support resource development, mainly as a means of fostering socioeconomic growth in their respective communities and jurisdictions. Second, there is a group of leaders who recognize the economic and political gains that resource development can bring but who also emphasize the protection of the Arctic environment. Last, there are those who express a greater degree of caution about embracing resource development and who highlight the potential negative environmental, social, and cultural impacts that such development is having on Inuit communities. A closer examination of these perspectives will demonstrate both the differences and the continuities between them.

The economic development perspective

Some Inuit regions, most notably Greenland, view resource development as a means to secure greater financial autonomy from their host states. The premier of Greenland, Kuupik Kleist, has repeatedly framed climate change in the Arctic as a source of future opportunity. He argues that while the effects of climate change—such as the change in sea ice—may have an impact on traditional ways, they also mean new economic prospects. In the speech he delivered in Copenhagen at the time of the 2009 15th meeting of the conference of parties on the framework convention on climate change, Kleist argued, "Greenland climate change ... offers new opportunities in terms of tapping the natural wealth of our country. Less ice means easier access to the sustainable harvesting of oil, gas and minerals. The ice-melt will also provide huge hydro-power resources ... all of which will be vital in securing our economic self-sufficiency."[7] The premier went on to defend, in this and other statements, the right of Greenland to develop economically, even if such development contributed to climate change, and cautioned against any climate agreement that blocked or limited its ability to do so. In June 2010, at the 11th general assembly of the ICC, Kleist reiterated many of the same themes, stressing the importance of oil and gas development to Greenland: "the exploitation of our enormous riches in oil and mineral resources is indisputably the most promising and real potential for a greater degree of economic self-sufficiency—at a scale that will secure Greenland's economy base and our future livelihoods.[8]

In Kleist's view, self-determination is directly related to economic development. This perspective does not preclude concerns about traditional ways being disrupted by climate change, nor does it reject some sense of Inuit unity. However, the perspective articulated by the Greenlandic premier privileges and, in fact, celebrates the potential of oil-and-gas development. It also focuses on the peoples he represents (and one gets the sense this is not the Inuit as a transnational group) and articulates a sense of difference that is then used as a way to silence criticism of Greenland's decisions. In this vein, Kleist stated, "These are decisive moments in our history and in the development of our Arctic home. Each of us will make choices, which others may think should have been made differently. Showing respect for one another's choices is also respecting one another's right of self-determination."[9]

---

7   Kuupik Kleist, "Opening speech by Kuupik Kleist for the Greenlandic parallel event: In the eye of climate change," 11 December 2009, http://uk.nanoq.gl. See also Kleist, "Inuit and Arctic indigenous peoples' day: Address by the premier of Greenland, Mr. Kuupik Kleist, at Inuit and Arctic indigenous peoples' day, North Atlantic house," 16 December 2009, http://uk.nanoq.gl; and Kleist, "Melting snow and ice: A call for action—speech by the premier of Greenland, Mr. Kuupik Kleist," Copenhagen, 15 December 2009, http://uk.nanoq.gl.

8   Kuupik Kleist, "Welcoming speech to ICC 11th general assembly in Greenland: Speech by premier of Greenland, Kuupik Kleist," Nuuk, Greenland, 6 June 2010, http://uk.nanoq.gl. This view has been echoed by Jimmy Stotts, the former chair of the ICC, who argued at the 2009 Copenhagen summit that northerners should be exempt from mandatory greenhouse gas emission cuts. According to one report, Stotts said that "Inuit people, who are based in developing countries, still have needs similar to developing nations when it comes to making their economies grow via such activities as mining and oil and gas exploration." See "Exempt northerners from emission cuts: Inuit leader," *CBC News*, 10 December 2009.

9   "Welcoming speech to ICC 11th general assembly."

In a recent editorial in *Nunatsiaq News*, the comments of the Greenlandic premier were framed as those of a "country now ready to embrace modernity" and representing the "voice of confidence." The same editorial labelled an Inuit leader from Nunavut who opposed Kleist's approach as representing the "voice of fear," "the fear of those who have been sorely wounded by rapid change, the fear of those who long for an Eden that will never return, and the fear of those for whom land, sea and wildlife are to be protected at all cost."[10] Kleist and his supporters are aware of the impact that climate change is having on Greenland and the Arctic region in general. They are also supportive of international efforts to slow the process of change.[11] At the same time, however, they stress the need for Inuit in Greenland and elsewhere to adapt to the changes and seize upon opportunities that these changes may present.

The "pragmatic" perspective

The second perspective is marked by a recognition that resource development will likely occur, but that when it does, the Inuit must be the primary beneficiaries. This is a view that has been expressed by, among others, Mary Simon, president of Inuit Tapiriit Kanatami and vice-president of ICC Canada. At the ICC resource summit in February 2011, she stated that "[w]e have agreed with the leaders that we [the Canadian Arctic] are open for business—on certain issues. ... We think it will be on a case-by-case basis [because] there are conditions that need to be met."[12] Simon expressed a similar view in 2010: "on the controversial issue of hydrocarbon development, we are realistic. We need non-renewable development if we are to achieve economic self-sufficiency. But the terms of such development must ensure the protection of our environment and the continuation of our ways of life. On that, there can be no compromise."[13]

Unlike the economic development perspective outlined above, however, Simon does not equate climate change with opportunity. She calls for continued efforts to reduce carbon emissions and she is critical of the narrow national self-interest that informs too many climate change policies. A central theme in many of her speeches is the importance and value of the "circumpolar Inuit declaration on sovereignty in the Arctic." This declaration states, among other things, that "Inuit consent, expertise and perspectives are critical to progress on international issues involving the Arctic, such as global environmental security, sustainable development, militarization, commercial fishing, shipping,

---

10 "Divided they stand," *NunatsiaqOnline*, 28 February 2011.

11 See Kleist's comments in an interview at the climate change summit in Cancun, Mexico, 2010, www.youtube.com/watch?v=R77BbLCSlSU.

12 Rogers, "ICC summit wraps up with lukewarm consensus."

13 Mary Simon "The Arctic and northern dimensions of world issues," Inuit Tapiriit Kanatami, 4 November 2010, www.itk.ca.

human health, and economic and social development."[14] In the pragmatic perspective, what we find then is a reflection of the diverse nature of the issues facing Inuit peoples, and what appears to be an attempt to balance the competing views in a way that ensures, first and foremost, Inuit sovereignty as understood from an Inuit perspective.

The environment-culture perspective

The third perspective we wish to highlight here is the environment-culture perspective. Consistent with the perspectives articulated above, it is multifaceted in nature but marked by a distinct set of themes that seem to dominate its articulation. We associate this perspective with such Inuit leaders as the current ICC chair, Aqqaluk Lynge, and former chair, Sheila Watt-Cloutier. It is also the perspective that was so negatively labelled above "the voice of fear." In it we find there is a much higher degree of caution associated with resource development, often referencing the case of Alaska as an example of why caution is needed. It also embodies a greater tendency to invoke traditional understandings of Inuit connections to the land as well as Inuit colonial experiences.

For example, during the climate change meeting in Copenhagen, Lynge noted that he was more concerned with the loss of Inuit language, identity, and "our beautiful ways, wonderful way of living and moving forward through time, than … with the possibility of being left behind the developed world and their increasing globalizing and conforming ways."[15] Similarly, a strongly worded speech by Watt-Cloutier at the Copenhagen meeting beautifully captures themes central to this perspective: she calls on Inuit peoples to be "wise stewards" of their land, to not give in to quick economic fixes, and to not compromise the values that have guided her people for millennia. Her words appear to be a direct challenge to those who advocate the economic development perspective articulated above. In Copenhagen she stated, "As wise stewards of our land, I would urge my own people to refuse the dangerous compromises between our principles and development that might diminish our own moral standing and claim to high ground as indigenous peoples. As we call on the world to change its ecologically degrading practices, we must not accept those practices at home no matter how desperate our need for jobs or economic development."[16]

Her views were shared by Lynge, who stated publicly that he agreed with Watt-Cloutier. While acknowledging the "paradox of development" faced by the Inuit, Lynge went on to say that "[i]f we develop as the colonizers and polluters have done before us, without regard to our environment, we may have a moral argument to do so, but the

---

14 "Circumpolar Inuit declaration on Arctic sovereignty," 2009, www.itk.ca.

15 George, "ICC moves to patch up Inuit climate change rift."

16 Sheila Watt-Cloutier, "Reclaiming the moral high ground: Indigenous peoples, climate change, and human rights," in *NunatsiaqOnline*, 21 December 2009.

approach will destroy us, and deny us the survival of our own Inuit culture."[17] This is not the voice of fear; rather, it is a voice that is much needed in a world that privileges economic growth over environmental wellbeing. It is a voice that reminds us all of the need to have a more holistic and sustainable approach to the world. It is, however, a voice competing to be heard.

...

Concluding Reflections

The ICC has been and continues to be a vital voice for the Inuit. While divisions over resource development do exist, we believe that it would be problematic for the ICC to either call it a day or turn its focus to areas that are primarily about economic development. Perhaps the most difficult question for the organization will be how to manage unity in diversity (a challenge its leaders have recognized). The successful management of the organization will not take place through the potential isolation or inward-looking tendency that comes from claims that sound strikingly similar to state-based claims of protecting that national interest. Historically, the ICC has been a forum for sharing best practices. It has advocated for the rights of Inuit peoples and reminded us all about the human face of climate change. No doubt, best practices will be needed in this era of rapid change and the social disparities faced by Inuit peoples are a shameful reminder of internal colonization. And we all need to be reminded of the human face of climate change, as much as we all need to be mindful of our relationship with the earth. The recent public reconciliation of the various perspectives does include these values, but whether or not they can be translated into action in the face of the forces of modernization remains to be seen.

---

17   George, "ICC Moves to patch up Inuit climate change rift."

Toward a Feminist Theory of Letting Go (2015)

Donna King

During an interview on NPR's *All Things Considered* (2011), David Greene asked Brian Henneman of the band The Bottle Rockets, "You've played with some pretty big names ... you guys have become big. [But] you're not as commercial ... as big as Wilco ... I mean, what takes you to the next level?" Henneman laughed and replied, "It's too late to go to the next level. We're too comfortable where we're at. Why would we want to move now if everything will just be more of a pain in the butt? So, yeah ... this is a real awesome comfortable place, and we like it. And by golly, that's our story, and we're sticking to it."

Setting aside the self-conscious coda, what strikes me about this exchange is Henneman's genuine satisfaction with his band's level of success. You can hear it in his voice, he means it. He is okay exactly where he is, with his band and in his life. He does not want to get to the top; he does not have to be the best. In fact, he foresees only headaches (or worse) lying in wait should he strive for bigger commercial success. Surely Henneman's social position—as a middle-aged working class musician from the Midwest, fronting a band that has played mostly in bars for over twenty years—has shaped his aspirational goals. I find it refreshing, nonetheless, to hear him say out loud and proud, "No thanks. I don't need to reach the top. I'm okay exactly where I am."

But then there is that conditional addendum, with its self-deprecating, defensive posturing, undercutting the message that good-enough is fine and implying instead that one must justify, explain, or make excuses for being satisfied with one's life as it is.

I question the core American imperative that says we must endlessly strive to be the best. My interest in this issue is both intellectual and personal. Like many women, I struggle to balance work life, home life, professional pursuits, creative endeavors, self-definition, and cultural mandates. And I ask: Does feminism provide theoretical supports for women who want to (or must) slow down, grow quiet, and let go of striving? Can one be simultaneously feminist and nothing special, a strong woman and a woman in touch with her real limitations?

I use the somewhat jarring term "nothing special" not to minimize or denigrate women, but rather to highlight cultural contradictions I see in a mainstream, white, affluent, "free market feminism" that promotes the relentless pursuit of personal and professional achievement while uncritically adopting a neoliberal ideology that conflates "female empowerment [with] the accompanying baggage of consumerism, individualism, radical inequalities of life chances [and] environmental degradation" (Eisenstein 2009, 221).[1]

As Hester Eisenstein (2009) argues in *Feminism Seduced*, "feminist energies, ideologies, and activism have been manipulated in the services of the dangerous forces of [a] globalized corporate capitalism" (viii) that views the majority of the world's women as "the cheap workforce of choice," (11) and co-opts privileged professional women, including many academic feminists, into an acritical (or defeatist) acceptance of the neoliberal agenda and its attendant "flight from the body" (220). As antidote to this cooptation, Eisenstein calls for a revitalized feminist critique of capitalism that "transcend[s] ... the differences between Third World and First World women to create a united international women's movement that can be a force for political and social change" (68). Primary among these forces for change, says Eisenstein, is a return to the body and to a social ethic of compassion, nurturance and care that "transform[s] maternalism, not as an essentialist definition of women's roles, but as a set of claims on the state" (x–xii) to provide child care, health care, sufficient nutrition, and adequate housing for all (229).

As Eisenstein's critique makes clear, there are contradictions in our culture, and within feminism, about how women should live our lives, particularly in terms of economic and cultural demands for high productivity, fast pace, pushing past limits, and denying the body. These pressures cut across race, class, work, and home. Many women are stuck in dead-end jobs with low wages, no job security, no autonomy, no respect, no control over their schedule, and unrelenting performance expectations. Professional women, despite their relative privilege, often face extraordinary demands on their time and energy. Home life, for many women, is rarely a safe haven from stress. Bearing and raising small children, dealing with teenagers, sending kids off to college, living with a partner or a dependent that is disabled or unhappily unemployed or clinically depressed or battling addiction—any potentially overwhelming experience that stretches us beyond our physical, mental, and emotional capacities leaves us ripe for a confrontation between so-called ideal and real women's lives.

We all face potential devaluation by family, friends, colleagues, peers, bosses, and perhaps most importantly by ourselves, when we do not "pull our weight" or "measure up" to socially defined standards of achievement. Many, if not most, women internalize impossible performance expectations, and it takes a tremendous force of will, or paradoxically, a complete letting go, to liberate ourselves from them.

---

1   Hester Eisenstein (2009:14) credits Jaqui Alexander and Chandra Talpade Mohanty for coining the term "free market feminism" to describe how in the 1990s the "Clinton administration was using mainstream feminism to sell 'free market' capitalism to the world."

I use Zen insight as a complement to Eisenstein's structural analysis of global neo-liberal capitalism to explore how close attunement to bodily experience allows some women with invisible chronic illness to let go of unreasonable expectations of productivity and pace. While Eisenstein is scathing in her criticism of feminist "postmodern analyses that focus on individual and private acts of resistance" (2009, 212), I argue that, much like a breaching experiment in which one consciously and publicly violates a behavior in order to make obvious its structure and social power, studying how women with invisible chronic illness navigate achievement expectations—under physically and mentally debilitating conditions—highlights oppressive and often unacknowledged productivity norms in a dramatic way and further supports Eisenstein's call for a broader social commitment to compassion and care.

I focus here on two explicitly feminist accounts of the chronic illness experience, Cheri Register's *Living with Chronic Illness* and Susan Wendell's *The Rejected Body*, and draw from Barbara Hillyer's *Feminism and Disability*. Reading the works of feminist women with disabilities reveals that they are uniquely positioned to address dominant cultural dictates in the most concrete and experiential way, through both their bodies and minds. As their bodies transform from reasonably healthy to seriously unwell, these women's lives and sense of self transform as well, sometimes in radically new and improbable ways. Many women with chronic illness live a path that moves from pain, fear, fatigue, frustration, and grief, through a gradual and often grudging acceptance of unwelcome and disabling limitations, toward a new found sense of inner peace and self-acceptance. They learn the hard way, through mortal necessity, how to let go.

Zen and the Art of Letting Go

When you are hungry, eat. When you are tired, rest.

—Zen instruction

Writing as an exhausted new mother, Zen teacher Karen Maezen Miller offers this paean to bone-tiredness:

> It is not something you would choose, like a spa vacation, but is something you can use, like a humidifier. ... It is a cure and a balm. Fatigue helps you forget. When you are tired, you let go. You drop what you no longer need and you do not pick it up again. You slow down. You grow quiet. You take comfort. You appreciate the smallest things. You stop fighting. (quoted in Harris 2006)

The idea that fatigue might be useful, rather than a problem to be solved, is counter-intuitive in our multitasking, wired, and information-overloaded world. Zen advice that we eat when hungry and rest when tired goes directly against American cultural norms that dictate we push past our limits in a tireless quest to succeed. What is it we drop when we slow down, grow quiet, and appreciate small things?

The Zen of letting go suggests a practice of paying attention to immediate experience and responding appropriately, including listening to the body and meeting bodily needs as they arise. This is emphatically not the same as seeking complete comfort and ease in life; an appealing but unattainable goal whose quixotic pursuit ironically leads directly to what Buddhists call *dukkha*, a Pāli word most commonly translated as "suffering" but perhaps better understood as anguish, fear, clinging, and/or dissatisfaction. We are all destined to feel multiple kinds of pain at multiple points in our lives, and for some this becomes a chronic mental, physical, and/or emotional state. But none of these kinds of pain need necessarily lead to suffering. For Buddhists, suffering is an add-on, a social construction that most often takes the form of chronic dissatisfaction with life as it is (see Loy 1996).

Letting go, in Zen terms, means dealing skillfully with whatever is going on without adding any storyline. Freedom from suffering comes from total involvement in simply being with what is—and in constantly letting go of our attachment to having things go a certain way. For the Zen practitioner, none of this is easy or ever fully accomplished. In fact, it is not even a goal. It is an ongoing practice and process with no end in sight (Beck 1989).

Far from simple passive acquiescence, however, Zen practice can explicitly critique the forces of corporate global capitalism and advocate for a political economy organized around care, compassion, and social justice (Loy 2003). As media activist and Buddhist practitioner David Edwards (2005) notes:

> When society subordinates its humanity to maximized revenues at minimum cost, then that society is well on the way to becoming lost, falsified, and in fact inhuman. If we are serious about combating selfishness and promoting compassion in the world, then is it not vital that we develop the tools of intellectual self-defense to deal with these assaults on our minds and hearts? The solution must lie in reversing the priorities, in subordinating dead things—money, capital, profits—to life: people, animals, the planet. … The antidotes to systemic greed, I am convinced, are political movements motivated by unconditional compassion for suffering.

Thus there is real potential for radical social change when we incorporate Buddhist insights with incisive critiques of neoliberal ideologies and practices that are colonizing our consciousness and the planet. We need not choose between inner awareness, listening to the body, and political activism for social justice. Activism can take many forms, and humanizing the global political economy and revitalizing a feminist commitment to a society based not on striving and "success" but on compassion and care may be just what is called for at this historical moment. But, as some feminists with invisible chronic illness attest, mainstream free-market feminism has not always accommodated the very real human need for retreat, reflection, and rest.

Living with Chronic Illness

In the mid-1980s, Patricia Fraser, a Harvard University Medical School physician working with chronically ill patients at Brigham and Women's Hospital in Boston, recognized that women with lupus—an invisible chronic illness that includes among other symptoms debilitating pain and extreme fatigue—face unique and painful challenges living up to the contradictory expectations society ascribes to all women:

> For most of us non-superwomen in good health, the discrepancy between the real and the ideal is clear and the ideal is used as a guideline to modify our lives. During periods of high energy and heightened motivation we may attempt to emulate features of the superwomen, but as we fatigue we drop back to somewhere near or slightly above where we started. Nothing is lost and something is gained in the experience; no harm is done. With lupus the issues and stakes are always higher, the risks magnified (Aladjem 1986, 61–62).

The risks Fraser refers to here include the very real, potentially fatal risks women with lupus and similar chronic illnesses face when they push themselves beyond their physical, mental, and emotional capacities and attempt to ignore their need for rest.

Irving Zola has noted that most research on illness narratives usually ignores any "detailed descriptions of the physical disability itself, especially its chronic aspects" (cited in Hillyer 1993, 37). Barbara Hillyer describes this omission as a "cultural silencing of embodied disability" (37). Susan Wendell agrees that "people with disabilities and illnesses learn that most people do not want to know about the suffering they experience because of their bodies ... interest in the subjective experience is rare" (1996, 91). But as Hillyer notes, "to disguise the pain denies the human connection, whether the disguise is meant to satisfy the demands of scholarly objectivity or those of political activism" (1993, 41). Thus it is important to look closely at the embodied subjectivity of women living with chronic illness as we trace the path of their self-transformation and its social implications. The precipitating event is a body that breaks down.

Living with Pain, Letting Go of Suffering

Pain can be a path to body knowing and self-centering like no other. For most healthy people feeling pain is a wake-up call. We look for the source, we seek relief, and we expect the pain to go away. Our experience of pain is not simply physical, however, as David Morris (1993, 3) makes clear when he observes that "pain is never the sole creation of our anatomy and physiology ... it emerges ... at the intersection of bodies, minds, and cultures." For women with chronic illness, living in pain brings body awareness into complete and total focus and initiates mental, emotional, and social challenges that require extraordinary effort to manage. As one woman reports:

> It seems to take everything in me to manage what I'm going through ... like people are going to suck some energy out of me that I don't have to give to them because I have to stay on top of this for myself. I think it takes such tremendous amounts of energy to have pain. (Register 1987, 81)

While the intensity and scope can vary, pain that never goes away is a fact of life for most women with chronic illness. Unrelenting opportunity and bitter necessity force many women, such as Eileen Radziunas (1989), to become "connoisseurs" of their pain. She describes in exquisite detail experiences that are invisible to others, who, over time and in the face of no firm diagnosis, may be inclined to deny their reality.

> Unlike other patients who I'd heard say "pain is pain," I knew there were different ways to describe it, because I felt it at such different levels. I detailed the deep, penetrating muscle pain, as opposed to the intense burning pain on the surface of my skin. I named the specific joints which ached routinely, and I pointed out that my tendons also hurt relentlessly, causing me as much pain at rest as during activity. I mentioned my transient blurry vision and excessive hair loss. It seemed superfluous to mention the bright red rash which ran across my cheeks and nose. (84)

For some, pain is so unpredictable and intense that it takes on a "terroristic" quality. Cheri Register (1987) describes her acute flare ups this way:

> I feel [like] concrete [is] filling my liver until it bursts and spills into my abdominal cavity, hardening as it is poured so that its rough edges grate against my diaphragm and the muscles between my ribs. I can't breathe, I can't lie down, and I can't imagine anything worse ... the knowledge that pain like this can come on at any time never leaves me, though I have good stretches when I don't have to dwell on it. Thus the threat of pain

determines, to a great extent, how I live my life, even though nothing I do can prevent it. Starting out the day is a little like heading down a dark street where a rape and an armed robbery have recently taken place. (180–81)

At these moments, when pain is the dominant mode of her existence, Register finds the possibility of acceptance and transformation remote, if not impossible: "When pain grows intense enough to force recognition, it demands complete attention. As I know it, severe pain is isolating and totally absorbing. I can't do anything but hurt. I simply have not learned how to "accept" these awful experiences. They undo me every time" (181).

But dealing with pain and rationing energy are at the heart of letting go and self-transforming for many women with chronic illness. Some women reach the point where their suffering and torment transmutes into "just pain":

> From my own and other people's experiences of chronic pain, I have learned that pain is an interpreted experience. ... For example, it is a fascinating paradox that a major aspect of the painfulness of pain, or I might say the suffering caused by pain, is the desire to get rid of it, to escape from it, to make it stop. A cultivated attitude of acceptance toward it, giving in to it, or just watching/observing it as an experience like others, can reduce the suffering it usually causes. (Wendell 1996, 181)

Susan Wendell's description here is reminiscent of a form of Zen meditation. Notice the pain (thought, sensation, emotion), recognize without attachment or resistance, and let it go. Watch as it changes or transforms. Perhaps this is how/why some women with chronic illness seem eventually to become happier than they were before their illness. Perhaps this focused attention to their bodies, coupled with their acceptance that they can't will their pain or bodily uncertainty away, but must learn to live with it, functions as a sort of an untutored and natural Zen practice. There seems to be a transformation of consciousness that comes through awareness and acceptance of the body in pain, as Wendell goes on to explain. "It is difficult for most people who have not lived with prolonged or recurring pain to understand the benefits of accepting it. Yet some people who live with chronic pain speak of 'making friends' with it as the road to feeling better and enjoying life" (109).

Paying more attention to our experience of our bodies can wake us up to what we are thinking, feeling, sensing, and provide an opportunity to choose how we will respond to the stimulus. But, according to Wendell, such an effort requires restructuring our lives to include more time for contemplation and rest. "In a sense I discovered that experiences of the body can teach consciousness a certain freedom from the sufferings and limitations of the body. ... Of course, it requires structuring my life so that I can rest and withdraw my attention into my body much more than healthy people my age normally do" (172).

Making time to rest becomes crucial for women with chronic illness who live with unrelenting pain and profound fatigue that is unpredictable and invisible to others. But how do they deal with unremitting social pressure in a neoliberal environment that tells them to push on, prove themselves, and be "productive"?

...

Transforming Selves, Transforming Societies

The lessons from Zen and women with invisible chronic illness seem to indicate that once we know ourselves in a deeply embodied way, we have the potential to free ourselves—from achievement mandates that tell us we are never good enough, accumulation mandates that tell us we will never have enough, attention mandates that tell us we don't count unless we are looked at and admired. Letting go of control over things we can't control, such as incurable illness, may enact a transformative process that allows for the rejection of social norms that have functioned to limit and constrain or push and exhaust, and for the rewriting of a new set of possibilities of being and time. A key transformative moment occurs when women accept "This is my body, these are my limits, these are my priorities, there is only this moment, I can let go of everything else." Is this a feminist breakthrough?

On its face letting go in this way challenges basic feminist tenets that women (as opposed to men) should control all aspects of women's lives and (more covertly) that women should excel in all pursuits. Superwoman expectations that emerged in the wake of feminist gains did and do exist for some women who "want to have it all." And some feminists who also happen to be disabled or responsible to care for someone who is disabled have written about this issue. As Barbara Hillyer (1993) notes:

> [In American culture] rushing from one activity to another is highly valued by others and oneself. It is not surprising, then, that "supercrip" and "superwoman" are roles that the movements for disability and women's rights are ambivalent about. We deplore the apparent necessity to be superhuman (stronger than able-bodied white males) but admire people who can do it and demand as much of ourselves. Better to be a superwoman than to be weak or dependent. (52)

Hillyer writes about the mainstream feminist bias for strong, highly productive, politically-active roles for women in society. She calls for a feminist theory that also acknowledges that "human beings are limited; that some losses cannot be repaired; and above all, that female strength and weakness must be integrated" (15). All of us are destined to age, decline, and die, says Hillyer, and women need a more intimate and grounded experience of body knowing and self-centering to help us navigate this inevitable developmental path. Hillyer describes a grief that arises from "being in touch with one's limitations," feeling less safe, recognizing one's vulnerability, and exploring

> the nature of one's own "real" condition—not idealized or misinterpreted by the culture. ... In a culture like ours that values optimism and a cheery willingness to minimize difficulties, it is very difficult to see oneself as a person with a serious problem ... recognition that she is a person with a serious difficulty defined from within forces a woman to find significance in her life as it is. (16)

Acknowledging human vulnerability and finding significance in life as it is has the potential not only for radical self-transformation, but for radical social transformation as well. As Hester Eisenstein argues, returning to the body is a crucial component in revitalizing a feminist politics that is critical of so-called "free-market" economies and advocates instead for a broad social compact committed to compassion and care. A feminist theory of letting go necessitates a radical rethinking of what it means to live as a woman in a culture that mandates we give it our all. And for some women, accepting limitations and rebuilding lives based on a slower, quieter and self-determined pace has—as an unintended consequence—not only self-transformation and the seeds of social transformation, but increased joy in life as it is.

References

Aladjem, Henrietta. 1986. *Understanding Lupus*. New York: Charles Scribner.

Beck, Charlotte Joko. 1989. *Everyday Zen: Love and Work*. San Francisco: Perennial/Harper & Row.

Bell, Inge, Bernard McGrane, and John Gunderson. 2011. *This Book is Not Required: An Emotional and Intellectual Survival Manual for Students*, 4th edition. Thousand Oaks, CA: Pine Forge.

Clarke, Jude. 2002. *The Language of Water: A Woman's Struggle with Systemic Lupus Erythematosus*. Saskatchewan, Canada: Thistledown.

Edwards, David. 2005. "Life or Death." *Tricycle Magazine*, Fall 2005. *www.tricycle.com/my-view/life-or-death*.

Eisenstein, Hester. 2009. *Feminism Seduced: How Global Elites Use Women's Labor and Ideas to Exploit the World*. Boulder, CO: Paradigm.

Harris, Leah. 2006. "If the Buddha Gave Birth: Review of *Mama Zen: Walking the Crooked Path of Motherhood*." *Literary Mama*, December 21. *www.literarymama.com/reviews/archives/2006/12/if-the-buddha-gave-birth.html*.

Hillyer, Barbara. 1993. *Feminism and Disability*. Norman, OK: University of Oklahoma.

hooks, bell. 2003. *Teaching Community: Toward a Pedagogy of Hope*. New York: Routledge.

Loy, David R. 1996. *Lack and Transcendence: The Problem of Death and Life in Psychotherapy, Existentialism, and Buddhism*. Amherst, NY: Humanity Books.

————. 2003. *The Great Awakening: A Buddhist Social Theory*. Boston: Wisdom.

Morris, David. 1993. *The Culture of Pain*. Berkeley: University of California.

National Public Radio (NPR) Staff. 2011. "The Bottle Rockets: Heartland Tales of Heartbreak." *All Things Considered Weekend Edition*, August 14. *www.npr.org/2011/08/14/139586886/the-bottle-rockets-heartland-tales-of-heartbreak*.

Radziunas, Eileen. 1989. *Lupus: My Search for a Diagnosis*. Claremont, CA: Hunter House.

Register, Cherry. 1987. *Living with Chronic Illness: Days of Patience and Passion*. New York: Free Press.

Wendell, Susan. 1996. *The Rejected Body: Feminist Philosophical Reflections on Disability*. New York: Routledge.

A Figment of Our (Civic) Imagination
(2016)

Henry Jenkins, Sangita Shresthova, Liana Gamber-Thompson, & Neta Kligler-Vilenchik

As OUR TEAM HAS SOUGHT TO understand the nature of participatory politics, we've increasingly been drawn toward the concept of the "civic imagination," which we define as the capacity to imagine alternatives to current social, political, or economic conditions. One cannot change the world unless one can imagine what a better world might look like, and too often, our focus on contemporary problems makes it impossible to see beyond immediate constraints. One also can't change the world until one can imagine oneself as an active political agent. For many of the young people we spoke with, the message they received on a daily basis was that what they had to say didn't matter; the social change organizations we studied work hard to help participants learn to trust their own voice. Here, we are drawing on Nick Couldry (2010), who describes political voice as the process of "giving an account of oneself," in ways which can help others to engage with your concerns and learn from your experiences. Such accounts may be autobiographical (as they often are among the DREAMer youth we have studied) but they may also involve sharing fantasies (as is more the case in the DREAMers' use of the superhero genre). For youth, this focus on potential civic roles is important since, as writers like Shakuntala Banaji and David Buckingham (2013) have suggested, young people are often excluded from playing an "actual" or "meaningful" role in the processes associated with institutionalized politics, their agendas are marginalized, and, as in current voter suppression efforts that make it harder for American youth to register to vote through their schools, they are disenfranchised. All of this is certainly true for young DREAMers who are fighting for their right to stay in this country and to participate in the "American Dream."

Yet, we've found that young people are learning to identify and frame political issues in language that speaks to them and their peers. Many of the youth we've interviewed told us that they felt discomfort embracing contemporary political rhetoric they found exclusive (insofar as you have to know much about the political system in order to understand what is being discussed) and repulsive (insofar as it is bound up with partisan struggles for power rather than an effort to find a consensus). In turning toward icons and narratives borrowed from popular media to express their civic identities and political concerns, they were seeking a way to bridge across divisions and differences that are making it hard for the political establishment to move forward to solve persistent problems.

This movement from private toward public imagination often depends on images already familiar to participants from other contexts, images drawn not from political rhetoric but popular fantasy. The image bank through which we forge the civic imagination shifts from generation to generation: for the civil rights movement in the 1950s, it might have been formed around the rhetoric of the black church with its talk of "crossing the River Jordan" and entering the "promised land," while for the American founding fathers, it might have been formed around motifs from classical history and mythology. But, the emerging generation of young activists maintains a strong, close relationship to American popular culture, and that shared vocabulary helps them to broker relations across different political groups.

...

"Waiting for Superman" Is a Bad Idea!

Marvel's efforts to incorporate American Muslim experiences into its superhero universe was a logical outgrowth of the efforts of the U.S. comic books industry to move beyond its jingoistic past in the wake of 9/11. As Henry Jenkins (2006, 79) wrote in an overview of how the comics industry depicted the tragedy, "Comic book artists rejected fisticuffs or vigilante justice in favor of depicting the superheroes as nurturers and healers. They are more likely to be standing tall against domestic racial violence than punching out terrorists." Making Ms. Marvel an American Muslim girl paralleled other recent decisions to grant an African American youth the mantle of Spider-Man or for Thor to adopt a female persona. Jenkins (2006) summed up his argument this way:

> Popular culture is the space of dreams, fantasies, and emotions. In that space, it matters enormously whether Captain America stands for fascism or democracy, whether Wonder Woman represents the strong arm of American cultural imperialism or whether she respects and understands third world critiques of her mission, whether Superman is more important than the average men and women who are accidental casualties of his power struggles or whether everyday people have the power to solve their problems without turning to superheroes for help. (98)

And for this reason, superheroes often get pulled into debates about what actions are appropriate for responding to contemporary social problems. We saw two rich examples of such debates in the course of our research.

The first involved the Nerdfighters. Nerdfighters participate in an informal online community revolving around the YouTube channel of the "VlogBrothers," John and Hank Green. Nerdfighters are united by a broad but shared identity as "nerds," as well as by a loosely defined civic mission to "decrease world suck." When Nerdfighters talk about "decreasing world suck," they may mean a broad range of things—helping a friend in need, creating a funny video to make others happy, or activities more traditionally conceived as civic engagement, such as donating to nonprofits and charities. Nerdfighters have shown impressive abilities to mobilize quickly with high impact, for example when in 2013 they raised over $870,000 in two days, which were then divided between charities for which Nerdfighters voted.

Uniting all these actions is a belief in a model of change in which every person counts, and small acts add up to make big change. Such an approach may be at odds with the superhero model, in which an extraordinary character saves the world, while ordinary people are powerless bystanders. This possible contradiction inspired a 2011 discussion entitled "I don't like superheroes," on a popular Nerdfighter forum, nerdfighters.ning. com. Nerdfighter Kat posted: "I don't hate them, it's just I don't like the idea of how one person wields the power to change things and fight crime, while the ordinary citizens are always sort of helpless and expect the superhero to save them; in real life, it's the ordinary people who change things, and they don't get special powers or are 'chosen,' and very often, they can't do it alone and have to band together."

Some Nerdfighters agreed with Kat. Other forum participants used the question of superheroes' popularity to make a wider statement about how humans respond to what often seems a chaotic and unjust world: "Superheroes are present for the same reason religions are, to restore order where we may see chaos. To enact morals where there may be none, to punish and reward." Others used superheroes as role models for "ordinary people," to make the argument that every person can make a difference—if they try hard enough. Another Nerdfighter, with the username Calibran explained: "Each and every one of those people has all the power they need to become a superhero in their own right." Superheroes thus offered the Nerdfighters a lens through which to discuss ideas about individual agency, civic responsibility, and models of change and thus to think more deeply about what motivates their own civic activities.

Similar analysis about which superheroes most embody a libertarian belief system can be found across the web, penned by range of libertarian authors, from casual bloggers to professional journalists. Witness writer and editor Franklin Harris's 2009 blog post from the Young Americans for Liberty website, "We Don't Need Another Hero." Harris focuses mostly on the libertarian appeal of Alan Moore and Dave Gibbons' 1986 graphic novel, *Watchmen*, adapted for film in 2009, but also identifies libertarian elements in the 2008 *Dark Knight* and *Iron Man* films: "While *Iron Man* and *The Dark Knight* both deal with issues of power and corruption, they ultimately side with their vigilante protagonists." The superheroes in *Watchmen*, on the other hand, have a more ambiguous relationship to social good, and they are often as vulnerable to established power structures as their human counterparts or, worse, wield their powers for evil and corruption. Following a similar logic to Thomas Andrea's critique of Superman as a law enforcer rather than as a champion of justice, Harris argues that *Watchmen* is so appealing to libertarians (and anti-statists in particular) because it is an allegory for the misuse of power:

> What are superheroes anyway, except unauthorized, unaccountable law-enforcement agents? Superheroes don't obtain search warrants. They don't read suspects their Miranda rights. If they screw up, they don't face disciplinary action. And it's almost impossible for a wronged party to sue them for misconduct. Just try serving a court summons to the Hulk. In short, all of the real-world problems associated with police misconduct are potentially worse when it comes to superheroes. They exist outside the rule of law.

Other libertarian writers have a less dystopian take on superheroes. Stacy Litz, a Drexel University student writing for *Examiner.com* in 2010, makes a case for the libertarianism of Iron Man, Tony Stark, who uses his private means to battle the military-industrial complex: "So, what did *Iron Man 2* prove to viewers? Government intervention results in a lot of unnecessary explosions. When striving to 'protect the country,' those in power will go through 'any means necessary' to achieve a sense of security, even by faking deaths, working with the enemy and stealing Iron Man suits. ... Private security is a reliable asset while public law enforcement is less than trustworthy."

Fred Roeder, blogging for Students for Liberty, agrees with Litz's assessment, including Stark in his June 2014 listicle/photo essay of "16 Libertarian Sci-Fi Heros." Roeder also includes the likes of V from *V for Vendetta*, Dr. Jean Grey from *X-Men*, Steve Rogers from *Captain America*, and even Unikitty from *The Lego Movie*.

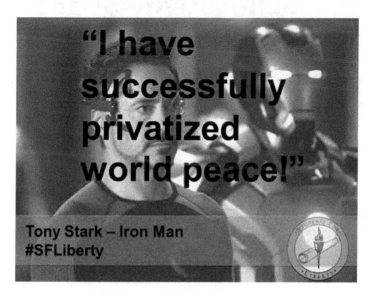

FIGURE 17.3   Artwork created by Fred Roeder of Students for Liberty.

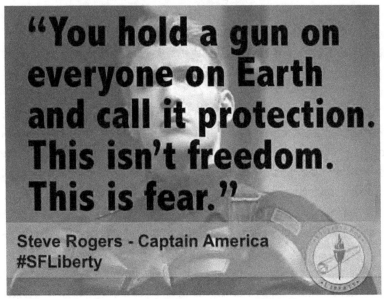

"You hold a gun on everyone on Earth and call it protection. This isn't freedom. This is fear."

Steve Rogers - Captain America
#SFLiberty

FIGURE 17.4   Artwork created by Fred Roeder of Students for Liberty.

"There is no government, no bedtimes, no baby-sitters, no frowny faces, no bushy mustaches, and no negativity of any kind."

Unikitty – The Lego Movie
#SFLiberty

FIGURE 17.5   Artwork created by Fred Roeder of Students for Liberty.

Both the Nerdfighters and the libertarians saw the superhero mythos as raising some core questions informing their civic and political lives. For the Nerdfighters, the key issue was whether change might come through the actions of everyday people working together toward common ends or whether it necessarily rested in the hands of elite institutions or exceptional individuals. For the libertarians, the question was how we should deal with the risks of concentrated power (especially when aligned with state interests).

Because participants already knew who these superheroes were, they were able to use them to encourage analysis and, through this process, to identify points of agreement or conflict in their underlying models of political life. Such debates may or may not spark action; they can also distract from more-grounded discussions of tactics for mobilization. Our focus on the civic differs from traditional understandings of ideology because of our focus on the bottom-up, participatory shaping of these narratives as part of larger cultural struggles over meaning and representation. We might read the superhero narrative as embodying particular ideologies about American exceptionalism and manifest destiny, meanings that can often be located in the official texts surrounding these characters. Superhero characters were deployed as part of propaganda campaigns during World War II, for example. Across the varied examples in this essay, we've also seen that these same figures can be and are deployed by a broader range of groups toward their own political ends—many of which challenge, contest, or even reverse that particular frame, allowing the superhero saga to speak for Sikhs, undocumented immigrants, or American Muslims who might otherwise be excluded from dominant ideological understandings of what constitutes an American hero. Any act of appropriation involves some reproduction of prevailing ideology but these examples also involve a remixing or rethinking of these core myths to express alternative perspectives. Our next section considers more fully what it means to "act" as superheroes in the political realm, looking at examples of performances within the Occupy Wall Street and Invisible Children movements.

Occupying Gotham

In an age when new media platforms have lowered the transaction costs for collective action and made it easier to share grassroots media with dispersed networks, young activists are often taking the civic imagination to the next level—performing these imagined identities through what Stephen Duncombe has described as "ethical spectacle." Duncombe (2012b) defines this concept in *Beautiful Trouble*, an online resource for contemporary activists:

> An ethical spectacle is a symbolic action that seeks to shift the political culture toward more progressive values. An ethical spectacle should strive to be:
>
> Participatory: Seeking to empower participants and spectators alike, with organizers acting as facilitators.

Open: Responsive and adaptive to shifting contexts and the ideas of participants.

Transparent: Engaging the imagination of spectators without seeking to trick or deceive.

Realistic: Using fantasy to illuminate and dramatize real-world power dynamics and social relations that otherwise tend to remain hidden in plain sight.

Utopian: Celebrating the impossible—and therefore helping to make the impossible possible.

Beautiful Trouble offers its own examples of the ways that the superhero has been mobilized for grassroots politics. On November 17, 2011, a coalition of labor organizers seeking to challenge austerity measures and to demand more jobs projected a Bat Signal on the side of Brooklyn's Verizon Building. As one of the event organizers (Read 2012) explained:

> The "bat signal" itself required no translation. It's a part of our cultural commons, part of the "spectacular vernacular" of global pop culture, a symbol we all understand to be a call for aid and an outlaw call to arms—after all, isn't that precisely what the Occupy movement is? Of course Batman is actually a quasi-sociopathic millionaire vigilante. A one-percenter, you might say. But by filling that symbol—by occupying it—with our own content—"99%"—we appropriated it for the rest of us. And in this reconfiguration, we were no longer waiting for some superhero, be it a masked vigilante or the first black president, to swoop in and save the day. Rather, we were the response to our own call for aid.

In his analysis of the Occupy movement, Manuel Castells (2012) talks about how its discursive and organizational practices created spaces for imagining alternatives, for expressing the movement's shared concerns about wealth inequalities, and for innovating new mechanisms for collaboration and deliberation. The Bat Signal, and especially the group's acknowledgment of its contradictory meanings, is a great illustration of these practices at work.

References

Banaji, Shakuntala, and David Buckingham. 2013. *The Civic Web: Young People, The Internet and Civic Participation*. Cambridge, MA: MIT Press.

Castells, Manuel. 2012. *Networks of Outrage and Hope: Social Movements in the Internet Age*. London: Polity.

Couldry, Nick. 2010. *Why Voice Matters: Culture And Politics After Neoliberalism*. London: Sage.

Duncombe, Stephen. 2012 b. "Theory: Ethical Spectacle." In *Beautiful Trouble: A Toolbox for Revolution*, ed. Andrew Boyd and Dave Oswald Mitchell. New York: OR Books. http://beautifultrouble.org/theory/ethical-spectacle.

Harris, Franklin. 2009. "We Don't Need Another Hero." *Young Americans for Liberty Blog*, October 30. http://www.yaliberty.org/node/13083.

Jenkins, Henry. 2006 a. *Convergence Culture: Where Old and New Media Collide*. New York: New York University Press.

Jenkins, Henry. 2006 b. "Captain America Sheds His Mighty Tears: Comics and September 11." In *Terror, Culture, Politics: Rethinking 9/11*, ed. Daniel J. Sherman and Terry Nardin, 69–102. Indianapolis: Indiana University Press.

Litz, Stacey. 2010. "Iron Man 2 Depicts Struggle Between Libertarian Super Hero and Intrusive Government." *Examiner.com*, May 8. http://www.examiner.com/article/iron-man-2-depicts-struggle-between-libertarian-super-hero-and-intrusive-government.

Read, Mark. 2012. "Case Study: 99 Percent Bat Signal." In *Beautiful Trouble: A Toolbox for Revolution*, ed. Andrew Boyd and Dave Oswald Mitchell. New York: OR Books; http://beautifultrouble.org/case/99-bat-signal.

Roeder, Fred. 2014. "16 Libertarian Sci-Fi Heroes." *Students for Liberty Blog*, June 16. http://studentsforliberty.org/blog/2014/06/16/16-libertarian-sci-fi-heros.

Kids Make History

(2021)

Colleen Bell

T HIS IS NOT A STORY OF adults using children as active participants in demonstrations, nor is it a story of college student activism. Rather, this article links two examples of how children develop political consciousness resulting in a sense of agency and justice-oriented action in the world. In the first example, a teenager acts directly against systemic racism in 1960s Mississippi; in the second, middle schoolers study that history and meet the key actor who is now in her sixties.

The following vignette is drawn from field notes I recorded during travel study with students from Southside Family School in Minneapolis, Minnesota. After months of discussing how young people participated in the Black freedom struggle of the 1950s and 1960s, students between the ages of 12 and 14 traveled by bus through Southern communities to meet with elders whose civil rights activism they had studied.

Brenda Travis Made History

Jackson, Mississippi, 2011. Two dozen middle schoolers circle up and press toward a wiry Black woman as she talks about growing up in McComb, Mississippi. Brenda Travis, now in her sixties, tells the children how deeply traumatized she was by the photo of Emmett Till's body in a 1955 *Jet* magazine. She was ten years old; Emmett Till was 14. The image of his tortured face in the casket was emblazoned in her mind; had Mamie Till not insisted on an open casket, that image would not have so powerfully imprinted the memories of generations of African American parents and children. In those moments, Brenda resolved to channel her anger and outrage into making Mississippi a better place for her family.

A few months after the Till murder, white police officers broke down the door of the Travis family home, pushed aside Brenda's grandmother, and grabbed her 13-year-old brother James who was sleeping on a pull-out couch in the living room. The police took James away, leaving the rest of the family in shock. Ten-year-old Brenda could not get Emmett Till's battered face out of her mind.

Brenda tells us that these searing events motivated her activism as a high school student. The children are rapt as Ms. Travis pauses. She fast-forwards six years to 1961 when she started volunteering with the Student Nonviolent Coordinating Committee (SNCC) to canvass in the Black community, inviting people to meetings and encouraging voter registration. As a 16-year-old, Brenda witnessed white people's violence and Black people's fear of it. SNCC organizer Bob Moses inspired her with his courage in the face of that violence.

The middle schoolers from Minnesota have learned about SNCC and Bob Moses and Brenda Travis in their classroom. They're eager to hear her version of the SNCC-in-McComb story. Ms. Travis talks about being trained in direct action, her face serious as she recalls lessons in maintaining dignity while breaking segregation laws and how violence would surely be the response to protestors' nonviolence. She recounts being the only girl and the only minor who volunteered to enter the Greyhound bus station and attempt to buy a ticket at the whites-only counter. That action resulted in her arrest and incarceration.

Brenda eventually faced a county judge who insisted that no 16-year-old could have decided to do this on her own and he asked her who had paid her for her actions.

Ms. Travis served 28 days in the county jail and missed the first month of her junior year in high school. When she returned to school and went to the office to register, she was expelled by order of the school board. Word of her expulsion spread quickly among the students and within hours, more than 100 students walked out of Burglund High School behind Brenda. They marched with dignity and calm, singing freedom songs on their way to a community gathering place, the McComb Masonic Temple.

The circle of Minnesota middle schoolers already know the story of the Burglund High School walk out but they hadn't heard it told by its lead actor. Their excitement bubbles up into questions: "What happened to your brother when you walked out?" and "Did your mother know you were going to walk out?" Ms. Travis is as engaged in telling her story as the children are in hearing it. She invites them to carry on: "we left a legacy … and we want you to tell the story when we're no longer here."

How Sociopolitical Consciousness Develops: Two Exemplars

Outrage at racial terror motivated Brenda Travis to violate segregation law as a 16-year-old Mississippian. She knew Emmet Till's murderers had not been held accountable, and she knew something like that could have happened to her brother James. It is clear from Brenda Travis's (2018) memoir that these harsh lessons in the dynamics of social power fueled her desire to act. Brenda's experience propelled her "capacity to think critically about systems and exercise political agency" (Kirshner 2015:18). This is a marker of sociopolitical development.

The county judge who failed to consider the possibility that Brenda thought critically about racism seriously underestimated her level of understanding. Not only did Brenda

Travis understand the system of racial domination but she was so outraged by its cruel consequences that she pledged to resist it. The judge's view that a 16-year-old girl would not be capable of what Brenda did demonstrates an ageist—actually, adultist—mindset. Ageism insists that elders and young people are unlike other people and negatively values both groups. Adultism—a belief that adults are better than young people—targets children and youth specifically (Love & Phillips 2007).

In the context of Brenda Travis's life, adultism, racism and likely, sexism exerted joint power. An adult white male judge saw a young Black female scofflaw as someone led astray by adults. In spite of being the only female and the only minor involved in the bus station protest, Brenda responded as an empowered social agent: an informed, deliberate political actor in collaboration with SNCC, a racial justice advocacy group she had joined.

Coming from a vastly different context, Southside Family School students who studied the Burglund High School walkout and met Brenda Travis also learned about power dynamics from her story. Although the Minnesota students did not experience this history directly, their teacher—Susie Oppenheim—authored a civil rights curriculum (titled *Kids Make History*) to deliberately center children as actors in history and literature. Susie's teaching encompasses far more than the stock story of the Southern Civil Rights Movement; her work to recover counternarratives from traditional histories demonstrates valuing children and youth as social and political agents who work for justice on behalf of their families and communities.

Reading about children as activists is certainly less vivid than engaging in or witnessing activism firsthand. Yet meeting Brenda Travis made a strong impression. Hearing her experiences of racial terror and her drive for justice offered the middle schoolers a chance to talk with a person who lived the history. Students' questions suggest that they identified with her young activist self; they wondered whether she was afraid of going to jail and how she felt when so many students walked out of the high school behind her and what has changed at Burglund High. The age difference between Ms. Travis and the middle schoolers was easily bridged in conversation about how young people make history. Clearly, Brenda Travis is one of this curriculum's "sheroes."

Barriers to Children's Sociopolitical Development

These two examples show how directly experiencing injustice, as Brenda Travis did, is a powerful way for young people to grasp the dynamics of social power. Those lessons were so violent and egregious that they motivated her to directly challenge white supremacy. Another path to children's sociopolitical development is learning history that does not exclude youth actors, that is, experiences designed to expand students' capacity to think critically about systems of power, as the middle schoolers from Minnesota do.

For anyone who has a choice, this second learning environment is preferable to learning as eyewitness.

There are barriers to social justice curricula in K-12 schools, one of which is adultism. If we see children as dependent, vulnerable and "less than" adults, we risk underestimating their capacities for critical thinking about systems of power. Assuming that children cannot "handle" certain topics will limit what is offered in classrooms. Adultism frames older people as appropriate models for children and as people whose accomplishments are worth studying; it discounts children's capacities and achievements. Scholar Terry Eagleton (1990) has challenged that practice, arguing:

> Children make the best theorists, since they have not yet been educated into accepting our routine social practices as "natural," and so insist on posing to those practices the most embarrassingly general and fundamental questions, regarding them with a wondering estrangement which we adults have long forgotten. Since they do not yet grasp our social practices as inevitable, they do not see why we might not do things differently. (34)

Politics of knowledge may be an even more daunting barrier. Whether public or private, formal schooling involves power dynamics: who benefits, who pays, what goals schools seek, how achievement will be measured, what texts are approved, and who governs schools. What is taught—whose history, whose knowledge—is core in this struggle. Commitments to dominant narratives of U.S. history are central to a vast majority of curricula and to standardized assessment; they reinforce educational business-as-usual. Counternarratives—those featuring young people engaged in justice struggles—when they are included, appear as margin notes and post scripts and this communicates their "place."

Concluding Notes

Youth scholar Ben Kirshner (2015) advocates for a "political account of youth" that locates their interests and actions "in a material and structural context" (167). Children don't wait until they are 18 or 21 to grapple with systems of power. They develop as political beings throughout childhood, practicing and participating in their social contexts, adjusting to their circumstances and building capabilities to act individually and collectively. If we understand children and youth as political beings, we must reconsider—as the *Kids Make History* curriculum does—how youth activism is fundamental to broader social change.

References

Eagleton, T. (1990). The significance of theory. Oxford: Blackwell Publishing.

Kirshner, B. (2015) Youth activism in an era of education inequality. New York: New York University Press.

Love, B.J. & Phillips, K.J. (2007) Ageism and adultism curriculum design. Pp. 359–377 in M. Adams, L.A. Bell & P. Griffin (eds) Teaching for diversity and social justice 2nd ed. New York: Routledge.

Travis, B. & Obee, J. (2018) Mississippi's Exiled Daughter: How My Civil Rights Baptism Under Fire Shaped My Life. Montgomery, AL: NewSouth Books.

What Can We Do? Unraveling the Gender Knot

(2006)

Allan G. Johnson

W HAT IS THE KNOT WE WANT to unravel? In one sense, it is the complexity of patriarchy as a system and worldview—the tree, from its roots to the smallest outlying twig. It is misogyny and sexist ideology that keep women in their place and men in theirs. It is the organization of social life around core patriarchal principles and the powerful dynamics of fear and control that keep it going. It is the fate of the Earth itself as the patriarchal obsession with control drives an economic system wreaking havoc on the environment on which we and every other species of life depend.

But the knot is also about our individual and collective paralysis when it comes to gender issues. It is everything that prevents us from seeing patriarchy and our participation in it, from the denial that patriarchy even exists to false parallels, individualistic thinking, and cycles of blame and guilt. Stuck in this paralysis, we cannot think or act to help undo the legacy of privilege and oppression.

To undo the patriarchal knot we have to undo the knot of our paralysis in the face of it. A good place to begin is with two powerful myths about how change happens and how we contribute to it.

Myth 1: It's Always Been This Way and Always Will Be

Given thousands of years of patriarchal history, it is easy to slide into the belief that things have always been this way. Even thousands of years, however, are a far cry from what 'always' implies unless we leave out the more than 90 percent of humanity's time on Earth that preceded it. Given all the archaeological evidence pointing to the existence of goddess-based civilizations and the lack of evidence for perpetual patriarchy, there are plenty of reasons to doubt that life has always been organized around some form of privilege [...]. When it comes to human social life, the smart money should be on the idea that *nothing* has always been or will be this way or any other, that the only thing we can count on is change. Reality is always in motion. Things may appear to stand still, but that is only because we have limited attention spans. If we take the long view—the *really* long view—we can see that everything is in process all the time.

Some argue that everything *is* process, the space between one point and another, the movement from one thing toward another. What we may see as permanent end points—global capitalism, Western civilization, advanced technology, and so on—are actually temporary states on the way to other temporary states. Even ecologists, who used to talk about ecological balance, now speak of ecosystems as inherently unstable. Instead of always returning to some steady state after a period of disruption, ecosystems are, by nature, a continuing process of change from one arrangement to another and never go back to the way they were.

Social systems are also fluid. A society is not some *thing* that sits there forever as it is. Because a system only happens as people participate in it, it cannot help but be a dynamic process of creation and re-creation from one moment to the next. In something as simple as a man following the path of least resistance toward controlling conversations (and a woman letting him), or being silent in the face of men's violence, the reality of patriarchy in that moment comes into being. This is how we *do* patriarchy, bit by bit, moment by moment. It is also how individuals can contribute to change—by choosing paths of greater resistance.

Since we can always choose paths of greater resistance or create new ones entirely, systems can only be as stable as the flow of human choice and creativity, which is no recipe for permanence. In the short run, patriarchy and its worldview may look stable and unchangeable. But the relentless process of social life never produces the same result twice in a row, because it is impossible for everyone to participate in any complex system in an unvarying and uniform way. Added to this are the dynamic interactions that go on among systems—between capitalism and the state, for example, or between families and the economy, or between ecosystems and human populations—that also produce powerful and unavoidable tensions, contradictions, and other currents of change. Ultimately, systems cannot help but change, whether we notice it or not.

Social systems often *seem* stable because they limit our lives and imaginations so much that we cannot see beyond them. This is especially true when a social system has existed for so long that its past extends beyond collective memory of anything different. As a result, it lays down terms of social life—including various forms of privilege—that can easily be mistaken for some kind of normal and inevitable human condition.

But this masks a fundamental long-term instability caused by the dynamics of privilege and oppression. Any system organized around an obsession with control is ultimately a losing proposition because it contradicts the uncontrollable nature of reality and does such violence to basic human needs and values. As the last two centuries of feminist thought and action have begun to challenge the violence and break down the denial, patriarchy has become increasingly vulnerable. This is one reason why men's resistance, backlash, and defensiveness can be so intense.[1] Talk radio is full of men complaining about their lot, especially the inability to realize ideals of control in relation to their own lives,[2] women, and other men. Fear and resentment of women are pervasive, from railing against affirmative action to worrying about being accused of sexual harassment or rape. Even the mildest criticism of men or mention of patriarchy is enough to elicit angry—and worried—charges of male bashing.

Patriarchy is also destabilized as the illusion of masculine control breaks down. As we saw in the financial collapse of 2008, corporate leaders alternate between arrogant confidence and optimism on the one hand and outright panic on the other, with banks becoming so large and complex that even their CEOs are no longer able to understand how they work. At the same time, governments lurch from one crisis to another, barely managing to stay in office, much less solving major social problems such as poverty, violence, terrorism and war, health care, middle-class angst, and, of course, the excesses and recklessness of global capitalism and the climate crisis it has caused. Computer technology supposedly makes life and work more efficient, but it does so by chaining people to an escalating pace of work and giving them less rather than more control over their lives.

The loss of control in pursuit of control is happening on a larger level as well. As the patriarchal obsession with control deepens its grip on everything from governments and corporations to schools and religion, the overall degree of control actually becomes less, not more. As out-of-control banks and other financial institutions illustrate, the scale on which systems are out of control simply grows larger. The stakes are higher and the capacity for harm is greater, and together they fuel an upward spiral of worry, anxiety, and fear.

As the illusion of control becomes more apparent, men start doubting their ability to measure up to patriarchal standards of manhood. We have been here before. At the turn of the twentieth century, there was widespread white male panic in the United States about the feminization of society and the need to preserve masculine toughness. From the creation of the Boy Scouts to Teddy Roosevelt's Rough Riders, a public campaign tried to revitalize manhood as a cultural basis for revitalizing a male-identified society and, with it, male privilege.[3] A century later, the masculine backlash is again in full

1   See Michael Kimmel, *Angry White Men: American Masculinity at the End of an Era* (New York: Nation Books, 2013).

2   This is what Warren Farrell means when he describes male power as mythical. In this case, he's right. See *The Myth of Male Power* (New York: Berkley Books, 1993). See also Molly Dragiewicz, *Equality with a Vengeance: Men's Rights Groups, Battered Women, and Antifeminist Backlash* (Boston: Northeastern University Press, 2011).

3   See Michael Kimmel, *Manhood in America*, 3rd ed. (New York: Free Press, 2011); and Richard Slotkin, *Gunfighter Nation: The Myth of the Frontier in Twentieth-Century America* (Norman: University of Oklahoma Press, 1998).

bloom with the warrior image re-emerging as a dominant ideal, from superhero movies to right-wing militias to images of war being invoked for everything from the search for a cancer cure to curbing illegal drug use.[4]

Neither patriarchy nor any other system will last forever. Patriarchy is riddled with internal contradiction and strain. It is based on the false and self-defeating assumption that control is the answer to everything and that the pursuit of more control is always better than contenting ourselves with less. The transformation of patriarchy has been unfolding ever since it emerged seven thousand years ago, and it is going on still. We cannot know what will replace it, but we can be confident that patriarchy will go, that it *is* going at every moment. It is only a matter of how quickly, by what means, at what cost, and toward what alternatives, and whether each of us will do our part to make it happen sooner rather than later and with less rather than more destruction and suffering in the process.

Myth 2: The Myth of No Effect and Gandhi's Paradox

Whether we help change patriarchy depends on how we handle the belief that nothing we do can make a difference, that the system is too big and powerful for us to affect. In one sense, the complaint is valid: if we look at patriarchy as a whole, it is true that we are not going to make it go away in our lifetime. But if changing the entire system through our own individual efforts is the standard against which we measure the ability to do something, then we have set ourselves up to fail. It is not unreasonable to want to make a difference, but if we have to *see* the final result of what we do, then we cannot be part of change that is too gradual and long term to allow that.

We also cannot be part of change that is so complex that we cannot sort out our contribution from countless others that combine in ways we can never grasp. Problems like patriarchy are of just that sort, requiring complex and long-term change coupled with short-term work to soften some of its worst consequences and lay the groundwork for what is to follow. This means that if we are going to be part of the solution to such problems, we have to let go of the idea that change does not happen unless we are around to see it and that what we do matters only if we *make* it happen. In other words, if we free ourselves of the expectation of being *in control* of things, we free ourselves to act and participate in the kind of fundamental change that transforms social life.

To get free of the paralyzing myth that we cannot, individually, be effective, we have to change how we see ourselves in relation to a long-term, complex process of change. This begins by changing how we relate to time. Many changes can come about quickly

---

4   See James William Gibson, *Warrior Dreams: Violence and Manhood in Post-Vietnam America* (New York: Hill and Wang, 1994).

enough for us to see them happen. When I was in college, for example, there was little talk about gender inequality as a social problem, whereas now there are women's studies programs all over the country. But a goal like ending male privilege takes far more time than our short lives can encompass. If we are going to see ourselves as part of that kind of change, we cannot use the human life span as a significant standard against which to measure progress.

To see our choices in relation to long-term change, we have to develop what might be called 'time constancy,' analogous to what psychologists call 'object constancy.' Infants lack object constancy in the sense that if you hold a toy in front of very young children and then put it behind your back while they watch, they cannot find the toy because they apparently cannot hold on to the image of it and where it went. In other words, if they cannot see it, it might as well not exist. After a while, children develop the cognitive ability to know that objects or people exist even when they are out of sight. In thinking about change and our relation to it, we need to develop something similar in relation to time that enables us to carry within us the belief that significant change happens even though we are not around to see it.

Along with time constancy, we need to get clear about how our choices matter and how they do not. Gandhi once said that nothing we do as individuals matters, but it is vital that we do it anyway. This touches on a powerful paradox in the relationship between society and individuals. In terms of the patriarchy-as-tree metaphor, no individual leaf on the tree matters. Whether it lives or dies has no effect on much of anything. But collectively, the leaves are essential to the whole tree because they photosynthesize the sugar that feeds it. Without leaves, the tree dies.

Leaves matter and they do not, just as we matter and we do not. What each of us does may not seem like much, because in important ways, it *isn't* much. But when many people do this work together, they can form a critical mass that is anything but insignificant, especially in the long run. If we are going to be part of a larger change process, we have to learn to live with this sometimes uncomfortable paradox rather than go back and forth between momentary illusions of potency and control and feelings of helpless despair and insignificance.

A related paradox is that we have to be willing to travel without knowing where we are going. We need faith to do what seems right without necessarily knowing the effect our actions will have. We have to think like pioneers who may know the *direction* they want to move in or what they would like to find, without knowing where they will wind up. Because they are going where they have never been before, they cannot know whether they will ever arrive at anything they might consider a destination, much less what they had in mind when they first set out. If pioneers had to know their destination from the beginning, they would never go anywhere or discover anything.

In similar ways, to seek out alternatives to patriarchy, it has to be enough to move *away* from social life organized around dominance and control and to move *toward* the certainty that alternatives are possible, even though we may not have a clear idea of what those are or may never experience them ourselves. It has to be enough to question how we think about and experience different forms of power, for example—how we see ourselves as gendered people, how privilege and oppression work and how we participate—and then open ourselves to experience what happens next. When we dare to ask core questions about who we are and how the world works, things happen that we cannot foresee, but they do not happen unless we *move*, even if only in our minds. As pioneers, we discover what is possible only by first putting ourselves in motion, because we have to move in order to change our position—and hence our perspective—on where we are, where we have been, and where we might go. Alternatives begin to appear as we imagine how things might be, but first we have to get past the idea that things will always be the way they are.

In relation to Gandhi's paradox, the myth of no effect obscures the role we can play in long-term transformations. But the myth also blinds us to our own power in relation to other people. We may cling to the belief that there is nothing we can do precisely because we know how much power we do have and are afraid to use it because people may not like it. If we deny our power to affect people, then we do not have to worry about taking responsibility for how we use it or, more significant, how we do not.

The reluctance to acknowledge and use power comes up in the simplest everyday situations, as when a group of friends starts laughing at a sexist or homophobic joke and we have to decide whether to go along. It is a moment in a sea of countless such moments that constitutes the fabric of all kinds of oppressive systems. It is a crucial moment because the group's seamless response to the joke reaffirms the normalcy and unproblematic nature of it and the system of privilege behind it. It takes only one person to tear the fabric of collusion and apparent consensus.

On some level, we each know we have this potential, and this knowledge can empower us or scare us into silence. We can change the course of the moment with something as simple as visibly not joining in the laughter, or saying, "I don't think that's funny." We know how uncomfortable this can make people and how they may ward off their discomfort by dismissing, excluding, or even attacking us as bearers of bad news. Our silence, then, is not because nothing we do will matter. Our silence is our not *daring* to matter.

Our power to affect other people is not simply about making them feel uncomfortable. Systems shape the choices people make primarily by providing paths of least resistance. We typically follow those paths because alternatives offer greater resistance or because we are not even aware that alternatives exist. Whenever we openly choose a different path, however, we make it possible for people to see both the path of least resistance they are following and the possibility of choosing something else.

The choice is both radical and simple. When most people get on an elevator, for example, they turn and face front without ever thinking why. We might think it is for purely practical reasons—the floor indicators and the door we exit through are at the front. But there is more going on than that, as we would discover if we simply walked to the rear wall and stood facing it while everyone else faced front. The oddness of what we were doing would immediately be apparent to everyone, and would draw their attention and perhaps make them uncomfortable as they tried to figure out why we were doing that. Part of the discomfort is simply calling attention to the fact that we make choices when we enter social situations and that there are alternatives, something that paths of least resistance discourage us from considering. If the possibility of alternatives in situations as simple as where to stand in an elevator can make people feel uncomfortable, imagine the potential for discomfort when the stakes are higher, as they certainly are when it comes to how people participate in oppressive systems like patriarchy.

If we choose different paths, we usually will not know if we affect other people, but it is safe to assume that we do. When people know that alternatives exist and witness other people choosing them, things become possible that were not before. When we openly pass up a path of least resistance, we *increase* resistance for other people around that path because now they must reconcile their choice with what they have seen us do, something they did not have to deal with before. There is no way to predict how this will play out in the long run, and there is certainly no good reason to think it will not make a difference.

The simple fact is that we affect one another all the time without knowing it. When my family moved to our house in the woods of northwestern Connecticut, one of my first pleasures was blazing walking trails through the woods. Sometime later I noticed deer scat and hoofprints along the trails, and it pleased me to think they had adopted the trail I'd laid down. But then I wondered if perhaps I had followed a trail laid down by others when I cleared 'my' trail. I realized that there is no way to know that anything begins or ends with me and the choices I make. It is more likely that the paths others have chosen influence the paths I choose.

This suggests that the simplest way to help others make different choices is to make them myself, and to do it openly so they can see what I am doing. As I shift the patterns of my own participation in patriarchy, I make it easier for others to do so as well—*and harder for them not to.* Simply by setting an example—rather than trying to change people—I create the possibility of their participating in change in their own time and in their own way. I can thus widen the circle of change without provoking the kind of defensiveness that perpetuates paths of least resistance and the systems they perpetuate.

It is important to see that in doing this kind of work we do not have to go after people to change their minds. In fact, changing people's minds may play a relatively small part in changing systems. Rather than turning die-hard misogynists into practicing feminists, we can shift the odds in favor of new paths that contradict core patriarchal values. We can introduce so many exceptions to the patriarchal worldview that the children or grandchildren of die-hard misogynists will start to change their perception of which paths offer the least resistance. Research on men's changing attitudes toward the male provider role, for example, shows that most of the shift occurs *between* generations, not within them.[5]

This same dynamic is what has driven the dramatic change in attitudes toward same-sex marriage in the United States. In the ten years between 2003 and 2013, for example, the percentage of Americans reporting favorable images of lesbians and gays rose from 38 percent to 58 and 54 percent, respectively, while the percentage supporting same-sex marriage rose from 51 to 72 percent. Much of this change reflects the greater level of LGBT acceptance among young people: 65 percent of those eighteen to twenty-nine years old support same-sex marriage, for example, compared with just 39 percent of those age sixty-five and older.[6]

All of this suggests that rather than trying to persuade individual people, the most important thing we can do is contribute to shifting entire cultures so that patriarchal forms and values begin to lose their 'obvious' legitimacy and normalcy and new forms emerge to challenge their privileged place in social life. And when this happens, the structures of privilege—the unequal and oppressive distribution of wealth, power, resources, and opportunities—become harder to maintain.

In science, this is how one paradigm replaces another.[7] For hundreds of years, for example, Europeans believed that the stars, planets, and the sun revolved around Earth. But Copernicus and Galileo found that too many of their astronomical observations were anomalies that did not fit the prevailing paradigm: if the sun and planets revolved around Earth, then they would not move as they did. The accumulation of such observations made it increasingly difficult to hang on to an Earth-centered paradigm. Eventually the anomalies became so numerous that Copernicus offered a new paradigm, for which he, and later Galileo, were persecuted as heretics. Eventually, however, the evidence was so overwhelming that a new paradigm replaced the old one.

---

5   J. R. Wilkie, "Changes in U.S. Men's Attitudes towards the Family Provider Role, 1972–1989," *Gender and Society* 7, no. 2 (1993): 261–279.

6   "A Survey of LGBT Americans: Attitudes, Experiences and Values in Changing Times," Pew Research Center, June 13, 2013, available at http://www.pewsocialtrends.org/2013/06/13/a-survey-of-lgbt-americans/; "In Gay Marriage Debate, Both Supporters and Opponents See Legal Recognition as 'Inevitable,'" Pew Research Center, June 6, 2013, available at http://www.people-press.org/2013/06/06/in-gay-marriage-debate-both-supporters-and-opponents-see-legal-recognition-as-inevitable/.

7   The classic statement of how this happens is in Thomas S. Kuhn, *The Structure of Scientific Revolutions* (Chicago: University of Chicago Press, 1970).

In similar ways, we can think of patriarchy as a system based on a worldview that shapes how we think about gender and organize social life in relation to it. The patriarchal worldview has been under attack for several centuries and the defense has been vigorous, with feminists widely regarded as heretics who practice the blasphemy of male bashing. The patriarchal worldview weakens in the face of mounting evidence that it produces unacceptable consequences. We help weaken it by openly choosing alternative paths in our everyday lives and thereby providing living anomalies that do not fit the prevailing paradigm. By our example, we contradict patriarchal assumptions and their legitimacy over and over again. We add our choices and our lives to tip the scales toward a worldview that does not revolve around control, privilege, and oppression. We cannot tip the scales overnight or by ourselves, and in that sense we do not amount to much. But on the other side of Gandhi's paradox, the poet Bonaro Overstreet reminds us that it is up to us to decide where to place "the stubborn ounces" of our weight.[8] It is in such small and humble choices that patriarchy and the movement toward something better actually happen.

Stubborn Ounces: What Can We Do?

There are no easy answers to the question of what to do about patriarchy. There is no twelve-step program, no set of instructions for turning it into something else. Most important, there is no way around or over it—the only way out is through.

We will not end oppression by pretending it isn't there or that we don't have to deal with it. Some may complain that working for change is divisive by drawing attention to oppressive systems of privilege. But when members of dominant groups mark differences by excluding or discriminating against subordinate groups and treating them as other, they are not accused of being divisive. Usually it is only when someone calls attention to how differences are used as a basis for privilege that the charge of divisiveness comes up.

In a sense, it *is* divisive to say that oppression and privilege exist, but only insofar as it points to divisions that already exist and to the perception that the status quo is normal and unremarkable. Privilege and oppression promote the worst kind of divisiveness because they cut us off from one another and, by silencing us, cut us off from ourselves as well. Not only must we participate in privilege and oppression by living in society, but we also must act as though they don't exist, denying the reality of our own experience and its consequences for people's lives, including our own.

---

8   Bonaro Overstreet, *Hands Laid upon the Wind* (New York: Norton, 1955), 15; see also Paula S. Rothenberg, *Invisible Privilege: A Memoir about Race, Class, and Gender* (Lawrence: University of Kansas Press, 2000).

What does it mean to go out by going through? What can we do about patriarchy that will make a difference?

Acknowledge That Patriarchy Exists

A key to the continued existence of every oppressive system of privilege is people being unaware of it, because privilege contradicts so many basic human values that it invariably arouses opposition when people know about it. The Soviet Union and its Eastern European satellites, for example, were riddled with contradictions that were so widely known among their people that the regimes fell apart with barely a whimper when given half a chance. Something similar happened in 2011 when Egypt's authoritarian ruler was deposed as a result of popular protests. An awareness of privilege can compel people to break the silence on which continued privilege depends. This is why most cultures mask the reality of privilege with a worldview that denies its existence, trivializes it, calls it something else, blames it on those most damaged by it, or draws attention to other things.

It is one thing to become aware and quite another to stay that way. The greatest challenge when we first become aware of a critical perspective on the world is to hang on to it. Every system's paths of least resistance invariably lead *away* from critical awareness of the system and how it works. Therefore, the easiest thing to do after reading a book like this is to forget about it. Maintaining a critical consciousness takes commitment and work. An alternative worldview is something we either maintain in the moment or don't. And the only way to hang on to an awareness of patriarchy is to make paying attention to it an ongoing part of our lives.

Pay Attention

Understanding how patriarchy works and how we participate is essential for change. It's easy to have opinions, but it takes work to know what we're talking about. The most available place to begin is to make reading about patriarchy part of your life. Unless you have the luxury of a personal teacher, you cannot understand patriarchy without reading, just as you need to read about a foreign country before you travel there for the first time. Many people assume they already know what they need to know about gender since everyone has a gender, but they are invariably wrong. Just as the last thing a fish would discover is water, the last thing we will discover is society itself.

This means you have to be open to the idea that what you think you know is, if not wrong, so deeply shaped by the patriarchal worldview that it misses most of the truth. This is why feminists talk with one another and spend time reading one another's work— seeing things clearly is tricky and difficult work. This is also why people who are critical of the status quo are so often self-critical as well, for they know how complex and elusive the truth really is and what a challenge it is to work toward it. People working for change are often accused of being orthodox and rigid, but they can be among the most self-critical people around.

There is a huge feminist literature available through any decent library and, increasingly, online, although you might never know it to judge from its invisibility in the mass media and mainstream bookstores. In fact, it is a good idea not to rely on mass media for meaningful analysis of privilege in any form. The media ignore most of what is known about privilege and routinely focus on issues that have the least to do with it ("Do men and women use different parts of their brains?"), that reflect the most flawed models of social reality ("Men are from Mars, ..."), and that set women against one another, especially when women attack other women. Most feminist work is virtually invisible to book reviewers, journalists, editorial writers, columnists, and publishers. So, to know what's going on, it may take an Internet search followed by a trip to the library or an interlibrary loan request or a special order at the bookstore. But we can do more than that—we can also tell librarians and bookstore managers how surprised we are that they do not stock such essential reading for understanding the world.

As you educate yourself, it is important to avoid reinventing the wheel. Many people have already done a lot of work that you can learn from. There is no way to get through it all, but you don't have to in order to develop a clear enough sense of how to act in meaningful and informed ways.

A good place to start is a basic text on women's studies. Men who feel there is no place for them in women's studies can start with books about patriarchy and gender that are written by men. Sooner or later, however, men will have to turn to what women have written, because women have done most of the work of figuring out how patriarchy works.[9]

Those who expect feminist writings to be full of animosity toward men should prepare themselves for a surprise. And while it is important not to swallow anything whole and uncritically, it is also important that men believe what women say about their experience of oppression under patriarchy. These are, after all, our mothers, sisters, daughters, lovers, wives, and friends telling us in a resounding collective voice of centuries of oppression from perspectives that we as men cannot duplicate. When the stories originate from women of so many ages and racial, class, and ethnic backgrounds, and when they echo across cultures and so much history, they call on men to have enough respect and humility to be silent for a while and listen.

Reading, though, is only a beginning. At some point you have to look at yourself and the world to identify what you are reading about. Once the phrase 'path of least resistance' entered my active vocabulary, for example, I started seeing them all over the place. The more aware I am of how powerful a path is, the more I can decide whether to go down it each time it presents itself. When this kind of awareness is shared openly

---

9   See the Appendix for a reading list.

among people, the possibilities for alternative paths multiply rapidly, especially when you realize that you don't have to feel guilty for what you're leaving behind.

If we focus on paths and people's choices in relation to them rather than on the content of their character, we can leave guilt and blame behind and work to identify new paths and support ourselves and other people in choosing them. It doesn't have to be about continually pointing to 'what's wrong' with ourselves or someone else, because the truth is that individuals are not the problem. The primary problem is the system we participate in and the consequences that result from the choices we make in relation to it. Seeing this and seeing how we can participate differently is not easy or fun. But it is a way for women and men to reclaim important parts of their lives that are now compromised, distorted, and damaged under patriarchy.

There are endless opportunities to participate in change, because paths of least resistance connect us to all kinds of systems. At work, the path of least resistance for managers is to mentor and promote people who most resemble themselves, which in most companies turns out to be white men. Whether at work or on the street, sexual harassment results from men following paths that define both male and female sexuality in male-dominated, male-identified, and male-centered terms. In everyday conversation, the path of least resistance is for men to dominate and be heard and for women to defer and be unheard. In school, patriarchal paths draw teachers to pay more and better attention to boys than to girls, draw boys to take advantage of it, and draw girls to expect less than they need or deserve. In politics, leaders routinely act as though compassion and compromise are weakness and domination and control are the only valid measures of strength and success. And on it goes, from one social situation and system to another, as the patriarchal worldview shapes how we perceive alternatives and how we choose among them without even knowing it. The challenge *is* to know it by becoming more aware of both the paths inherent in those situations and the choices we make about them.

It helps to be like anthropologists, participant observers who watch and listen to others and ourselves, who notice patterns that come up over and over in social life. We can pretend we are strangers in a strange land who know nothing about where we are and *know* that we know nothing. This keeps us open to mistaken assumptions and the surprise of realizing that things are not what they seem.

This is especially challenging for men, whose privilege tells them they should not have to work to figure out someone else, that it's up to others to figure them out. It is easy for men to fall into the trap of being like impatient, arrogant tourists who do not take the initiative to educate themselves about where they are and their place in it. But taking responsibility means men not waiting for women to tell them what to do, to point out what is happening, or to identify alternatives. If men are going to take their share of responsibility, it is up to men to listen, watch, ask, and listen again, to make it their business to find out for themselves. If they do not, they will slide down the oblivious path of male privilege. And then they will be *just* part of the problem, and they *will* be blamed, and they will have it coming.

Learn to Listen

This is especially difficult for members of dominant groups. If someone confronts you with your own behavior that supports privilege, step off the path of least resistance that encourages you to defend and deny. Do not tell them they're too sensitive or need a better sense of humor, and do not try to explain away what you did as something else than what they are telling you it was. Do not say you didn't mean it or that you were only kidding. Do not tell them what a champion of justice you are or how hurt you feel because of what they're telling you. Do not make jokes or try to be cute or charming, since only privilege can lead someone to believe these are acceptable responses to something as serious as privilege and oppression. Listen to what is being said. Take it seriously. Assume for the time being that it is true, because given the power of paths of least resistance, it probably is. And then take responsibility to do something about it.[10]

A student of color in one of my classes, for example, once told me that she noticed me cutting her off during class, something she did not think I did with white students. I could have weighed in with my professorial authority and said it wasn't true, that she was imagining it, that I treat all my students the same, that she was being too sensitive, that I travel all over the country speaking about issues of inequality and injustice, so certainly I was above such things. But what I said to her was that I was truly sorry she'd had that experience. I was not aware of doing that, I told her, but the fact that I did not consciously mean to was beside the point.

To respond in this way, I had to decenter myself from my position of privilege and make her experience and not mine the point of the conversation. I ended by telling her I would do everything I could to pay attention to this in the future to make sure it did not happen in my classes.

It is important to note that my goodness or badness as a person was not the issue. The issue was the existence of pervasive racist patterns through which privilege is enacted every day and whether I was unconsciously reproducing those patterns and, most important, whether I was willing to take responsibility for paying attention to my own behavior as a participant. I believe that most of the time, members of subordinate groups are not looking for dominant groups to feel ashamed or guilty, because this will do nothing in itself to improve their own lives. In my experience, the true goal is to end privilege and oppression and to get dominant groups to commit themselves to doing whatever they can to make that happen.

---

10 The examples in this paragraph are based on suggestions from Joanne Collahan. My thanks go to her for making me aware of this issue.

Little Risks: Do Something

The more you pay attention to what is going on, the more you will see opportunities to do something about it. You do not have to mount an expedition to find them, because they are all over the place, beginning in ourselves.

As I became aware of how I gravitated toward controlling conversations, for example, I also realized how easily men dominate group meetings by controlling the agenda and interrupting, without women objecting to it. This pattern is especially striking in groups that are mostly female but in which most of the talking nonetheless comes from a few men. I would find myself sitting in meetings and suddenly the preponderance of male voices would jump out at me, an unmistakable hallmark of male privilege in full bloom.

I have had to decide what to do about this little path of least resistance and my relation to it that leads me to follow it so readily. With some effort, I have tried out new ways of listening more and talking less. At times it has felt contrived and artificial, like telling myself to shut up for a while or even counting slowly to ten (or more) to give others a chance to step into the silence. With time and practice, new paths have become easier to follow and I spend less time monitoring myself. But awareness is never automatic or permanent, for patriarchal paths of least resistance will be there to choose or not as long as patriarchy exists.

You might be thinking at this point that everything comes down to changing individuals after all since doing something is a matter of people's behavior. In a sense, of course, it is true that, for us, it all comes down to what we do or do not do as individuals since that is what we are. But the key is always to connect our choices to the systems we participate in. When we *openly* change how we participate in a system, we do more than change our own behavior, for we also change how the system itself happens. When we change how a system operates, we change the social environment that shapes other people's behavior, which, in turn, further changes how the system operates. And when we do that, we also change the consequences that come out of the dynamic relationship between systems and individuals, including patterns of privilege and oppression.

Sometimes stepping off the path of least resistance is a matter of directly calling attention to the system and how it is organized. As we will see shortly, for example, it might involve calling attention to the distribution of power and resources in an organization: Why are all the secretaries women and all the executives men? Why is the custodial staff mostly people of color and the management staff entirely white? Choosing to call attention to such patterns means changing our own behavior, but it does more than that, because the focus of our actions is the system itself.

In short, since the world happens as it does through the dynamic relationship between individuals and social systems, changing the world has to involve both.

As we see more of what is happening, questions will come up about what goes on at work, in the media, in families, in communities, in religion, in government, on the street, and at school—just about everywhere. The questions do not come all at once (for which we can be grateful), although they sometimes come in a rush that can feel overwhelming. If we remind ourselves that it isn't up to us to do it all, however, we can see plenty of situations in which we can make a difference, sometimes in surprisingly simple ways. Consider the following possibilities:

Organize, organize, organize was the advice given by the writer, abolitionist, and former slave Frederick Douglass. Work with other people. This is one of the most important principles of participating in social change. From expanding consciousness to taking risks, it makes all the difference in the world to be in the company of people who support what you are trying to do. You can read and talk about books and issues and just plain hang out with other people who want to understand and do something about patriarchy. Remember that the modern women's movement's roots were in consciousness-raising groups in which women did little more than gather to talk about themselves and their lives and try to figure out what that had to do with living in patriarchy. It may not have looked like much at the time, but it laid the foundation for huge social movements. One way down this path is to share a book like this one with someone and then talk about it. Or ask around about local groups and organizations that focus on gender issues, and go find out what they're about and meet other people. After reading a book or article that you like, write to the author in the care of the publisher or by e-mail. Don't be stopped by the belief that authors do not want to hear from interested readers, because the truth is that they usually welcome it and respond. Make contact and connect to other people engaged in the same work. Do whatever reminds you that you are not alone in this, and in so doing, you will remind others that they are not alone either.

Make noise, be seen. Stand up, volunteer, speak out, write letters, sign petitions, show up. Like every oppressive system of privilege, patriarchy feeds on silence. Breaking the silence is especially important for men, because it undermines the assumption of male solidarity that patriarchy depends on. If this feels too risky, men can practice being aware of how silence reflects their investment in solidarity with other men. This can be a place to begin working on awareness: "Today I said nothing, colluded in silence, and this is how I benefited from it. Tomorrow I can try something different."

Find little ways to withdraw support from paths of least resistance and people's choices to follow them, starting with yourself. It can be as simple as not laughing at a sexist joke or saying you don't think it's funny. Or writing a letter to the editor objecting to sexism in the media. When my local newspaper ran an article whose headline referred to sexual harassment as "earthy behavior," for example, I wrote a letter pointing out that harassment is anything but.

The key is to interrupt the flow of business as usual. You can disrupt the assumption that everyone is going along with the status quo by *not going along yourself.* This stops the flow, if only for a moment, and in that moment other people can notice and start to think and question. It is a perfect time to suggest the possibility of alternatives such as humor that is not at someone else's expense or of ways to think about harassment and violence that do justice to the reality of what it is and how it affects people's lives.

We often like to think of ourselves as individuals—especially in the United States. But it is amazing how much of the time we compare ourselves to other people as a way to see how well we fit in. Anything that disrupts this process in even the smallest way can affect taken-for-granted assumptions that underlie social reality. It might help to think of this process as inserting grains of sand in an oyster to irritate it into creating a pearl of insight, or as a way to make patriarchy itch, stir, and scratch and thereby reveal itself for others to see, or as planting seeds of doubt about the desirability and inevitability of the way things are, and, by example, planting seeds of what might be.

Dare to make people feel uncomfortable, beginning with yourself. At the next local school board meeting, for example, ask why principals and other administrators are almost always men, while the teachers they control are mostly women, especially in elementary school. Ask how students are being prepared to deal with gender issues in their lives, including men's violence and the use of social media to stalk and harass women and girls.

It may seem that such actions do not amount to much until you stop for a moment and feel your resistance to doing them—your worry, for example, about how easily you could make people feel uncomfortable, including yourself. If you take that resistance to action as a measure of power, then your potential to make a difference is plain to see. The potential for people to feel uncomfortable is a measure of the power for change inherent in such simple acts of not going along with the status quo.

Some will say that it isn't nice to make people uncomfortable, but patriarchy does a lot more than make people feel uncomfortable, and it certainly isn't nice to allow it to continue. Besides, discomfort is an unavoidable part of any meaningful process of education. You cannot grow without being willing to challenge your assumptions and take yourself to the edge of your competencies, where you are bound to feel uncomfortable. If you cannot tolerate ambiguity, uncertainty, and discomfort, then you will never go beneath the superficial appearance of things or learn or change anything of much value, including yourself.

Openly choose and model alternative paths. As you identify paths of least resistance—such as women being held responsible for child care and other domestic work—you can identify alternatives and then follow them openly so that other people can see what you are doing. Patriarchal paths become more visible when people choose alternatives, just as rules become more visible when someone breaks them. Modeling new paths creates tension in a system, which moves toward resolution (like the irritated oyster). You do not have to convince anyone of anything. As Gandhi put it, the work begins with us as we work to be the change we want to see happen in the world. Anyone who thinks this has no effect need only watch how people react to the smallest departures from paths of least resistance, at how much effort people expend trying to ignore or explain away or challenge those who choose alternative paths.

Actively promote change in how systems are organized around patriarchal values and male privilege. There are almost endless possibilities here because social life is complicated and patriarchy is everywhere. You can, for example:

- Start where you live by paying attention to and speaking out on issues of gender equity in your family. Cultural ideas about wives and husbands, mothers and fathers are linchpins of male privilege.

- Speak out for equality in the workplace.

- Promote awareness and training around issues of privilege.

- Support equal pay and promotion for women.

- Oppose the devaluing of women and the work they do, from the dead-end jobs most women are stuck in to the glass ceilings that keep women out of top positions.

- Support the well-being of mothers and children and defend women's right to control their bodies and their lives.

- Object to the punitive dismantling of welfare and attempts to limit women's access to contraception and other reproductive health services.

- Speak out against violence and harassment against women wherever they occur, whether at home, at work, or on the street.

- Object to media coverage of men's violence in all its forms that ignores gender.

- Support government and private support services for women who are victimized by men's violence.

- Volunteer at the local rape crisis center or battered women's shelter.

- Call for and support clear and effective antiharassment and abuse policies in workplaces, unions, schools, professional associations, government, religious institutions, and political parties, as well as public spaces such as parks, sidewalks, and malls.

- Join and support groups that intervene with and counsel men who perpetrate violence against women.

- Object to pornography in theaters, fraternities, and neighborhoods and on the Internet. This does not require a debate about censorship—just the exercise of freedom of speech to articulate pornography's role in patriarchy and to express how its opponents feel about it.

- Ask questions about how work, education, religion, family, and other areas of social life are shaped by core patriarchal values and principles. Some accept women's entry into combat branches of the military or the upper reaches of corporate power as progress, for example. But others question what happens to people and societies when political and economic institutions are organized around control, domination, 'power over,' and, by extension, competition and the use of violence. Is it progress to allow selected women to share control with men over oppressive systems of privilege?

- Speak out to expose the connection between patriarchy and the way social institutions are organized—how the masculine obsession with control, for example, is connected to militarism and war, ways of responding to and defending against terrorism, government surveillance and the invasion of privacy, the exploitation and destruction of the natural environment, and the oppression or working people and people of color.

Openly support people who step off the path of least resistance. When you witness someone else taking a risk—speaking out, calling attention to privilege and oppression—do not wait until later to tell them in private that you are glad they did. Waiting until you're alone makes it safer for you but does them little good. Support is most needed when the risk is being taken, not later on, so do not wait. Make your support as visible and public as the courageous behavior that you're supporting.[11]

> *Because discrimination and persecution targeting gay, lesbian, bisexual, and transgender people is a linchpin of patriarchy, support the right of women and men to be who they are and to love whom they choose.* Raise awareness of homophobia and heterosexism. Ask school officials and teachers about what is happening to LGBT students in local schools. If they do not know,

---

11 I thank Joanne Callahan for this example.

ask them to find out, since it is a safe bet that LGBT students are being harassed by other students and in other ways oppressed at one of the most vulnerable stages of life. If you find alternatives to heterosexuality to be unacceptable for moral or religious reasons, then consider how the treatment of LGBT people is used to perpetuate patriarchy and the oppression of women. Whether in the media or among friends, when gender identity and sexual orientation are discussed, raise questions about their relation to patriarchy. Remember that it is not necessary to have answers to questions in order to ask them. Offer support to those who question and challenge the rigid dualisms of sex and gender, female and male, masculine and feminine, on which the patriarchal worldview depends.

Because patriarchy is rooted in principles of domination and control, pay attention to racism and other forms of oppression that draw from those same roots. There has been a great deal of struggle within women's movements about the relationship between patriarchy and other forms of privilege, especially those based on race, social class, and sexual orientation. There has also been debate over whether some forms of privilege are more important to attack first or produce more oppressive consequences than others.

One way out of this conflict is to realize that patriarchy is not problematic just because it emphasizes *male* dominance but because it promotes dominance and control as ends in themselves. In that sense, all forms of privilege draw support from common roots, and whatever we do that draws attention to those roots undermines them *all*. If working against patriarchy is seen as enabling some women to get a bigger piece of the pie, then some women will succeed at the expense of others who are disadvantaged by race, class, or sexual orientation. But if we identify the core problem as *any* society organized around privilege, then changing *that* requires attention to all forms of privilege and oppression. Whether we begin with race or gender or disability status or class, if we name the problem correctly, we will wind up going in the same direction.

Do not keep it to yourself. A corollary of looking for company and organizing is not to restrict your focus to the tight little circle of your own life. It is not enough to work out private solutions to social problems like patriarchy and other forms of privilege and keep them to yourself. It is not enough to clean up your own act and then walk away, to find ways to avoid the worst consequences of patriarchy at home and inside yourself and think that is taking responsibility. Patriarchy is not a personal problem and it cannot be solved through personal solutions alone. At some point, taking responsibility means acting in a larger context, even if it means letting only one other person know what you are doing. It makes sense to start with yourself, but it is equally important not to *end* with yourself.

If all of this sounds overwhelming, remember again that we do not have to deal with everything. We do not have to set ourselves the impossible task of letting go of everything or transforming patriarchy or even ourselves. All we can do is what we can *manage* to do, secure in the knowledge that we are making it easier for other people—now and in the future—to see and do what *they* can do. So, rather than defeat yourself before you start:

- *Think small, humble, and doable rather than large, heroic, and impossible.* Do not paralyze yourself with impossible expectations. It takes very little to make a difference. Small acts can have radical implications. If the main requirement for the perpetuation of evil is that good people do nothing, then the choice is not between all or nothing but between nothing or *something.*

- *Do not let other people set the standard for you.* Start where you are and work from there. Make a list of all the things you could actually imagine *doing*—from reading another book about patriarchy to suggesting policy changes at work to raising questions about who cleans the bathroom at home—and rank them from the most risky to the least. Start with the least risky and set reasonable goals ("What small risk for change will I take *today*?"). As you get more experienced at taking risks, you can move up your list. You can commit yourself to whatever the next steps are for you, the tolerable risks, the contributions that offer some way—however small it might seem—to help balance your inability to avoid being part of the problem. As long as you do something, it counts.

In the end, taking responsibility does not have to be about guilt and blame, about letting someone off the hook or being on the hook yourself. It is to acknowledge your obligation to make a contribution to finding a way out of patriarchy and to find constructive ways to act on that obligation. You do not have to do anything dramatic or earth-shaking to help change happen. As powerful as patriarchy is, like all oppressive systems, it cannot stand the strain of many people coming together to do something about it, beginning with the simplest act of speaking its name out loud where others can hear.

A New Way Ordered by Love

(2018)

Sonya Renee Taylor

A World for All Bodies Is a World for Our Bodies

Perhaps you have missed it thus far, but I have an agenda to which I am obnoxiously wedded. It's a simple agenda. I want to change the world by convincing you to love every facet of yourself, radically and unapologetically, even the parts you don't like. And through this work, illustrate for you how radical love alters our planet. Radical self-love is an internal process offering external transformation. How we show up to life reflects how we show up to ourselves. When we strip away the veneer of self-reliance and individualism and allow ourselves access to our most vulnerable truths, we can't help but be heartbeat present to the fact that our relationship with other bodies mirrors in tangible ways our relationship with our own body. Yes, we have been cutting and cruel to ourselves and have watched our internalized shame spill over into how we parent, how we manage employees, how we show up to friends and family. Yes, we believed that our bodies were too big, too dark, too pale, too scarred, too ugly, so we tucked, folded, hid ourselves away and wondered why our lives looked infinitesimally smaller than what we knew we were capable of. Yes, we have been less vibrant employees, less compassionate neighbors, less tolerant of the bodies of others, not because we are bad people but because we are guilty of each of those counts against ourselves.

Our lens to the outside world is an interior lens projecting our experience in our bodies onto our external landscape. A shame-clouded interior lens can only project shame and judgment. Employing a radical self-love ethos is like squirting Windex on our daily lives: suddenly we can see ourselves as employees or employers, as parents and friends, as neighbors and community members, as leaders, thinkers, doers—as humans, distinctly connected to other humans. Applying radical self-love to each facet of these roles and responsibilities alters the very fabric of humanity, ultimately creating a more just, equitable, and compassionate world.

Radical Reflection

The least compassionate politician and the most rigid authority figure are demonstrating to us how they are with themselves. We can practice compassion for them while demanding accountability from them.

Speaking French and Implicit Bias

Bridging the gap between radical self-love and radical human love may feel like a Herculean task. "Sonya, it is hard enough to try this radical self-love stuff on myself! Now you want me to love the world?" What I am proposing is that radical human love is not an altruistic endeavor. We want a world that works for our bodies. There is one superhighway free of the debris of body shame and terror that gets us there, and that is radical human love. This means we must become the architects of a world that works for everybody and every body. Our responsibility to humanity is to unearth the ways in which we have been sabotaging the blueprints and thwarting the radical self-love efforts of others.

Right this minute, we are sauntering across someone's radical self-love path like a lumbering bovine. Removing ourselves as a barrier to other folks' radical self-love only becomes possible when we are willing to fear-facingly examine our beliefs. It is not enough to transform our relationship with our physical and emotional selves and leave the world around us unexamined or unaltered. Messages we received about the validity and invalidity of our own bodies did not occur in a vacuum. We were simultaneously receiving and spreading those messages. Dismantling oppression and our role in it demands that we explore where we have been complicit in the system of body terrorism while employing the same compassion we needed to explore our complicity in our internalized body shame. Regrettably this is where too many of us choose to exit the radical self-love train. We desperately want our good intentions and niceness to be enough. Although each of us is inherently "enough" to be loved; valued; cared for; and treated with respect; our efforts to raze systems of oppression and injustice will require more than our niceness. "But I am a good person; I am nice to everyone" has never toppled one systemic inequity nor interrupted the daily acts of body terrorism leveled against humans throughout history. *You* are enough. Being good or nice is not.

> **Unapologetic Inquiry #22**
>
> *Think of three times when your choice to be "nice" or "polite" mode you complicit in body shame or body terrorism.*

Why do we avoid looking at the ways in which we uphold systems of body shame and terror? For the exact same reasons we avoid exploring uncomfortable thoughts about our own bodies and lives: we are in a constant struggle to distinguish our indoctrinated beliefs and behaviors from our true, radically self-loving beings. Remember that we are not the sum of our thoughts or even actions. When we fail to make that distinction, we avoid exploring our ideas and continue to cause harm to ourselves and others. Seeing our thoughts and behaviors as part and not the whole of us allows us to transform our way of being with other bodies. In my "Ten Tools for Radical Self-Love" workshops, I describe our unconscious collusion with the system of body terrorism using the example of French.

If you were born into a francophone family, at around six to eight months of age you would utter your first mumbling word. Likely it would be *mère* (mother) or *père* (father). Your language would be an extension of the world around you, which would likely consist of your French-speaking primary caregivers. Between eighteen months and two years of age, you would develop sentences. Again, those sentences would reflect the language you had been immersed in since birth. Unless your caregivers spoke or regularly exposed you to other languages, you undoubtedly would still be speaking French, even without ever having picked up a book or taken a single class. You would become a fluent French speaker. As you were exposed to more information, resources, and social systems, all in French, you would gain even greater proficiency. Your default language would be French. You'd think your thoughts in French. If you desired to learn a new language, you would have to study it, take classes, practice speaking it with others who had aptitude. It would take effort. On occasion, despite your new linguistic pursuits, you would return to speaking French. You might even subconsciously translate the new language back to French. Likely, no matter how proficient you became in another language, even if you stopped speaking French altogether, sometimes you would still think in French.

Body terrorism is our universal native tongue, our French. We learned the language in our formative years. We were the small child in the grocery store [...], learning the language of ableism and being taught by our mothers to scurry off and whisper in shame and secrecy about the disabled body. We were five-year-old ballerinas in dance class being told by our teacher that we must wear nude tights with our leotards, only to discover that the default for "nude" in every store was pink or tan, never brown. It was in that class that we learned the default hierarchy of white bodies. We were children in the school cafeteria singing "Fatty, fatty, two by four, can't fit through the kitchen door." Or chanting "Keisha, Keisha Bald Spots" on the bus. Whether we chanted and sang along or not, we knew with certainty that we never wanted to be the people in those bodies being targeted. We learned the language of fatphobia and weight stigma, the language of difference-shaming. We were becoming fluent in body terrorism, either as perpetrators or as inactive bystanders, not because we were bad people but because we were in an immersion school of shame. As adults, we have likely done much to disengage from the overtly callous messages we received about many bodies. But without an intentional free dive into the subconscious ways in which we still adhere to those beliefs, enact them in our lives, and project them onto the bodies of others, we will continue to speak body terrorism—ahem, French— whether we want to or not.

Radical Reflection

When we practice awareness, we will notice that we "speak French" all day long, "What is that person wearing? She is too big to wear that!" "He needs to stop being such a wimp." The only way to stop speaking French is to notice when we are.

Researchers have a term for the phenomenon I'm describing with my French analogy: implicit bias. The term refers to the "attitudes or stereotypes that affect our understanding, actions, and decisions in an unconscious manner."[1] Implicit bias can be favorable or unfavorable, but its key component is that it is involuntary: without an individual's conscious awareness or control. If you are prone to a heightened need for control, the concept of implicit bias might make your head explode. "What do you mean I am thinking things I don't think I'm thinking?" I know it can be maddening. Our brains are highly sophisticated organs encoding trillions of responses that control everything from scratching your head to jumping when someone startles you. Our embedded behaviors are so vast it would be impossible to notice them all. However, we do have the ability to raise some of these functions to conscious awareness.

Early on we discussed the theory of in-group out-group bias. This theory can help us understand the origins of implicit bias and see its interruption as a pivotal tool in dismantling a world of body terrorism. Humans are predisposed to social categorization. We subconsciously evaluate who is part of our group and who is not. These assignments happen within seconds, directing our subsequent engagement and influencing our treatment of others. These biases most generously benefit the bodies we consider "normal" while fettering millions of folks on the path of radical self-love. None of us are solely culprits or solely victims. We all get a bit of what we give. Each person in a society is obstructing someone's road to radical self-love while simultaneously being obstructed on their own road. Unexamined implicit bias upholds the hierarchy of bodies in our society, reaffirming our system of default bodies and codifying structures of body-based oppression. Implicit bias proves that just as we have internalized messages of body shame, so too have we been willful and unintentional agents of body terrorism. Through the exploration of how body shame has obstructed our own path, and by making a personal commitment to the creation of a just and compassionate world, we open up to the fear-facing examination of how our indoctrination has hindered the paths of others. Systems and structures of body terrorism are constructed, governed, and operated by humans—that is (cough, cough), by us. We built them, and only our intentional, concentrated efforts to deconstruct body terrorism in ourselves and in our world will tear them down.

---

1   "Understanding Implicit Bias." Kirwan Institute for the Study of Race and Ethnicity, accessed January 30, 2017, http://kirwaninstitute.osu.edu/research/understanding-implicit-bias/.

Beating Body Terrorism from the Inside Out

Describing body terrorism as a systemic and structural issue underscores how our political, economic, and social systems uphold the marginalization of bodies based on race, gender, age, size, ability, sexual orientation, and a variety of other markers.

Unapologetic Inquiry #23

Destroying the system of body terrorism requires an investigation into our unconscious beliefs about other bodies. Remember, we are not our beliefs. We can examine them without judgment and shame. From a place of curiosity and compassion, explore the social, culture, and political messages you have received about the bodies listed below. How have those messages informed your relationship with those bodies?

- *Fat bodies*
- *Bodies of other races*
- *Lesbian or gay bodies*
- *Transgender bodies*
- *Disabled bodies*
- *Aging bodies*
- *Bodies with mental illness*

Bodies are not the only designators of oppression, but all oppression is enacted on the body. To discuss oppression as a manifestation of body terrorism is to move the conversation out of the abstract and return it to its site of impact, the body. Otherwise we risk forgetting that oppression in its many variations is a shared experience. Everybody with a body is affected. Understanding body terrorism as a function of systems and structures does not abdicate our responsibility for working toward its eradication. We do not get to say, "Oh well, racism/sexism/ weight stigma/ageism/homophobia/transphobia/etc. is just so big. Boy, I sure hope 'they' figure it out." Systems do not maintain themselves; even our lack of intervention is an act of maintenance. Every structure in every society is upheld by the active and passive assistance of other human beings.

Let's take the example of body terrorism in the form of ableism. One structural manifestation of ableism is access. If you rented a space for an event and never considered whether that space had ramps, elevators, or disability restrooms, you would be individually upholding the system of ableism by not ensuring that a person with a disability could access your event. No, you didn't build the inaccessible building, but you did rent it, never considering its accessibility for all bodies, thus furthering the erasure of people with physical disabilities and their needs. The architects, investors, and builders who failed to include accessible accommodations for the building project participated in upholding the structural system of ableism by creating a barrier to access for people with disabilities in public life. Each of us is responsible for a sphere of influence.

We are lawyers, salesclerks, teachers, loan officers, physicians, customer service representatives, counselors, judges, law enforcement agents—an inexhaustible list of humans whose jobs impact the lives of other humans every single day. As a human in a body sharing this planet with other humans in bodies, I have a responsibility to interrupt body terrorism, as do you.

This responsibility is distinct from some sort of savior complex in which radical self-love emboldens you to save the poor and downtrodden of Earth. Radical self-love is a manifestation of our interdependence. Lilia Watson, an Aboriginal Australian artist and activist, along with the activists of 1970s Queensland are credited with saying, "If you have come to help me, you are wasting your time. If you have come because your liberation is bound up with mine, then let us work together."[2] Our freedom from body terrorism is bound together. We each have a role in dismantling its systems and structures if we desire a free and spacious road to radical self-love. The first step is to interrupt the ways in which body terrorism resides in us.

Changing Hearts

Civil and labor rights activist Grace Lee Boggs died in 2015, leaving a legacy of work that exemplified her willingness to fear-facingly wrestle with how we create sustainable social change and justice. As a philosopher, she grappled with the delineation between rebellion and revolution. Her exploration of these nuances led her to focus her later writings on what she saw as an unyielding connection between our personal transformation and a transformed world. She wrote:

> Being a victim of oppression in the United States is not enough to make you revolutionary, just as dropping out of your mother's womb is not enough to make you human. People who are full of hate and anger against their oppressors or who only see Us versus Them can make a rebellion but not a revolution.... Therefore, any group that achieves power, no matter how oppressed, is not going to act differently from their oppressors as long as they have not confronted the values that they have internalized and consciously adopted different values.[3]

---

2   L. Watson, Lilia: Internation Women's Network, January 27, 2010, https://lillanetwork.wordpress.com/about/.

3   G. L. Boggs, *Living for Change: An Autobiography* (Minneapolis: University of Minnesota Press, 2016), 146.

Boggs tells us that the only sustainable foundation for a changed world is internal transformation. We need look no further than our present political and social realities to see this premise in action. Social uprisings and upheaval are ineradicable foundations of human history. Laws, rules, and institutions are impermanent and fragile. They have been written, revised, and removed thousands of times over, and yet each new attempt at social change seems to be a mutation of a previous system of body terrorism. The PBS documentary *Slavery by Another Name* describes the post-Civil War practice of convict leasing: a system of leasing incarcerated people to local planters or industrialists in exchange for a minimal fee plus food and board.[4] Low initial cost to the people doing the leasing and increased revenue to the local prisons ballooned the practice, and soon wealthy entrepreneurs were buying and selling convicts between themselves. Laws like the "Black Codes" restricted Black life and freedom while disproportionately targeting Blacks for incarceration.[5] The body terrorism of slavery found its structural mutation in the form of convict leasing and Jim Crow laws. Today, mass incarceration serves the same function, according to legal scholar and author Michelle Alexander. She details the comparison in her groundbreaking book, *The New Jim Crow*:

> In the era of colorblindness, it is no longer socially permissible to use race, explicitly, as a justification for discrimination, exclusion, and social contempt. So, we don't. Rather than rely on race, we use our criminal justice system to label people of color "criminals" and then engage in all the practices we supposedly left behind. Today it is perfectly legal to discriminate against criminals in nearly all the ways that it was once legal to discriminate against African Americans. Once you're labeled a felon, the old forms of discrimination—employment discrimination, housing discrimination, denial of the right to vote, denial of educational opportunity, denial of food stamps and other public benefits, and exclusion from jury service—are suddenly legal. As a criminal, you have scarcely more rights, and arguably less respect, than a black man living in Alabama at the height of Jim Crow. We have not ended racial caste in America; we have merely redesigned it.[6]

Shortly after being inaugurated U.S. president, Donald Trump signed a series of executive orders targeting Muslims and Latinos. The orders ranged from banning visa

---

4 *Slavery by Another Name* (documentary), directed by Samuel D. Pollard, aired February 13, 2012, accessed January 30, 2012, http://www.pbs.org/tpt/slavery-by-another-name/themes/convict-leasing/.

5 "Black Codes," History.com, 2010, http://www.history.com/topics/black-history/black-codes.

6 M. Alexander, *The New Jim Crow* (New York: New Press, 2012), 2.

holders from seven mostly Muslim countries, to blocking the acceptance of Syrian refugees, to ordering a wall built on the border of Mexico, to increasing immigration raids on undocumented families.[7] These actions emboldened national racism and xenophobia and harkened to a long history of state-sanctioned body terrorism. The Chinese Exclusion Act of 1882 placed a decade-long moratorium on the immigration of Chinese people into the United States, with the result of scapegoating them for the country's economic woes and limiting their rights for the next fifty years. Citing fears of Nazi spies, Franklin D. Roosevelt drastically limited the number of Jewish refugees allowed into the country during World War II, taking less than a quarter of the twenty-six thousand he had authorized annually. This decision meant that in June 1939 the ocean liner SS *St. Louis,* which carried nearly one thousand Jewish passengers, was turned away from multiple ports and forced to return to Europe. More than a quarter of its passengers are believed to have been killed in the Holocaust.[8]

We do not have to travel far back through history to describe the shape-shifting nature of body terrorism. Homophobia and xenophobia led to an immigration ban in the United States against HIV-positive persons. The ban remained in place for more than two decades (until 2009), sanctioning social stigma and embedding it into foreign policy.[9] These legal and political decisions illuminate that shape-shifting power of centuries of body terrorism.

Why do we keep reinventing new forms of body terrorism? To answer that question let's explore a conversation between former presidential candidate Hillary Clinton and a group of Black Lives Matter activists that took place in New Hampshire during the 2015 primaries. In a reportedly tense meeting, the soon-to-be Democratic nominee chided the young activists for what she saw as a naïve and unrealistic approach to addressing police violence against unarmed Black citizens, "Look, I don't believe you change hearts," Clinton said, arguing that the movement couldn't change deep-seated racism. "I believe you change laws, you change allocation of resources, you change the way systems operate. You're not going to change every heart. You're not."[10] Certainly, candidate Clinton felt she was offering sage advice at the time, highlighting the dangers of placing idealism above political pragmatism. Surprisingly, a year later Clinton,

---

7   M. Kennedy, "Trump's Immigration Order Is 'Not a Ban on Muslims,' Homeland Security Chief Says," January 31, 2017, http://wwwnpr.org/sections/thetwo-way/2017/01/31/512678699/trumps-immigration-order-is-not-a-ban-on-muslims-homeland-security-chief-says.

8   "Six Other Times the US Has Banned Immigrants," AlJazeera.com, January 29, 2017, http://www.aljazeera.com/indepth/features/2017/01/times-banned-immigrants-170128183528941.html.

9   "Immigration," HIV Law and Policy, accessed January 30, 2017, https://www.hivlawandpolicy.org/issues/immigration.

10   D. Merica, "Hillary Clinton Speaks with Black Lives Matter Activists," CNN.com, August 18, 2015, http://www.cnn.com/2015/08/18/politics/hillary-clinton-black-lives-matter-meeting/.

released a campaign video in collaboration with the Human Rights Campaign that opens with her stating, "Equality is, of course; about changing laws, but it's also about changing hearts and minds."[11] Perhaps the final year on the campaign trail gave Hillary a peek into the true social and cultural consequences of our historical unwillingness to work to change hearts. Failing to change hearts makes body terrorism a centuries-old shell game of guessing what new law it is hiding beneath now.

Juan Manuel Montes was a twenty-three-year-old undocumented immigrant who, despite being protected under the Deferred Action for Childhood Arrivals (DACA) program, was deported in early 2017 to Mexico, a country he had not lived in since age nine.[12] Body terrorism is not a historical aberration, it is the lived experience of millions of people at this very moment. As Chinese immigrants, Jews turned away at port, Leelah Acorn, and Juan Manuel Montes would tell you if they could, the consequences of unchanged hearts are life and death. Body terrorism is made of both systems and structures, hearts and minds. It is the constant stratification of bodies, placing us into hierarchies where we are valued and denigrated often at the same time, in the same body. Propagating a world of radical self-love is both a practice of individual transformation and a commitment to collective transformation. It is a practice of personal and global thinking, doing, and being. Radical self-love necessitates changed hearts, beginning with our own. Quite simply, we cannot build in the world that which we have not built in ourselves.

Unapologetic Agreements

Moving from a radical self-love that transforms you to a radical love that creates justice and equity in the world may feel like a tall order, but you are already on your way. As we cultivate new ways of being in our own bodies, we develop new ways of *being* on this planet with other bodies. A return to radical self-love requires our commitment to building shame-free, inclusive communities that uplift one another while honestly addressing body terrorism in all the ways it manifests as oppression based on age, race, gender, size, ability, sexual orientation, mental health status, and all other human attributes. Some will deride our efforts with charges of playing to "identity politics." We should remind those people that they, too, have identities that are informed by their bodies. Their lack of awareness about those identities generally means their body falls

---

11 "Hillary Clinton: Equality Is About Changing Hearts and Minds," YouTube video, October 21, 2016, https://www.youtube.com/watch?v=kuxdbBPSnas.

12 A. Gomez and D. Agren, "First Protected DREAMer Is Deported Under Trump," *USA Today*, April 18, 2017, https://www.usatoday.com/story/news/world/2017/04/18/first-protected-dreamer-deported-under-trump/100583274/.

into a multiplicity of default identities that uphold the social hierarchy of bodies. The luxury of not having to think about one's body always comes at another body's expense. We should, with compassion, remind them that oppression oppresses us all, even those who are default. Not even they will always have a body at the top of the ladder. No one wins in a world of body terrorism.

At this very moment someone is wringing their hands in worry. "But what if I make a mistake, Sonya? What if I say or do the wrong thing?" If it is you who are worrying, let me calm your precious nerves by assuring you that you will make a mistake ... and then reminding you to revisit pillar 4. Creating a radical self-love world requires our willingness to have challenging conversations about privilege, power, history, culture, inequality, pain, and injustice. We will mess up and say something in French. That doesn't mean we quit. It also doesn't mean we become defensive and retreat to judgment and blame. It means we apologize and try again, holding fast to our intention to connect with other humans in different bodies from a place of compassion and shared humanity. As you move the conversation of radical self-love from an internal dialogue out into your family, community, and world, try on the Unapologetic Agreements that appear below. Commit to engaging in the type of radical self- love communication that grows our understanding of ourselves and one another—the type of communication that fosters global change.

1. **Be a body-shame-free friend.** Eliminate language that disparages bodies based on race, age, size, gender, ability, sexual orientation, religion, mental health status, or any other attribute. Compassionately challenge others you hear using body-shame language to describe themselves or others. This includes "health or concern trolling" (making unsolicited comments about a person's health based on their physical appearance).

2. **Engage and encourage curiosity-driven *dialogue*, not debate or arguing.** Practice the value of sharing and listening to the perspectives of others. The goal of dialogue need not be to change anyone's mind, but to *offer* and *receive* a perspective for consideration and curiosity.

3. **Embrace multiple perspectives.** Avoid having conversations from the assumption of right and wrong. Even if every cell in your body disagrees with someone's perspective, remember that making people "bad" and "wrong" will never build connection and understanding. People who feel judged and attacked often only become further entrenched in their ideas.[13]

4. **Have compassion for and honor people's varied journeys.** Not everyone has read the books you've read or had the experiences you've had. There was

---

13 M. Inman, "You're not going to believe what I am about to tell you," The Oatmeal.com. July 23, 2017, http://theoatmeal.com/comics/believe.

a time when you had not had them either. Our journeys are unique and varied. Compassion births patience.

5. **Expect and accept discomfort.** Conversations about centuries-old oppressions are *hard!* If they were not, the world would be rid of body terrorism and oppression by now. Honor how we all have been indoctrinated into systems of oppression that we each must unlearn. Unlearning is challenging. Do not expect neat, tidy resolutions or assume that we will instantly "fix" the world's ills in a single dialogue. We can, however, get closer to those goals if we are willing to be uncomfortable. Remember, fear is not necessarily danger.

6. **Acknowledge intent while addressing impact.** It is possible to be well-meaning and still cause harm. No matter our intention, we practice accountability when we are willing to acknowledge the impact of our words and actions on others. Likewise, people's words and behaviors may have an impact on us, but they are rarely actually about us. The way we respond to situations is most often a reflection of our own journey. Refraining from personalization makes accepting discomfort easier.

7. **Take breaks for self-care.** Talking with friends, family, and community about radical self-love, body terrorism, and body shame can be joyous and eye-opening. It can also be challenging and triggering. These conversations often involve issues that have caused great trauma in the world—and in our own lives. Some dialogues may bring up painful memories, old wounds, present hurts, and current resentments. We place a premium on self-care as a tool of radical self-love! Do what you need to do to navigate your mental, emotional, and physical wellbeing. Step away from conversations when needed. Focus on yourself, and come back when you are recentered. Radical self-love dialogue depends on your wellness.

8. **Interrupt attempts to derail.** Oftentimes, conversations about body terrorism and oppression bring up such discomfort that we immediately attempt to change the conversation to something that feels more comfortable. Before you know it, the conversation turns to pickle farmers in Europe when we started out talking about fat shaming. Work to keep the focus on the subject being addressed, and avoid the desire to derail.

9. **Remember that personal attacks, name-calling, heavy sarcasm, and general unkindness are unhelpful.** The fastest way to devolve a dialogue is to turn to mean or hurtful language. Our anger need not be expressed as cruelty. We should work to speak from our "inside voice."

10. **Practice unapologetic inquiry.** Part of helping people sort through their ideas and beliefs is to ask questions about those ideas. That includes asking *ourselves* hard questions: "Why do I believe this? What am I afraid of? What am I gaining or losing by trying on a new perspective?" The answers that stick with us

over time are the answers we come up with ourselves. Good questions get us to good answers.

11. **Have conversations based on what was actually said.** Often our translations of people's ideas are not accurate depictions of what they were sharing. Be sure to engage with people based on their actual words and not what you assume those words meant. If you are unsure, ask for clarity.

12. **Assume the best about one another.** It is exceptionally painful to be dismissed, called a liar, or accused of making up your experiences. Start from the assumption that people's experiences are *real* and that they are the expert on their experience. We *may* have shared experiences, but this is not always true. Ask to learn more about other people's truths, rather than erasing them. Start from the assumption that we are all doing our best at any given moment with the tools we have.

13. **Celebrate difference.** Identifying difference is a way to embrace how we can all show up as our fullest, most authentic selves without shame. Acknowledge and embrace those things that are varied in us. Notice when difference is absent, and interrogate why. Ask who is not in the room. Our love of difference translates into creating a movement that welcomes everybody and every body.

14. **Make the goal of the conversation radical, unapologetic love.** The desire for a world free of body terrorism is a desire born out of love. Activist Che Guevara once said, "At the risk of seeming ridiculous, let me say that the true revolutionary is guided by a great feeling of love."[14] Allow your conversations to be guided by the primary principle of love.

"Sonya, will following these agreements keep me from arguing with my racist, fat-phobic Aunt Martha during Thanksgiving dinner?" Listen, love, I cannot promise that you will never again storm out of the house and finish your holiday meal at the local Denny's. However, I can tell you that I have seen the Unapologetic Agreements transform hostility into human connection and acrimony into camaraderie. Like all radical self-love principles, they will take time and effort to master. But keep working at it. "You will be amazed before you are even halfway through."[15]

---

14 J.L. Anderson, *Che Guevara: A Revolutionary Life* (New York: Grove Press, 2010), 178.

15 A.A., S, (n.d.). Promises—Alcoholic Anonymous. Retrieved from https://step12.com/promises.html.

Refer back to the reading selections in this unit to help you correctly respond to each of the questions below.

1. In 1964, 57% of Americans felt that, in the past year, Black people's actions in the civil rights movement were violent, 63% thought the civil rights movement was moving "too fast," and 58% believed that Black people's actions for the movement hurt their own cause.[1] This was the broader public opinion context for Martin Luther King Jr.'s letter, and for his response to fellow clergymen's criticisms of civil rights activities being "unwise and untimely."

   • How does King address these criticisms? What support does he give for why direct action in the civil rights movement is, in fact, both wise and timely?

   • What are some examples of direct actions in the contemporary Movement for Black Lives? How are these similar to and different from tactics deployed in the 1960s civil rights movement?

   • What is the public sentiment around whether present-day racial justice direct action tactics are violent, too fast, or hurting the cause? Have you heard any of these critiques leveraged against today's Movement for Black Lives? How is this public sentiment similar to and different from that of the 1960s? What do you think about direct action tactics deployed today?

2. What does Audre Lorde mean by "the interdependence of mutual (nondominant) differences"? What role does this approach to understanding social difference play in effecting change and social justice?

3. How does bell hooks define "engaged pedagogy"? How can engaged pedagogy contribute to social change? How has or hasn't engaged pedagogy been a part of your educational classroom experiences?

4. Segregation is often viewed as a barrier to social justice. However, Sharon Groch's research points to how physical segregation can facilitate social movement activism.

   • Compare and contrast how physically segregated "free spaces" contributed to the creation of an oppositional consciousness among deaf and blind people.

   • Can you think of other examples of how free spaces have facilitated or continue to facilitate social justice activism?

---

1   Massie, Victoria M. 2016. "Americans Are as Skeptical of Black Lives Matter as They Were of the Civil Rights Movement." *Vox*. July 27. Retrieved May 6, 2021 (https://www.vox.com/2016/7/24/12236580/black-lives-matter-support-civil-rights-movement).

5. Gary Wilson and Heather Smith outline three competing Inuit perspectives on resource development.

   • Name and describe these three perspectives.

   • For each perspective, explain whether the claims being made about justice are distributive, nondistributive, or a combination of both (see Reading 2.1).

6. Henry Jenkins, Sangita Shresthova, Liana Gamber-Thompson, and Neta Kligler-Vilenchik offer some examples of how young people use new media to participate in politics.

   • How is Jenkins et al.'s social justice analysis of the use of new media similar to and different from Vicente Rafael's discussion of lighter and more mobile cameras and how this new technology resulted in a proliferation of colonial photography in the early 1900s (see Reading 3.9)?

7. How is the social justice curriculum described by Colleen Bell an example of a counternarrative against (a) ageist narratives of U.S. history and (b) adultist narratives of U.S. history?

8. Consider the following concepts: oppositional consciousness (see Reading 4.4), civic imagination (see Reading 4.7), and sociopolitical development (see Reading 4.8).

   • Define each of these concepts.

   • What do these concepts have in common?

   • How do they each contribute to social change?

9. Allan Johnson discusses two powerful myths about how social change happens and how we contribute to social change.

   • Name and describe these two myths.

   • Have you ever experienced or internalized these myths?

   • Can you provide an example (or examples) of when you either bought into or rejected these myths?

10. Allan Johnson discusses "the path of least resistance."

    • What does Johnson mean by "taking the path of least resistance"?

    • Name a time when you chose to step off the path of least resistance. Now, name a time when you chose to stay on the path of least resistance. In each case, describe what happened and how you felt about the situation.

11. Consider Donna King's concept of "letting go" and Sonya Renee Taylor's concept of "radical self-love."

   - How are these two social change strategies similar?

   - How are they different?

   - Do you enact these two social justice strategies in your own life? If so, give an example of this. If you do not enact these strategies, explain why not.

12. Johnson and Taylor both conclude their readings with a list of tangible actions to take in order to enact social justice and social change.

   - Select three actions from each list, and explain how they combat one or more of the defensive tactics listed by Cornel Pewewardy (see Reading 2.8).

Afterword

Nico Van Ostrand

When I was first invited to help select readings for this anthology, I was finishing my BA in social justice and women's studies, unsure of my job prospects but entirely sure that I was studying exactly what I needed to. I trusted that following my morals would open the right kinds of doors and feed my soul along the way. So far, I've found this to be true.

The invitation to support the creation of a social justice textbook was an opening of the right kind of door. Some days, my role involved standing at the copy machine to scan and print pages of texts before sorting them into 3-ring binders for reading and consideration. Some days found me sprawled out on my living room, making notes on each reading and turning them over and over in my mind. But my favorite days, the ones that continue to stick with me, were the ones where Valerie and I slipped into the natural flow of laughter and conversation that was a central part of my undergrad experience. On those days, I felt so clearly that I had crossed the threshold and joined the social justice community I'd spent the last five years reading about.

As I write this afterword, I am an organizer and educator who holds a bachelor's degree, and while I believe I am beloved and respected in my circles, I am not the kind of well-established scholar often granted this honor. I don't say this to diminish my knowledge and skill or my career's progress but rather to point out that I am out of place next to the usual afterword authors.

Since you just finished reading this anthology, you have an understanding of social inequities; you may already be drawing the connections between those inequities and inaccessible higher education. You can appreciate how problematic it is to reinforce the elitism of higher education by only uplifting known academics. The invitation to write this afterword did not counter decades of established academic norms. It did, however, place value on my ideas, experiences, and writing. This choice, and hopefully my writing, offer one example of how to do things differently.

I don't know what you are feeling as you reach the end of this anthology. At the end of my first few social justice texts, I carried with me a terrible sense of helplessness and overwhelm. As I learned more and more about the massive, intertwined problems in our world and institutions—problems that harm and kill people daily—I got stuck in a feedback loop of hopeless urgency. I felt so small in the face of these massive, systemic problems. I felt that even if I did everything I could every second of every day for the rest of my life, it still wouldn't make even a dent in social inequity. Yet how could I do anything else?

Looking back, I can recognize the problematic individualism in that line of thinking. And while I still feel hopeless every so often, understanding that I don't have to fix everything by myself was vital to making my work and life sustainable. Just as none of the theories or stories in this anthology were the result of one person, my social justice praxis could never be confined to my efforts alone.

Let me note that realizing I needed a community to lean on was much easier for me than actually finding and connecting with such a community. I began by attending one event, hosted by a Filipino social justice organization. I loved it and knew I wanted to interact with that group more. I also knew that I didn't have capacity at the time for meeting a bunch of new people, something that has always been difficult for me.

Though I didn't use this particular framework at the time, that event several years ago sparked the idea that I needed to understand my own personal definition of "sustainable." At first, sustainable meant following the organization on social media for a few years while my attention and energy were elsewhere. Later, sustainable came to mean I needed to devote energy to connecting with a circle of people doing the same difficult work I was doing. I attended a few more events hosted by the Filipino organization, offered them my time and skills, and soon became active in leadership. Now, the people I've met in organizing circles are among the most important to me.

Sustainable has also come to mean finding pockets *within* my community where justice is being done right. I added this to my definition after cohosting an event about abolishing the police and creating a safer community. At this event, I watched a beloved elder name aloud the programs and systems she thought would be required for a safe, police-free community. I witnessed in real time her realization that many of those programs already exist in small ways, and the ones that don't currently exist would be difficult, but very possible, to create. Her example made clear something I already knew—that pockets of effective efforts are vital reference points for my own efforts in the context of larger societal change.

Though all of the problems and unjust systems will not be righted in my lifetime, my community is doing incredible things in the here and now. My community is creating pockets of justice in the midst of those massive, intertwined problems with our world and institutions. I understand my role in the creation of this anthology and afterword as another pocket of social justice. Again, my involvement in this project does not irrevocably alter academia, but it is one example of how to do academia differently. This pocket doesn't need to solve everything; it just needs to exist in all its wonder. My responsibility then is to notice this pocket and others like it, because on my bad days they are the only reason I am able to stay engaged in social justice work; on my good days they are points of inspiration that help me bring other pockets into being.

I'll wrap up by saying that my most recent evolution of what sustainable means now includes a need to dream and imagine. When I started from the hopeless place of understanding the truly grim picture painted by my first social justice texts, what saved me were those pockets of goodness and my ability to dream beyond them. Not all imaginings are practical, and many of the dreamings that I think are brilliant likely won't become real in my lifetime.

Dreaming gets me pointed in the right direction. And I've also come to understand that reaching the dream is not a realistic goal. My dreams are aspirations, and every time I inch closer—alongside my community—I know it's worthwhile.

So my invitation to you is to dream. Dream and imagine the most beautiful, equitable future for yourself and your community.

Then live pockets of it into being, and in doing so, inspire someone else's dreamings.

CPSIA information can be obtained
at www.ICGtesting.com
Printed in the USA
LVHW061134130821
695181LV00002B/8